THE TOTAL WORK OF ART

SPEKTRUM: Publications of the German Studies Association

Series editor: David S. Luebke, University of Oregon

Published under the auspices of the German Studies Association, Spektrum offers current perspectives on culture, society, and political life in the German-speaking lands of central Europe—Austria, Switzerland, and the Federal Republic—from the late Middle Ages to the present day. Its titles and themes reflect the composition of the GSA and the work of its members within and across the disciplines to which they belong—literary criticism, history, cultural studies, political science, and anthropology.

Volume 1: **The Holy Roman Empire, Reconsidered**
Edited by Jason Philip Coy, Benjamin Marschke, and David Warren Sabean

Volume 2: **Weimar Publics/Weimar Subjects**
Rethinking the Political Culture of Germany in the 1920s
Edited by Kathleen Canning, Kerstin Barndt, and Kristin McGuire

Volume 3: **Conversion and the Politics of Religion in Early Modern Germany**
Edited by David M. Luebke, Jared Poley, Daniel C. Ryan, and David Warren Sabean

Volume 4: **Walls, Borders, Boundaries**
Spatial and Cultural Practices in Europe
Edited by Marc Silberman, Karen E. Till, and Janet Ward

Volume 5: **After The History of Sexuality**
German Genealogies with and Beyond Foucault
Edited by Scott Spector, Helmut Puff, and Dagmar Herzog

Volume 6: **Becoming East German**
Socialist Structures and Sensibilities after Hitler
Edited by Mary Fulbrook and Andrew I. Port

Volume 7: **Beyond Alterity**
German Encounters with Modern East Asia
Edited by Qinna Shen and Martin Rosenstock

Volume 8: **Mixed Matches**
Transgressive Unions in Germany from the Reformation to the Enlightenment
Edited by David M. Luebke and Mary Lindemann

Volume 9: **Kinship, Community, and Self**
Essays in Honor of David Warren Sabean
Edited by Jason Coy, Benjamin Marschke, Jared Poley, and Claudia Verhoeven

Volume 10: **The Emperor's Old Clothes**
Constitutional History and the Symbolic Language of the Holy Roman Empire
Barbara Stollberg-Rilinger
Translated by Thomas Dunlap

Volume 11: **The Devil's Riches**
A Modern History of Greed
Jared Poley

Volume 12: **The Total Work of Art**
Foundations, Articulations, Inspirations
Edited by David Imhoof, Margaret Eleanor Menninger, and Anthony J. Steinhoff

The Total Work Of Art

Foundations, Articulations, Inspirations

Edited by

DAVID IMHOOF, MARGARET ELEANOR MENNINGER,
AND ANTHONY J. STEINHOFF

berghahn
NEW YORK • OXFORD
www.berghahnbooks.com

First published in 2016 by

Berghahn Books

www.berghahnbooks.com

Library of Congress Cataloging-in-Publication Data

Names: Imhoof, David Michael, 1970- editor. | Menninger, Margaret Eleanor, editor. | Steinhoff, Anthony J. editor.
Title: The total work of art : foundations, articulations, inspirations / Edited by David Imhoof, Margaret Eleanor Menninger, and Anthony J. Steinhoff.
Description: New York : Berghahn Books, 2016. | Series: Spektrum : publications of the German Studies Association ; volume 12 | Includes bibliographical references and index.
Identifiers: LCCN 2015047943| ISBN 9781785331848 (hardback : alk. paper) | ISBN 9781785331855 (ebook)
Subjects: LCSH: Arts, German--Philosophy. | Senses and sensation in art.
Classification: LCC NX550.A1 T68 2016 | DDC 709.43--dc23 LC record available at http://lccn.loc.gov/2015047943

British Library Cataloguing in Publication Data

A catalogue record for this book is available from the British Library

Printed in the United States on acid-free paper.

ISBN: 978-1-78533-184-8 hardback
ISBN: 978-1-78533-185-5 ebook

The creative act is not performed by the artist alone; the spectator brings the work in contact with the external world by deciphering and interpreting its inner qualifications and thus adds his contribution to the creative act.

—Marcel Duchamp, "The Creative Act" (1957)

~: CONTENTS :~

List of Illustrations and Tables vii

Foreword viii
Celia Applegate

Acknowledgments xiv

Introduction 1
Margaret Eleanor Menninger

Part I. Foundations

1. The Play's the Thing: Schiller, Wagner, and Gesamtkunstwerk 21
Nicholas Vazsonyi

2. From Gesamtkunstwerk to Music Drama 39
Sanna Pederson

3. Richard Wagner, *Parsifal*, and the Pursuit of Gesamtkunstwerk 56
Anthony J. Steinhoff

Part II. Articulations

4. Epic Gesamtkunstwerk 81
Joy H. Calico

5. Gesamtkunstwerk, Gestaltung, and the Bauhaus Stage 95
Melissa Trimingham

6. Exposing the Political Gesamtkunstwerk: Hanns Eisler's *Nuit et Brouillard* 115
Amy Lynn Wlodarski

7. Reconciling the "Three Graceful Hellenic Sisters": Wagner, Dance, and Song-Ballets Set to Richard Strauss's *Vier letzte Lieder* 133
Wayne Heisler, Jr.

Part III. Inspirations

8. The "Translucent (Not: Transparent)" *Gesamtglaswerk* 157
Jenny Anger

9. Quiet Audience, Roaring Crowd: The Aesthetics of Sound and the Traces of Bayreuth in *Kuhle Wampe* and *Triumph of the Will* 183
Theodore F. Rippey

10. The Will to Heal: Gesamtkunstwerk and Memorial Music since 1945 206
Julia Goodwin and Margaret Eleanor Menninger

11. Consuming Voices: Musical Film and the Gesamtkunstwerk of Mass Culture 228
David Imhoof

Afterword: Gesamtkunstwerk as Epistemic Space 249
Kevin S. Amidon

Select Bibliography 259

Index 273

∾: ILLUSTRATIONS :∾

Figure 5.1. Lyonel Feininger. Cathedral of Socialism for the Program of the State Bauhaus in Weimar, 1919

Figure 8.1. Bruno Taut. Glashaus (Glass house). Cologne, 1914

Figure 8.2. Robert Delaunay. *Simultaneous Windows (1st Part, 2nd Motif, 1st Replica)*, 1912

Figure 8.3. Anna Scheerbart. Front endpapers to Paul Scheerbart, *Glasarchitektur*, 1914

Fig. 8.4. Anna Scheerbart. Back endpapers to Paul Scheerbart, *Glasarchitektur*, 1914

∾: TABLES :∾

Table 7.1. Selective Inventory of Song-Ballets

~: FOREWORD :~

CELIA APPLEGATE

This volume has the distinction of not having been conceived as a contribution to the Richard Wagner bicentenary. Its authors did take part in the bicentenary's many events and publications in 2013, Nicholas Vaszonyi as editor-in-chief of *The Cambridge Wagner Encyclopedia* most centrally of all. But one of the strengths of this volume is that it makes us think about more than Wagner when we think about the *Gesamtkunstwerk*. In his *New Yorker* essay on the "Wagner Summer" of 2013, Alex Ross was right to say that "Richard Wagner will not be ignored," and this volume does not ignore him. Nor is he made to sit in the corner for being Hitler's favorite composer, the most common and laziest move that Wagner commentators perform. Instead he is placed in conversation with people who came before him, his contemporaries, and people who came after him. We find him conceiving of, distancing himself from, renaming, rethinking, revising, and realizing the artistic ideal he once (or twice) called the Gesamtkunstwerk. We see him through the eyes of those who admired him, those who learned from him without admiring him, and those who denied learning from him but did anyway. Some of the time we do not see him or hear him talked about at all.

Ross rightly regretted the absence of a "raft of fresh insights" in the Wagner bicentenary year, with the important exception of what went on in "scholarly precincts."[1] This volume, a product of the lively, multidisciplinary precinct that is the German Studies Association Annual Meeting, is unabashedly and splendidly scholarly, and in it, fresh insights about Wagner, as well as much else, abound. Although the range of places mentioned in these chapters point to a world of artistic activity, their focus remains German Europe and their concerns the traditions, the ideas, the practices, and the people who tried to create and experience this complete communion of the arts. All aspects of the Gesamtkunstwerk have points of reference in the life and works of Richard Wagner. Yet what emerges most strongly in this volume is the dynamic energy, the eclecticism, the attention to the past, and the activist understanding of the role of art in the present that defined and continues to define the German cultural space as a whole. Wagner was a part of that, just as important in integrating and reinventing aspects of the past as he was in bringing forth wholly new experiments in aesthetic experience. So too was the Gesamtkunstwerk a characteristic product of this distinctive cultural milieu, perhaps the most complete effort to express its disparate, sometimes clashing energies.

Still, even if one manages to create some thinking space between Wagner and the Gesamtkunstwerk, one would still have the problem of thinking about the thing itself, marked by one of those German words that seem designed to defy deconstruction. Over the past decade or so, there have been a number of works that grapple with the term, trying in various ways to pin down the phenomenon to which it refers, producing lists of characteristics, connotations, and connections. The sheer range of scholarship cited in the chapters that follow is testimony to the usefulness of such efforts, even if by their nature they are doomed to an academic version of the incompleteness that haunts—and taunts—the would-be producers of Gesamtkunstwerk. But as the introduction makes clear, this collection does not aim at completeness. Indeed essay collections as a scholarly genre acknowledge the incompleteness and open-endedness of knowledge. They are never definitive; they celebrate the process of testing and discovery. This one tests the many definitions of Gesamtkunstwerk that have been proposed recently by confronting generality with specificity and exceptionality. That is the least of its achievements. Long before crowd-sourcing and swarming became buzzwords, essay collections demonstrated the wisdom that emerges from the accumulation of disparate parts, and this one is no exception.

What wisdom, then, does this collection impart? First, it suggests the benefits of understanding phenomena through genealogies, of which this volume offers a rich palette. Nicholas Vazsonyi analyzes the crucial importance of Friedrich Schiller to Wagner's ideas about the "transformative experience" of theater. Sanna Pedersen illuminates the genealogy in Wagner's own thought, by which one idea—Gesamtkunstwerk—appeared and gradually evolved, through experiment, experience, and cogitation, into the music drama. Melissa Trimingham explores the "radical recasting" of Goethe's idea of *Einheit* (unity) through Wagner to the Bauhaus. Joy Calico finds the direct ancestor of Brecht's epic theater in the "modernist struggle" with Wagner and from there to Wagner himself. But the genealogies are not confined to those that run to and through Richard Wagner. Wayne Heisler illuminates the various lineages of modern theatrical combinations of dance, music, and theater, which look subtly different from other Gesamtkunstwerk histories when dance is made a central focus of the genealogy. And Jenny Anger suggests that the Gesamtkunstwerk is but one instance in a "German tradition of constructing utopian neologisms out of constitutive parts"—though the outlines of that intriguing tradition remain as yet undetermined.

Genealogies themselves do more than explain how one thing led to another. For Nietzsche, the point of the genealogy was to reveal essential things that had been forgotten but should not have been; to know where something came from was to know what it was. Less ambitiously but useful nevertheless, they can reveal branches growing in unexpected directions on the family tree. Too large to be accidental, a cluster of left-wing artist-intellectuals emerges from these chapters, each drawn in some way to the search for a unified theory and practice of the arts. Rejecting the Wagnerian version of it did not mean embracing some *a cappella* ideal of artistic purity. To the contrary, it meant aspiring to, if not the totality of the arts, then at least a great deal of interaction and simultaneity among them. As Calico puts it in regard to Brecht, the "poles are bound together by the current flowing between them," and so it was too, though less powerfully, in the case of men like Hanns Eisler, Slatan Dudov, Bruno Taut, and Oskar Schlemmer (discussed in the chapters by Theodore Rippey, Amy Wlodarski, Jenny Anger, and Melissa Trimingham). The ideal of unity expressed by Gesamtkunstwerk appealed because it seemed like a purposeful and effective way of acting in the world. It was, in other words, political and, to a large extent, revolutionary.

If these essays illuminate by exploring genealogies, they also illuminate by contracting and expanding, accordion-like, the term itself, with and without reference to Wagner. This effect is produced by the variety of ways through which the authors approach the phenomenon and the range of actors and activities they include in it. Careful readings of Wagner's writings yield one set of insights into what this possibly unattainable ideal of unity meant and was meant to do. Both Vaszonyi and Pedersen maintain a sharp focus on Wagner's own aspirations, and Anthony Steinhoff makes the case for understanding *Parsifal* as the ideal realized. But other essays attempt to expand the reach of the term as a means to make sense of new and hybrid kinds of artistic work, all after Wagner's death. It would be interesting to know more about Wagner's imitators during his life or about contemporaries of Wagner who independently worked through the legacy of Schiller and Goethe to come up with their own versions of Gesamtkunstwerk, outside the magic circle of Bayreuth. In any case, after his death modernism in architecture and staging developed at least in part against the kind of cultural hegemony that Wagner represented—but in the case of new media, he had (of course) nothing to do with their advent. Twentieth-century examples of total art projects both did and did not need Wagner. Anger's essay on architectural uses of glass, both translucent and transparent, finds an artistic practice that brought "many media and people together, far across time and space" into a totalizing, if not total, experience. Trimingham demonstrates that Wagner and Bauhaus thespians both relied on the medium of the stage production to achieve their aesthetic visions of totality, even if the Bauhaus preferred to speak of this in terms of form (*Gestaltung*). The new medium of film, on the other hand, practically demanded that artists find new ways to integrate the arts, and the essays of Ted Rippey, David Imhoof, and Amy Wlodarski tease out a great variety of artistic *gesamt-ness* or "coming together" in films as disparate as the *Blaue Engel, Kuhle Wampe* and *Night and Fog*. And Julia Goodwin and Margaret Eleanor Menninger show how powerful—and total—could be the musico-dramatic performances of the postwar era that provided rituals of mourning and commemoration. Britten's performance of his *War Requiem* in 1962 emerges in their account as a deeply purposeful effort to use every aspect of performance to effect reconciliation among former enemies.

The third kind of wisdom that this volume imparts is the wisdom of including the audience in any effort we make to understand art's aspirations. That audiences matter is in some sense obvious; much harder to explain is why they matter, beyond the economic imperative, and how they work, beyond a general sense that a good audience energizes a performance. Even college professors, those dinosaurs who "basically spout out ideas that nobody ever does anything about," know that one lectures better to a crowd, and better yet to a crowd undistracted by gadgetry.[2] Many of these chapters bring the crowd into their analysis, indeed make it a constituent part of what constitutes Gesamtkunstwerk: no audience, no total experience. An exquisite awareness of the importance of spectator-participants has marked the practice of totalizing art from Schiller through Wagner to Brecht, Britten, and beyond, but only recently is the history of audiences coming into clearer focus. Sometimes we have evidence for what the audience thought; often we have to speculate, based on the likely effects of certain causes, as in familiar music or startling juxtapositions or particular configurations of space and choices of time. No one can read these essays without going away with a far more nuanced understanding of what it meant—and means—to be a member of an audience. That is perhaps the second greatest achievement of this volume. The first is that one comes to understand—as one scholar after another picks up and examines the idea of the Gesamtkunstwerk, turning it around to catch the light in different ways, seeing what it does when you drop it or spin it or wind it up—that there is no "there", no definite achievement of a total work of art, just the far more interesting process of trying to arrive.

1. Alex Ross, "Wagner Summer: A New 'Ring' in Bayreuth; 'Die Meistersinger' in Salzburg," *The New Yorker* (26 August 2013).
2. "GOP: Chris Christie's Professorial Putdown," *Boston Globe* (23 August 2013).

Celia Applegate is William R. Kenan, Jr. Professor of History and Affiliate Professor of Musicology at Vanderbilt University. She is author of *Bach in Berlin: Nation and Culture in Mendelssohn's St. Matthew Passion* (Cornell, 2005), co-editor of *Music and German National Identity* (Chicago, 2001), and is completing a work entitled *Variations on a German Theme: Music in Central European Society and Culture*.

ACKNOWLEDGMENTS

The idea for this volume emerged from some lively exchanges that took place during a series of panel sessions devoted to the "Total Work of Art" at the Thirty-Fourth Annual Meeting of the German Studies Association, held in Oakland, CA in 2010. That fact that the series itself was even organized owed much to a suggestion that Celia Applegate had offered the year before. We would thus like to thank all those who participated in these sessions and in the subsequent conversations about how to turn the ideas that emerged from these discussions into a suitable publication.

In the course of preparing the volume, we have received valuable assistance from many quarters, which we are delighted to acknowledge here. To our contributors, first, we offer our deep gratitude for your professionalism, good humor, and, above all, patience with what has turned out to be a rather long process. We also appreciate that our respective academic institutions—Susquehanna University (David Imhoof), Texas State University (Margaret Eleanor Menninger), and the University of Tennessee-Chattanooga and the University of Quebec at Montreal (Anthony J. Steinhoff)—have given us financial, library, and moral support for this endeavor. Without that aid, this volume would never have seen the light of day. We are likewise grateful to Jean-François Hughes for assistance with the volume bibliography and to the University of California Press for permitting Joy Calico to incorporate into her chapter material that previously appeared in her book, *Brecht at the Opera* (2008). To David Luebke, the *Spektrum* series editor, thank you for your early interest in the project, for serving as a sounding board, and for advice on how to turn a big idea into a manageable book. The anonymous trio of readers for the *Spektrum* series shared comments that proved enormously useful in fine-tuning all of the contributions prior to publication. We are also indebted to the staff at Berghahn Books, especially Chris Chappell, for transforming our manuscript into a published volume.

∾: INTRODUCTION :∾

MARGARET ELEANOR MENNINGER

The broad influence of *Gesamtkunstwerk*, routinely if imperfectly translated as the "Total Work of Art," on modern European cultural and political activity is unmistakable.[1] Called the stuff of "campfire stories" by one scholar, Gesamtkunstwerk is such an evocatively protean idea that it is hardly surprising that its genealogy and application remain lively subjects, even as its precise taxonomy remains elusive.[2] In the realms of music, literature, art, architecture, and theater, the idea of Gesamtkunstwerk continues to be a potent means of telegraphing a particular set of aesthetic goals for practitioners and analytical practices for scholars. But beyond these usual suspects, it has also been used as a descriptor for virtual reality and as a means of considering pedagogy in the new millennium, all in places far beyond its original geographic and disciplinary locus.[3] Perhaps the concept of the total work of art has even become the victim of its own success; indeed, it may have evolved into a "label with no meaning."[4] But should it be completely jettisoned?[5]

The participants in this collection hew to the premise that the ideal of Gesamtkunstwerk has always revolved more around a central idea of promise rather than of delivery, functioning as a "recurrent dream" as one critic has put it.[6] The exact contents and manner of such a promise may themselves be subject to change, but this essentially aspirational aspect of Gesamtkunstwerk has proven its worth over time to artists, performers, and scholars. It is the durability of the idea rather than the specific details of its content and meaning that continue to make it worthy of study. The sheer number of works on the subject that have appeared in the past twenty years would seem to support the claim that there is still much to be considered about the total work of art vis-à-vis cultural and intellectual life in the nineteenth and twentieth centuries. Yet the extant literature has its own peculiarities.

If "in the beginning" was *not* Richard Wagner, his ideas exerted and continue to exert the greatest gravitational pull on how scholars and the general public discuss the total work of art. Indeed, Gesamtkunstwerk oftentimes seems to function as a means of identifying an aesthetic-political pathway that leads either to or from Richard Wagner (if not as a shorthand term of reference for his works in general).[7] The road toward Wagner is relatively well trodden;

it focuses for the most part on the German Romantic tradition and those thinkers' understanding of earlier Greek and Roman ideals of political and artistic unity.[8] Wagner's particular "brand" of Gesamtkunstwerk, as Nicholas Vazsonyi calls it, was a uniquely innovative means of packaging ideas about art and universalism that had origins in the eighteenth century in both Germany and France, a point echoed by David Roberts.[9] That brand had and continues to have important aesthetic and political resonance for the middle of the nineteenth century, as seen in Udo Bermbach's specific focus on the 1840s and 1850s in *Der Wahn des Gesamtkunstwerks* and his attention to the political dimensions of Wagner's aesthetic project.[10]

The path away from Wagner gets a bit thornier. After his death, Gesamtkunstwerk becomes thickly entwined with Wagnerism as an international, and particularly pan-European, cultural-intellectual phenomenon. [11] For example, while Timothée Picard's primary focus is on the "totality" of the Gesamtkunstwerk (as is evident from his use of *L'art total* in his title), he also sees it as one of several ways Wagnerism and Wagnerian tropes persisted, particularly in literature, long after the composer's death. Kevin C. Karnes, following Picard, seeks to return Wagner to the center of his study of the arts in fin-de-siècle Vienna, highlighting in particular Wagner's influence on the emergence of a "utopian imagination in Vienna's creative culture."[12] Marcella Lista, likewise, has illuminated the relationship between the notion of Gesamtkunstwerk (and its reinterpretation) and the emergence of early twentieth-century avant-garde movements.[13] And in *Modernism after Wagner*, Juliet Koss proposes that Wagner's specific concept of Gesamtkunstwerk continued to provide a framework for understanding the interrelation of various art forms from the mid-nineteenth century through the 1930s, including the very European workshop that was the Bauhaus.[14]

In all these works, Wagner's remains the version of a total work of art to adopt, adapt, or reject outright. Collectively these scholars point toward a broader European understanding and employment of the idea of the total work of art after Wagner's death, a project that embraces cultural production up to the end of the twentieth century and beyond.[15] Scholarship presenting variations of Gesamtkunstwerk maintains these broadly international perspectives in terms of the type of artistic creation examined. In essence, the total work of art has developed into an "aesthetic aspiration to borderlessness," both in terms of disciplines and nationalities.[16] Anke Finger and Danielle Follett's collection, *The Aesthetics of the Total Artwork*, highlights this broadening of perspective that enables the concept to be extended to many fields while it pushes the examination of Gesamtkunstwerk from modernity into postmodernity.[17]

Thus, in a European and international context, the road away from Wagner is one that runs ever on. In the German context, however, the road seems to have a very definite dead end. It ends in 1933, or perhaps more properly in

1935, with National Socialism and *Triumph of the Will*. Even in works such as Josef Chytry's *The Aesthetic State*, Gesamtkunstwerk only plays a part insofar as it relates to Wagner and further to National Socialism.[18] To be sure, scholars have noted the impact of Gesamtkunstwerk on the work of Brecht, Kandinsky, Schoenberg, and many others who shared neither Hitler's philosophy nor the nastier elements of Wagner's worldview. However, even these efforts to include progressive creative activity in the narrative of Gesamtkunstwerk ultimately become part of a trajectory that smashes into the triumph of a totalizing and totalitarian aesthetic vision. In the words of Adrian Daub, efforts to rescue the total work of art in Germany from a fascist fate belong to the "losing side of the Gesamtkunstwerk."[19] Ralf Biel, echoing Jürgen Söring, is even more deterministic: "[T]he idea of the *Gesamtkunstwerk* … mutates step by step into the total artwork of German totalitarianism."[20]

We would beg to differ. Even as much of the scholarship on the total work of art in the last twenty years or so has been explicitly European, the redolence of "Teutonic profundities" remains.[21] Of course the centrality of Wagner, German modernism, and National Socialism to most discussions of the total work of art during the nineteenth and twentieth centuries inevitably nudges any study toward a German center. But much of the research, especially that of more recent vintage, seems not to consider German cultural production since 1945 to any great degree; furthermore, the scholarship on Gesamtkunstwerk that views the idea as an ongoing theme or phenomenon within German cultural history in particular is underdeveloped.[22] This collection is a step toward correcting that oversight. Above all, pushing the trajectory of Gesamtkunstwerk in the German-speaking world beyond World War II forces us to consider the longer life of Daub's "losing side of the Gesamtkunstwerk" and how artists and audiences, in the context of ambitious, large-scale, audience-focused works, have come to terms with Nazism's legacies.

This volume thus explores Gesamtkunstwerk primarily within a German context. Collectively, the chapters reflect on German cultural history and the relationship between culture and politics in German-speaking Europe. We understand this scope mainly in two ways. First, expectedly, the essays focus on events and developments that took place in German Europe or were intimately associated with it. Second, we include essays that examine artistic engagement with creative works of Germanic provenance. Our chronological focus, from the early nineteenth century through to the early twenty-first, also makes clear that the evolution of German thinking about the total work of art has been varied and multidirectional. The road runs in many directions, and National Socialism neither exhausts the possibilities along the way nor serves as the terminus.

The essays here contribute to trends in the extant literature that acknowledge but also reconsider Wagner's central presence in the discourse and writing on

Gesamtkunstwerk, both inside and outside "Germany." They question the need to understand Gesamtkunstwerk only as an idealization of totality, above all in the sense of an impulse towards creating monumental, synthetic works where the component parts are neatly integrated into an overarching whole. Perhaps, following early twentieth-century artists like Wassily Kandinsky, we need also to be attuned to readings of "totality" that strive not for unity in art, but only inclusivity—to the point even of embracing discord and incongruity.[23] At the very least, it seems that we need to be aware of the degree of conflict inherent in the creation of Gesamtkunstwerk. Along these lines, Matthew Wilson Smith has recently argued that dialectical struggles in the name of total aesthetic experience—art vs. commerce, organicism vs. mechanization, political ideologies of the left vs. the right—have determined the history of the Gesamtkunstwerk.[24] He suggests, thus, that the key to understanding this evolution is to look for the clashes beneath the smoother external surface of the work itself—that is, to study the way a would-be Gesamtkunstwerk attempts to mask the conflicts fundamental to its meaning. It is in the "relationship between the total work of art, technology, and mass culture" where Gesamtkunstwerk's functional and creative history is most clearly found.[25]

Put another way, a total work of art could be likened to *Lohengrin*'s swan: appearing all serene above the waterline but frantically paddling against the current below. That image points not only to the dynamism of the underlying creative process but also leads us to question the semblance of overall coherence in the final result, at least in those takes on Gesamtkunstwerk that strive for synthetic unity. The term may be parsed in other ways too. For, when considering Gesamtkunstwerk, the question of what "*gesamt*" means remains critical: most commonly translated to mean "total," it may also be understood in terms of the "communal" or the "collective," as Josef Chytry, Marcella Lista, and Matthew Wilson Smith have pointed out.[26] Anke Finger refines this distinction slightly, observing that where a "Gesamt-Kunstwerk" may represent a single work presented as a total artwork, a "Gesamtkunst-Werk" should be understood as a "collaborative product."[27] Deconstructing the components of the term differently points toward any number of analytical pathways, some easier to navigate from the perspective of one discipline than from another. But all raise fundamental questions about the consequences of an image of surface unity, however completely achieved, that covers up (or attempts to cover up) the struggle to paddle against currents generated by the tensions among the various component elements.

This collection is itself a collaborative product that aims to propel Gesamtkunstwerk into new and less charted waters. It began as an informal conversation at the end of a panel devoted to music, history, and cultural studies at the 2009 German Studies Association Conference in Washington DC, when it was suggested that the panelists ought to organize a series of conference sessions to explore and question the idea of Gesamtkunstwerk as multidisciplinary praxis in the nineteenth and twentieth centuries. Taking cues from all the above-mentioned studies, the present volume collectively investigates a large number of Gesamtkunstwerk's potential and actual permutations. It does not provide its own complete or totalizing account of Gesamtkunstwerk in German-speaking Europe, and this is intentional. The diverse approaches to, and understandings of, Gesamtkunstwerk over the nineteenth and twentieth centuries are themselves indicative of twists and turns in the evolution of German culture itself in the same period. Thus, at the same time that this series of essays collectively explores Gesamtkunstwerk against the backdrop of a highly dynamic cultural landscape, it seeks to shed new light on our understanding of that cultural heritage.

First, these essays demonstrate that politics—broadly construed—has been critical to the total work of art in both theory and practice. Gesamtkunstwerk is not just about creating multimedia, synthetic products: it involves art with a purpose, even when the politics are worn lightly. That a total work of art ought to have a political message may not seem much of a news flash, but in our view the types of political messages associated with it have been too narrowly categorized, and again have been made to follow a very specific evolutionary route running from revolutionary idealism in 1849 to totalizing authoritarianism in 1935. Scholars' ongoing emphasis on totality, and especially a very specific understanding of that totality as the central definitional thrust of the term, one that is unitary rather than collaborative, has also tended to obscure the fact that many different types of political messages can find their way into Gesamtkunstwerk.

Second, we seek to focus more attention on the consumption of Gesamtkunstwerk—above all in the sense of how audiences received such works and, even more so, actively collaborated in investing them with meaning. Gesamtkunstwerk has been intimately reliant on reception, not merely the creation of would-be "total" worlds or worldviews.[28] This book's focus on Gesamtkunstwerk's communal and collective elements keeps the spotlight, so to speak, on the performance—the reality of making and presenting a work—and on the audience. Many of the essays have profited from the categorization of the total work of art advanced in Anke Finger and Danielle Follett's collection. Their proposed trinity of elements—aesthetics, politics, and metaphysics—provides a useful, informal baseline from which to analyze potential "total works of art." Nevertheless, one of the conclusions that emerges from the contributions here is that two more elements should be added to the mix: process (or production) and experience (or reception). Indeed, the contributors to this volume show clearly that the practical factors of creation help shape how we understand the constitution of a total work of art in the moment, and how the practice (and practicality) of creation affects the end result.

Third, this book considers Gesamtkunstwerk's aspirational nature. As we noted earlier, the total work of art has always worked better as ideal than blueprint.[29] This is true for both performers and scholars. Treating Gesamtkunstwerk as an ideal—stated or implied—that may inform the experience of cultural activity or practice opens up possibilities for employing it as a heuristic device to arrive at richer understandings of cultural phenomena and their specific social contexts. These possibilities are largely obscured if we focus on the nostalgic dimensions of Wagner's Gesamtkunstwerk concept, that is, as a way to return to a world that has been lost. But, if we think about Gesamtkunstwerk as a collaborative model—not just among different branches of art, but also among creator, performers, and audience—then it can serve not so much as a criterion for deciding whether a work is or is not deemed to be a total work of art, but rather as a way to highlight and reflect on what the apparent similarities or dissonances between ideal and realization might mean. This approach also opens the way to exploring art works in terms of the total work of art, even if their creators did not conceive them as such, and to examining aspects of the collaborative process that do not even focus on the artwork itself. In their various ways, each essay in this collection engages with this notion of Gesamtkunstwerk as collaborative practice and communal experience. But if Gesamtkunstwerk emerges from these analyses as a stable ideal, it is one where the content and meaning have undergone and undergo continuous revision.

The book divides the eleven chapters into three parts. Part I considers the genesis or **Foundations** of Gesamtkunstwerk and its use by Richard Wagner; Part II looks at its deliberate re-engineering after Wagner's death, or **Articulations** of the idea; and Part III sees Gesamtkunstwerk as **Inspiration**, in which the authors probe the concept's aesthetic boundaries and its value for analyzing cultural production and consumption. In one way or another, all of these broad topics of investigation study the dialectic and myth of unity that seems to be inherent in the concept of Gesamtkunstwerk. They also demonstrate the ways in which the idea of Gesamtkunstwerk has remained an important theme in German cultural history since the early nineteenth century. A further testament to the breadth of Gesamtkunstwerk is the fact that this collection brings together scholars from a wide range of disciplines: history, music, dance, literature, and art history. Under these three headings, the essays that follow explore the ways in which (1) nineteenth-century thinkers and practitioners, including Wagner, created the idea of Gesamtkunstwerk; (2) artists in a variety of fields subsequently employed, reworked and extended the concept; and (3) how the idea's potent yet contentious afterlife may help us explore and understand dimensions of German cultural life from the early twentieth century to the present day.

Specifically in the "Foundations" section, the authors consider how early nineteenth-century Romantics developed the idea of a total work of art, revealing the utter lack of consensus on how to use the term.[30] As the contributors point out, the foundation of the Wagnerian total work of art, as it was understood by later artists, was built both on what he wrote in 1849 and what he later did on stage, particularly in *Parsifal*. For Nicholas Vazsonyi (Chapter 1), it is Friedrich Schiller's vision of drama's liberating potential that most effectively showed Wagner the path to imagining Gesamtkunstwerk as dramatic process and revolutionary participatory ideal. In particular, Vazsonyi stresses, Schiller (and other Romantics) inspired Wagner to regard performance as central to any understanding of the total work of art. Critically, this position implies that the audience is itself an essential element in the realization of Gesamtkunstwerk. As Vazsonyi puts it, the ultimate goal of any performance, particularly anything aspiring to the status of Gesamtkunstwerk, was "the fundamental impact on the recipient" of the drama in question. The goal of such an impression was not merely to wow the viewers; it was to use the emotional response to the spectacle to drive home a moral point. Gesamtkunstwerk in performance thus creates a communal, shared experience as well as an opportunity to "catch the conscience" of the audience.

Sanna Pederson (Chapter 2) focuses directly on the two main texts where Wagner developed his ideas about the total work of art. She argues that while Wagner's formulation of Gesamtkunstwerk in *The Artwork of the Future* (1849/50) was both strikingly original and politically radical, he rapidly retreated from that position. His text *Opera and Drama* (1851), in particular, presents a less revolutionary analysis where Gesamtkunstwerk as such is not even named. Pederson suggests, too, that Wagner had to change his earlier vision of Gesamtkunstwerk in part to fit his practice (or perhaps his planned practice, as he only actively returned to composition in 1854), having realized that his earlier cooperative and inclusive vision of art would inevitably founder on the shoals of actual performance. Even if Wagner found the ecstatic union of the three sister arts (music, dance, poetry) to be inspiring and seductive, when it came time to think practically about the realities of the artist as creator, it made sense to simplify. But the procreative analogy of the union of music and drama, while more compelling as a means of description of how to "create" an artwork, still left control in too many hands. Ultimately, Pederson concludes, Wagner opted for the creative force of one.

Anthony Steinhoff (Chapter 3) is not quite so pessimistic about the survival of Wagner's early vision of Gesamtkunstwerk, although he locates its best expression some thirty years later than Pederson's end point. Steinhoff agrees that, in assessing Wagner's writings about the total work of art, we must distinguish between the theoretical and the concrete. "We may need to make a clearer distinction," he suggests, "between the fundamental problems Wagner hoped to address (the 'thesis') and the specific solutions (the 'hypotheses') he proposed to them." Wagner did not stop thinking about Gesamtkunstwerk in the 1850s; rather he continued to investigate the notion from a variety of angles for the rest of his life. Steinhoff finds in *Parsifal,* Wagner's final opera, the idea of Gesamtkunstwerk to be most completely realized. By then the Bayreuth "workshop" had given Wagner the requisite time and artistic conditions to develop his earlier vision of a revolutionary Gesamtkunstwerk into a performance that approached his unified vision of the musical, the aesthetic, and the dramatic, all reunited with a sense of political program.

If Steinhoff cautions us not to fall into the trap of turning Wagner's idea of Gesamtkunstwerk into an eternal verity, the chapters grouped in the "Articulations" part offer a series of reflections on Gesamtkunswerk's meaning and application post-Wagner. During the last decades of the nineteenth century and the first half of the twentieth century, a time when his and Bayreuth's influence were particularly controversial, many of those engaged with the production and reception of Gesamtkunstwerk fought against Wagner's concept. Thinkers such as Friedrich Nietzsche, Walter Benjamin, and Theodor Adorno expressed their concern over Wagner's legacy.[31] Meanwhile practitioners and observers increasingly paid attention to the political implications of Wagner's ideas.

The articulations of Gesamtkunstwerk expressed here are, in their way, all essays on "the reception of Wagner-reception," as Gerd Rienäcker first put it and as Amy Wlodarski points out in her contribution.[32] For the artists working after the Great War, Wlodarski notes, the "received" Wagnerian Gesamtkunstwerk put enormous and, in their eyes dangerous, emphasis on music.[33] Its creative function as the dominant element in a total work of art threatened to leave the listener with dangerous cravings and numbed senses.[34] Integrating a greater number of disciplines and media into the total art work offered one way to prevent this harm. Bauhaus artists, for instance, were known for adding architecture and film to the three sisters of music, poetry, and dance. But the essential point upon which the artists discussed in this section of the volume saw their work turning remained the issue of unity or, in Joy Calico's words, the "totalizing impulse." As a group, the chapters in Part II reveal that the goal of unity (or totality) remained a central concern for these artists even as they rejected Wagner's—or their understanding of Wagner's—method(s) for achieving it.

Joy Calico (Chapter 4), notably, contends that Bertolt Brecht used Gesamtkunstwerk to express his own ideas about totality in opera and theater. Brecht, conventionally depicted as the polar opposite to Wagner in operatic terms, was engaging with a particular iteration of the total work of art, the "Nietzsche-Wagner brand," as we might put it, which had come to stand in for Wagner proper. But if we look carefully, she points out, Brecht's vision of theater has a great deal in common with Wagner's early models of

Gesamtkunstwerk in terms of both theory and practice. Like Wagner, Brecht was also confronted with the problem of how to achieve his ideas on an actual stage. The pragmatic problems of production (of particular concern because Brecht could not supervise the staging of his works while in exile) have to be factored into how Brecht understood the theory of what he was achieving. For Calico, thus, Brecht's epic theater projects can be understood as consciously articulating the elements of a total work of art, albeit in a way as far from that of Wagner as possible. And yet in straining to pull away from "planet Wagner," Brecht's own totalizing impulse shows distinct similarities to the Schillerian ideals of a total work of art with drama serving as the sun.

In her exploration of Oskar Schlemmer and the Bauhaus theater, Melissa Trimingham (Chapter 5) notes that efforts to create a sense of unity within the Bauhaus were often haunted by the Wagnerian brand of Gesamtkunstwerk. Yet, she insists, the Bauhaus was also very much inspired by pre-Wagnerite ideals of unifying the arts in terms of the works that were produced there. In particular, Oskar Schlemmer's theatrical performances embraced the broad potential of the stage reminiscent of Goethe and Schiller—even as the performances deliberately downplayed music as part of the formal presentation. Schlemmer and others at the Bauhaus, however, did not ban music from their vision of the unified arts. Indeed, music played a central role in the everyday life at the Bauhaus. The collaborative and communal aspects of total work of art were part of the ordinary practice of those who worked—and partied—there. Nevertheless, Trimingham views the stage work of Schlemmer and his co-workers as a practical and material realization of the unity of the arts expressed by the early Romantics. That is, the modernist theater of Schlemmer and his colleagues, stripped of any nineteenth-century embellishment, nonetheless tapped "into a vision of cultural harmony" that reached back to before Wagner.

Even artists who explicitly rejected Gesamtkunstwerk as a Wagnerian trope nevertheless still made use of a "total" concept to create an artificial unity in their work, which in turn could inspire revolutionary thought. Indeed, as Trimingham tellingly remarks, "Wagner and the Bauhaus become radically different embodied manifestations of what is essentially the same impulse." This observation, and the other essays in Part II, point to the extraordinary political malleability of the total work of art. Gesamtkunstwerk could be used as effectively by those on the left as by those on the right, despite the legacy of National Socialist exploitation of Wagner. The analytical implications of these findings are particularly significant, for they suggest that we ought not to conflate the artistic drive towards unity with political definitions of "total" or "totalitarian" as was done by both Adorno and Benjamin. The framework they developed has encouraged a far more manipulative take on totality as it pertains to Gesamtkunstwerk than was necessarily present in the striving towards unity undertaken by the artists of the Bauhaus or in Brecht.[35]

In her exploration of Alain Resnais' film *Nuit et Brouillard* (Night and Fog, 1955) with music by Hanns Eisler, Amy Wlodarski (Chapter 6) shows once more how the conscious rejection of Wagner's idea of Gesamtkunstwerk, in particular its alleged trance-inducing musical totality, could result in works that articulated a modernist vision of unity. For Eisler, as for Brecht and those in the Bauhaus, unity was best articulated in works that re-engineered the components of Gesamtkunstwerk to reject one form of totality while in a sense creating another. Eisler's film score (music), Wlodarski concludes, serves to bring together the elements of *Night and Fog*, so that it reads as a "political retort to totalitarianism" that undercuts "Wagnerian conventions," even while embracing some of the same techniques.

That said, the impulse to push back against Wagnerian ideas (or at least a particular take on them) was not always as combative. Wayne Heisler (Chapter 7) investigates articulations of unity in the total work of art by reclaiming the "graceful Hellenic sister" all too often left by the side of the road in later iterations of Gesamtkunstwerk: dance. Perhaps more than Brecht or the artists of the Bauhaus, Heisler shows that twentieth-century dancers and choreographers found productive and positive ways to fuse Wagnerian models of totality and unity in their efforts to create ballet as a "total" theatrical form. At the same time, they gave new impetus to the ideas of Gesamtkunstwerk. In the case of dancers such as Martha Graham, and such choreographers as Maurice Béjart and Rudi van Dantzig, ballet as Gesamtkunstwerk resembled more "reconciled artworks" rather than total ones. Heisler suggests that this element of reconciliation can be seen particularly in the "song ballets," especially those based on Richard Strauss' *Vier letzte Lieder* (Four Last Songs). The ballets set to these particular songs, with their emphasis on the themes of grief and acceptance, demonstrate, in Heisler's view, a resurgence of a particularly Romantic variant of Gesamtkunstwerk that Wagner had bypassed, proving that, in some cases, recapitulation can be articulation.

The contributions to the third and final section, "Inspirations," all seek to push the envelope with respect to how we think about Gesamtkunstwerk and about aesthetic practice, cultural consumption, and audiences more generally. Each author approaches Gesamtkunstwerk not so much as a label to be affixed to an artistic endeavor, but rather as a complex of aesthetic-cum-political ideas that can be employed analytically, either en bloc or à la carte, to enrich our understanding of art and its sociopolitical contexts, especially over the course of the twentieth century. Admittedly, the cases examined in this section were never conceived, at least in any direct sense, as works of total art. Rather, by viewing them through the lens of Gesamtkunstwerk and, thereby, shifting focus from aesthetic model to analytical concept, the authors in this section seek to open up new perspectives on our understanding of the creative process, the connections between art and politics, above all in the age of mass media.

In this way these pieces appropriately echo the variety of Gesamtkunstwerke discussed in parts I and II, illustrating that a willingness to step out of Wagner's shadow can provide us with a more insightful and analytically useful vision of this concept.

Theorists ever since Schiller have invariably considered the audience as central to their understanding of a total work of art. But frequently their analyses treat the audience as if it receives a total work of art as an already completed unit. The contributors in this section argue that we must also consider the audience's active reception of the artwork as part of the artwork itself. Thinking about the audience, in turn, forces us to think about how "total" a total work of art actually was before it was seen or heard. To put the question another way: does Gesamtkunstwerk only take place between a person's ears or in front of a person's eyes? Is the act of consumption the crucial final piece of Gesamtkunstwerk? Or, to return to the title of Nicholas Vazsonyi's essay, is the play really the thing, or is it the audience?

In their respective chapters, Jenny Anger and Theodore Rippey engage directly with two basic means of reception: visual and auditory. Combining what David Roberts calls the "two great recurrent symbols of the total work of art"—the theater and the cathedral—in an analysis of Bruno Taut's 1914 *Glashaus*, Jenny Anger (Chapter 8) demonstrates how using a new term, *Gesamtglaswerk* (total glass work), offers a means of reclaiming the "utopian spirit" of unity in Gesamtkunstwerk.[37] In the case of Taut's piece, this spiritual recovery is achieved by combining the site-specific theatricality of the translucent Glashaus as an architectural space with the spiritual sense of "purity" and "unity" reported by those who visited it.[38] The medium through which this is accomplished is glass, thanks to the ways in which glass and light interact. In the Gesamtglaswerk, it is light, blended light, that spiritually unifies the arts, but with light and sight rather than music and hearing as the binding agents. Gesamtglaswerk incorporates the effects of collaborative production as well as the promise of that most utopian of projects: the political and spiritual unity of mankind.

For Theodore Rippey (Chapter 9), sound is the element at Gesamtkunstwerk's center, and not just as music. He argues that noise was also an important part of the soundscape, particularly for those in the 1930s who were inspired by Wagner's approach to sight and sound at Bayreuth and also committed to the ideal of Gesamtkunstwerk as "an object for and maker of an audience." The films *Kuhle Wampe* and *Triumph of the Will*, he contends, show how crowd noise functions as part of the performance the audience hears and as something that the audience contributes to the aesthetic, cinematic experience. Noise thus redirects the experience of the audience/viewer and adds something new to Gesamtkunstwerk's artistic "palette." This attention to sound and noise also leads Rippey to challenge the conventional wisdom that Leni Riefenstahl's

Triumph best realizes Gesamtkunstwerk's aesthetic ideal. Instead, he suggests that honor be bestowed on Slatan Dudov's *Kuhle Wampe*, on account of its more natural, inclusive approach to cinematographic sound. Not only does this analysis undermine *Triumph*'s putative status as the apotheosis of a totalitarian Gesamtkunstwerk, it reminds us yet again that the political range of the total work of art has too often been narrowly defined.

More than any other contributors to this collection, Julia Goodwin, Margaret Eleanor Menninger, and David Imhoof resist the centripetal force of Wagner's Gesamtkunstwerk by situating their analyses of total works of art at the point where it is furthest away from the artist's control. Their respective essays contend that the process of consumption completes the Gesamtkunstwerk; that is, that reception is a crucial part of performance. The essay by Goodwin/Menninger (Chapter 10) re-centers music within the total work of art in a manner that Wagner would likely have endorsed. But they propose a new way of using the ideals of unity so prized by the early nineteenth-century Romantics. Namely, they propose that we understand performances of memorial music designed for ceremonial acts of reconciliation as enactments of total works of art themselves. Using the example of Benjamin Britten's *War Requiem*, they show that the choice of specific performers, "symbolic casting," was also an important factor in the creation of these total works of art, which strove to be transformational for the psyche as well as for the spirit. Memorial music itself, Goodwin and Menninger suggest, becomes Gesamtkunstwerk through the articulation of specific conditions for particular performances and through the experience of reception.

In his piece, David Imhoof (Chapter 11) likewise shows how audiences, especially in their roles as consumers of mass culture, worked to manufacture a sense of unity around particular musical films. He reveals that German viewers' familiarity with stories, soundtracks, and stars of musical films provided hooks that enabled them to connect their specific experiences of these movies with their broader cultural consumption habits. Through such links, consumers could foster a semblance of unity in their cultural lives. Placing virtually all the agency for creating a total work of art in the hands of the audience, Imhoof takes us farthest from the creators of artistic products discussed elsewhere in this collection. His radical emphasis on Gesamtkunstwerk as a mythical whitewashing of complex connections and contradictions in cultural life may be the logical extension of Gesamtkunstwerk as *Lohengrin*'s swan serenely covering the vigorous paddling below the surface. Ultimately Imhoof maintains that using Gesamtkunstwerk as an analytical lens can help us understand the ways that mass consumer culture functioned in Germans' lives.

The idea of Gesamtkunstwerk continues to inspire and vex us. Humans still thrill to the promise of experiencing a moment of transcendent unity through art, despite all the evidence of the potential for misuse and the passionate arguments against the dangers of totality. Perhaps the tendency to cling stubbornly to the ideal of Gesamtkunstwerk remains in part because it is so difficult to pin down objectively. Indeed one might almost be moved to remark, as Supreme Court Justice Potter Stewart did in 1964 about obscenity, that we know Gesamtkunstwerk when we see it.[39] Strange as it may sound, this use of an uncertain yet certain definition has more merit than is immediately apparent. Like the fragmentary origins of the idea of the total work of art, Stewart's decision was one of seven separate opinions deciding the case. Moreover, Stewart's phrase has developed a life of its own, not only in everyday speech but also in legal opinion.[40] Beyond these rather surface points of similarity, however, Stewart's "analytical category" is worth revisiting, especially in the context of using the idea of Gesamtkunstwerk for analysis, both from the point of view of the final recipient—the audience—and that of the scholar. In an article on the linguistic afterlife of Stewart's decision, legal scholar Paul Gerwitz declares that he wishes to "identify and celebrate various ways in which non-rational as well as rational elements enter judicial decisions."[41] Here is the place where Stewart's decision can be helpful. Like him, we are "faced with the task of trying to define what may be indefinable," even if we recognize the absence of any universally agreed upon criteria. That act of recognition is based in part at least on instinct and emotion as much as on conviction.

If we go along with the idea that we know a Gesamtkunstwerk when we see one, or perhaps experience one, we are ultimately acknowledging the force of irrational and individual subjectivity as an indispensable component of the notion of "totality" (or "integration" or "commonality") inherent in the total work of art. If we further agree that the pursuit of unity remains a pedal point in the harmonic structure of the total work of art, we might conclude that the way to find that utopian total is within the fractured individuals we are. Embedded within the idea of knowing what one sees when one sees it are some important resonances which we hope this volume will address. In the case of Gesamtkunstwerk, we know it when we see it; yet when we do, we all see it differently. It is in collaboration that the outlines of a total work of art are clearest. Only from a cooperatively constructed foundation can the chorus of articulations and inspirations begin. In that sense, this volume may be understood as a *Lehrstück* in the way that Brecht envisioned it—what Joy Calico calls a means of "communal participation." It is our collective hope that a project initially designed for the education of the participants has moved some way toward being a full-fledged performance. Its potential to rise to heights beyond that we leave to the experience of the reader.

Notes

Although the introduction bears only one of our names, it and the entire project have been a joint venture; my thanks to David Imhoof and Anthony J. Steinhoff.

1. While it ultimately proved necessary to incorporate this English rendering of Gesamtkunstwerk into the collection's title, this chapter, and many of the contributions that follow, view "The Total Work of Art" as only one of several possible ways of translating and thinking about Gesamtkunstwerk. Thus, throughout the volume, we have opted to retain the original German term, supplementing it as appropriate with the standard English translation.
2. "Ein mythischer Begriff in Erzählungen am Kaminfeuer..." See Harald Szeemann, "Vorbereitungen," in *Der Hang zum Gesamtkunstwerk: Europäische Utopien seit 1800*, ed. Harald Szeemann (Aarau, 1983), 17.
3. See Matthew Wilson Smith, *The Total Work of Art: From Bayreuth to Cyberspace* (New York, 2007) especially 157–86; and Margaret Eleanor Menninger, "The Classroom as a 'Total Work of Art': Pedagogy, Performance and 'Gesamtkunstwerk,'" *Ubiquitous Learning: An International Journal* 3, no. 3 (2011): 97–104. I am grateful for the thoughts of Mark Guzdial and Amy Bruckman on the application of the concept of Gesamtkunstwerk to education and technology. See also Mark Guzdial and Allison Elliott Tew, "Imagineering Inauthentic Legitimate Peripheral Participation: An Instructional Design Approach for Motivating Computing Education," ICER '06 *Proceedings of the Second International Workshop on Computing Education Research* (New York, 2006), 51–58.
4. See Nicholas Vazsonyi, "The Play's the Thing: Schiller, Wagner, and Gesamtkunstwerk," in this collection.
5. In their introduction, Danielle Follett and Anke Finger suggest detonation: "Dynamiting the Gesamtkunstwerk: An Introduction to the Aesthetics of the Total Artwork," in *The Aesthetics of the Total Artwork: On Borders and Fragments*, ed. Anke Finger and Danielle Follett (Baltimore, 2011), 1–25. See also Roger Fornoff, *Die Sehnsucht nach dem Gesamtkunstwerk: Studien zu einer ästhetischen Konzeption der Moderne* (Hildesheim, 2004), 18.
6. David Roberts, "Review Essay: The Total Work of Art," *Thesis Eleven* 83 (November 2005): 104.
7. See, for example, Sven Oliver Müller, *Richard Wagner und die Deutschen: Eine Geschichte von Hass und Hingabe* (Munich, 2013), 25–45 passim.
8. See Simon Shaw-Miller, "Opsis Melos Lexis: Before and Around the Total Work of Art," in *Rival Sisters, Art and Music at the Birth of Modernism, 1815–1915*, ed. James H. Rubin and Olivia Mattis (Farnham, 2014), 37–51.
9. Nicholas Vazsonyi, *Richard Wagner: Self-Promotion and the Making of a Brand* (Cambridge, 2010). See also Timothée Picard, *L'Art total: grandeur et misère d'une utopie (autour de Wagner)* (Rennes, 2006), 23–26; and David Roberts, *The Total Work of Art in European Modernism* (Ithaca, 2011), 15–33. The point about French interest in Gesamtkunstwerk is also made very specifically for early nineteenth-century French literature in Matthias Brzoska, *Die Idee des Gesamtkunstwerks in der Musiknovellistik der Julimonarchie* (Laaber-Verlag, 1995).
10. Udo Bermbach, *Der Wahn des Gesamtkunstwerks: Richard Wagners politisch-ästhetische Utopie*, 2nd, revised and expanded edition (Stuttgart, 2004).

11. Juliet Koss, *Modernism after Wagner* (Minneapolis, 2010), xi. See also David Clay Large and William Weber, eds, *Wagnerism in European Culture and Politics* (Ithaca, 1984).
12. Kevin C. Karnes, *A Kingdom Not of This World: Wagner, the Arts, and Utopian Visions in Fin-de-Siècle Vienna* (Oxford and New York, 2013), 3 and 30–31. See also Picard, *L'Art total.*
13. Marcella Lista, *L'Œuvre d'art totale à la naissance des avant-gardes 1908–1914* (Paris, 2006).
14. Koss, *Modernism.*
15. See, for example, Danielle Cohen-Levinas, ed., *Le Renouveau de l'art total* (Paris, 2004).
16. Finger and Follett, *Aesthetics,* 4. Walter Scheel echoes this suggestion remarking that, with respect to art, "Totale Kunst—oder der Traum von ihr—hat mehr mit individueller, schöpferischer und grenzenloser Freiheit zu tun…" Scheel, "Zum Geleit," in Szeemann, *Der Hang zum Gesamtkunstwerk,* 8.
17. In addition to the work in Finger and Follett, see particularly Georges Banu, "*Gesamtkunstwerk* et kabuki," and Hélene Bouvier, "Le théâtre à Madura (Indonésie), un totalité artistique et sociale," both in *L'Oeuvre d'art totale,* ed. Denis Bablet and Élie Konigson (Paris, 1995), 325–32 and 333–40; as well as Marcella Lista, "Des correspondences au *Mickey Mouse Effect*: l'œuvre d'art totale et le cinema d'animation," in *L'Oeuvre d'art totale,* ed. Jean Galard and Julian Zugazagottia (Paris, 2003), 109–38.
18. Josef Chytry, *The Aesthetic State: A Quest of Modern German Thought* (Berkeley, 1989). This is not to say that other models of totalitarian rule are ignored. On Stalin, see Roberts, *Total Work of Art,* 207–31. Other arguments in favor of a natural link between Gesamtkunstwerk and totalitarianism may be found in Hans Jürgen Syberberg, "Hitler und die Staatskunst: Die mephistophelische Avantgarde des 20. Jahrhunderts," in *Realismus: Zwischen Revolution und Reaktion 1919–1939,* ed. Günter Metken (Munich, 1981), 382–87; and Erich Michaud, "Oeuvre d'art totale et totalitarisme," in Galard and Zugazagottia, *L'œuvre,* 35–66.
19. Adrian Daub, *Tristan's Shadow: Sexuality and the Total Work of Art after Wagner* (Chicago and London, 2013), 76.
20. Ralf Beil, "'For me there is no other work of art': The Expressionist Total Artwork—Utopia and Practice," in *The Total Artwork in Expressionism: Art, Film, Literature, Theater, Dance and Architecture, 1905–1925,* ed. Ralf Beil and Claudia Dillmann (Darmstadt, 2011), 39. Beil references Jürgen Söring, "Gesamtkunstwerk," in *Reallexikon der deutschen Literaturwissenschaft,* vol. 1, ed. Klaus Weimar (Berlin, 1997), 711.
21. Roberts, *Total Work of Art,* 144.
22. Bazon Brock's consideration of the work of Hans Jürgen Syberberg and Anselm Kiefer offers a counterexample. See Brock, "Der Hang zum Gesamtkunstwerk: Pathosformeln und Energiesymbole zur Einheit von Denken, Wollen und Können," in Szeemann, *Der Hang zum Gesamtkunstwerk,* 22–39.
23. See, Élie Konigson, "Introduction" and Didier Plassard, "Approches de l'art monumental: Kandinsky et la synthèse des arts," in Bablet and Konigson, *L'Oeuvre,* 13–19 and 111–28.
24. The contributors in Denis Bablet and Élie Konigson's edited volume explore the quest to create a "total work of art" for the stage, although Odette Aslan and Didier Plassard prefer to call the result "complete theater" and "monumental art" respectively. See Odette Aslan, "Le *Christophe Colomb* de Claudel, du théâtre 'complet' à l'acteur 'total,'" in Bablet

and Konigson, *L'Ouevre*, 195–214; and Plassard, "Approches de l'art monumental." See also Cohen-Levinas, *Renouveau*.

25. Smith, *Total Work of Art*, 3 and 6.
26. Chytry, *The Aesthetic State*, 289; Lista, *L'Œuvre*, 11–15; Smith, *Total Work of Art*, 8–9. See also Beil and Dillmann, *The Total Artwork*, 14.
27. Anke Finger, *Das Gesamtkunstwerk der Moderne* (Göttingen, 2006), 80. Variations of this observation may also be found in Odo Marquard, "Gesamtkunstwerk und Identitätsystem: Überlegungen im Anschluss an Hegels Schellingkritik," in Szeemann, *Der Hang zum Gesamtkunstwerk*, 40–41.
28. In literature, for example, Proust, Mann, and Tolkien all imagined worlds that have caused scholars to designate them as total works of art. See, for example, Antoine Compagnon, "L'hypertexte proustien," in Galard and Zugazagottia, *L'œuvre*, 93–108, as well as the discussions in Picard and Daub.
29. It should be noted that in its entirety, *Der Hang zum Gesamtkunstwerk* was an exhibition of utopias in Europe since 1800, and that the project itself was supported by the European Union as a gesture towards unifying European arts from both the West and the East. See Scheel, "Zum Geleit," 7–10, Szeemann, *Der Hang zum Gesamtkunstwerk*.
30. In doing this, the authors tend not to follow David Roberts' lead in assigning credit for the idea to both German and French sources.
31. Adorno posits that "the totalitarian and seigneurial aspect of atomization, that devaluation of the individual vis-à-vis the totality" and further contends that "Wagner's anti-Semitism," expressed in part through the music dramas, "assembles all the ingredients of subsequent varieties." Theodor Adorno, *In Search of Wagner* (London, 2005), 40–41 and 16. Then, in the 1963 essay, "Wagner's Relevance for Today," he asserts, "The form of nationalism that he embodied, especially in his work, exploded into National Socialism." Adorno, "Wagner's Relevance for Today," in *Essays on Music*, ed. Richard Leppert and trans. Susan H. Gillespie (Berkeley and Los Angeles, 2002), 585. See also Walter Benjamin, "The Work of Art in the Age of Mechanical Reproduction," in *Illuminations*, ed. Hannah Arendt and trans. Harry Zohn (New York, 1968), 217–51; and the related discussion in Roberts, *Total Work of Art*, 238–44 and 255; as well as, among others, Harald Szeemann and Jean Clair in Szeemann, *Der Hang zum Gesamtkunstwerk*, 16–21 and 93–104 passim; and Fornoff, *Sehnsucht*, 526–87.
32. Gerd Rienäcker, *Musik Theater im Experiment; fünfundzwanzig Aufsätze* (Berlin, 2004), 201.
33. Juliet Koss called the assessment of many of these artists a "reverent misunderstanding" of the term. Koss, *Modernism*, xvi.
34. Koss, *Modernism*, esp. 245–73; and Koss, "Invisible Wagner" in Finger and Follett, *Aesthetics*, especially 168–69 and 187–90.
35. Although Fornoff concludes his book with a study on the links between Gesamtkunstwerk and the Hitler and Stalin regimes, he does not hold that the total work of art naturally tends towards totalitarianism. He observes, "Auf diesem Wege wird sich zudem zeigen, dass das Konzept 'Gesamtkunstwerk' insofern quer zum politischen 'Links-Rechts-Schema' steht, als sich in ihm emanzipatorische und reaktionäre, progressive und regressive, demokratische und antidemokratische Aspekte und Tendenzen durchdringen und nahezu unentwirrbar miteinander verknüpfen," *Sehnsucht*, 553. This remark also has resonance with Walter Scheel's declaration,

"Der totale Staat is Antithese, ist Feind der totalen Kunst." Scheel, "Zum Geleit," 8, in Szeemann, *Der Hang zum Gesamtkunstwerk.*

36. Dance reinterpreted as movement was a part of the larger Bauhaus universe. See Koss, *Modernism*, 207–14 and 232–43.
37. Roberts, *Total Work of Art*, 159.
38. Adolf Behne, "Das Glashaus," *Die Umschau* 18 (1914): 712–16.
39. The key statement in Stewart's opinion finding that the film *The Lovers* (directed by Louis Malle) was not obscene, which overturned two previous court decisions, reads as follows: "I shall not today attempt further to define the kinds of material I understand to be embraced within that shorthand description [of obscenity]; and perhaps I could never succeed in intelligibly doing so. But I know it when I see it, and the motion picture involved in this case is not that." *Jacobellis v. Ohio*, 378 U.S. 184 (1964) at 197.
40. As of 1996, the phrase had been used in over 150 separate opinions in the federal courts. See Paul Gewirtz, "On 'I Know It When I See It,'" *The Yale Law Journal* 105, no. 4 (1996): 1024–25.
41. Ibid., 1025–26.
42. Stewart, *Jacobellis v. Ohio*.

Margaret Eleanor Menninger is NEH Distinguished Teaching Professor in the Humanities and Associate Professor of History at Texas State University. She has published articles on the history of cultural philanthropy in both the United States and Germany, and was a contributor to *The Cambridge Wagner Encyclopedia*. She is completing a book entitled *A Serious Matter and True Joy: Philanthropy, the Arts, and the State in Nineteenth-Century Leipzig*.

I

Foundations

CHAPTER 1

The Play's the Thing
Schiller, Wagner, and Gesamtkunstwerk

NICHOLAS VAZSONYI

Gesamtkunstwerk—A Label with No Meaning

One issue that makes the case of Wagner so unusual is that he comes with a special vocabulary all his own—terms associated with him either exclusively or in the first place: *Leitmotiv, music drama, Festspiel, Gesamtkunstwerk*. Ironically, most of these labels were not coined by Wagner, some of them Wagner never used in connection with his own work, some he even rejected. Nevertheless, they are now part of that distinct and distinctive package I have been calling the Wagner "brand."[1] With the possible exception of leitmotif, none of these terms has had as complex a history, or as rich an afterlife beyond Wagner, as Gesamtkunstwerk.

This special vocabulary of Wagnerian terms—and particularly the ideas that accompany them—almost never begin with Wagner. So, while the complete "package" that he put together is distinctly and uniquely Wagnerian, the specific elements that make up that package were all taken from established sources and then adapted to suit his own purpose. This is as true of the music festival (based on the ancient Greek model, then revived in the early nineteenth century) as it is of the musical motif that is repeated and takes on some form of meaning in the process. It is no different with Gesamtkunstwerk, which, as an idea, predates Wagner by almost a century in terms of the aesthetic and ideological motivations that are its driving forces. In order to construct his own theory, which he would marry to the term Gesamtkunstwerk, Wagner borrowed elements from a number of different sources, ranging from Schiller to the first generation of Romantic authors. None of these predecessors used the actual term Gesamtkunstwerk which, as Alfred Neumann has shown, was first used in 1827. It is unclear whether Wagner would have been aware of this.[2] When Wagner did use the term, it was only on six occasions, in the course of two essays and one letter, and none of them was directly in connection with one of his own works. Nevertheless, because of Wagner's uncanny ability to make noise about himself and his project, the term Gesamtkunstwerk stuck and quickly became the label used perhaps most often to describe the goal, if not the reality, of his mature project and the resulting works for the stage. If and when the word Gesamtkunstwerk is used today, the Wagnerian stamp is an essential component, even if the aim is to oppose or ignore him.

The problem is that, as with much else that essentially starts with Wagner, for a variety of reasons its afterlife often does not have much to do with him anymore. Indeed a brief survey of recent literature on Gesamtkunstwerk leaves the sobering conclusion that the term has by now been applied to so many different aesthetic projects and has been used in so many different situations that it can mean almost anything. In other words, through overuse, it has been virtually emptied of meaning, as Erika Fischer-Lichte noted already in 1989, and Roger Fornoff repeated in his massive study of 2004.[3]

I suspect that Anke Finger would disagree with this conclusion, but she nevertheless addresses the same phenomenon by observing that, after his death, "Wagner's original idea" was "set free from Wagner himself."[4] Randall Packer completes this thought by adding that the idea of the total artwork "has been a catalyzing force through which artists from a myriad of artistic disciplines have freed themselves from the constraints of traditional artistic thinking."[5] Indeed. Not unlike the fatal consequences of the destabilized tonality in Wagner's *Tristan und Isolde,* artists have grabbed on to the term Gesamtkunstwerk, and used its seemingly "unsteady" definition as a license to apply it to any form of artistic project with some claim to a multimedia or totalizing dimension. The fate of the so-called "Tristan" chord has been no different. While Wagner's harmonic instability is totally dependent on the existence of a powerfully functioning tonal system—in other words, the "instability" can only be perceived as such against "stability"—Wagner's gesture was nevertheless taken as an opening gambit that would lead to the elimination of tonality per se. Clearly, artists are free to do as they please, and modernism would have happened sooner or later, with or without Wagner. Nevertheless, the arbitrary or, better said, sloppy use of terminology has become symptomatic of our times. In the case of Gesamtkunstwerk, I am suggesting that it also derives from a misunderstanding of its Wagnerian conception. This is not the case for all uses of the term after Wagner, which do indeed continue and further develop his main ideas. However, in the case of artists who subsequently used the term freely without any sense of obligation to further develop Wagner's concept, I submit that they should have devised a different, more meaningful and appropriate expression. There are also those who have modified or played with the term, again to the point of meaninglessness. For instance, Roy Ascott uses "Gesamtdatenwerk" to describe a global art project on the internet,[6] and Simon Shaw-Miller talks of music as a "Gesamtsensorischeswerk" which "becomes a Gesamtkunstwerk when other art forms are joined with it."[7] Rainer Guldin suggests that "another way of achieving" the Gesamtkunstwerk "is by juxtaposing and mixing different languages" in a work of literature.[8] Really?

In the following, I would like to tease out the fundamental criteria that inform the Gesamtkunstwerk idea at the heart of Wagner's project, a term that he wisely did not apply to any of his completed works, not because he was unclear on what he meant by the term, but because he went one better by assigning unique and specific genre terms for most of his later works: *Handlung* (*Tristan*), *Bühnenfestspiel* (*Ring*), *Bühnenweihfestspiel* (*Parsifal*)—arguably yet one more way of branding his products.

Gesamtkunstwerk—A Brief Genealogy

As four recent books emphasize, Gesamtkunstwerk as an idea is bound up with the project we call modernity.[9] For Danielle Follett and Anke Finger, there are essentially "three aspects of the total artwork": aesthetic, political, and metaphysical.[10] Different artists at different times have emphasized these three to varying degrees, sometimes to the point of ignoring one or more entirely. In the hands of some, the Gesamtkunstwerk has meant an aesthetic means to rectify everything that is wrong with modernity, politically and spiritually; for others, the Gesamtkunstwerk, if realized, would be the quintessential expression of modernity, an expression in the aesthetic realm of everything that modernity promises: liberation from old forms, a joy in experimentation and innovation, human enlightenment and, perhaps most of all, an all-encompassing work that, like modernity itself, leaves nothing untouched. Both conceptions invest tremendous power in the redemptive or regenerative potential of the artwork and, by extension, in the artist who creates such works. It is an extraordinary power, in part because it has both a social/political and a spiritual/emotional dimension. Such a transcendent potential is expressed most clearly in the Romantic notion of *Kunstreligion* (religion of art), an idea Karl Friedrich Schinkel formulated succinctly in 1809/10: "Die Kunst selbst ist Religion,"[11] an idea that had already begun to dominate eighteenth-century discussions of art, linked, as they are, to the Enlightenment understanding of Greek antiquity which offered a holistic symbiosis of religion and art.

Most genealogies of the Gesamtkunstwerk, perhaps because of this, settle on the pioneers of German Romanticism as the original architects of the concept, and cite them as the immediate antecedents of Wagner's notion, even if the Romantics did not specifically coin the term. Such approaches tend to ignore the specifically political dimension of the Gesamtkunstwerk, a lacuna that David Roberts seeks to rectify in his recent and comprehensive genealogy by adding the French Revolution and its socio-aesthetic outcomes to the mix.

According to Roberts, while Wagner is the "dominant reference" for subsequent theorizing on the term, he is at the nexus of two separate strands (German and French) originating in the late eighteenth century.[12] Both of these are rooted in a reception of ancient Greece, though importantly, Roberts argues that the French sociopolitical model originates in Sparta, while the German aesthetic strand is rooted in Athens.[13] The festival idea, so crucial to Wagner's project, with its celebratory and communal elements that transcend the architectural and formal constraints of the established theater, is an outgrowth of the French Revolution—an attempt, Roberts argues, to realize in palpable terms Rousseau's "general will" as well as eliminate the boundary between actor and audience. The currently scant literature on the German music festivals of the early nineteenth century—foremost the Rhine music festival—notes their link to ancient Greek models, but makes little mention of French influences.[14] Given the geopolitical situation in the Rhine area during the Napoleonic years, though, it does seem plausible that there would have been a French impetus. Even if this were not the case, it is difficult to discard the direct significance that French models might have had on Wagner's ideas, given the profound impact of Wagner's stay in Paris between 1839–42, which, as I have argued elsewhere, must be viewed as the formative experience that triggered his mature project, including the Gesamtkunstwerk, even if it was not until 1849/50 that he came to formulate these ideas forcefully.[15]

Turning to Germany, Roberts argues that the country with no political revolution waged its campaign for reform not, as the French had done, in deeds, but in thought. This familiar trope from the early 1800s of Germany as the land of "poets and thinkers",[16] which later led to Friedrich Meinecke's distinction between the *Staatsnation* ("political nation," namely France) and the *Kulturnation* ("cultural nation," namely Germany), actually undermines Roberts' thesis about the twin roots of the Gesamtkunstwerk.[17] In the absence of a political revolution, German thinkers posited their ideas about social reform in theory, articulated perhaps foremost in the realm of aesthetics, with the argument that it would be the artwork that would have the capacity to change men's hearts and mold a new society. This flight into the realm of art was as much a reflection of the political impossibility of revolution in the loose conglomerate that was Germany as it was prompted by horror at the brutal realities of the recent upheavals in France. Roberts bases much of his evidence on Matthias Brzoska's compelling study of the Gesamtkunstwerk concept in France around 1830.[18] However, as Brzoska himself concedes, much of the impetus for these ideas can actually be traced back to German influences. So, I would argue that it is the German aesthetic reaction to modernity in general and the French Revolution in particular, and not so much the French models for communal events, that lie at the heart of the Gesamtkunstwerk project as it came to be formulated. It is precisely the notion that the sociopolitical, and resultant spiritual, problems of modernity can best be resolved in the aesthetic realm that is the German, and not the French, idea. If Wagner did briefly toy with physical revolution in 1848–49, he retreated into aesthetics shortly thereafter and remained true to his German ideological roots for the remainder of his career.

Nevertheless, Roberts' comprehensive and inclusive study is perhaps the most authoritative to date, which makes all the more interesting what he neglects or to what he pays insufficient attention. Foremost among these is Friedrich Schiller who, as I will argue in the core of this essay, is something like Gesamtkunstwerk's spiritual godfather as an aesthetic project with sociopolitical consequences. True, Roberts titles one of his subchapters "Aesthetic Education: Schiller," but this is largely cosmetic, as the discussion of Schiller's theories spans little more than a single page.[19] Roberts also misses the point, by looking at Schiller's post-revolutionary writing—especially *Über die Ästhetische Erziehung des Menschen* (*On the Aesthetic Education of Man*)—as his contribution to the discourse, with the consequence that while the untranslatable concept of *Bildung* (human character formation) is addressed, however briefly, Schiller's vitally important discussion of theater is ignored. Schiller's theater project actually predates the French Revolution, while his essay on aesthetic education is a reaction to it. So, by his own selective attention to German ideas, Roberts yet again privileges the French Revolution and its consequences. Without wanting to minimize or dismiss the legitimacy of such a contention, I suggest that Schiller's work prior to the revolution already conveys what I argue is the core complex of issues that the Gesamtkunstwerk, as Wagner formulates it, entails. The French Revolution only intensified for Schiller the role of art and its creator. In other words, the Gesamtkunstwerk project, as Wagner understood it, is inconceivable without Schiller, and to some extent, the prerevolutionary one at that.

Instead of Schiller, Roberts is more focused on Hölderlin, Schelling, and Hegel.[20] It is unnecessary to restate his arguments here, save to point to Schelling's highly relevant discussion of a "mixed media" format in his call for the reunification of the same three sister arts—poetry, music, and dance—that also becomes the centerpiece for Wagner's early essays on the subject.[21] Schelling is unclear on the issue of form, which had eluded many of his contemporary Romantics, pointing directly to the theater, indeed musical theater, as the ideal mode of presentation—one already "perfected" in the drama of antiquity (*Drama des Altertums*), which has become a mere "caricature" of itself in modern day opera.[22] While he leaves the specific answer open, he at least points in a direction.

Strangely, Roberts makes no mention of Friedrich Schlegel's famous *Athenäum* Fragment number 116, which equates the Romantic project per se with something he terms "*progressive Universalpoesie*" (progressive universal poesy). Importantly, "poesy" here is to be understood as poesis/poetics rather than "poetry." Schlegel similarly leaves open the question of form,[23] the issue that was never clearly resolved by the Romantics in connection with their aesthetic experiments. When Schlegel does mention a specific form, it is the novel (*Roman*). For example, Novalis's unfinished *Heinrich von Ofterdingen* explores the nature of what a mixed-genre work might look like, though it can hardly be described as mixed-media, since it is solely a literary text. This is an important distinction as I will explain below, because there can be several genres within a certain medium, so multi-genre is not necessarily multimedia.

Nevertheless, taken in isolation, Schlegel's catchphrase and the subsequent explanation he offers bears a striking resemblance to Wagner's own, albeit much later description of a unifying artwork. As such, his has been regarded as perhaps the foundational statement for the notion of "mixed-media" and "boundary-crossing" that is fundamental to historic interpretations of the Gesamtkunstwerk idea; so the fact that Roberts never mentions it inexplicable. Nevertheless, Schlegel's proposition has been misconstrued. He may mention as examples the "sigh" (*Seufzer*) and the "kiss" (*Kuß*), that is several different "media" of expression, but in technical terms, he only uses the word "genres" (*Gattungen*), that is, not "media" at all. This is an important distinction. The words "medium/media" indicate different modes of communication/transmission and sensory reception (e.g., audio, video, tactile), whereas "genre" refers to different forms within an art form (e.g., within music: symphony, concerto, quartet). Using this definition, opera is an example of a multimedia art form and, in the absence of film, the modality best suited for adaptation to the Gesamtkunstwerk concept.

Along these lines, the somewhat later Romantic author E.T.A. Hoffmann was, according to Dieter Borchmeyer, the first to use the term "music drama,"[24] though his fictional imaginings of the term are quite far from the reality of Wagner works. Around the same time, as Matthias Brzoska has argued, there was rampant discussion in Paris of the total work of art as a concept, though again the term itself was not used.[25] So, when Wagner came to Paris in 1839, it had not only been an idea preoccupying the leading thinkers of his own country for a half century, but was also an established discourse in Paris. Small wonder, perhaps, that he begins to explore the idea of a "*musikalisches Drama*" in his successful and highly readable novella, *Eine Pilgerfahrt zu Beethoven* (A Pilgrimage to Beethoven) of 1840.[26]

Clearly, it would be wrong to deny the essential connection between the Romantics and Wagner, and thereby to deny the role the Romantics had in constructing the idea of the Gesamtkunstwerk as Wagner came to discuss it. But I would submit that, of the "three aspects"—i.e., aesthetic, political, and metaphysical—the Romantics' primary interest was in aesthetics, and in the metaphysical consequences of the aesthetic experience, hence Roberts' focus on the French in an attempt to recuperate the political. This emphasis on Romantic origins has not gone away. Indeed, subsequent iterations of the Gesamtkunstwerk idea, especially more recent elaborations of multimedia art, are almost exclusively oriented around the synthetic boundary-crossing theories of Romanticism, thus ignoring much of what concerned Wagner.

For Wagner, the aesthetic, boundary-crossing, multimedia issues, meaning the artwork itself, were the means to an end, not the end in itself. In a most perceptive essay, Christiane Heibach contrasts Wagner with "early romanticism's insistence on the idea that every art ought to direct itself first and foremost to the inner sense of the imagination; structural boundary crossings between the arts are possible on this view, but their medial relationship disappears into the background."[27] This is because Wagner "seeks a performance model for his word-time drama in which text and score are made manifest to the audience's external senses."[28] Wagner's art form was not complete until it was performed, as Carl Dahlhaus states explicitly: "Drama is not reproduced but actually comes into existence through the process of staging, which Wagner understood as *realization*."[29] And so any Gesamtkunstwerk that does not involve performance—meaning the "medium" of human, lived, and live experience—is already a departure from and, I submit, a fundamental misunderstanding of the Wagnerian idea. This, Heibach explains, is why Wagner "had to act as the creator of not only the text and the score but also of the performance."[30] Indeed, Wagner was not only the conductor of his works but stage director, a profession only just beginning in the mid nineteenth century, and for which Wagner was one of the pioneers.[31] However, even the performance is not Wagner's ultimate goal, but rather the fundamental impact on the recipient induced by the performed artwork: this was originally Gesamtkunstwerk's "sociopolitical" dimension, so key to Roberts' discussion, but which, I argue, dwindled in significance for Wagner the further away he got from 1849. Having said this, the notion of Wagner's project as a "national undertaking" (*nationale Unternehmung*) was never fully abandoned.[32]

Schiller

The missing and often ignored element in discussion of the Gesamtkunstwerk's genealogy is Friedrich Schiller. He, too, never used the word Gesamtkunstwerk, nor did he outline a mixed-media or even a mixed-genre aesthetic vision. Nevertheless, the politically utopian and fundamentally ethical stakes inherent in the work of art, its existence as a response to the social and ethical environment in which it is created, and the significance of the artist who creates such works, are formulated by him with a forcefulness and an eloquence that are unprecedented. Secondly, Schiller left no doubt on the issue of genre, and his statements find a remarkable and insufficiently noted echo in Wagner, though an echo with crucial differences owing largely to the changed cultural and political circumstances in which Wagner wrote.[33] The Gesamtkunstwerk project, as Wagner understood it, is inconceivable without Schiller, and it is a misuse of the term to apply it as a label to describe an artistic project that does not include what I will call the "Schillerian" element.

Schiller's theories from the 1780s on, and refined during the 1790s in the wake of the French Revolution and its disastrous phases, are based on a critique of modernity for which, again, Schiller may have provided the first coherent articulation. I differentiate between Schiller's and Rousseau's respective critiques because Rousseau—as crucial as he was to political and ideological developments in the latter half of the eighteenth century and beyond—was also analyzing the conditions of people in society, irrespective of historical period. Schiller, by contrast, develops an enduring model that mounts a conceptual resistance to what some, primarily European intellectuals, perceive as the social, economic, and ultimately ethical problems of modernity in particular. According to the critique, these have caused or resulted in a series of traumatic ruptures, all of which constitute a loss. The growth of cities has replaced organic communities with the alienating individualism of mass society; the development of industrial production has replaced the artisanal craftsman with the specialized laborer, and so on: all this Schiller juxtaposed with an idealized image of a holistic Greek antiquity perhaps most succinctly formulated in his essay, *Über naïve und sentimentalische Dichtung* (*On Naive and Sentimental Poesy*, 1795).

While the malaise, melancholy, and despair that modernity has triggered for some also lie at the heart of the Romantic project, its flight into the aesthetic realm is precisely what Schiller did not foresee as the role of art. More importantly still, for Schiller, there was no doubt that the most effective aesthetic medium for the transmission of ideas to a public in need of moral, ethical, and political persuasion was the drama to be performed on the stage. Under Schiller, and especially in the wake of the failed French Revolution, the theater was the institution that could undertake humanity's re-education and moral redemption, and the creative artist became nothing less than the designated guide. For Schiller, the work of art becomes a tool to achieve the aesthetic state through peaceful revolution, where all modernity's ruptures and tensions would be resolved. This is the political-utopian dream that lies at the heart of the Gesamtkunstwerk as Wagner adopted it a half century later. It is the centrality of the drama as form, and the theater as site for the ideal artwork that becomes blurred for the Romantics in their desire for transcendence, perhaps because of theater's physicality.[34] Wagner also recuperates the idea of theater with reference to an idealized vision of ancient Greek culture and, by integrating music, opens up the theatrical stage to the possibilities of transcendent experience. Adaptations and variations of the Gesamtkunstwerk idea after Wagner that apply a mixed-media or boundary-crossing form that lacks a performative element thus constitute a departure from Schiller's (and by extension Wagner's) principles, and are conceptually more indebted to the theories of German Romanticism, or possibly even the legacy of the French Revolution, as Roberts presents it.

What is it about the stage that, according to Schiller, provides such an ideal forum? In a remarkable and remarkably short lecture titled "Die Schaubühne als eine moralische Anstalt betrachtet" (The Theatrical Stage Contemplated as a Moral Institution, 1784), Schiller rehearses an argument that Wagner echoed in his Zurich writings of 1849/50.[35] Schiller draws from the well-established eighteenth-century discourse concerning the pedagogical value of the theater, as articulated by Gottsched and Lessing, but then adds a post-Rousseauian socially-critical and social-utopian element that is distinctly his own. Schiller takes as his starting point quotidian life and the need for an appropriate experience in the theater: "Exhausted by higher mental exertions, worn down by the monotonous, often oppressive duties of work, and bombarded by sensuality, man necessarily felt an inner emptiness which clashed with his eternal desire for activity."[36] He clarifies:

> Human nature cannot bear the constant and unrelenting grind of daily business; and sensual excitement simply dies with its own gratification … The businessman is in danger of developing ulcers in return for a life generously dedicated to the state; the scholar is in danger of degenerating into a dull pedant; the common man, into a beast. The stage is the institution where instruction and pleasure, exertion and repose, culture and amusement are wedded.[37]

The ideal outlet for the troubled and burdened spirit is "theater above all else, since it opens up infinite horizons to the spirit thirsting for activity, providing nourishment to the soul's every power without overtaxing any single one, and uniting the cultivation of the mind and heart with the noblest entertainment."[38]

Schiller draws the crucial comparison between performed drama on stage and religion, which has the greatest hold on our civil and moral conduct, an influence exerted with equal force by the stage.[39] For Schiller, religion and the stage similarly bypass the intellect and operate instead on a visceral level: "Religion generally acts more upon the sensual side of people—indeed, it probably has this infallible effect only through the sensuous … —and how does the stage achieve its effect?"[40] This is exactly what Wagner also meant, when he talked about "die Gefühlswerdung des Verstandes" (the transformation of the intellect into feeling).[41] When Schiller is talking about religion, he means religion as "church-performance," rather than the peaceful contemplation of the Bible at home. Religion tries to address all aspects of life, but, as Schiller adds, "the stage extends its sphere of influence further still. Even in those regions where religion and law deem it beneath their dignity to accompany human sentiment, the theater is still at work for our upbringing."[42]

For Schiller, the stage is nothing less than an institution that promotes what he later terms mankind's aesthetic education: "The stage is, more than any other public institution, a school of practical wisdom, a guide to our daily lives, an infallible key to the most secret accesses of the human soul."[43] Its moral dimension also has a political function in that it binds together people of a distinct culture, and aids them in finding a unity of taste, conduct, and cultural identification that makes them different from another culture. This was already the case in ancient Greece,[44] and Schiller believes it will be no different in the case of the project to form a (German) national identity:

> I cannot possibly overlook the great influence that a good standing theater would have upon the spirit of the nation. I define a people's national spirit as the similarity and agreement of its opinions and inclinations concerning matters in which another nation thinks and feels differently. Only the stage is capable of producing such accord to so great a degree.[45]

After the French Revolution, and especially after it turned ugly, Schiller added an important element to this aesthetic philosophy articulated before 1792. Hence, the *Ästhetische Erziehung des Menschen* is all about finding a way to improve humanity and revolutionize society without the need for a bloody political upheaval. For Schiller, the artwork turns out to be the way to achieve a bloodless revolution; and so, in a corrupted age, it is the role of the artist to imagine a different world and to represent that idea in the artwork—a role that defines the modern "sentimental" artist against that of his "naive" predecessor.

Wagner's Schiller

Wagner's library in Dresden, a collection that grew between 1843 and 1849, contained a twelve-volume edition of Schiller's complete works as well as a separate volume of his correspondence with Goethe.[46] From this and written evidence, we know that Wagner read Schiller in the years just before he began to formulate his major theories, and did so evidently for the remainder of his life. Schiller is everywhere in Wagner's writings, from his published essays and correspondence to his and Cosima's diaries. Apart from the predictable near-obsession with Schiller's "Ode to Joy," which provided the text for Beethoven's all-important Ninth Symphony, Wagner mainly writes about Schiller's dramas which, together with Goethe's, he considers the pinnacle of German writing for the theater, though in that genre he elevates Schiller even above Goethe as "our greatest dramatist" (unser[ ] größte[r] dramatsiche[r] Dichter).[47] His references to Schiller's dramatic or aesthetic theories are far more limited, though he was clearly familiar with Schiller's ideas.[48] In his essay "Über das Dirigiren" (On Conducting, 1869), he makes direct references to Schiller's *Über naïve und sentimentalische Dichtung*.[49] In the closing words of *Über die Bestimmung der Oper* (*The Destiny of Opera*, 1871) Wagner cites Schiller directly when he projects the salvation of the German nation by way of the artist (*Künstler*) and the German theater.[50] Wagner uses a sentence from Schiller's letter to Goethe of 17 August 1795 to launch his own late essay "Religion und Kunst" (Religion and Art, 1880), whose first sentence is perhaps Wagner's own most succinct formulation of the *Kunstreligion* idea: "One might say that where Religion becomes artificial, it is reserved for art to save the kernel of religion by recognizing the figurative value of the mythic symbols which the former would have us believe in their literal sense, and revealing their deep and hidden truth through an ideal presentation."[51] The fact that Wagner does not engage directly with Schiller's theories is neither surprising nor unusual. The same is true for the philosophers Ludwig Feuerbach and Arthur Schopenhauer, both of whom were central to Wagner at different points in his life. As opposed to the latter two, though, Schiller and the ways in which he interpreted modernity and articulated the centrality of the theatrical experience are embedded in Wagner's language; they are constantly present in his prose writings. Schiller's ideas are also more complex than the genre-mixing impulse and the desire for transcendence bequeathed by Romanticism.

Interestingly, the historical situation that prompted Wagner has much in common with that of Schiller. In both cases, a time of ferment resulted in violent political revolution that failed to achieve its goals, and prompted artists to write aesthetic manifestos of broad sweep. But there were differences also. Conceived in the context and immediate aftermath of the 1848 revolutions in general and, specifically, the failed Dresden uprising of May 1849 in which Wagner took an active role, the now fugitive Wagner wrote a series of aesthetic manifestos in his Zurich exile starting that same year. For Wagner, revolution is the driving political force of his long-term aesthetic project, a connection he makes in the title of the first essay of his series, *Die Kunst und die Revolution* (*Art and Revolution*, 1849). Revolution and the relationship between the artwork, political activism, and political change is Wagner's starting point, which would tend to justify Roberts' emphasis on the French Revolution as the impulse for the Gesamtkunstwerk idea that here finds its first formulations as such. However, this relationship, initially outlined in *Art and Revolution*, rapidly undergoes a transformation as a consequence of political realities, which pushes Wagner from what must be characterized as idealistic utopianism to a more resigned and realistic evaluation of both the potentialities of political change, as well as the possible effectiveness of the artwork to effect that change. Wagner moves decisively away from the notion of political revolution, and even seems less certain about Schiller's proposition of political change through art, but he never abandons the interrelated concepts of drama and performance as the basis of his own agenda: the salvation of humanity.

The notion of *Gesammtkunstwerk* [*sic*] is introduced in this first essay, *Art and Revolution*, a label Wagner uses twice to describe his vision of Greek drama. For Wagner, it was not just that in Greek drama the sister arts—dance, music, and poetry—had found a unified expression, but that the circumstance of the performance itself had also been ideal: dramas were given during public holidays, making them communal events that all members of society regardless of rank could attend for free. Gesamtkunstwerk for Wagner was never "just" about the artwork itself.

There are three key words here: holiday, event, and free. Wagner, like Schiller, responds to the soul-killing monotony of the bourgeois workday. But, unlike Schiller, Wagner's answer does not lie in an evening's entertainment, however morally uplifting. Instead, there must be a total caesura between the quotidian lifestyle and the aesthetic experience. This idea was there from the start, and the actuality of Bayreuth in no way constitutes a change of heart. Wagner recalls the holidays in ancient Greece and the idea of going to a special place for its celebration, the performance becoming an event. This gesture is certainly one of retreat from the sociopolitical sphere, where all would come together regardless of politics. For Schiller, the theater establishes and cements national identity, an idea Wagner echoes when he talks of the Bayreuth project as a "*nationale Unternehmung*" (national undertaking).[52] The third element, which Wagner still planned for Bayreuth but ultimately had to give up, was free admission. In other words, for Wagner, the idea of Gesamtkunstwerk was never solely about aesthetics. From the beginning, it also had performative, sociological, and economic components.

In his next essay, *Das Kunstwerk der Zukunft* (*The Artwork of the Future*, 1849/50), Wagner again uses the term "Gesammtkunstwerk," this time on three occasions. But now, he adapts his own term originally applied to describe Greek drama by adding the epithet "of the future" (i.e., Gesammtkunstwerk der Zukunft).[53] Wagner changes the focus to his own project, even if he never draws an explicit connection between the Gesamtkunstwerk and a specific composition of his own. The "Gesamtkunstwerk der Zukunft" represents the recovery of a Greek idea for a unified artwork to be performed under ideal circumstances. Moreover, and in a pseudo-Marxist vein that Wagner quickly abandoned, the creator of this new artwork will be the people (*das Volk*), indeed a newly awakened people, again with echoes of the French Revolution.

But the political revolution never took place. And so, after the initial burst of revolutionary writings, Wagner becomes increasingly apolitical and engages in a series of retrenchments that have earned him the accusation ever since of being inconsistent and confused. But was Wagner not being true to his original 1849 definition of and aspirations for the Gesamtkunstwerk in that he never described one of his completed works as one? In the case of Wagner, and even more *for* Wagner, the Gesamtkunstwerk as originally defined never came into being, and nor could it. Wagner's operatic project then represents a compromise that takes into account the realities of the sociopolitical situation of his time.

Wagner's Gesamtkunstwerk

Within a year or two of his first using the term, Gesamtkunstwerk was seized upon to such an extent that Wagner was moved to add the following comment in a letter to Franz Liszt where he discusses the founding of a new music journal: "Above all, nothing of this unfortunate Gesamtkunstwerk in the title!!! Enough already!" (16 August 1853).[54] This self-distancing is symptomatic for Wagner, and we have similar examples when it comes to leitmotif and music drama.

Still, in Wagner's hands, Gesamtkunstwerk becomes, like modernity itself, a project in the process of becoming. So what, if anything, can we say about Wagnerian Gesamtkunstwerk? What remains from the initial Schiller-influenced impetus of the idea? Thomas Grey once wrote that the Gesamtkunstwerk comes "with batteries included."[55] The context of his comment suggests that he was talking about the completeness of the aesthetic package which, in Wagner's case, is much more than just the writing of the text and composition of the music. Grey's catchphrase becomes the definitive expression of a venture so wide ranging that it has yet to be exceeded, even with the advent of electronic technologies and the phantom worlds of cyberspace. Wagner was a pioneering conductor and practically invented the role of the modern stage director. He had a hand in set design and was the co-architect of his own theater. All of these constitute elements of the "total" in "total work of art," because they span the theoretical conception, the composition, the space, and the performance.

Not unlike Disneyland, Bayreuth itself is a performance. Wagner was obsessed with the construction and retention of a perfected illusion: the sunken orchestra pit, the invisible orchestra and conductor, the series of proscenium arches, the use of smoke and steam, the totally darkened theater (though this was not originally intended), all of which contribute to the experience's totality and must properly be considered part of Gesamtkunstwerk. Beyond this, even, the entire evening is choreographed, from the audience's walk up the hill towards the Festival Theater, to the timing of the performance itself starting at 4 PM, to the brass band that plays on the outside balcony of the theater to indicate the end of the intermission for ticketholders and spectators alike. So the audience becomes part of this performance, part of the pageantry of the occasion, watching and being watched from all sides.

This brings me, in conclusion, to my particular interest in Wagnerian Gesamtkunstwerk. The totality of Wagner's project goes beyond even the aesthetic and the performative, because it also entails a business and marketing model that is integral to the undertaking—an aesthetic project that both rhetorically resists and yet tangibly embodies modernity. As Theodor W. Adorno and Andreas Huyssen have shown specifically in the case of Wagner, and Pierre Bourdieu has argued in the case of Wagner's French contemporaries, Baudelaire and Flaubert, the artwork that announces its existence as a rejection of the market is nevertheless beholden to the imperatives of the marketplace. Bayreuth may be a utopia for some and a dystopia for others, but it is a totally commodified one. From the moment one steps off the train under the shadow of the Festspielhaus, Wagner and Bayreuth are for sale. Here we see the full realization of Thomas Grey's comment about the Gesamtkunstwerk coming "with batteries included," a standard phrase on the packaging of toys and gadgets that require something in addition to the product itself for it to be enjoyed fully. Wagner delivers not only the artwork (the product), but a complex explanatory apparatus to help understand that artwork from the inside (remember to read the directions before using). And, if you go to Bayreuth, you get the "authentic experience" that delivers a total physical package, one that addresses all the senses, including smell and taste, making you, the audience member, an integral part of the performance.

All this takes us quite far away from anything Schiller envisaged or, to be fair, could have envisaged. Wagner, as I suggested at the beginning, was adept at taking a multitude of impulses and fusing them into something uniquely his own. But at its core, the Bayreuth festival is about resisting the alienation precipitated by modern life, creating in its stead a sense of community through the performance of a stage work that is intended to deliver a transformative experience, and that is all Schiller.

Notes

1. Nicholas Vazsonyi, *Richard Wagner: Self-Promotion and the Making of a Brand* (Cambridge, 2010).
2. Used by Karl Friedrich Eusebius Trahndorff, *Aesthetik oder Lehre von der Weltanschauung und Kunst* (Berlin, 1827), 2: 312; quoted in Alfred R. Neumann, "The Earliest Use of the Term 'Gesamtkunstwerk,'" *Philological Quarterly* 35 (1956): 192–93.
3. Erika Fischer-Lichte, "Das 'Gesamtkunstwerk.' Ein Konzept für die Kunst der achtziger Jahre?," in *Dialog der Künste: Intermediale Fallstudien zur Literatur des 19. und 20. Jahrhunderts. Festschrift für Erwin Koppen*, ed. M. Moog-Grünewald and Christoph Rodiek (Frankfurt am Main, 1989), 63. See also, Roger Fornoff, *Die Sehnsucht nach dem Gesamtkunstwerk: Studien zu einer ästhetischen Konzeption der Moderne* (Hildesheim, 2004), 18.

4. Anke Finger, "Idea/Imagination/Dialogue: The Total Artwork and Conceptual Art," in *The Aesthetics of the Total Artwork: On Borders and Fragments*, ed. eadem and Danielle Follett (Baltimore, 2011), 117.
5. Randall Packer, "The Gesamtkunstwerk and Interactive Media," in Finger and Follett, *Aesthetics*, 158.
6. Packer, "Gesamtkunstwerk," 164.
7. Simon Shaw-Miller, "Music as Imminent *Gesamtkunstwerk*: Absolute Music, Synesthesia, and *The Lucky Hand*," in Finger and Follett, *Aesthetics*, 191. Shaw-Miller has written his own book on the topic: *Visible Deeds of Music: Art and Music from Wagner to Cage* (New Haven, 2002).
8. Rainer Guldin, "Polyglot Poetry: Multilingualism and the Aesthetics of the *Gesamtkunstwerk*," in Finger and Follett, *Aesthetics*, 307.
9. Matthew Wilson Smith, *The Total Work of Art: From Bayreuth to Cyberspace* (New York, 2007); Juliet Koss, *Modernism after Wagner* (Minneapolis, 2010); Finger and Follett, *Aesthetics*; and David Roberts, *The Total Work of Art in European Modernism* (Ithaca, 2011).
10. Finger and Follett, *Aesthetics*, 5.
11. Quoted in Fornoff, *Sehnsucht*, 111.
12. Roberts, *Total Work of Art*, 8.
13. Ibid., 10.
14. See foremost Cecilia Hopkins Porter, "The New Public and the Reordering of the Musical Establishment: The Lower Rhine Music Festivals, 1818–67," *19th-Century Music* 3, no. 3 (1980), 211–24. More recently, see also Ryan Minor, *Choral Fantasies: Music, Festivity and Nationhood in Nineteenth-Century Germany* (Cambridge, 2012), esp. 23–26. Minor does briefly mention the post-revolutionary French culture of public festivals, but argues that "in Germany, by contrast, the festival culture worked in almost the opposite direction," 27.
15. See Vazsonyi, *Richard Wagner*, Chapter 1.
16. Repeated even by Wagner in his essay "Deutsche Kunst und deutsche Politik," *Samtliche Schriften und Dichtungen* (hereafter *SSD*), 8:45.
17. Friedrich Meinecke, *Weltbürgertum und Nationalstaat. Werke*, vol. 5, 1st edn 1907 (Munich, 1962), see esp. 9–26.
18. Matthias Brzoska, *Die Idee des Gesamtkunstwerks in der Musiknovellistik der Julimonarchie* (Laaber, 1995).
19. Roberts, *Total Work of Art*, 38–44. After page 39, Roberts leaves Schiller and moves to Schelling and Hölderlin.
20. See ibid., 40–53.
21. Friedrich Wilhelm Joseph Schelling, *Philosophie der Kunst* (1802–3).
22. It is uncertain whether Wagner might have known of Schelling's arguments. Schelling, *The Philosophy of Art*, ed. and trans. Douglas Stott (Minneapolis, 1989): 280.
23. "[U]nd doch gibt es noch keine Form, die dazu gemacht wäre, den Geist des Autors vollständig auszudrücken," Friedrich Schlegel, *Kritische Schriften*, ed. Wolfdietrich Rasch (Munich, 1964), 39.
24. Dieter Borchmeyer, *Das Theater Richard Wagners: Idee—Dichtung—Wirkung* (Stuttgart, 1982), 100; he mentions E.T.A. Hoffmann's *Die Serapionsbrüder* (1819–21).
25. Brzoska, *Idee des Gesamtkunstwerks*.
26. See Vazsonyi, *Richard Wagner*, 31–40, esp. 38.

27. Christiane Heibach, "Avant-Garde Theater as Total Artwork? Media-Theoretical Reflections on the Historical Development of Performing Art Forms," in Finger and Follett, *Aesthetics*, 213.
28. Ibid.
29. "Durch die Inszenierung, die Wagner als Verwirklichung begriff, wird das Drama nicht reproduziert, sondern überhaupt erst hervorgebracht," Carl Dahlhaus, *Wagners Konzeption des musikalischen Dramas* (Munich, 1990): 27. See also Udo Bermbach, *Der Wahn des Gesamtkunstwerks: Richard Wagners politisch-ästhetische Utopie*, 2nd, revised and expanded edition (Stuttgart, 2004). Bermbach succinctly points to the two "constitutive" elements of the Gesamtkunstwerk for Wagner: the synthesis of individual arts and the production of the artwork in public (210).
30. Heibach, "Avant-Garde Theater," 224.
31. We have a detailed account of Wagner's work as a stage director of the first complete production of the Ring: see Richard Fricke, *Richard Wagner auf der Probe: das Bayreuther Tagebuch des Ballettmeisters und Hilfsregisseurs Richard Fricke* (Stuttgart, 1983), trans. and ed. George Fricke, James Deaville, and Evan Baker, *Wagner in Rehearsal, 1875–1876: The Diaries of Richard Fricke* (Stuyvesant, 1998).
32. Vazsonyi, *Richard Wagner*, 179–89.
33. One of the few exceptions is Udo Bermbach, who devotes a section of *Der Wahn des Gesamtkunstwerks* to a comparison of Schiller and Wagner along the lines I am suggesting here, see 241–48, especially 246.
34. Similarly, it is not the people's festival as a demonstration of solidarity and "general will" in the wake of a successful revolution, but precisely the transformative "Volksfest" that takes the place of the revolution that motivated Wagner.
35. The lecture, held on 26 June 1784, was published under the title "Was kann eine gute stehende Bühne eigentlich wirken?" *Schillers Werke*, Nationalausgabe Bd. 20.1 [hereinafter NA 20.1], ed. Norbert Oellers et al. (Weimar, 2001): 87–100.
36. "Erschöpft von den höheren Anstrengungen des Geistes, ermattet von den einförmigen, oft niederdrückenden Geschäften des Berufs, und von Sinnlichkeit gesättigt, mußte der Mensch eine Leerheit in seinem Wesen fühlen, die dem ewigen Trieb nach Thätigkeit zuwider war" (NA 20.1: 90).
37. "Die menschliche Natur erträgt es nicht, ununterbrochen und ewig auf der Folter der Geschäfte zu liegen, die Reize der Sinne sterben mit ihrer Befriedigung ... Der Mann von Geschäften ist in Gefahr, ein Leben, das er dem Staat so großmüthig hinopferte, mit dem unseligen Spleen abzubüßen—der Gelehrte zum dumpfen Pedanten herabzusinken—der Pöbel zum Thier. Die Schaubühne ist die Stiftung, wo sich Vergnügen mit Unterricht, Ruhe mit Anstrengung, Kurzweil mit Bildung gattet" (NA 20.1: 99–100).
38. "[D]ie Bühne, die dem nach Thätigkeit dürstenden Geist einen unendlichen Kreis eröffnet, jeder Seelenkraft Nahrung gibt, ohne eine einzige zu überspannen, und die Bildung des Verstandes und des Herzens mit der edelsten Unterhaltung vereinigt" (NA 20.1: 90).
39. "[D]ie schwankende Eigenschaft der politischen Geseze, welche dem Staat die Religion unentbehrlich macht, bestimmt auch den ganzen Einfluß der Bühne" (NA 20.1: 91).
40. "Religion wirkt im Ganzen mehr auf den sinnlichen Theil des Volks—sie wirkt vielleicht durch das Sinnliche allein so unfehlbar ...—und wodurch wirkt die Bühne?" (NA 20.1: 91).

41. Wagner, *Opera and Drama*, in *Richard Wagner's Prose Works*, trans. William Ashton Ellis, 8 vols (London, 1892–99), 2:208 (translation modified).
42. "Aber der Wirkungskreis der Bühne dehnt sich noch weiter aus. Auch da, wo Religion und Geseze es unter ihrer Würde achten, Menschenempfindungen zu begleiten, ist sie für unsere Bildung noch geschäftig" (NA 20.1: 94). Schiller reinforces this point again and again. See also: "So gewiß sichtbare Darstellung mächtiger wirkt, als todter Buchstabe und kalte Erzählung, so gewiß wirkt die Schaubühne tiefer und dauernder als Moral und Geseze" [As assuredly as a visible presentation is more effective than the dead letter and cold narration, so too is the impact of the stage deeper and more lasting than morals and laws] (93), and "Tausend Laster, die jene [Religion N.V.] ungestraft duldet, straft sie [Bühne N.V.]; tausend Tugenden, wovon jene schweigt, werden von der Bühne empfohlen. Hier begleitet sie die Weisheit und die Religion" [The (stage) punishes thousands of vices which (Religion) tolerates unpunished; Thousands of virtues, which Religion never mentions, are recommended from the stage. In this way, the stage accompanies wisdom and religion] (NA 20.1: 93).
43. "Die Schaubühne ist mehr als jede andere öffentliche Anstalt des Staats eine Schule der praktischen Weißheit, ein Wegweiser durch das bürgerliche Leben, ein unfehlbarer Schlüssel zu den geheimsten Zugängen der menschlichen Seele" (NA 20.1: 95).
44. "Was kettete Griechenland so fest aneinander?" [What held Greece so firmly together?] (NA 20.1: 99).
45. "Unmöglich kann ich hier den großen Einfluß übergehen, den eine gute stehende Bühne auf den Geist der Nation haben würde. Nationalgeist eines Volks nenne ich die Aehnlichkeit und Uebereinstimmung seiner Meinungen und Neigungen bei Gegenständen, worüber eine andere Nation anders meint und empfindet. Nur der Schaubühne ist es möglich, diese Uebereinstimmung in einem hohen Grad zu bewirken" (NA 20.1: 99).
46. Curt von Westernhagen, *Richard Wagners Dresdener Bibliothek 1842–1849. Neue Dokumente zur Geschichte seines Schaffens*, Mit 6 Abbildungen und Kunstdrucktafeln (Wiesbaden, 1966).
47. Wagner, *SSD* 8:93.
48. See, e.g., Wagner, "Deutsche Kunst und deutsche Politik," *SSD* 8:44–45 and 8:77–78.
49. Wagner, "Über das Dirigiren," *SSD* 8:287.
50. Wagner, *SSD* 9:155–56.
51. "Man könnte sagen, daß da, wo die Religion künstlich wird, der Kunst es vorbehalten sei den Kern der Religion zu retten, indem sie die mythischen Symbole, welche die erstere im eigentlichen Sinne als wahr geglaubt wissen will, ihrem sinnbildlichen Werthe nach erfaßt, um durch ideale Darstellung derselben die in ihnen verborgene tiefe Wahrheit erkennen zu lassen" (*SSD* 10:211). Translation from *Richard Wagner's Prose Works*, 6:213.
52. E.g., "Schlußbericht über die Umstände und Schicksale, welche die Ausführung des Bühnenfestspieles 'der Ring des Nibelungen' bis zur Gründung von Wagner-Vereinen begleiteten," (Final Report of the Circumstances and the Fortunes that Accompanied the Execution of the Stage-Festival-Play "The Ring of the Nibelungen" Down to the Founding of the Wagner Societies), *SSD* 9:317.
53. See Sanna Pederson, "From Gesamtkunstwerk to Music Drama," in this volume.
54. "Vor Allem aber auch nichts von dem unglücklichen »Gesammtkunst« in den Titel!!! Genug davon!"
55. Thomas S. Grey, *Wagner's Musical Prose: Texts and Contexts* (Cambridge, 1995), 318.

Nicholas Vazsonyi is Jesse Chapman Alcorn Memorial Professor of German and Department Chair of Languages, Literatures & Cultures at the University of South Carolina. Amongst his publications are *Wagner's Meistersinger: Performance, History, Representation* (University of Rochester Press, 2003) and *Richard Wagner: Self-Promotion and the Making of a Brand* (Cambridge University Press, 2010). He was editor of the Cambridge Wagner Encyclopedia (2013).

CHAPTER 2

From Gesamtkunstwerk to Music Drama

SANNA PEDERSON

More than any other individual composer's music, Wagner's music has its own special terminology. "Gesamtkunstwerk," "absolute music," "music drama," "*Stabreim*," "music of the future," "leitmotifs" and other terms formed part of an aesthetic theory that he developed in a series of publications, the so-called Zurich writings, from 1849 to 1851.[1] However, in their original context, these terms were used so casually that it is hard to believe Wagner was aware he was coining new catchwords. It was in the response to his writings, where they were summarized, explicated, interpreted, and criticized by both advocates and detractors that the terms emerged and crystallized. They became part of the Wagner lexicon, despite the fact that Wagner himself rejected some of them and favored others that did not catch on. In this chapter, I offer the perspective of a music historian. My aim lies not in examining how the term "Gesamtkunstwerk" came to take on a life of its own and be interpreted creatively, a task that falls more to the volume as a whole. Rather, I offer a historical account of the circumstances and influences that led Wagner to use the term in the first place, as well as a hypothesis about why he did not favor it as a descriptor for his stage works.

The term Gesamtkunstwerk appears in *Das Kunstwerk der Zukunft* (*The Artwork of the Future*, 1849) but not in the following treatise *Oper und Drama* (*Opera and Drama*, 1851). My essay surveys the main points of scholarly contention regarding these Zurich texts, all the while recognizing that there is no foreseeable end to the quest to understand writings that, at times, verge on complete opacity. By examining key passages where Wagner describes how the different arts come together to make up an opera, my reading finds that Wagner's outlook changes significantly from one text to the other. My excavation of the way Wagner himself used the term before it started being widely used has consequences for understanding the crucial issue of Wagner's political ambitions for his artworks. In particular, I propose that "Gesamtkunstwerk" properly refers to Wagner's plans for a politically motivated artwork, in distinction to "music drama" (*Musikdrama*) which speaks primarily to Wagner's views on operatic reform. Of course, Gesamtkunstwerk will continue to accrue different meanings for which Wagner's original definition is irrelevant.[2] But for those interested in how it relates to Wagner, I offer a musicological investigation of his distinction between Gesamtkunstwerk and music drama as a way to understand some central issues in Wagner's thought. Briefly stated, I suggest that the differences between the two terms can function heuristically to articulate differences between theory and practice, and between his political and aesthetic priorities.

I begin with a brief overview of the history of opera as a total work of art in order to put Wagner's aesthetics in musical-historical context. Then, I trace the emergence of the term Gesamtkunstwerk and how it became part of the special vocabulary associated with Wagner. A discussion of recent scholarship on Wagner's aims for Gesamtkunstwerk follows, which reveals a range of opinions regarding the extent and duration of Wagner's political commitment. Against this background, I explore Wagner's aspirations by comparing the two major Zurich writings, *Das Kunstwerk der Zukunft* and *Oper und Drama*. Finally, I examine Wagner's shift in views over this relatively short period with reference to a change in his use of rhetoric. In sum, I contend that Wagner's writing gradually shed the political hortatory style evident during the revolutionary years of 1848–1849 and became more figurative, relying increasingly on extended metaphors and analogies to describe his plans for creating a new kind of opera. In *Das Kunstwerk der Zukunft*, Wagner envisions a Gesamtkunstwerk by and for the people. By the time he writes *Oper und Drama*, though, he depicts his new kind of opera as the result of music and drama coming together like woman and man in the act of sexual love.

The Gesamtkunstwerk in the History of Opera

The concept of the "total work of art" is much larger than a chapter on Wagner in the history of opera. In fact, the history of debates about opera's integration of its individual components is as long as opera itself. As Christopher Morris has recently observed:

> Measured against the possibility of rediscovering a lost unity—between poetry and music in Hellenic theatre—a conviction shared by so many of the theorists and practitioners of opera, from the Florentine Camerata through the eighteenth-century philosophers to Wagner—opera was always haunted by an ancient ghost and found wanting by comparison. That ghost was Aristotle.[3]

Aristotle's requirements for unity were part of the discussions of the Florentine Camerata, which is credited with creating the first works in the operatic genre at the end of the sixteenth century. Their reconstruction of ancient Greek tragedy was based on the idea that it had been sung rather than spoken throughout, so that the meaning of the words was inseparable from the expressive and musical aspects of their sound.[4] Although this background was well known to musicologists in the eighteenth century and had been extensively described by early nineteenth-century historians and critics, Wagner never acknowledged that the first works in the operatic repertoire came into being as an attempt to bring together arts that had gone their separate ways.[5]

Wagner's lengthiest theoretical text, *Oper und Drama,* includes his most detailed historical account of opera. As part of a polemic attacking the opera of his time, his version departs from the standard narrative that had been established by the mid nineteenth century, and presents opera's history as a descent into corruption. Any historical attempts to restore dramatic unity to opera that Wagner deigns to mention are dismissed. This includes the reforms called for in the eighteenth century by Christoph Willibald von Gluck, who famously supported the call to make the music subordinate to the drama in a formulation that is close to Wagner's own declaration in bold type at the onset of *Oper und Drama,* "that a Means of expression (Music) has been made the end, while the End of expression (the Drama) has been made a means."[6]

Oper und Drama devotes far more pages to decrying how the whole has been split into isolated parts than to strategizing how to restore unity. It follows the premise of the other Zurich writings in attributing the downfall of art to its being severed from sociopolitical life and becoming merely commercial entertainment. But nowhere else does Wagner go so far in denigrating music as an art unto itself. Music on its own here is deemed "absolute" music, meaning "just" music or "only" music in a dismissive sense. For Wagner, the problem with absolute music is precisely that it is "absolute"—so autonomous that it has no relationship to anything but itself. Gluck, Weber and Mozart were, in his eyes, first and foremost composers (or, as he calls them, absolute musicians), and therefore could not subordinate music in order to achieve a greater integration in their operas. In contrast, Wagner presents himself as the anti-absolute: selflessly reaching out to create connections (words as well as music) for the sake of the drama.

Wagner did know about other manifestos addressing the need to reform opera and integrate its individual elements. His reading of music criticism by the previous generation, especially E.T.A. Hoffmann and Carl Maria von Weber, influenced his own writing tremendously. For instance, the term "music drama," now a fixed part of the Wagnerian lexicon, appears in E.T.A. Hoffmann's praise of Gluck in 1810: "While most of the newer operas are only concerts given on the stage and in costume, Gluck's opera is the true music drama ["das wahre musikalische Drama"] in which the action proceeds without stopping, from moment to moment."[7]

Weber's writings on opera appear to have given Wagner even more food for thought. In his review of Hoffmann's 1816 opera *Undine,* Weber declared: "Of course when I speak of opera I am speaking of the German ideal, namely a self-sufficient work of art in which every feature and every contribution by the related arts are molded together in a certain way and dissolve, to form a new work."[8]

Using these passages and others, John Warrack has argued that "the ideal of a Gesamtkunstwerk (if not by this name) had a long history in Germany ... [and] what tended to distinguish the German writings from those of other nations was the ideal of a genuine fusion of the arts, rather than their simultaneous stage presence."[9] In *Carl Maria von Weber and the Search for a German Opera,* Stephen Meyer has also presented evidence that demonstrates that the issue of unifying the arts into an operatic whole pre-dates Wagner and even Weber in Germany.[10] In sum, although the concept of Gesamtkunstwerk is overwhelmingly attributed to Wagner, the aim of transforming the separate arts into a single artwork has long been central to the history of opera, and of German opera in particular.

The Problem with Naming the Gesamtkunstwerk

Wagner did not take credit for the Gesamtkunstwerk concept, nor for the term itself. As Nicholas Vazsonyi's chapter in this volume points out, the fact that Gesamtkunstwerk and music drama became Wagnerian "trademarks" had little to do with Wagner himself; both terms are largely absent from his writings. Vazsonyi shows that the term Gesamtkunstwerk appeared in print before Wagner "coined" it, and I have found evidence that it was used without reference to Wagner for a time both before and after his "appropriation" of it.[11] As previously mentioned, Wagner does not use Gesamtkunstwerk at all in the most elaborate exposition of his artistic system, *Oper und Drama,* preferring instead the simple "Drama" or occasionally "Drama der Zukunft" (Drama of the Future) or "Kunstwerk der Zukunft" (Artwork of the Future) as the genre he proposes to create. It is worth remembering, too, that the titles of the main Zurich essays refer to a "Kunstwerk" and a "Drama" not a "Gesamtkunstwerk" and a "Music Drama." In his most forthright statement from the Zurich years, Wagner declared: "Because I do not care to invent any arbitrary name for these works, I will simply call them dramas, since that at least indicates the standpoint from which they are to be understood."[12]

Gesamtkunstwerk as a Wagner trademark emerged rather slowly. Music periodicals started using the term with any frequency only in the 1870s.

Significantly, it appeared most often in the *Musikalisches Wochenblatt*, an independent pro-Wagner journal, and in the *Bayreuther Blätter*, founded in 1878 with Wagner's encouragement. But for the vast majority of music journals in the late nineteenth century, the term is only used once or twice in passing. Moreover, there is no mention of Gesamtkunstwerk in places where we might well expect it. It is altogether absent from contemporary writings on the first Bayreuth Festival in 1876, such as Friedrich Nietzsche's "Richard Wagner in Bayreuth."[13] The term also does not seem to have figured in the tremendous effort to promote *Der Ring des Nibelungen* and its first complete performance at the theater for which it was specially built.[14] If the number and variety of reference works or guides for Wagner enthusiasts had dramatically increased by the end of the nineteenth century, it was only in the twentieth century that such publications began to employ Gesamtkunstwerk as an essential term for understanding Wagner's works.[15]

In a recent article, Lydia Goehr calls attention to the many notable inconsistencies in recent scholarship when it comes to designating Wagner's works as operas or music dramas. Her thesis is that "a significant part of the tension regarding naming and titling, as it manifests itself in Wagner's oeuvre, turns on a move Wagner encouraged, to cease thinking about names and titles as merely descriptive or classificatory and to start thinking about them as pointing toward an *unnamable* ideal."[16] However true this might have been about Wagner's intention, in practice the terms took on a life of their own, as others sought to explain Wagner and his works. To give just one relatively recent example, Jürgen Kühnel, in his excellent overview of the prose writings for *The Wagner Handbook*, calls *The Artwork of the Future*: "A general aesthetic theory which centers on what Wagner referred to only in passing as the Gesamtkunstwerk."[17] He continues by stating that "*Oper und Drama* finally gives concrete form to the aesthetics of the Gesamtkunstwerk as the aesthetics of music drama."[18] He could have said more clearly and more simply that *Oper und Drama* finally gives concrete form to the general aesthetic theory of *Das Kunstwerk der Zukunft* without ever using the terms "Gesamtkunstwerk" and "music drama."[19] But these "buzz words" are tempting not because they explain the concept, but rather because they substitute labels for definitions.[20]

Assessing the Political Dimension of Wagner's Works

In general, the explication of Wagner's aesthetics is complicated by the long span of his life, his stylistic evolution, his massive corpus of critical writings (which often contradict each other), and his multiple roles as poet, musician, and thinker. The Wagner literature exhibits a whole range of interpretations on the relationship among Wagner's writings, dramatic works, and political beliefs. After World War II, Wagner's works were "denazified" by focusing on the analysis of the music's formal features. Carl Dahlhaus, the pre-eminent German musicologist of the second half of the twentieth century, authored many influential books and essays on Wagner, in which he contended that "political convictions meant nothing to Wagner except in relation to the idea of musical drama, the measure of all things for him ... Art was the only idea in which Wagner believed."[21] American musicologists such as Thomas Grey, Anthony Newcomb, and William Kinderman concurred on this point, citing Wagner's later writings, where he seemed to assert the primacy of music in the total artwork.[22] They generally agreed that Wagner abandoned the ideal of the Gesamtkunstwerk following his reading of Schopenhauer, and subsequently reinstated music to its position as the highest of the arts.[23] The corollary to this view, whether or not explicit, was that Wagner invoked Gesamtkunstwerk only when he was most directly concerned with art's political function.

Starting in the 1990s, after the end of the Cold War, scholars outside the discipline of musicology approached the tendentious question of Wagner's importance as a political thinker and how this dimension affected the definition of Gesamtkunstwerk. David J. Levin, James Treadwell, Lydia Goehr, Marc Weiner, Linda and Michael Hutcheon, and Slavoj Žižek are examples of scholars from other disciplines who have emphasized Wagner's original, political formulation of the unity of the arts.[24]

In German musicology, the most prolific and prominent figure who has argued that politics was the driving force behind Wagner's creative activity is Udo Bermbach. His 1994 book, *Der Wahn des Gesamtkunstwerks*, is the most prominent and extensive presentation of his argument about Gesamtkunstwerk's fundamentally political nature, a position he has reiterated in many other books and articles. According to Bermbach, Wagner distinguished his views on artistic union from earlier synesthetic concepts by inverting a basic Romantic premise: instead of aiming to aestheticize "real" life, Wagner insisted that life must inform and infuse the artwork.[25]

Bermbach asserts that it is Wagner's new conception of the *Volk* that lies at the heart of the connection between politics and Gesamtkunstwerk. "For him the Volk has social and political significance, and it is only because it is unified socially and politically that it can realize its potential for artistic productivity."[26] Because the Volk is a free association of creative people—an "artistic fellowship of the future" as Wagner put it in *Das Kunstwerk der Zukunft*—only an artwork that is created communally can embody the ideals of a post-revolutionary social order.[27] Bermbach draws special attention to a section at the end of *Das Kunstwerk der Zukunft*, where Wagner envisions an ideal society that would provide for "higher, universal, spiritual needs," through flexible cooperatives of artists that form and dissolve as needed.[28] In one of his most radical statements, Wagner declares:

> Each dramatic artwork, as it enters upon life, will therefore be the work of a new and never-hitherto-existing, and thus a never-to-be-repeated fellowship of artists: its communion will take its rise from the moment when the poet-actor of the hero's role exalts his purpose to the common aim of the comrades whom he needed for its exposition, and will be dissolved the very instant that this purpose is attained.[29]

A political scientist as well as a musicologist, Bermbach is struck by Wagner's grasp of modern organizational theory, calling this passage "a plan for flexible organizational structures, which follow changing demands and in which there is no more place for institutional consolidation and stable, hierarchically ordered rankings."[30] He sees intriguing parallels to initiatives of grassroots democracy where citizens come together in ad hoc organizations for a specific purpose. Bermbach argues, too, that Wagner continued to be informed by his political idealism to the very end. He bases this view on the late essay "Religion und Kunst" (Religion and Art, 1880) and characterizes the 1876 Bayreuth Festspiele as the realization of the Gesamtkunstwerk concept he first outlined in 1849:

> Wagner intended the Festspiel as a celebration of the revolution, as the interpretation of revolutionary events in a particular theatrical form ... With the idea of the Festspiel, the final component that constitutes the concept of Gesamtkunstwerk is specified ... It is based upon music drama, on the synthesis of the individual arts that it achieves, but it reaches far beyond that. It represents above all the performance of Wagnerian music drama in the space of a theatrical festival, a festival play, in a theater whose architecture removes every social distinction; in a social public space where the separation of stage and spectator no longer exists, in which the people take part in the performance, both producing and consulting, and in which life, including politics, is subsumed aesthetically into a perceptible representation.[31]

In sum, Bermbach seizes on the most radical passages from 1849 that propose to dissolve the traditional distinctions of author, work, and audience in order to transform society. He asserts that these aims informed Wagner's projects to the end of his life.

Another, equally prominent, German musicologist who has written extensively about Wagner, Dieter Borchmeyer, takes the opposite view. His entry for "Gesamtkunstwerk" in the current edition of *Die Musik in Geschichte und Gegenwart* (*MGG*), the most prestigious German encyclopedia of music, presents the provocative thesis that "Wagner's idea of the Gesamtkunstwerk, insofar as it actually aims at uniting all the arts, is a purely ideological construct (soon abandoned) without any concrete significance for his dramaturgy."[32] He argues that the proof is in the pudding: the operas that were actually completed and performed do not realize any of the political aims expressed in the Zurich writings.

That two pre-eminent scholars have arrived at such different conclusions regarding Wagner's political commitment over the course of his career demonstrates that the question of the political dimension of Wagner's Gesamtkunstwerk is far from settled. My re-examination of the evidence draws attention to two factors: the specific historical setting and Wagner's rhetorical strategies. This involves, in particular, focusing in on the critical period in 1849 after the revolutions failed, when Wagner had to run for his life after participating in the May uprising in Dresden. Against this context, and drawing on an analysis of major shifts in Wagner's metaphors and figures of speech in the major Zurich texts, I show how and why Wagner's priorities shifted from theory to practice, from politics to aesthetics, and from Gesamtkunstwerk to music drama.

Gesamtkunstwerk and *Das Kunstwerk der Zukunft*

Compared to Wagner's other writings, *Das Kunstwerk der Zukunft* stands out for its enthusiasm for the Young Hegelian philosopher Ludwig Feuerbach, to whom it is dedicated. In his autobiography, Wagner recalled reading Hegel and Feuerbach before he embarked on his own writings at this time. These authors, with their difficult prose, seem to have influenced Wagner's already ponderous writing style, pushing the Zurich-period works toward almost complete opacity. While Feuerbach's philosophy was a crucial influence on critical thought in the lead-up to the revolutions of 1848–49, his popularity waned soon after. His impact on Wagner seems to have taken a similar trajectory. Wagner's discovery of Schopenhauer in 1854 also mirrored a general philosophical trend that favored a resurgence of metaphysics, and treated Feuerbach like yesterday's news.

While under his spell, Wagner expounded mainly on Feuerbach's ideas on the contribution of mutual love to human society and freedom. In the work that, by his own admission, struck Wagner most forcefully, *Gedanken über Tod und Unsterblichkeit* (*Thoughts on Death and Immortality*), Feuerbach stated:

> Without love, you are inseparable from your particular existence; in love, you and your particularity become nothing. But at the same time this perishing is a new and more excellent state of being. Accordingly, you exist and do not exist in love; love is being and not-being in one, life and death as one life. Love gives life and takes it away, destroys and engenders life.[33]

In Part I of *Das Kunstwerk der Zukunft*, Wagner echoes Feuerbach when he declares repeatedly that the highest human need is love. Love also appears in a section where Wagner calls for reuniting all the arts: not only music, poetry, and dance, but also architecture, sculpture, and painting. Despite this attempt at inclusiveness, dance, music, and poetry receive the most attention, to the point that Wagner's Gesamtkunstwerk could more accurately be described as a "Dreikunstwerk."[34] The other arts are certainly superfluous in Wagner's vivid description of how these three "muses" form a single artwork. The detailed imagery, possibly inspired by Botticelli's painting "La Primavera," ends with a picture of the three "sisters" kissing and wrapping around each other to make a single figure:

> As we gaze at this entrancing circle of the purest and most high-born muses of the artistic man, we see the three first stepping forward, each with their loving arm entwined around the other's neck; then, now this one and then the other, slipping out of their entwinement, as though to show the others her beautiful figure in its independence, only brushing with her fingertips the hands of the others; now the one, entranced by the view of the double figure of her two firmly clasped sisters, leaning towards them; then the two, enchanted by the one, greet and do her homage—until finally all, tightly clasped, breast to breast, limb to limb, with heated love-kisses join together into a single blissfully living figure.[35]

Wagner's further commentary on the relationship of the three to each other sounds very similar to Feuerbach's theory that love annihilates the individual in order to give life to a greater whole:

> When at last the pride of all three arts in their own self-sufficiency shall break to pieces, and pass over into love for one another; when at last each art can only love itself when mirrored in the others; when at last they cease to be dissevered arts—then will they all have power to create the perfect artwork; and their own desistence, in this sense, is already of itself this Art-work, their death immediately its life.[36]

If any of the arts is given priority here, it is dance. Wagner declares that dance was the original art because of its primal basis, rhythm, which is also what connects it to music. Towards the end of *Das Kunstwerk der Zukunft* he returns to the image of the three sister arts and how important love is for their ability to lose their individuality and gain a higher unified existence.

Oper und Drama: Love and Procreation

Wagner began work on *Oper und Drama* about two years after *Das Kunstwerk der Zukunft*.[37] As discussed above, some scholars see a continuity in the political aims; others detect a shift in *Oper und Drama* from an explicit political program to a more aesthetically oriented discussion of Wagner's plans for the remaking of art. In this much longer essay, Wagner developed different imagery.[38] Instead of three sisters as creators of the artwork, he now described how a loving woman (music) gives herself up to man (poetry) in order to create the artwork through their sexual love. The three arts have now been reduced to two. Wagner's earlier formulation of dance as the original art is cast differently, so that its rhythmic dimension demotes it to being a part of music. The transformation of Wagner's imagery from three sisters to a man and woman coming together to procreate can be read in a number of ways. In his recent book, Adrian Daub argues for taking the sexual imagery seriously; he "posits that there is a logic to the entwinement of these two fields, opera and sexuality, at this precise point in history—that it was necessitated by a concern with totality that attained renewed importance in aesthetics in the wake of Wagner and with the advent of modernism."[39]

Daub, however, does not find it necessary to distinguish between love and sexuality. He uses the words "erotic," "sexual," and "love" interchangeably. He also elides gender roles and sex by assuming that the nineteenth-century concept of the complementarity of masculine and feminine features is the equivalent of the same era's understanding of procreation. I contend that we need to use these terms more carefully, precisely because of the changing ways in which Wagner's analogies and imagery make use of notions of gender, love, and sex. Wagner's preoccupations and priorities about art shift as he moves away from seeing artwork as the result of the entwining of three loving sisters to the consequence of a loving couple having sex. Wagner's avid description of the sisters' embraces and kisses is erotically charged, but this image does not mark the sisters as sexual females capable of childbearing. Their erotic touching leads to a literal meltdown, which results in the formation of a single being or artwork. In *Oper und Drama*, music is singled out and characterized as a woman. The way Wagner stresses this is rhetorically different than his use of other metaphors. He announces: "*Music is a woman.* The nature of Woman is love; but this love is receiving and in receiving an unreservedly *surrendering*, love."[40] It seems to me that this strident declaration tries to push beyond metaphor, to say "music is not *like* a woman, music somehow *is* a woman." Wagner was trying to understand composition as a natural biological process so that he could create actual works by using music/woman as the receptacle for the man's/the poet's fertilizing seed. Like others at this time, Wagner was in the dark about how and what exactly the woman contributes to the child to which she gives birth. But he takes care to minimize as much as possible the woman's role, making the distinction that although music as woman gives birth, she does not beget music drama ("die Musik ist die Gebärerin, der Dichter der Erzeuger").[41]

By *Oper und Drama*'s conclusion, Wagner abandoned any pretense and named himself as the one person who could create music drama. The original vision of a communal creation and a coming together of all the arts, not just music and poetry, was no longer in evidence. There is a possible pragmatic explanation: once Wagner started thinking in terms of actual operas, he acknowledged that he was going to do it all himself. Rather than admit that his expertise did not extend to all the arts, he focused on the way the librettist and composer came together to create a new artwork, implying with his imagery that a new opera only requires words and music. In "Eine Mitteilung an meine Freunde" (A Communication to my Friends), which was written soon after *Oper und Drama*, he more clearly described that the masculine and feminine interactions occur within the one person of the artist. Instead of feminine music and masculine poetry, he equated the feminine with art and the masculine with real life. Wagner acknowledged the danger that the artist's receptive force could be completely absorbed by art, leading to writing absolute music, becoming an absolute artist, and therefore absolutely feminine. But if the artist's receptive force was able to form his ability to receive life impressions, his masculinity could be retained and his life force channeled into an artistically productive force. By the time he was writing "A Communication," Wagner had completely adjusted his theories so that they pointed directly to himself. But I believe Wagner also moved away from his radical long-term vision of a Gesamtkunstwerk because of a pressing need to address the immediate future of art.

The Doubtful Future for not only Gesamtkunstwerk, but *any* Kunstwerk

After the revolutions of 1848–49 failed, most writers on art abandoned their political rhetoric and tried to regroup. The fear could hardly be suppressed that art had come to a dead end; it had lost its vital force and was petering out. Metaphors and comparisons of art to a living organism that is either dead or dying abound.[42] Empirical evidence indicating that composers' creativity had already dried up was offered as early as July 1848. Leipzig's *Neue Zeitschrift für Musik* noted a significant drop in the quantity of new music being published. After conceding that being inundated by "floods" of music in previous years had not been optimal either, the anonymous writer described the current situation with revulsion: "Now look where the flood has receded, look at the creeping plants, the weeds that overrun it, look at the vermin that live there, the breed that wiggles and squirms in the slime! Who would want to inspect these grounds?"[43] In the aftermath of the wave of revolutions, only the lowest forms of life and art had not been washed away.

This image of repulsion was echoed in Wagner's notorious contribution to the same journal in 1850, "Das Judenthum in der Musik" (Jewishness in Music). Towards the end of the text, he depicted art as a corpse, with the Jews as the worms that decomposed the body:

> As long as the separate art of music had real, organic life necessity in itself, up to the time of Mozart and Beethoven, a Jewish composer was nowhere to be found; it was impossible that a completely foreign element could occupy a part of the

> living organism for the formation of this life. Only after the inner death of a body was evident did the elements lying outside win the power to seize it, but only in order to decompose it. Then the flesh of this body disintegrated in the teeming life of worms: who looking at this body would take it as still alive? The spirit, that is, *life*, flew from this body to kindred bodies, and that is only life itself: *and only in real life can we also find again the spirit of art, not in the worm-devoured corpse.*[44]

Like the earlier article's image of the filth left behind from a receded flood, Wagner's view of art as a corpse betrays charged feelings of revulsion and disgust with the musical situation. Wagner expresses abhorrence of the corpse, but adds to this his revulsion of the devouring worms. While Wagner spent most of his essay venting his anxiety and frustration over the loss of music's vitality by denigrating the Jews, this particular image sees art as already dead and the Jews as worms living off it.

While his contemporaries seemed mostly resigned to a period of decline, Wagner continued to spout political rhetoric and plans for new artworks, which did not go down well, as he acknowledged in his preface to *Oper und Drama*: "A friend has told me that, with my earlier utterances on Art, I angered many persons far less by the pains I took to unmask the grounds of the barrenness of our nowadays art-making, than by my endeavors to forecast the conditions of its future fruitfulness."[45]

Wagner's claim that his contemporaries were hostile toward any plans for Art's future is supported by another scandal. Contentious exchanges in the musical press that began towards the end of 1852 centered on the term *Zukunftsmusik* (Music of the Future). The origin of the term is not clear, but several common phrases that use Zukunft were "in the air" and probably engendered it together.[46] The vehemence surrounding "Music of the Future," as opposed to the more muted skepticism regarding other terms and concepts, indicate that it hit closest to home in the overall controversy about Wagner. The musicologist Dietmar Strauß has also argued that this term was the most important for characterizing the polarizing debate between musical camps, starting in 1853: "At this time the concept of the future was a central point of discussion, from which the concepts of program music, Neudeutsche, Gesamtkunstwerk and music drama were distinguished as secondary."[47] Wagner's subsequent behavior is also telling: in 1861 he felt compelled to write to Berlioz and disavow any responsibility for the phrase. He even wrote an essay later that year entitled, *Zukunftsmusik* (*The Music of the Future*) in which he attributed the "invention of the specter of a music of the future" to popular reports in the press, which merely picked up on a title without trying to understand his writings. Attention was focused on Wagner because he dared to plan new artworks. His dejected and pessimistic contemporaries split into two groups: those who were angered and those who were inspired by his grandiose plans.

Conclusion: The Difference between *Das Kunstwerk der Zukunft* and *Oper und Drama*

Oper und Drama tries to specify how a new artwork can be generated. Wagner evidently abandoned the imagery in *Das Kunstwerk der Zukunft* because it could not supply the necessary details. He found the biological procreative analogy, a basic and common trope used over and over in religious, philosophical, and literary imagery, more "naturally" compelling as a depiction of how to make an artwork, while the image of three sisters entwining their limbs provided only a salacious picture.

One can conclude that Gesamtkunstwerk, standing in for the whole of the text *Das Kunstwerk der Zukunft,* is the more political, more utopian, and more egalitarian vision for opera. Love is seen as a universal that ennobles every human being. It is the "glue" that melds people into a single whole, where they give up their individuality in order to be part of a higher unity. *Oper und Drama* is much more focused on the problem of the artist as creator of vital artworks in a pessimistic period when music as a natural resource seemed to have dried up. The creator of music drama, the term usually associated with the thoughts expressed in *Oper und Drama,* is not the human race, or even the three arts of dance, music, and poetry. The creator is a single artist, a poet, who uses music to serve his needs. This difference can be noted by distinguishing between Gesamtkunstwerk and music drama. As fruitful as the term "Gesamtkunstwerk" has been in other contexts, for a true evaluation of its significance to Wagner we must read it in the light of his constantly developing musical style and aesthetics.

Notes

1. See, for example, explication in Josef Chytry, *The Aesthetic State: A Quest in Modern German Thought* (Berkeley and Los Angeles, 1989), 287–88.
2. For instance, Gottfried Kiesow, *Gesamtkunstwerk—die Stadt: zur Geschichte der Stadt vom Mitteralter bis in die Gegenwart* (Bonn, 1999); Rudolf Sühnel, *Der Park als Gesamtkunstwerk des englischen Klassizismus am Beispiel von Stourhead* (Heidelberg, 1977); and Christian Breuer, *John Lennon und Yoko Ono als Gesamtkunstwerk* (Munich, 1999).
3. Christopher Morris, "'Too Much Music': The Media of Opera," in *The Cambridge Companion to Opera Studies,* ed. Nicholas Till (Cambridge, 2012), 95.
4. See Tim Carter, "Early Opera," in *Music in Late Renaissance and Early Baroque Italy* (Portland, OR, 1992), 202–21.
5. Some treatments of the early history of opera that could have been available to Wagner include: Johann Georg Sulzer, "Oper; Opera," in *Allgemeine Theorie der schönen Künste in einzeln, nach alphabetischer Ordnung der Kunstwörter auf einander folgenden Artikeln abgehandelt,* exp. ed. (Leipzig, 1787) 3:466–91; Friedrich Rochlitz, "Entstehung der Oper (Schreiben an einen Freund)," in *Für Freunde der Tonkunst* (Leipzig, 1824),

2:281–330; Carl von Winterfeld, *Johannes Gabrieli und sein Zeitalter* (Berlin, 1834); Gottfried Wilhelm Fink, "Merkwürdiges Berühmtwerden der Oper zur Zeit als sie noch nicht ihren Namen erhalten hatte," in *Wesen und Geschichte der Oper: ein Handbuch für alle Freunde der Tonkunst* (Leipzig, 1838), 83–105.

6. Richard Wagner, *Opera and Drama*, in *Richard Wagner's Prose Works*, trans. William Ashton Ellis (London, 1900), 2:17. For the sake of consistency, I refer to Wagner's writings using their German titles, even if I have often relied on Ellis' translations of the prose works.
7. Cited in John Warrack, *German Opera: From the Beginnings to Wagner* (Cambridge, 2001), 272.
8. Carl Maria von Weber, *Writings on Music*, ed. John Warrack, trans. Martin Cooper (Cambridge, 1981), 201–2.
9. Warrack, *German Opera*, 392.
10. Stephen Meyer, *Carl Maria von Weber and the Search for a German Opera* (Bloomington, 2003).
11. Christian Hermann Weisse's *System der Aesthetik als Wissenschaft von der Idee der Schönheit* uses Gesamtkunstwerk as early as 1830. Friedrich Theodor Vischer's important *Aesthetik, oder Wissenschaft des schönen* uses it in 1854 with regard to ancient Greek music, not Wagner, as does Josef Bayer's *Aesthetische Untersuchungen* (Prague, 1863). Julian Schmidt uses it with reference to Goethe in his *Bilder aus dem geistigen Leben unserer Zeit* (Berlin, 1870). A.W. Ambros actually argues that the Gesamtkunstwerk does not occur in the theater, as Wagner says, but rather in the church with sacred music; see A.W. Ambros, *Die Grenzen der Musik und Poesie: eine Studie zur Aesthetik der Tonkunst* (Leipzig, 1872).
12. Wagner, "A Communication to My Friends," as cited in Thomas Grey, "A Wagnerian Glossary" (entry on "Music Drama") in *The Wagner Compendium: A Guide to Wagner's Life and Music*, ed. Barry Millington (London, 2001), 236.
13. Indeed, Nietzsche does not appear to have ever used the term "Gesamtkunstwerk" in his published writings.
14. None of the following titles, for example, employ the term "Gesamtkunstwerk": F. Filippi, *Richard Wagner: eine musikalische Reise in das Reich der Zukunft* (Leipzig, 1876); Gustav Engel, *Das Bühnenfestspiel in Bayreuth: kritische Studie* (Berlin, 1876); Oskar Berggruen, *Das Bühnenfestspiel in Bayreuth im Hinblick auf die bildende Kunst* (Leipzig, 1877); Paul Lindau, *Nüchterne Briefe aus Bayreuth* (Breslau and Leipzig, 1877); Martin Plüddemann, *Die Bühnenfestspiele in Bayreuth, ihre Gegner und ihre Zukunft* (Colberg, 1877); Heinrich Porges, *Das Bühnenfestspiel in Bayreuth. Eine Studie über Richard Wagner's "Ring des Nibelungen"* (Munich, 1877); Max Kalbeck, *Das Bühnenfestspiel zu Bayreuth: eine kritische Studie* (Breslau, 1877).
15. None of these popular guides from the late nineteenth century, for instance, use the term: Carl Giessel, *Bayreuth: Ein Wegweiser durch die Stadt und Umgebung unter besonderer Berücksichtigung der Bühnenfestspiele. Zugleich eine kurze Chronik von Bayreuth …* (Bayreuth, 1889); Max Chop, *Vademecum für Wagnerfreunde: Führer durch Richard Wagner's tondramen (mit über 400 notenbeispielen)* (Leipzig, 1893); Friedrich Wild and Richard Pohl, *Bayreuth …: Praktisches Handbuch für Festspielbesucher* (Leipzig, 1896).
16. Lydia Goehr, "From Opera to Music Drama: Nominal Loss, Titular Gain," in *Wagner and His World*, ed. Thomas Grey (Princeton, 2009), 66. Emphasis in original.
17. Jürgen Kühnel, "The Prose Writings," in *Wagner Handbook*, ed. Ulrich Müller and Peter Wapnewski, trans. John Deathridge (Cambridge, MA and London, 1992), 582.

18. Ibid.
19. Jack Stein also refers to *Opera and Drama* as Wagner's "central exposition of the Gesamtkunstwerk," in *Richard Wagner and the Synthesis of the Arts* (Detroit, 1960), 6.
20. Nicholas Vazsonyi, *Richard Wagner: Self-Promotion and the Making of a Brand* (Cambridge, 2010), 161.
21. John Deathridge and Carl Dahlhaus, *The New Grove Wagner* (New York, 1984), 95–96. In my view, Dahlhaus overreaches by attempting to derive Wagner's concept of "absolute music"—a term that was unmistakably pejorative for him—directly from the Romantic glorification of music as the ultimate art. See Dahlhaus, *The Idea of Absolute Music*, trans. Roger Lustig (Chicago, 1989); and Sanna Pederson, "Defining the Term 'Absolute Music' Historically," *Music & Letters* 90, no. 2 (2009): 240–62.
22. Carl Dahlhaus, "The Music," in Müller and Wapnewski, *Wagner Handbook*, 297–314; Dahlhaus, "Wagners Begriff der 'dichterisch-musikalischen Periode'," in *Beiträge zur Geschichte der Musikanschauung im 19. Jahrhundert*, ed. Walter Salmen (Regensburg, 1965), 179–94; Thomas S. Grey, "Wagner and the Problematics of 'Absolute Music' in the Nineteenth Century," in *Wagner's Musical Prose: Texts and Contexts* (Cambridge, 1995), 1–50; Klaus Kropfinger, "Beethoven's Role in Wagner's Writings on Art," in *Wagner and Beethoven: Richard Wagner's Reception of Beethoven* (Cambridge, 1991), 68–154; Anthony Newcomb, "The Birth of Music out of the Spirit of Drama: An Essay in Wagnerian Formal Analysis," *19th-Century Music* 5, no. 1 (Summer 1981): 38–66; Newcomb, "Those Images That Yet Fresh Images Beget," *Journal of Musicology* 2, no. 3 (Summer 1983): 227–45; William Kinderman, "Dramatic Recapitulation in Wagner's 'Götterdämmerung,'" *19th-Century Music* 4, no. 2 (Autumn 1980): 101–12.
23. Dieter Borchmeyer, *Richard Wagner: Theory and Theater*, trans. Stewart Spencer (Oxford, 1991), 66, 111–15.
24. David J. Levin, ed., *Opera Through Other Eyes* (Stanford, 1993); James Treadwell, *Interpreting Wagner* (New Haven and London, 2003); Lydia Goehr, *The Quest for Voice: On Music, Politics, and the Limits of Philosophy* (Berkeley and Los Angeles, 1998); Slavoj Žižek and Mladen Dolar, *Opera's Second Death* (New York, 2002); Marc A. Weiner, *Richard Wagner and the Anti-Semitic Imagination* (Lincoln, 1995); Linda Hutcheon and Michael Hutcheon, *Opera: Desire, Disease, Death* (Lincoln, 1996).
25. Udo Bermbach, *Der Wahn des Gesamtkunstwerks. Richard Wagners politisch-ästhetische Utopie* (Frankfurt am Main, 1994), 229.
26. Ibid., 247.
27. Wagner, *Artwork of the Future*, 196.
28. Ibid., 203–4.
29. Ibid., 204.
30. "Jahre, denn Wagner entwirft hier—sicherlich mit großen Strichen gezeichnet und in eine weite Perspective hineingestellt—den Plan von flexiblen Organisationsstrukturen, die je wechselnden Bedürfnissen folgen sollen und in denen für institutionelle Dies ist gewiß eine der erstaunlichsten Stellen in den politische- ästhetischen Schriften der Züricher Verfestigungen und dauerhaft hierarchisch gestufte Ordnung kein Platz mehr ist." Bermbach, *Wahn des Gesamtkunstwerks*, 250.
31. "Wagner will im Festspiel die Feier der Revolution, die Interpretation der revolutionären Ereignisse in singulärer theatralischer Form … Mit der Festspielidee ist die letzte konstitutive Komponente der Konzeption des Gesamtkunstwerks benannt … Er gründet sich auf das Musikdrama, auf die in ihm geleistete Synthetisierung aller Einzelkünste, aber er reicht weit darüber hinaus. Er meint vor allem auch die Aufführ-

rung des Wagnerschen Musikdramas im Rahmen eines theatralischen Festes, eines Festspiels, und zwar in einem Theater, in dem schon durch die Architektur alle gesellschaftlichen Unterschiede wahrnehmbar beseitigt sind; in dem als einem öffentlichen gesellschaftlichen Raum die Trennungen von Bühne und Zuschauerraum nicht mehr existieren, das ›Volk‹ produzierend wie konsultierend an der Aufführung teilnimmt, das ›Leben‹, also auch die Politik, im Musikdrama ästhetisch aufgenommen und zur sinnhaften Darstellung gebracht wird." Bermbach, *Der Wahn des Gesamtkunstwerks*, 266, 270.

32. "Wagners Idee des Gesamtkunstwerks, insofern sie wirklich auf eine Vereinigung aller Künste zielt, eine bloße (bald aufgegebene) ideologische Konstruktion ist—ohne jegliche konkrete Bedeutung für seine Dramaturgie." Borchmeyer, "Gesamtkunstwerk," *Die Musik in Geschichte und Gegenwart*, 2d edn (Kassel, 1995), 3:1285.
33. Ludwig Feuerbach, *Thoughts on Death and Immortality: From the Papers of a Thinker, Along with an Appendix of Theological-Satirical Epigrams*, ed. James A. Massey (Berkeley and Los Angeles, 1980), 38.
34. Frank Glass makes this point in his book *The Fertilizing Seed: Wagner's Concept of Poetic Intent* (Ann Arbor, 1983).
35. "Beim Anschauen dieses entzückenden Reigens der ächtesten, adeligsten Musen, des künstlerischen Menschen gewahren wir jetzt die drei, eine mit der andern liebevoll Arm in Arm bis an den Nacken verschlungen; dann bald diese bald jene einzelne, wie um den anderen ihre schöne Gestalt in voller Selbstständigkeit zu zeigen, sich aus der Verschlingung lösend, nur noch mit der äußersten Handspitze die Hände der anderen berührend; jetzt die eine, vom Hinblick auf die Doppelgestalt ihrer festumschlungenen beiden Schwestern entzückt, ihr sich neigend; dann zwei, vom Reize der einen gerissen, huldigungsvoll sie grüßend—um endlich Alle, fest umschlungen, Brust an Brust, Glied an Glied, in brünstigem Liebeskusse zu einer einzigen wonniglebendigen Gestalt zu verwachsen." Wagner, *SSD*, 3:83.
36. Wagner, *Das Kunstwerk der Zukunft*, 155.
37. Klaus Kropfinger, "Nachwort," in Richard Wagner, *Oper und Drama*, ed. Klaus Kropfinger (Stuttgart, 1994), 449–53.
38. See Thomas S. Grey, "Metaphor," in *The Cambridge Wagner Encyclopedia*, ed. Nicholas Vazsonyi (Cambridge: Cambridge University Press, 2013), 297–99.
39. Adrian Daub, *Tristan's Shadow: Sexuality and the Total Work of Art after Wagner* (Chicago and London: The University of Chicago Press, 2014), 11.
40. *Opera and Drama*, 1:111. Emphasis in the original.
41. *Opera and Drama*, 3:315.
42. See my "Romantic Music under Siege in 1848," in *Music Theory in the Age of Romanticism*, ed. Ian Bent (Cambridge, 1996), 57–74.
43. "Sehet nur jetzt, da die Fluth zurückgedrängt ist, den Boden an, sehet die Schlingpflanzen, das Unkraut, das ihn überwuchert, blicket an das Ungeziefer, das darinnen lebt, das Gezücht, das sich im Schlamme krümmt und windet! Diesen Boden zu untersuchen, wer hätte dazu Lust?" "Kritischer Anzeiger" of 1 July, *Neue Zeitschrift für Musik* (hereafter *NZfM*) 29 (1848): 7.
44. "So lange die musikalische Sonderkunst ein wirkliches organisches Lebensbedürfniß in sich hatte, bis auf die Zeiten Mozart's und Beethoven's, fand sich nirgends ein jüdischer Componist: unmöglich konnte ein, diesem Lebensorganismus gänzlich fremdes Element an den Bildungen dieses Lebens Theil nehmen. Erst wenn der innere Tod eines Körpers offenbar ist, gewinnen die außerhalb liegenden Elemente die Kraft, sich

seiner zu bemächtigen, aber nur um ihn zu zersetzen. Dann löst sich wohl das Fleisch dieses Körpers in wimmelnde Viellebigkeit von Würmern auf: wer möchte bei ihrem Anblicke aber wohl der Körper selbst noch für lebendig halten? Der Geist, das ist: *das Leben*, floh von diesem Körper hinweg zu wiederum Verwandtem, und das ist nur das Leben selbst: *und nur im wirklichen Leben können auch wir den Geist der Kunst wieder finden nicht bei ihrer würmerzerfressenen Leiche*." K. Freigedank, "Das Judenthum in der Musik," *NZfM* 33 (1850):111.

45. "Ein Freund teilte mir mit, daß ich mit dem bisherigen Ausspruche meiner Ansichten über die Kunst bei vielen weniger dadurch Ärgernis erregt hätte, daß ich den Grund der Unfruchtbarkeit unseres jetzigen Kunstschaffens aufzudecken mich bemühte, als dadurch, daß ich die Bedingungen künftiger Fruchtbarkeit desselben zu bezeichnen strebte." Wagner, *Oper und Drama* (Stuttgart, 1984), 7.
46. Besides *Das Kunstwerk der Zukunft*, Wagner had given Part III of *Oper und Drama* the subtitle "Dichtkunst und Tonkunst im Drama der Zukunft" (Poetry and Music in the Drama of the Future). For a detailed investigation of the term's origin, see Christa Jost and Peter Jost, "'Zukunftsmusik'. Zur Geschichte eines Begriffs," Musiktheorie 10 (1995): 119–35.
47. Dietmar Strauß, "Eduard Hanslick und die Diskussion um die Musik der Zukunft," in *Eduard Hanslick. Sämtliche Schriften. Historisch-kritische Ausgabe*, ed. Dietmar Strauß, Band I, 4 Aufsätze und Rezensionen 1857–1858 (Vienna, Cologne and Weimar, 2002), 407.

Sanna Pederson, who specializes in German music history and culture in the nineteenth century, has been the Mavis C. Pitman Professor of Music at the University of Oklahoma since 2001. Her most recent work has been engaged with the aesthetic theories of Richard Wagner, and she contributed eleven articles in *The Cambridge Wagner Encyclopedia* related to that topic.

CHAPTER 3

Richard Wagner, *Parsifal*, and the Pursuit of Gesamtkunstwerk

ANTHONY J. STEINHOFF

In a diary entry dated 29 March 1881, Cosima Wagner recorded the following declaration of her husband, Richard: "Gobineau says the Germans were the last card Nature had to play—*Parsifal* is my last card."[1] Unfortunately, the entry provides no further clues to help clarify what Wagner intended to assert through this comparison. For scholars such as Robert Gutman, Hartmut Zelinsky, and Marc Weiner, Wagner's point was obvious. The association branded *Parsifal* as an essentially racial and, given the prominence of anti-Semitic discourse in much of Wagner's writing on race, anti-Semitic work.[2] While this argument has merit, it does not exhaust the interpretative possibilities for this profoundly ambiguous statement. Clearly, Wagner's reference to Gobineau served to do more than just announce that *Parsifal* would be his final stage composition—but what? To answer this question, we would need to reflect at greater length on how Wagner envisioned the creation of *Parsifal* as equivalent to what Nature had accomplished in "producing" Germans, noting too that Gobineau's discussions of race were largely devoid of anti-Semitic overtones.[3] That is, we would need to assess how *Parsifal* figured in Wagner's broader artistic-*cum*-political agenda. Viewed from this perspective, I suggest, a rather different conclusion emerges. Namely, *Parsifal* was Wagner's "last card" in that it represented the culmination of his decades-long pursuit of the ideal of Gesamtkunstwerk.

On a number of levels, this proposition seems to run counter to the scholarly consensus on Wagner and Gesamtkunstwerk. To begin with, as Nicholas Vazsonyi and Sanna Pederson point out in their respective contributions to this volume, Wagner himself disliked this term. It was also conspicuously absent from the branding strategy that Team Wagner pursued in the 1870s and 1880s.[4] Hence, Wagner would not have explicitly framed the comparison between Germans/Nature and *Parsifal*/Wagner's oeuvre in terms of Gesamtkunstwerk.

In addition, scholars frequently point out that Wagner's encounter with Arthur Schopenhauer's *Der Welt als Wille und Vorstellung* (*The World as Will and Representation*) in 1854 prompted him to abandon most of the ideas about art, politics, and theater that he had advanced in the Zurich writings of 1849–1851 (above all, *Art and Revolution*, *The Artwork of the Future*, *Opera and Drama*), which had come to be summed up by the term "Gesamtkunstwerk," at least in the public imagination. Dieter Borchmeyer, for instance, has stated that, post-Schopenhauer, Gesamtkunstwerk existed only as an aesthetic-dramaturgical concept, stripped of the utopian and revolutionary positions advanced in the Zurich writings.[5] Accordingly, what passed for Gesamtkunstwerk after 1854 was only a pale reflection of its "true," revolutionary self. And whatever content we might want to place in the Gesamtkunstwerk "box," by 1881 Wagner no longer regarded it as a core element of his creative mission.

Nonetheless, there are good grounds for resisting the notion that Wagner was essentially through with "Gesamtkunstwerk" by the mid-1850s. Indeed, by declaring *Parsifal* to be his last and perhaps most important card to play in the pursuit of Gesamtkunstwerk, I contend that realizing Gesamtkunstwerk was as an ongoing artistic-social-political project for Wagner in which his fleshing out of ideas in the Zurich essays (and their partial realization in *Rheingold* and the first act of *Die Walküre*) was just a beginning, not the end. Admittedly, Wagner refused to embrace the label "Gesamtkunstwerk." But then, as Nicholas Vazsonyi and Lydia Goehr have demonstrated, Wagner was notoriously picky about labels and terms, both because he wished to control how people talked about his oeuvre and because he was anxious to avoid closing down the field of creative activity that the act of naming normally engendered.[6] Consequently, we should not equate the rejection of a label with the absence of an artistic-political ideal to which the term roughly corresponded. Above all, *Die Meistersinger von Nurnberg* and even more so *Parsifal* reveal that Wagner's desire to use musical theater and the stage to explore and expound upon notions of society, community, and the role of (German) art remained powerful well after the encounter with Schopenhauer. Indeed, *Parsifal* not only treats a mythic (or more accurately, legendary) subject, but is itself myth-like, at least in the way that Wagner talked about myth in *Opera and Drama*. That is, it is suggestive, open to continual articulation by poets and actors across time and, arguably, across space. In short, even if an "ideal that shall not be named," Gesamtkunstwerk remained a critical part of Wagner's creative-cum-political agenda, and not merely in terms of aesthetics and dramaturgy.

In addition to underscoring Gesamtkunstwerk's ongoing salience to Wagner's creative agenda, identifying *Parsifal* as his final statement on the subject prompts a needed reappraisal of what he did mean by the term, not just in theory—which was never his strong suit—but also in practice. In recent writing on Gesamtkunstwerk, scholars have duly stressed *Parsifal*'s importance both for Wagner and for his aesthetic legacy. *Parsifal* is thus understood either as a source of inspiration for aesthetic synthesis and experimentation or as a forerunner of the twentieth century's totalizing aesthetic experiences.[7] But, much as Nicholas Vazsonyi suggests in his essay here, these discussions largely downplay what was key to Wagner: the importance of theater *qua* theater. His commitment to music drama reflected his own professional interests, to be sure. But it also reflected a conviction that music theater, properly conceived and executed, had an incredible capacity to ennoble and teach. It was this sense of drama, which he believed had existed in classical Greece, that Wagner wanted to resurrect and refashion for modern times in order to promote the virtues of Art and, thereby, strengthen the German spirit and people. For Wagner, thus, public theater was inherently political and social. This perspective powerfully informed the Zurich writings and how he thought about "*gesamt*" and "*Kunstwerk*," especially in the context of the aesthetic choices and experiments manifest in the stage pieces from the *Ring to Parsifal*.

Having shuffled the deck, it is time now to deal out the cards and commence play. In the first round, we will revisit the emergence of a vision of Gesamtkunstwerk in Wagner's Zurich writings. But, critically, I propose that we understand this package as an initial articulation of problems and dreams, rather than a completed, finite creative-political statement. In the second round, we will examine Wagner's ongoing engagement with the Gesamtkunstwerk ideal, most notably in connection with his ideas on festival theater, culminating with the first Bayreuth Festival of 1876. Then in a final round we explore *Parsifal* as the *summa* of Wagner's achievements in his pursuit of Gesamtkunstwerk.

Gesamtkunstwerk, Music Drama, and the Theatrical Ideal

A year after *Opera and Drama* was published, Wagner felt compelled to comment on the apparent discrepancies between the principles he espoused in that text and his previous compositional practices. The result was "A Communication to my Friends," an essay Wagner addressed only to the "friends" who "[felt] a need and inclination to understand" him.[8] "A Communication" presents a fascinating discussion of Wagnerian theory and practice, but it is telling that Wagner acknowledges here the difficulties contemporaries—not just friends, but foes too, we must assume—faced in comprehending the maze of ideas he advanced in the Zurich writings, particularly with respect to what I will continue to call Gesamtkunstwerk. As Sanna Pederson observed in the previous chapter, part of the challenge (then and now) lies in penetrating the fog of Wagner's murky prose style. But an even deeper problem, it seems, is the very way Wagner went about developing his ideas in the Zurich texts. For while he presents these essays as theoretical statements and explications of fundamental principles, he nonetheless simultaneously denies them any prescriptive validity. They communicate his own reflections on the "artwork of the *future*," namely, his views on its goals and its basic qualities. But throughout this discussion, Wagner tacitly acknowledges that this artwork, if realized, still might not take the form that he has envisioned. In part this reflects the very uncertainty of looking into the future, but also the real and multiple challenges involved in moving from theory, and the realm of ancient Greece, to practice, and conditions in modern, nineteenth-century German Europe.

It seems to me, thus, that in talking about the ideas in the Zurich writings that came to be grouped together as Wagner's "Gesamtkunstwerk idea," it might be fruitful to adopt a strategy similar to that used by the French priest, Félix Dupanloup, to explain Pope Pius IX's *Syllabus errorum* of 1864. In short, Dupanloup, a liberal Catholic, sought to make the pope's reactionary list of modern errors palatable to Catholics by referring to the *Syllabus* as a "thesis"—what is ideally and eternally true—which he then distinguished from the "hypothesis"—that which could be realized in practice given prevailing social, cultural, and political conditions.[9] Admittedly, this analogy has its limits, since Wagner did not regard his Geneva texts as "eternally true" statements of principle. Rather, they were essays, literally attempts in thinking through how to translate what he viewed as the core forces of classical Greece's intertwining of art, politics, and social life into the modern German present. In the 1861 essay *Zukunftsmusik* (*The Music of the Future*), he even confesses to having a certain repugnance towards this "labyrinth of theoretical speculation" that he wrote while "in a thoroughly abnormal state of mind."[10] While introducing the Zurich writings for the 1872 edition of his *Gesammelte Schriften*, he owns up to his own shortcomings as a theorist in these texts. He characterizes the essays as an "impassioned tangle of ideas" (eine gewisse leidenschaftliche Verwirrung) that reflected more the ebbs and flows of his own thinking on how to translate the classical Greek past into a modern German present than an effort to announce a distinct, rigorous aesthetic-"philosophic system."[11]

Nonetheless, central to all of Wagner's Zurich essays is this notion, very similar to Dupanloup's idea of a "thesis," that classical Greece indeed presented an ideal to which Wagner aspired, not in an exact reproduction of the artistic forms or social relationships, but in the creation of a truly German vision that was consistent with the spirit of that Greek ideal. And from this vantage, the analogy has real merits for reorienting the discussion of Wagner and Gesamtkunstwerk in productive ways. With respect to the Zurich pieces in particular, it suggests that we may need to make a clearer distinction between the fundamental problems Wagner hoped to address (the "thesis") and the specific solutions he proposed for them (the "hypothesis") in these texts. This is not to suggest that we should simply reduce the web of concepts and concerns that Wagner raises in these pieces to a single PowerPoint slide. Nor do I propose that we ignore their specific historical context—that is, their intimate ties to Wagner's reading of Ludwig Feuerbach and his situation as a political exile following the failed Dresden uprising of 1849.[12] But thinking about the Zurich writings in terms of "thesis vs. hypothesis" does prompt us to distinguish more clearly between surface features of this discourse, which have tended to attract the greatest degree of popular and even scholarly attention, and the central aesthetic, dramaturgical, and even political challenges that Wagner sought to address via these treatises.

Much has been made in the literature about the revolutionary, utopian spirit that infuses Wagner's Zurich writings[13]—and rightly so. It is one of these texts' most striking features. Furthermore, mid-century readers were fascinated by, if also often critical of, it. In his account of the origins of drama in classical Greece and its role in the life of the Greek *polis*, at least during the glory days of Aeschylus and Sophocles, Wagner paints a picture of drama as artwork that stood in marked contrast to the conditions prevailing in contemporary Europe: artwork as communal product versus art as commercial good; the people (Volk) as co-creators of art, rather than mere consumers; the artist as "translator" of the national spirit for the benefit of the Volk, instead of alienated (and egotistical) worker; and organic union of arts in the artwork versus their separation and individual corruption by modern tastes. To overcome this sorry state of affairs, especially in the German lands, Wagner does call for revolution that would need to occur along two more or less simultaneous fronts. First, it would be necessary to create the "artwork of the future," that is, in an ideal type of (music) theater. Second, it would be essential to promote the social, cultural, and political conditions that would ensure the proper reception of that artwork.

Perhaps no element of the Zurich essays, especially *The Artwork of the Future* and *Opera and Drama*, has been the subject of more interest and debate than Wagner's musings over the form and content of the future artwork, which came to be labeled Gesamtkunstwerk. It is tempting to regard this as the most utopian element of all, inasmuch as Wagner seems to call for re-establishing a long lost synthesis among the arts, much as Sanna Pederson described in the previous chapter. Moreover, as Anke Finger observes, this creative and aesthetic synthesis in the "total artwork" was itself emblematic of the larger communitarian dimension of Wagner's thought. "The Wagnerian total artwork project is," she writes, "thus, an aesthetic, social, and political interdependency intertwining both art and human being (not just the artists) and the artist as human being."[14]

And yet, even in the context of this post-revolutionary moment and Wagner's own efforts to realize some of these ideas in the composition of *Das Rheingold* and the first parts of *Die Walküre*,[15] it seems more productive to regard much of his, admittedly lengthy, reflection on the ideal relationship among the arts as surface detail, rather than as central problem. Indeed, one weakness in much of the discussion of Wagner and "Gesamtkunstwerk" has been this very tendency to parse the word as "Gesamtkunst-Werk," whereby the stress is laid on the synthetic, amalgamated character of the final creative product or *Werk*. Accordingly, Wagner has been criticized either for encouraging the creation of some sort of unwieldy all-encompassing creative construct or for ignoring his theories altogether by producing merely "two-art" or "three-art" works.[16] While this might seem justification enough to jettison the term altogether, much as Wagner himself recommended, Matthew Smith's comments on the word, and the challenges that translating it poses, in fact help us move from the surface detail to the central problem. He writes:

> The most frequent translation of the word is "total work of art," but even this is by no means straightforward: other possibilities include "communal work of art," "collective work of art," "combined work of art," and "unified work of art." Indeed, the concept includes all of these ideas, for it is an art-form as much about collectivity as about unity, about community as about totality.[17]

By exploring the different meanings packed into the element "Gesamt-," Smith calls attention to the importance of unified purpose and synergy in the genuine "work of art," which is arguably Wagner's paramount focus in the Zurich texts.

Perhaps nowhere is this clearer than in *Opera and Drama*, where he devotes the first two parts to deploring the state of modern drama, above all in contemporary German Europe. In part, his attacks on contemporary opera and theater were completely self-serving, functioning to defend and advance his own dramatic and theatrical vision. But the passionate critique cannot be fully reduced to personal motive. For running through this text, as with the other essays, is a deep-seated commitment to theater, especially as social practice. Properly created and executed, Wagner believed, theater served to articulate and present values common to the Volk. At the same time, though, it helped to nurture and instill within the Volk those same values and sentiments. The initial realization of Gesamtkunstwerk, as David Roberts has stressed, would indeed have a revolutionary, regenerative function. But, for Wagner, the transformative power of theater was not just a matter of ritual or a Rousseauian civil religion, as Roberts suggests.[18] It was also intimately associated with the theater's role as a type of a moral-educational institution, such that we might even read individual theater pieces as *Lehrstücke* (anticipating, perhaps, the theories of Bertolt Brecht).[19] And given the theater's capacity to enlighten and teach, by example and through the shared experience, Gesamtkunstwerk would promote the type of spiritual renewal in Germany that Wagner believed essential so that "Germany" could take real form as a cultural-political entity in modern times. He states the connections between drama and national sentiment quite clearly in *Art and Revolution*: "The Greeks considered dramatic art to be the most perfect; it was the epitome of everything in Greek culture that could be expressed. It was the Greek nation itself, in intimate connection with its history, which saw itself mirrored in the drama presented on stage."[20]

The key point in all of these musings on (music-)drama, the Volk and the public (or national) spirit, is that for the drama to have its desired function, it had to be properly created and executed. Wagner ultimately identifies two elements as essential. First, the proper subject of drama is myth. In a clear indication of how classical Greece serves not as a template but only a source of inspiration, Wagner famously states that Germanic legend should be the mythic source for proper German drama.[21] In this context, we see too—and it is worth emphasizing—that a central concern in all of these writings is the creation of "proper" musical theater for Germany. It may well be that the Gesamtkunstwerk idea could be applied to other national contexts, but here, as in later writings, Wagner is focused almost exclusively on Germans and Germany. Second, and here we return more directly to the notion of Gesamtkunstwerk, each of the separate arts needs to work together in harmony to realize a common purpose. Or, as Wagner notes in *The Artwork of the Future*, "[t]he true Drama is only conceivable as proceeding from a common drive of all the arts towards the most direct presentation to a common public."[22] Again, in the context of mid-nineteenth-century German Europe, this aim is doubly revolutionary in that it requires not just a new aesthetic-*cum*-dramaturgical practice, but also a social–political environment in which the Volk could see itself as constituting a common public.

Admittedly, in *Art and Revolution*, and again in *Opera and Drama*, Wagner repeatedly mentions that this collaboration of the several arts in the creation and production of drama enables both drama and each art to attain their highest degrees of fullness. But, echoing a point Nicholas Vazsonyi raises earlier in this volume, in the final analysis, what matters most here really is the Drama, the collective end product, rather than the individual component pieces. Accordingly, the artwork of the future would be free of *Effekt*, gratuitous moments of artistic egoism, which he viewed as symptomatic of modern depravity in the contemporary theater and opera house. But it would also be characterized by the harmonious coordination among the various arts, each one contributing to the common goal according to its particular nature. Thus, rather than invoke the Hegelian notion of *Aufhebung* to comprehend Wagner's notion of the type of synthesis that occurs in the context of Gesamtkunstwerk, we might resort most fruitfully to the corporeal metaphors regularly employed by St. Paul to discuss the Christian community: "For just as each of us has one body with many members, and these members do not all have the same function" (Romans 12:4), so it is with the Gesamtkunstwerk. But whereas the human body already existed, and the relationships among its parts essentially defined, the *Artwork of the Future* that Wagner imagined still had to be created. Critically, this act of creation did not entail bringing to life a long-dead Greek model. Rather, it entailed fashioning a collaborative artwork for contemporary times, something that would entail considerable thought and experimentation with respect to the ideal relationship among the component arts. The Zurich writings, thus, represented an initial effort to think through the possibilities and modalities of this new drama, this Gesamtkunstwerk. But, as Wagner's subsequent work and writing reveals, the quest to realize Gesamtkunstwerk hardly ended in 1851.

Theaters, Festivals, and Drama

The fact that Wagner distanced himself early on from the term "Gesamtkunstwerk" is not necessarily a reason in and of itself for contending that Wagner also lost interest in the underlying concept once he shifted his attentions away from theoretical reflection. Following the arguments Nicholas Vazsonyi has advanced in his study of the Wagner "brand," we can understand this rejection as part of Wagner's ongoing efforts to control public discourse on his creative production by insisting on the proper terminology to be employed vis-à-vis his "product line." Inasmuch as Wagner himself had little role in promoting Gesamtkunstwerk as a concept to describe his aesthetic-dramatic-political vision, it makes sense that he preferred not to endorse the label.[23] But, more importantly, this reticence also reflects Wagner's own unwillingness to view the points made in the Zurich essays as constituting a specific course of action, musico-dramatic or otherwise. Again, these were think pieces, in which Wagner sought to show the merits of exploring and understanding the Greek past as a way to prepare Germany's future. The central point, as Udo Bermbach has underscored, was that art, or the aesthetic realm, was essential to bringing about necessary cultural, social and political reform in German-speaking Europe.[24] What changed most after the publication of "A Communication to my Friends" in 1851, thus, was not Wagner's conviction about the intimate connection between art and public life and hence politics, but that realizing Gesamtkunstwerk required not just theoretical reflection, but also actual creative activity.

During the quarter century following the publication of the Zurich writings, the aspect of the Gesamtkunstwerk concept that Wagner explored most visibly was what Udo Bermbach has called its "formal" dimension. Bermbach uses this notion primarily to designate the essential conditions surrounding the production of music theater: from the preparation and performance of singers and orchestra members to the architecture and technological capacities of the theater itself. But, critically, this formal side of Gesamtkunstwerk also encompasses the broader social–political context of the production, in terms of both the artists and their public responsibilities and the public and its "new" relationship to art.[25] A major indication of Wagner's engagement with these issues was his promotion of theater reform in German-speaking Europe. In fact, the start of his literary efforts to improve conditions in Germany's theaters preceded the Zurich essays, as evidenced by the 1848 essay, "Entwurf zur Organisation eines deutschen National-Theaters" (Plan for the Organization of a German National Theater for the Kingdom of Saxony). And in the midst of writing *Opera and Drama*, he published "Über die musikalische Direktion der Züricher Oper" (On the Musical Direction of the Zurich Opera) (1850). Thereafter followed, between 1851 and 1872, eight more texts, including such considerable essays as "Ein Theater in Zürich" (A Theater in Zurich) (1851), "Das Wiener Hof-Operntheater" (The Vienna Court Opera House)" (1863), and "Bericht an Seine Majestät den König Ludwig II. von Bayern über eine in München zu errichtende deutsche Musikschule" (Report to His Majesty King Ludwig II of Bavaria on a German School of Music to be Established in Munich) (1865).

In short, from roughly 1850 to 1872, Wagner continued his discourse on Gesamtkunstwerk, focusing now on the questions of the performance and the staging of musical theater. Many of these essays adopted a self-consciously practical perspective to questions of theatrical production, from theater design and stage technology to musical direction and acting. But, as Dieter Borchmeyer has noted, Wagner the visionary was also omnipresent in these works.[26] This is especially apparent in the two institutional proposals, the one for the Kingdom of Saxony (of 1848), the other for Munich (of 1865), in which he sought to lay the foundations for the long-term health of German theater by creating a model that could be adopted by other regional theaters (the Saxony proposal) and by establishing a model for the proper training of artists (singers, actors, instrumentalists) for the theater (both proposals).

The ties between these texts and the Zurich writings, and hence between the former and the concept of Gesamtkunstwerk, do not end with the mere enumeration of subject matter. As Jürgen Kühnel has stressed, Wagner's first articulation of what came to be called Gesamtkunstwerk occurred, in fact, not in any of the Zurich writings, but in the proposal for the National Theater for Saxony.[27] For Wagner prefaces his proposal by observing: "In the art of the theater all the arts are united, to a greater or lesser degree, to create an impression on the public that is more immediate than any one of them is able to produce alone."[28] In addition, these writings share with the Zurich essays, and with *Opera and Drama* in particular, the conviction that theater reform is not just an aesthetic or a dramaturgical project, but a political-national one. In the proposal for the Kingdom of Saxony, Wagner makes this point almost immediately following his observation on drama as a "collaborative" endeavor, by claiming that "the extraordinary effect [of the theater's] accomplishments upon the taste and manners of a nation has been actively recognized by leaders of the State at different epochs," a situation that has also justified state support for the theater.[29] Similarly, in 1863, Wagner points out that in establishing the two Court Theaters in Vienna, Joseph II specifically charged them "to contribute to the ennobling of the nation's manners and taste."[30] In the proposal to Ludwig II to create a music school for Munich, as well, Wagner contends that the objective should not be to create a conservatory, since there does not yet exist a German national style to be conserved. Rather, the goal should be to establish an institution that can help develop and then train individuals in a German style, which would "eventually prove of utmost benefit to German art."[31]

Ultimately, none of Wagner's reform plans came to fruition, at least as he intended, namely in the form of new, state-led initiatives and institutions. Dieter Borchmeyer has explained these failures as stemming largely from the projects' internal weaknesses. Wagner's vision, however powerful, lacked the clarity and conceptual consistency necessary to effect a project's realization. Moreover, time and again, he made utterly unrealistic assessments about what the particular political and financial circumstances would allow, which made it all the easier for court officials to dismiss his proposals as utopian musings.[32] Nonetheless, they remain valuable indications of Wagner's ongoing efforts to help bring about the institutional and artistic conditions that he viewed as essential for realizing Gesamtkunstwerk. In addition, a number of the ideas presented in these proposals did later find tangible expression in the context of launching the first Bayreuth Festival.

The story of the creation of the Bayreuth Festival has received enough attention in the scholarly literature that we do not need to dwell on it at length here.[33] But a few observations are necessary to highlight the fundamental connections between this endeavor and the broader, ongoing Gesamtkunstwerk project. First and foremost, as Wagner's initial reflections on the festival concept and the performance of the *Ring* indicate, the notion of mounting a theater festival was intimately connected with the idealism and Philhellenism expressed in the Zurich writings. David Roberts thus contends that the Bayreuth Festival represents a concrete effort to resuscitate not only the ancient Greek theater festival, but also what he calls the Greek "art religion."[34] Whether we must necessarily ascribe to Wagner's festival idea the explicitly religious and cultic dimensions that Roberts proposes is debatable. Clearly, Wagner's belief in theater's capacity to edify and promote a national spirit owed much to its ritual dimensions. The theater festival was especially propitious to the raising of national consciousness, since, by its very nature, it occurred outside of "ordinary time." Not only were the festival events marked as special, but because people were temporarily liberated from common temporal constraints, they also had greater leisure to experience them to the fullest.[35] Wagner's eventual selection of Bayreuth as the site for his festival further promoted this "festive climate," at least in principle, because it required participants to separate themselves physically from their normal worlds in the interest of national art. However, as scholars such as Catherine Bell have noted, while ritual is intimately connected with religion, all that is ritualistic is not necessarily religious.[36] For instance, National Socialist, Fascist and even Communist regimes also invoked ritual to promote particular values, worldviews, and notions of community at various points in the twentieth century, but the conclusion that such regimes were thus "political religions" remains sharply contested.[37]

Second, as Udo Bermbach has usefully stressed, the Bayreuth project's idealism was intimately political and nationalistic.[38] Wagner intended this festival to be a true German *Volksfest* (people's or national festival), inspired as much by the festivals he witnessed while in exile in German-speaking Switzerland as by his imaginings of the Greek past.[39] Accordingly, the festival would be organized around a "German" theater piece, namely, the *Ring*, with its subject based on Germanic legend. Finally, public financial support would permit the Volk free admission to the festival. As is well known, the more this dream approached reality, the less "popular" the Bayreuth Festival became. Wagner's efforts to obtain federal funding for the festival following the establishment of the German Empire in 1871 came to naught. Similarly, the subscription campaign launched in 1871 came up well short of expectations. Financial necessities, thus, forced him to give up on his dreams of a truly popular festival, an event that could speak to all Germans regardless of their social background. It is this lack of public support for the Bayreuth project that helps to explain Wagner's unwillingness to have "his" theater described as a "national theater," a point he made during the ceremony for the laying of the theater's foundation stone in 1872.[40] Yet, as Cosima Wagner reports in a diary entry dated 6 January 1873, her husband continued to regard Bayreuth as a national theater: "Bismarck hat Deutschland, R. ein *deutsches* Theater geschaffen ([Otto von] Bismarck created Germany, R[ichard] a *German* theater).[41]

Finally, whereas such scholars as Matthew Smith and Juliet Koss have emphasized the role that the Bayreuth stage played in advancing the notion of Gesamtkunstwerk as "total art," a place whose technical apparatus seduces and captivates the audience in the name of Art, in the lead up to the first festival we need also think about Bayreuth as a workshop for creating Gesamtkunstwerk, that is a collaborative, multidisciplinary artistic product.[42] In fact, at one level, we might consider all of Wagner's post-1850 dramatic works as essays in Gesamtkunstwerk, even if halfway through *Die Walküre* Wagner stopped trying to follow the principles he announced in *Opera and Drama*. That is, from *Das Rheingold* to *Götterdämmerung* (we will look at *Parsifal* in the following section), Wagner never stopped experimenting with how to write musical theater so as to maximize the dramatic message and experience. In part, this involved exploring new ways to negotiate the relationship between music and text. It also led to further development of the orchestra as a dramatic "actor," above all through its handling of a work's leitmotifs.[43] But these experiments also entailed grappling with the challenge of explicating myth—Germanic legend—on stage. Of course, with *Die Meistersinger von Nürnberg,* Wagner opted to treat a historical rather than a legendary subject. Yet, the ways in which Germanness—notions of the Volk, German spirit and German culture—pervade this music drama also permit regarding it as a trial run in using historical material to create effective musical theater.

Above all, the conditions at Bayreuth provided Wagner with his first opportunity to shape pretty much every aspect of the actual production and performance of his dramatic works. The theater's specific features, from the famed sunken pit to the simple approach to audience seating, all reflected his intent to realize as fully as possible his views on staging musical theater. Likewise, the technical capabilities of the performance space were developed (and, in part, invented) so as to accommodate the considerable demands of works like the *Ring.*[44] Last, but not least, Wagner succeeded in establishing an unusually long rehearsal period for the inaugural performances of the *Ring* in 1876. Of course, the festival's musical ensemble and production team did have to mount two world premieres (namely *Siegfried* and *Götterdämmerung*) as well as revive two other operas (*Das Rheingold* and *Die Walküre*) that summer; nevertheless, contemporary accounts reveal that Wagner also used the lengthy rehearsal period as a sort of short course in performing musical theater as Gesamtkunstwerk.[45] With respect to that artistic ensemble, as is well known, Wagner decided neither to establish a permanent corps of instrumentalists and singers (wise, given the shaky financial situation of the entire venture), nor to hire a specific existing orchestra or chorus to perform at the festival. Rather, he formed a "national ensemble," hiring talented musicians from the various German theaters to perform the solo parts, play in the orchestra and sing in the chorus.[46] In sum, although Wagner could not obtain an ideal *völkisch* audience for the Bayreuth experiment of 1876, in pretty much every other respect the festival represented a truly impressive effort to realize key formal and substantive dimensions of Gesamtkunstwerk. An all-German team of artists presented a cycle of "multidisciplinary" musical theater pieces based on Germanic legend in a model theater in the heart of Germany.

The *Bühnenweihfestspiel Parsifal*

With the *Ring* performances at the first Bayreuth Festival, Wagner scored a major artistic triumph. Piotyr Illyich Tchaikovsky concluded his review of the festival by calling it "[a]n event of the greatest importance to the world, an epoch-making work of art."[47] It also represented Wagner's most important effort to date to realize the concept of Gesamtkunstwerk (even if, again, neither he nor those in his circle employed that specific term). He himself realized that in some key respects, the festival experience fell short of the ideal. Writing in the *Bayreuther Blätter* in 1878, Wagner continued to lament the lack of imperial financial sponsorship, which prevented the festival from attracting a more truly "German" public. In fact, the festival finished with such a large deficit that all plans for a second festival had to be put on hold until the financial situation improved.[48] Despite the heroic efforts of the team led by Wagner's technical advisor at Bayreuth, Karl Brandt, there were also numerous difficulties with stage technology and equipment, as might be expected in a brand new theater, which occasionally undercut the composer-*cum*-producer's dramatic intentions.[49] And while some contemporary observers, like the Austrian critic Max Kalbeck, praised Wagner for having made the *Ring* "stageable," others later pointed out that the composer's staging was not always in keeping with his own dramatic goals.[50]

After *Götterdämmerung*, Wagner completed only one other score, that for the *Bühnenweihfestspiel Parsifal*. This was ultimately a result of his death early in 1883, just a few months after the work's successful premiere at the second Bayreuth Festival of 1882. But even while working on *Parsifal*, Wagner had announced that it would be his final stage work; thereafter he would only write "symphonic dialogues."[51] Thus, *Parsifal* stands as Wagner's last card vis-à-vis Gesamtkunstwerk, not just because he did not have a chance to write more, but because he intended it to be his final stab at creating "real" German musical drama.

The formal designation for the work, *Bühnenweihfestspiel* or "Festival Stage Dedication Play," alludes to a first facet of *Parsifal*'s significance as a contribution to Wagner's ongoing Gesamtkunstwerk project. Namely, it is the only work in the Wagnerian opus specifically written for Bayreuth. In a sense, of course, *Siegfried* and *Götterdämmerung* were also written for the Bayreuth stage. However, in these latter two cases, Wagner was finishing the scores while the theater itself was being constructed. He knew how he wanted the theater to sound and what technical capacities were required for these works, but in reality he was composing for an imaginary theater. After three series of *Ring* performances in 1876, however, Wagner had acquired a very good idea of what his theater was capable of and how he might exploit its possibilities. And it is this experience, these insights that worked a powerful influence on the *Parsifal* score, on which Wagner began work in early 1878. Taking advantage of the famed covered orchestra pit, for instance, he could write for a larger and frequently louder orchestra without cost to the vocal production or intelligibility of the singers. Similarly, coupled with the hall's unique acoustics, the large orchestra enabled Wagner to produce musical colors and textures in *Parsifal* that he would never have dared in his other scores.[52] Indeed, so intimate was the union between score and theater in *Parsifal* that Wagner's heirs, and a good number of disciples too, later claimed that only Bayreuth was capable of giving a "true" performance.[53] Although the argument failed to convince German legislators in 1912–13 that *Parsifal* warranted special copyright protection, this effort to extend the "work concept" to include the stage underscores just how much Wagner achieved in integrating stage and drama in the Bühnenweihfestspiel.[54]

Parsifal is not just noteworthy as a singular accomplishment in the realization of Gesamtkunstwerk's formal dimension. In this dramatic work, Wagner returns to a number of the political and social concerns that were prominent in the Zurich writings. In other words, pace Udo Bermbach, *Parsifal* explicitly engages the dimension of Gesamtkunstwerk's actual content. Just as *The Artwork of the Future* and *Opera and Drama* criticized the political and cultural state of Germany at mid century, so too does *Parsifal* register Wagner's frustration, indeed dissatisfaction, with the results of German unification under Prussian auspices. Accordingly, Germany was still in need of regeneration and redemption—two themes that pervade both *Parsifal* and a number of Wagner's final prose compositions, notably "Wollen wir hoffen?" (Shall We Hope, 1879) and "Religion und Kunst" (Religion and Art, 1880). Wagner also persisted in his insistence that art had a major role in bringing about this regeneration-*cum*-revolution.

As Fritz Stern has observed, this idealistic position placed Wagner firmly in the ranks of the cultural pessimists, with whom he also shared such other political and social positions as anti-Semitism and an increasingly chauvinistic nationalism.[55] For our purposes, it is not necessary here to enter into the lengthy debates over what Wagner intended to say on these subjects in *Parsifal*.[56] The main point is that he viewed these sociopolitical concerns as integral aspects of his dramatic project, asserting once more the fundamental connection between art and politics. In this context, finishing *Parsifal* and holding a second Bayreuth Festival took on added significance. On the one hand, *Parsifal* became the once and future Artwork, there for the German Volk when it was ready to understand it. Similarly, Bayreuth was akin to a German "field of dreams." Wagner had built it—he succeeded in organizing a second festival there in 1882, devoted exclusively to *Parsifal*—and now it remained to be seen if the Germans would come.

Admittedly, in 1882, the institutionalization of the Bayreuth Festival as an almost yearly event still lay in the future. That this step could be taken and that viewing *Parsifal* in Bayreuth acquired the trappings of a pilgrimage experience, however, owed much to the success of the run of sixteen performances in 1882. One crucial indication of this triumph was financial: the festival netted some 135,600 Marks, which in turn demonstrated that it could have a long-term future.[57] Even more importantly, *Parsifal* was deemed an artistic coup—as Gesamtkunstwerk. Reflecting on the *Parsifal* performances after the festival,

Wagner delighted in how wonderfully everything had come off. There were glitches, most notably involving the moving scenery for the transformation scenes in Acts I and III.[58] But overall, Wagner was thrilled with the high degree of perfection in the execution of musical, scenic, and dramatic detail that summer. Tellingly, he attributed the successes neither to the talent of this or that artist nor even to the virtues of the dramatic poem and score, but rather to the harmony achieved by the artists' and production team's single-minded efforts to realize a common dramatic objective:

> These fine successes, which in and of themselves could have been won only through the special talents of all the artists, would nevertheless have been impossible to achieve solely through the technical arrangements and agreements mentioned here, had not from every side the scenic-musical element also contributed with the same effectiveness.[59]

Wagner was not alone in regarding *Parsifal*'s triumphant debut as a vindication of the possibility—even desirability—of modern Gesamtkunstwerk. Throughout 1882 and into 1883, critics repeatedly commented on how successfully, both in the score and on stage, *Parsifal* managed to integrate different artistic components into a whole that was indeed greater than the sum of its parts. Writing in the *Neue Evangelische Kirchenzeitung*, Hermann Messner observed: "Already at first glance it is clear that with respect to the standard opera text, here too more is accomplished dramatically then usual ... the entire arrangement of the piece, as is typical of Wagner, is fit for the stage and effective (*wirksam*)."[60] In the *Berliner Börsen-Courier*, George Davidsohn concurred:

> In no other of Wagner's works does the particular nature of his artistry manifest itself so clearly, in no other does the internal imperative of the chosen means of representation show itself, in no other is the rapport between content and form so convincing as in [Parsifal]. And none, with regard to its effect [*Wirkung*], is as completely dependent on the joint effect of word and tone, on the dramatic poetry and the symphonically handled orchestra, and on the scenic pictures and the art of presentation as this one ... Indeed, so completely unique is this work that it requires its own theater, its own form of presentation and—its own public.[61]

Even Eduard Hanslick, one of Wagner's most trenchant critics, found much to praise in *Parsifal*:

> It is a skillfully contrived drama with completely new, sometimes brilliant situations ... It represents, moreover, a welcome advance (or healthy retreat) in diction [over the Nibelungen poem] ... The finale [of Part I] belongs unquestionably among those dazzling musico-scenic achievements in which Wagner has no rival ... The third act may be counted as the most unified and the most atmospheric

... Although [the libretto] is utterly inadequate as a "dramatic poem," it is a better opera text. It is, in a word, more musical.[62]

To be sure, Hanslick was critical of other aspects of *Parsifal*. He suggested, for instance, that the listener would need to ignore "its logical and psychological impossibilities" as well as its "false religious-philosophical pretensions."[63] Nevertheless, even these observations underscore Hanslick's recognition of the work as Wagner's most significant effort to realize the ideal of Gesamtkunstwerk. From the libretto and the scoring to the staging and performance, *Parsifal* was an impressive essay in creating integrated music drama that sought not merely to entertain but also to enlighten artists and audience alike in a theater devoted to German art.

Conclusion

"What's in a name?," Juliet asks in Shakespeare's immortal play, *Romeo and Juliet*. "That which we call a rose / By any other name would smell as sweet."[64] This is precisely the question, it seems, that we need to pose vis-à-vis Wagner and Gesamtkunstwerk. It is certainly important to recognize that, for all practical purposes, Gesamtkunstwerk was not a term Wagner cared to use or endorse, either at mid century or towards the end of his life. Although partly a matter of "brand control," this posture was arguably even more so a reflection of Wagner's unwillingness to determine, through the act of naming, a concept and an idea that—at least circa 1849/50—was still very much in flux. In the final analysis, even after completing the Zurich essays, Wagner's vision of a new approach to music theater, a vision inspired by the Greeks but oriented towards the cultural and spiritual needs of the German Volk in the nineteenth century, remained quite rudimentary. Again, Wagner was writing with an eye towards the future, idealizing an artwork, artists, and an audience that did not yet exist and, thus, would need to be created. Exactly in what form and in what time frame this might occur, was obviously an open question. But, much as Juliet opined with respect to rose, there was something tangible to which Wagner aspired and, to a certain degree, it matters not whether we call it "Gesamtkunstwerk," "Gesamttheaterstück," or something else. To return to the title of Nicholas Vazsonyi's essay, the play was the thing, not the name per se.

In part, the decision here to proclaim *Parsifal* Wagner's "last card" in his pursuit of Gesamtkunstwerk aims to legitimate the analytical use of the term "Gesamtkunstwerk." Even though Wagner avoided this label, it does point usefully to a central aspect of his creative endeavors from roughly 1849 forward: a desire to create a new type of theatrical experience that integrated the component elements into a unified whole whose sum was to be greater than the individual parts. We should, however, refrain from equating Gesamtkunstwerk with a Weberian ideal type, because whereas Wagner's ideal of an integrated, socially and politically meaningful experience of German music theater was constant, the way to achieve that idea in practice was subject to constant revision. This observation leads to the second contention in presenting *Parsifal* as the summa of Wagner's efforts with respect to Gesamtkunstwerk: namely, the Zurich writings represented just a first step in articulating how both the formal and substantive aspects of Gesamtkunstwerk might be realized. Only thereafter, and most notably in the context of composing the *Ring* and mounting the first Bayreuth Festival, did Wagner move from the realm of theory to that of practice. Just as Wagner's ideas evolved considerably from one Zurich essay to the next, so too did the notion of Gesamtkunstwerk continue to undergo revision and refinement as Wagner wrote about theater conditions and composed his music dramas. But as such prose texts as "Was ist Deutsch?" (What is German) and "Religion and Art" make clear, Wagner's conviction that art (and drama) could be a vehicle for cultural, social, and political change never flagged.

Parsifal was not just the last, but arguably Wagner's most concerted effort to gather together into a meaningful, final whole the various strands of Gesamtkunstwerk thought and activity. As noted earlier, much of this occurred at the level of what Borchmeyer has called the "aesthetic-dramaturgical level":[65] the intimate interdependency of libretto and score, text and music; consideration of specific acoustic and technical conditions throughout the compositional process; and "mood setting" practices, such as the decision to forbid applause following the first act. But the ideological/political aspects are there too, represented by the theme of community (embodied in the Grail knights as well as their negative counterparts, the Flower maidens) and by the fact that Parsifal explicitly served to dedicate the "German" theater at Bayreuth. Similarly, Matthew Smith has recently referred to *Parsifal* as embodying a "*Gesamtkunstwerk* of presence," in that "Wagner at last declared totality, organic community, and real presence in the here and now of *Parsifal*."[66]

For Smith, Wagner's success in mounting *Parsifal* as an all-encompassing, all-engrossing, seductive spectacle anticipates Gesamtkunstwerk's future in the age of mass politics, twentieth-century technology, and totalitarianism.[67] And yet, Wagner's very achievement with *Parsifal* exposed real limitations to Gesamtkunstwerk's future viability, at least as Wagner had conceived it. Ultimately, this feat was the consequence of special circumstances: Wagner's unique gifts as composer, librettist, and theater producer; the availability of his own stage and talented musicians; and *Parsifal*'s origins as a work destined for Bayreuth. To a very real degree, thus, *Parsifal* as Gesamtkunstwerk was heavily dependent on Bayreuth's existence, even had Wagner not also insisted that it only be performed there.[68] The intensity of this link between work and theater became especially apparent in discussions of the first productions of Parsifal after it entered the public domain in 1914. Take, for instance, Karl Maria Klob's review of the Vienna Hofopfer's staging for *Bühne und Welt*: "The Viennese production was certainly radiant and all those involved … clearly offered their best." Nevertheless, if it still failed to deliver the pleasure many expected of it, "this owed much to the peculiar nature of the work that demands such peculiar performance conditions and that Bayreuth alone is capable of offering." In particular, Klob had in mind the sonic effects produced by the covered pit, which, "no matter the director's artistry, an exposed orchestra would not be able to reproduce."[69]

Nonetheless, while *Parsifal* remained the centerpiece of each Bayreuth Festival down to 1914, it had lost much of its status as Art. As an act of piety towards her deceased husband, in continuing the Bayreuth Festival after 1882, Cosima transformed *Parsifal* into a museum piece. Whereas Wagner might well have opined, "My production of *Parsifal* in 1882 was as good as I could accomplish given the available resources and stage technology," Cosima proceeded from the premise that the 1882 production was the ideal realization of the work on stage. Thus, apart from some minor changes to costumes and a bit of second act scenery, there was no new *Parsifal* production at Bayreuth until 1934.[70] Even at the premiere run of performances, though, individuals like the reviewer for Munich's *Allgemeine Zeitung* noted that there could never be a fixed way of realizing the score (a *typisch feststehende Vollendung*), given the considerable variation in how the roles were performed by the different casts (there were three different Parsifals, three Kundrys and two Klingsors over the course of the 1882 festival).[71] Moreover, in those areas of stage production where Wagner was less gifted or where the technical means did not yet exist to carry out some of Wagner's wishes, there was indeed considerable room for improvements. For instance, at the turn of the century, the Swiss architect and designer Adolphe Appia hoped to rescue *Parsifal* by taking fuller advantage of new lighting technology and a fresh approach to the relationship between music and scenery to create sets that were more dramatically effective (and less naturalistic). Cosima Wagner was fundamentally opposed to Appia's vision, but his ideas ended up having considerable influence on production practice during the 1914 "Parsifal year."

In short, while *Parsifal* at Bayreuth in 1882 indeed represented the high point of Wagner's efforts to realize musical theater as Gesamtkunstwerk, his very successes that year testify to the essential truth in Wagner's musings from his Zurich days, namely, that even for a talented and gifted person like Wagner, "doing Gesamtkunstwerk" was ultimately a collaborative project in which the poet and composer were only part of the larger ensemble of players. In retrospect, *Parsifal*'s triumph as Gesamtkunstwerk seems to have been as much that of Wagner the director and producer, as Wagner the writer and composer. Or, to paraphrase Matthew Smith, *Parsifal* at Bayreuth was a Gesamtkunstwerk of presence, not merely by declaring totality to the audience, but also by engaging the audience to participate in and associate themselves with the sense of community generated through the act of performance.

Notes

1. Cosima Wagner, *Die Tagebücher*, ed. Martin Gregor-Dellin and Dietrich Mack, 2 vols. (Munich, 1977), 2:718.
2. Robert W. Gutman, *Richard Wagner: The Mind, His Mind, and His Music* (New York, 1968), 418–40; Harmut Zelinsky, "Der verschwiegende Gehalt des Parsifal" and "Richard Wagners letzte Karte," in *Parsifal: Texte, Materialen, Kommentare*, ed. Attila Csampi and Dietmar Holland (Reinbek, 1996), 244–56; Marc A. Weiner, *Richard Wagner and the Anti-Semitic Imagination* (Lincoln, 1995).
3. On Gobineau's ideas on race and nature, see Edward Beasley, *The Victorian Reinvention of Race: New Racisms and the Problem of Grouping in the Human Sciences* (London, 2010), esp. 44–62.
4. In addition to his contribution to this volume, see Nicholas Vazsonyi, *Richard Wagner: Self-Promotion and the Making of a Brand* (Cambridge, 2010).
5. Dieter Borchmeyer, *Richard Wagner: Theory and Theatre* (Oxford, 1991), 65–68.
6. Cf. Vazsonyi, *Richard Wagner*, 107–8; and Lydia Goehr, "From Opera to Music Drama: Nominal Loss, Titular Gain," in *Wagner and His World*, ed. Thomas S. Grey (Princeton, 2009), 68–72.
7. See notably, Matthew Wilson Smith, *The Total Work of Art: From Bayreuth to Cyberspace* (New York, 2007); Anke Finger and Danielle Follett, eds., *The Aesthetics of the Total Artwork: On Borders and Fragments* (Baltimore, 2011); and David Roberts, *The Total Work of Art in European Modernism* (Ithaca, 2011).
8. Richard Wagner, "Eine Mittheilung an meine Freunde," in *Sämtliche Schriften und Dichtungen* (hereafter *SSD*), vol. 4 (Leipzig, 1911), 231.
9. Cf. Nicholas Atkin and Frank Tallett, *Priests, Prelates & People: A History of European Catholicism Since 1750* (Oxford, 2003), 135–36.
10. Wagner, *Zukunftsmusik*, in *SSD* 7:89.
11. Wagner, "Einleitung zum dritten und vierten Band," in *SSD* 3:4. The sentence in full reads: "Hieraus entsprang eine gewisse leidenschaftliche Verwirrung, welche sich als Voreiligkeit und Undeutlichkeit im Gebrauche philosophischer Schemata kundgab." See also, James Treadwell, "The Urge to Communicate: The Prose Writings as Theory and Practice," in *The Cambridge Companion to Wagner*, ed. Thomas S. Grey (Cambridge, 2008), 179–91, esp. 182–90.
12. See, most recently, the remarks in Barry Millington, *The Sorcerer of Bayreuth: Richard Wagner, His Work and His World* (Oxford, 2012), 78–97.
13. See especially, Udo Bermbach, *Der Wahn des Gesamtkunstwerks. Richard Wagners politisch-ästhetische Utopie*, 2nd, revised, and expanded edition (Stuttgart, 2004); Borchmeyer, *Richard Wagner: Theory and Theater*, 65; Anke Finger, "Idea/Imagination/Dialogue: The Total Artwork and Conceptual Art," in Finger and Follett, *Aesthetics*, 110–27, especially 110–15; and Roberts, *Total Work of Art*, 73–76.
14. Finger, "Idea/Imagination," 113–14.
15. Cf. Millington, *Sorcerer of Bayreuth*, 96.

16. See Frank Glass, *The Fertilizing Seed: Wagner's Concept of Poetic Intent* (Ann Arbor, MI, 1983), 22.
17. Smith, *Total Work of Art*, 8–9.
18. Roberts, *Total Work of Art*, 74–76.
19. Here, again, we return to Wagner's debts to Schiller, as discussed by Vazsonyi in this volume. On Brecht's notion of the *Lehrstück* and opera, see especially Joy Calico, *Brecht at the Opera* (Berkeley and Los Angeles, 2008), 16–23, as well as her contribution to this volume.
20. Wagner, *Art und Revolution, SSD*, 3:28–29.
21. See especially Wagner's remarks in *Opera and Drama, SSD* 4:30–34. On Wagner's approach to myth and the discourse on German nationalism, see too George Williamson, *The Longing for Myth in Germany: Religion and Aesthetic Culture from Romanticism to Nietzsche* (Chicago, 2004), esp. 180–210.
22. Wagner, *The Artwork of the Future, SSD* 3:150.
23. Vazsonyi, *Richard Wagner*, 1 and 194–97.
24. Bermbach, *Wahn der Gesamtkunstwerk*, 215.
25. Ibid., 210.
26. Borchmeyer, *Richard Wagner: Theory and Theater*, 15.
27. Jürgen Kühnel, "The Prose Writings," in *Wagner Handbuch*, ed. Ulrich Müller and Peter Wapnewski, trans. and ed. John Deathridge (Cambridge, 1992), 580.
28. Wagner, "Plan for the Organization of a National Theater for the Kingdom of Saxony," *SSD* 2:235.
29. Ibid.
30. Wagner, "On the Vienna Court Opera House," *SSD* 7:274–75.
31. Wagner, "Report to His Majesty King Ludwig II of Bavaria on a German School of Music to be Established in Munich," *SSD* 8:131–32.
32. Borchmeyer, *Richard Wagner: Theory and Theater*, 21.
33. In addition to Frederic Spotts, *Bayreuth: The History of the Wagner Festival* (New Haven, 1994), esp. 29–54, see also Michael Karbaum, *Studien zur Geschichte der Bayreuther Festspiele* (Regensburg, 1976), and Bermbach, *Wahn des Gesamtkunstwerks*, 251ff.
34. Roberts, *Total Work of Art*, 101–5.
35. See here especially, Carl Dahlhaus, "Richard Wagners 'Bühnenfestspiel': Revolutionsfest und Kunstreligion," in *Das Fest*, ed. Walther Haug and Rainer Warning (Munich, 1989), 592–609.
36. See, for instance, Catherine Bell, *Ritual Theory, Ritual Practice* (Oxford, 1992).
37. Cf. Hans Maier, "Political Religion: A Concept and Its Limitations," *Totalitarian Movements and Political Religions* 8, no. 1 (2007): 15–16.
38. Udo Bermbach, "Nationalismus in deutschen Festspielen? Zur Idee und Praxis der Bayreuther Festspiele," in *Politische Erinnerung. Geschichte und kollektive Identität*, ed. Harald Schmid and Justyna Krzymianowska (Würzburg, 2007), 53–66.
39. Cf. Borchmeyer, *Richard Wagner: Theory and Theater*, 19.
40. Wagner, "Das Bühnenfestspielhaus zu Bayreuth. Nebst einem Berichte über die Grundsteinlegung desselben," SSD 9: 323–45, esp. 328.
41. Cosima Wagner, *Tagebücher*, 1:624, emphasis added.
42. Smith, *Total Work of Art*, 22–47; Juliet Koss, "Invisible Wagner," in Finger and Follett, *Aesthetics*, 168–90.
43. Cf. Spotts, *Bayreuth*, 19; and Carolyn Abbate and Roger Parker, *A History of Opera* (New York, 2012), 355–57.

44. Cf. Patrick Carnegy, *Wagner and the Art of the Theatre* (New Haven, 2006), 69–106.
45. Cf. Richard Fricke, *Wagner in Rehearsal, 1875–1876: The Diaries of Richard Fricke*, ed. James Deaville with Evan Baker, *Franz Liszt Studies* 7 (Stuyvesant, 1998); and Heinrich Porges, *Wagner Rehearsing the Ring: An Eye-Witness Account of the Stage Rehearsals of the First Bayreuth Festival*, trans. Robert L. Jacobs (Cambridge, 1983).
46. Spotts, *Bayreuth*, 20.
47. Quoted in Millington, *Sorcerer of Bayreuth*, 232.
48. Wagner, "Rückblick auf die Bühnenfestspiele des Jahres 1876," *SSD* 9:103–17, esp. 103–6 (originally published in the December 1878 edition of the *Bayreuther Blätter*).
49. See Carnegy, *Wagner and the Art of the Theater*, 94–102.
50. Carnegy, *Wagner and the Art of the Theater*, 104; Millington, *Sorcerer*, 232.
51. Carl Friedrich Glasenapp, *Das Leben Richard Wagners*, 6 vols (Leipzig, 1905) 6:137.
52. On the orchestration of *Parsifal* and the acoustic conditions at *Bayreuth*, see Stephan Mösch, *Weihe Werkstatt Wirklichkeit: Wagners Parsifal in Bayreuth* (Kassel, 2009), 141–52.
53. See, Anthony J. Steinhoff, "Embracing the Grail: Parsifal, Richard Wagner and the German Nation," *German History* 30 (2012): 380–81.
54. On Wagner and the concept of the musical work, see Lydia Goehr, *The Imaginary Museum of Musical Works: An Essay in the Philosophy of Music* (Oxford, 1992), 89–120.
55. Fritz Stern, *The Politics of Cultural Despair: A Study in the Rise of the Germanic Ideology*, 2d edn (Berkeley and Los Angeles, 1974).
56. A useful overview of the literature here appears in Glenn Stanley, "Parsifal: Redemption and Kunstreligion," in *The Cambridge Companion to Wagner*, ed. Thomas S. Grey (Cambridge, 2008), 151–75, esp. 169–75.
57. Karbaum, *Studien zur Geschichte der Bayreuther Festspiele*, II:150.
58. For a more thorough discussion of the trials and tribulations of the 1882 *Parsifal* premiere, see Mösch, *Weihe Werkstatt Wirklichkeit*, 152–58.
59. Wagner, "Das Bühnenweihfestival in Bayreuth 1882," *Bayreuther Blätter* 5 (November–December 1882): 321–29.
60. Herman Messner, "Richard Wagner's 'Parsifal,'" in *Neue Evangelische Kirchenzeitung* 13, August 1882, reprinted in Susanna Großmann-Vendrey, *Bayreuth in der deutschen Presse*, vol. 2 (Regensburg, 1977), 55.
61. George Davidsohn, "Die Aufführung des 'Parsifal,'" in *Berliner Börsen-Courier*, Nr. 361 (27 July 1882), reprinted in Großmann-Vendrey, *Bayreuth*, 69.
62. "Parsifal," in Eduard Hanslick, *Music Criticisms 1846–99*, trans. and ed. Henry Pleasants (Baltimore, 1950), 189, 200–1, 206.
63. Ibid., 205.
64. *Romeo and Juliet*, II, ii 1–2.
65. Borchmeyer, *Richard Wagner: Theory and Theater*, 65.
66. Smith, *Total Work of Art*, 46.
67. Smith, *Total Work of Art*, 41–42 ; see also, Thomas Mann, "The Sorrows and Grandeur of Richard Wagner," in *Thomas Mann, Pro and Contra Wagner*, trans. Allan Blunden (Chicago, 1985), 129.
68. On the history of Wagner's request that *Parsifal* be exclusive to Bayreuth, see Steinhoff, "Embracing the Grail," 374–77.
69. "Die Erstaufführung des 'Parsifal' in der Wiener Hofoper," *Bühne und Welt* (1914): 465–66.

70. The most thorough account of the initial 1882 production is now Mösch, *Weihe Werkstatt Wirklichkeit*.
71. "Die Parsifal-Aufführungen in Bayreuth," *Allgemeine Zeitung*, Nr. 216 (4 August 1882).
72. A good overview of Appia's theories on Wagnerian theater production appears in Carnegy, *Wagner and the Art of the Theatre*, 175–207.

Anthony J. Steinhoff is Associate Professor of History at the Université du Québec à Montréal. A specialist in modern German and French cultural and social history, he is the author of *The Gods of the City: Protestantism and Religious Culture in Strasbourg, 1870–1914* (Brill, 2008) and the translator of Rita Kuczynski, *Wall Flower: A Life on the German Border* (University of Toronto Press, 2015). He is currently writing a cultural history of the first hundred years of Richard Wagner's *Parsifal* in German-speaking Europe.

II

Articulations

CHAPTER 4

Epic Gesamtkunstwerk

JOY H. CALICO

In the thirty years between 1926, when he began working with Kurt Weill, and his death in 1956, Bertolt Brecht undertook roughly two dozen opera projects. The vast majority of these were never completed, but the fact remains that he actively pursued plans for many different operas over the course of three decades, nursing projects and frequently returning to them over time as he completed other pieces. This engagement took many forms: the completed texts he identified as operas; the use of operatic models in his theoretical writings and plays; an unacknowledged, perhaps inadvertent, debt to pre-Wagner opera and the theories of other opera reformers; the incomplete fragments that formed the backdrop for his creative activity; and, most importantly for our purposes, his preoccupation with Richard Wagner, which waxed and waned but never disappeared. Opera, or what Brecht understood opera to be as an artistic genre and as a social institution, informed his texts for the stage, the use of music therein, and their modes of performance practice. Much of "what Brecht understood opera to be" derived from Wagner's music dramas filtered through Nietzsche. In fact, in his efforts to counter the Nietzschean version of the Gesamtkunstwerk, Brecht's epic theater wound up being quite indebted to Wagner's original concept. In this chapter, I begin with an overview of Brecht's engagement with Wagner, and then propose two ways in which the notion of Gesamtkunstwerk manifested itself in his epic theater: a new audience contract and a reconsideration of the relationship between gesture and music.

Brecht, Wagner, Nietzsche

The specter of Wagner looms large in any study of Brecht and opera. The trajectory of his Wagner reception began with youthful obsession, moved to dismissal on aesthetic, social, and political grounds, and culminated in repudiation of the composer as a forerunner of fascism.[1] Wagner and Brecht were frequently arranged as polar opposites in the debates on the fate of German opera in the 1920s, and that perception has become conventional wisdom.[2] Yet Brecht's mature relationship to Wagner is not just one of opposition; as in any polarity, the poles are also bound together by the current flowing between them. Furthermore, beginning with the superficial, one can compile an extraordinary list of biographical parallels. Each enjoyed enormous financial success with a theater piece at age thirty, was a revolutionary driven into exile, showed an interest in using as models *Measure for Measure* and Sophocles' *Antigone*, and persuaded political leaders to give him his own theater and to support it. Wagner was a composer who became a librettist; Brecht was a poet/playwright who became a librettist (although this was a title to which he objected strenuously). Politics and aesthetics were closely linked for both, for each saw theater as an instrument with the potential for social revolution.

But the similarities go far beyond biography to the stage genres in which they worked. Epic theater typically features a non-linear, episodic plot replete with disruptions and characters who may address the audience directly, but the attributes most strongly associated with it pertain to production, and are frequently applied to stage-works that are not otherwise epic, such as the use of projections and placards and highly stylized, non-naturalistic acting. Its aesthetic is rooted in the conviction that audience members should not be passively entertained by illusion but be actively engaged with the experience, never forgetting that they are attending the theater and observing actors rather than participating in real life. Scholars such as Christoph Nieder, Ernst Schumacher, Marianne Kesting, and Hilda Meldrum Brown have recognized certain aspects of epic theater in Wagner's music drama, such as the prevalence of narrative and monologue, and even the work of the leitmotif.[3] In 1963 Adorno wrote that "one might speak, in regard to the entire *Ring* and other works of the mature Wagner, of epic theater—although the rabid anti-Wagnerian Brecht would not have wanted to hear this and would be at my throat."[4] Conversely, there are also ways in which the epic is Wagnerian. Matthew Wilson Smith argues that Brecht's attempt to develop a comprehensive theory of the theater experience in opposition to Wagnerian theatricality—what will become epic theater—actually reinscribes the totalizing experience of Wagnerian Gesamtkunstwerk. By using "discontinuity and contradiction … as a means to the creation of the 'unified whole' rather than [as] a subversion of it" he created "a kind of unity through juxtaposition," thus perpetuating an aesthetic of totality.[5] The title of the present essay, "Epic Gesamtkunstwerk," is meant to acknowledge that debt, while simultaneously highlighting Brecht's positioning of epic theater as ostentatiously anti-Wagner. Martin Puchner argues that the entire modernist theater project was a reaction against the Wagnerian theatricality that had come to dominate the stage.[6] Puchner does not emphasize the fact that Wagner was not only a man of the theater but also an opera composer, and therefore does not pursue this argument to what I see as its tantalizing, fantastical conclusion: what he posits amounts to an assertion that modernist theater is directly descended from the modernist struggle with Wagner. Since no one engaged more fully in that battle than Brecht, then it stands to reason that modernist theater, of which epic theater has long been the standard bearer, may be the illegitimate child of opera.

Brecht may or may not have been aware of the extent to which his epic theater was indebted to Wagner's original Gesamtkunstwerk as devised in the 1840s and 1850s because, like virtually every other modernist of his day, the version he imbibed was filtered through Nietzsche. *Nietzsche contra Wagner*, the essay the philosopher assembled in 1888–89, is a critique that took the composer to task for everything from his conversion to Christianity, which Nietzsche dismissed as a sign of weakness, to the painful somatic responses his music induced in listeners. Since the 1870s, recovering Wagnerians have been as numerous as practicing disciples. Each new generation of disillusioned devotees takes some cold comfort in the knowledge that even Nietzsche was bamboozled by endlessly unresolved chromatic harmony, perpetual melody, and the confluence of the arts into the mishmash of the Gesamtkunstwerk. Nietzsche decried the Gesamtkunstwerk as a blend in which the arts were hopelessly indistinguishable from one another, resulting in an overwhelming, anaesthetizing experience for the audience. By the turn of the century this interpretation had come to stand in for Wagner proper, so that Brecht's epic theater project was a reaction against what he understood Wagner to be—that is, the Nietzschean interpretation, as confirmed by Brecht's own experience in the opera house. Nietzsche's hyperbolic critique of the Gesamtkunstwerk concept is not unfounded, but it is not entirely accurate, either. As Sanna Pederson's contribution to the present volume makes clear, Wagner had been quite explicit in *Das Kunstwerk der Zukunft* that the three sister arts of poetry, music, and dance (and any others introduced along the way) should retain their individuality and "artistic purity" within the total work of art, believing that the audience would become a unified, ennobled community as a result of its engagement with such a performance.[7] To that end, Juliet Koss makes the case that Wagner's agenda was primarily about spectatorship.[8] While I prefer the broader term "audience experience" ("spectatorship" being too exclusively visual and passive, even for Wagner's expectations for his audience), we are in agreement that Wagner was focused on what an audience member saw, heard, felt, and thought during a performance.

The aforementioned qualifier, "what Brecht understood opera to be," is worth reiterating. When Brecht criticized "opera" in his theoretical writings, his language reflected Wagner's own criticisms of the genre and was characterized by the modernist tendency to take a rather simplistic interpretation of Wagner's music drama as representative of *all* opera. According to Lawrence

Kramer, "Wagner became both central and radically extrinsic to the institution of Opera, both its primary model and its primary antagonist, its authentic self, beyond emulation, and its monstrous Other."[9] Brecht's complaints about the narcotic effects of continuous music refer to Wagner and his followers, and not to Mozart, whose operas he admired, although he consistently opposed the ways in which opera production and operagoing as cultural practices participated in the reproduction of social hierarchies. (He also applied the generic designation "opera" to some of his own projects, an indication that the meaning was context specific.) The rhetorical inversion whereby music drama was transformed from a subgenre of opera to its definitive, negative, generic essence is symptomatic of the anti-Wagnerism that underpins Brecht's modernism. It is worth noting that Wagner criticized the operatic tradition against which he rebelled in much the same terms in which Brecht later excoriated Wagner. Where Wagner dismissed Rossini with talk of "the intoxication of an opera-night's narcotic fumes,"[10] Brecht subsequently railed against the intoxicating effects of Wagner's Gesamtkunstwerk.

Opera + *Lehrstücke* = New Audience Contract of Epic Theater

Wagner's Gesamtkunstwerk was initially and primarily concerned with creating a new experience for the audience, and that experience was partly didactic. The same was true for Brecht's epic theater, which aimed to negotiate a new contract for the audience in the theater, and decried Wagnerian opera as the most extreme offender of the audience's rights. The new terms emerged from Brecht's simultaneous work in two musical genres in the 1920s: *Lehrstücke* (learning plays) and opera, which occupy opposite ends of the continuum for audience experience in musical theater. Brecht observed that the social contract in effect for opera audiences not only stipulated that participants empathize with characters, suspend disbelief, and submit to emotional manipulation, but that they do so under the influence of the powerful narcotic of continuous music. Brecht countered this in two ways in the 1920s: from within the system, in his two operas (*Die Dreigroschenoper* and *Aufstieg und Fall der Stadt Mahagonny*); and from outside the system, in his four Lehrstücke (*Der Lindbergflug, Lehrstück, Der Jasager*, and *Die Massnahme*). According to Brecht, the latter did not require an audience, although scholars have subsequently muddied the waters by erroneously claiming that the Lehrstücke required the exclusion of an audience, demonstrating the ease with which the absence of necessity becomes the necessity of absence.[11] As such, Lehrstücke could effectively render attendees a non-audience by transforming them into participants, or, at the very least, prospective participants. Brecht ran the Lehrstück experiment concurrently with the opera experiment, thereby attacking the problem of the audience contract from both sides at once and generating the theory of epic theater. Its primary goal: renegotiating the audience's pact with the theater and, by extension, the citizen's contract with society.[12]

Brecht worked out some of his ideas about a new audience contract through his attempts to rehabilitate the corrupted opera genre from within. He and his operatic collaborator Kurt Weill disagreed on many, if not most, aspects of opera, and their partnership did not survive long beyond *Mahagonny*. Brecht's essay "Notes on the *Opera Mahagonny*" was a response to several articles Weill had published about their work, and what began as a screed against the institution and art form of opera (and, it must be said, against Weill) became the blueprint for epic theater and its audience contract. The description of epic theater contained therein is couched in both operatic and anti-operatic terms, a reflection of his simultaneous immersion in opera and Lehrstück. His wide-ranging critique of opera in this essay can be distilled to a renunciation of the way in which the opera treats its spectating audience, particularly where the music is concerned. The operatic apparatus, or culture industry, serves its own needs by reproducing the society that facilitates its survival, and gains the complicity of that society by drugging its citizens. This sedation comes courtesy of the music, which aids and abets the apparatus in insidious ways:

> The opera *Mahagonny* pays conscious tribute to the senselessness of the operatic form. The irrationality of opera lies in the fact that rational elements are employed, solid reality is aimed at, but at the same time it is all washed out by the music. A dying man is real. If at the same time he sings we are translated to the sphere of the irrational. (If the audience sang at the sight of him the case would be different.) The more unreal and unclear the music can make the reality … the more pleasurable the whole process becomes: the pleasure grows in proportion to the degree of unreality.[13]

This paragraph warrants scrutiny because it makes several claims for music's culpability that subsequently determine its use in epic theater. First, music is the agent of irrationality in opera. The implication is that the genre might otherwise exist in an apparently desirable state of rationality and realism, but the power of music is so overwhelming that its mere presence precludes that possibility. Second, Brecht reasons that music transforms reality into unreality, and the amount of pleasure experienced by an audience member is determined by the degree of unreality; the more music, the more irrational the situation becomes, and the more pleasurable. The word he uses for pleasure is *Genuß*, with its connotations of hedonism and excessive indulgence, an experience akin to narcosis, and music is the source of that pleasure. Third, his parenthetical remark hints at the role he is developing for music in the epic theater. Because the audience does not spontaneously burst into song at the sight of a dying man onstage, the fact that the dying man continues to sing *should* be a moment of estrangement for the audience. This does not happen in his operatic example, presumably because the wash of continuous music, the excess of narcotic, has dulled the audience's senses. But in a music theater work in which the music is mostly limited to song-sized doses in the context of speech, music *could* have the effect of making strange. For the critical audience member, music should become a marker of the unreal.

Elsewhere in the essay Brecht famously argues for the separation of the elements because the Gesamtkunstwerk was guilty of bewitching the audience. This famous passage has been widely quoted, but Matthew W. Smith's close reading of it is enlightening. He notes that the statements usually cited as the most damning are in fact introduced equivocally: "*so long as the* expression 'Gesamtkunstwerk' means that the integration is a muddle, *so long as* the arts are supposed to be 'fused' together [emphasis added in Smith]."[14] This suggests that Brecht still held out hope for the opera genre, and for opera audiences, if they could be liberated from an audience experience that Koss describes as "a loss of self and an overidentification with the object of attention."[15] Smith also interprets this as a rejection of a particular manifestation of the total work of art, but not of the concept per se. Brecht assigns a very particular role to music in the undesirable muddle or fusion: "the process of fusion extends to the spectator, who gets thrown into the melting pot too and becomes a passive (suffering) part of the total work of art. Witchcraft of this sort must of course be fought against. Whatever is intended to produce hypnosis, is likely to induce sordid intoxication, or creates fog, has got to be given up."[16] Having established that music is the irrational force that corrupts an art form by rendering it unreal (thus calling into question the viability of opera at all), then music is also the active ingredient in the alchemy that produces the (con)fusion of Gesamtkunstwerk. Separation is necessary to guard against music's tendency to dominate the rest of the text as well as the audience. Even so, Brecht does not take the draconian measure of banishing music from the epic theater. The act of quarantine acknowledges the danger, but controlled retention of the musical element admits its efficacy. Epic theater confined music exclusively to the song where it was always mediated by Brecht's lyrics, and Brecht gave music new responsibilities in the epic theater. The music "communicates," "sets forth the text," "takes the text for granted," "takes up a position," and "gives the attitude."[17] Gone was the continuous, beguiling euphony of Wagner's music drama. These new duties are clearly designed to limit the opportunity for music to do the traditional work of intoxication.

The Lehrstücke, on the other hand, appear to be the anti-opera musical genre in virtually every regard, beginning with their not inconsiderable resemblance to the oratorio. Early reviewers described *Die Massnahme* as an oratorio long before the composer Hanns Eisler revealed that he and Brecht had used J.S. Bach's *St. John Passion* as a model.[18] Historically the oratorio has been the sacred, un-staged counterpart to opera, and now the Lehrstück appropriated the oratorio's most distinctive, anti-operatic features (prominent chorus, narrative text, and static staging), augmented by the possibility of audience participation, to mark the new genre as a populist, activist, alternative to opera. The Lehrstücke also unified the production and consumption of art in a single reciprocal process, challenging the concept of audiences as mere consumers of cultural products: a Lehrstück may have a spectating audience, but its primary function is not to play to it; it is primarily about communal participation. The principle that theater required performers and an audience, and that those participants had to be discrete entities, had been the premise of all previous audience contracts in the theater, so the Lehrstücke represented a radical affront to that basic tenet. Here, in the desire to blur the distinctions between and even unify the modes of production and consumption, we see clear evidence of the totalizing impulse Brecht shared with Wagner.

Therefore, the audience contract of epic theater emerged from Brecht's negotiation between innovation (writing Lehrstücke, pieces that required no audience whatsoever) and renovation (rehabilitating opera), during which two different roles for music emerged, both pertaining to the audience: structural and communal for the Lehrstück, means of gestus and estrangement for the opera. The new contract meant that the apparatus—the impresario, librettist, composer, actor-singer—no longer dictated audience response because participants were emancipated to behave as self-actualizing entities. Ideally, it permits and facilitates an independent, conscious, critical response from audiences unaccustomed to being in that position. (Make no mistake, however: in Brecht's epic theater there *is* a correct response, even though the playwright may have liked for audiences to choose it freely.) The new contract was intended to redistribute the balance of power between the spectating audience and the stage. Brecht thought it represented a radical affront to the Gesamtkunstwerk as well, but it is not so different from what Wagner had originally envisioned for his own audiences. Wagner endorsed the shared reception of a group audience, which he conceived as active. Like the individual arts that were brought together to form the Gesamtkunstwerk, members of the unified audience were to be participants in its creation, not merely passive witnesses; their collective presence was central to the creative power of the work of art.[19] There is no doubt that Wagner's definition of "audience participation" was not Brecht's, but at the same time, in a very real way, Brecht's *new* contract with the audience was actually quite similar to Wagner's *old* contract with the audience, even if Brecht would not have recognized it as such thanks to the Nietzschean filter through which he imbibed his theory of the Gesamtkunstwerk.

Music and the Body Onstage

Another way in which the epic theater is connected to the Gesamtkunstwerk has to do with the relationship between the music and the body onstage. During the mid-1930s, thanks to the disruptions of life in exile, Brecht was forced to develop a highly pragmatic performance theory because his pieces were now being performed without the benefit of his direct supervision. Whereas he had previously situated gestus almost exclusively in the performer's visible body in motion and stasis, new circumstances prompted him to locate the gestus in the fixed, notated score, which was then realized via the performer's temporal, sounding body. According to Brecht, gests are stylized behaviors designed to reveal the socially constructed nature of human interaction. However abstract or ill-defined Brecht's notion of gestus may have been, Peter Ferran's summation that it always contains three essential elements—"social behavior; attitudinal perspective; demonstrative enactment"—is useful.[20] Gestus is revealed in music because the rhythm, melody, and style of a character's music are established in musical notation in a way that pacing, inflection, and characterization cannot be fixed in the libretto. Pointing prospective directors and performers toward the music as the bearer of gestus was intended to ensure more appropriate interpretations of *Die Mutter* (1932) and *Die Rundköpfe und die Spitzköpfe* (1936) in particular. Brecht limited music's presence to song-sized doses that were too brief to intoxicate, and in which the music's effect was always tempered by his own lyrics.

According to Mary Ann Smart, "Wagner remained undecided about whether physical gesture was properly the premise or the result of musical expression."[21] Brecht faced a similar dilemma. Ambivalence about the triangulation of music, gesture, and the body is another thing the two artists had in common,[22] as Brecht's gestus and Wagner's gestural music are both indebted to the nineteenth-century operatic stage practice of mimesis. One strand of its development appears to have been highly musicalized from the start. The system of codified stage movements developed by François Delsarte (1811–1871), uncle of George Bizet and a singer with the Paris Opéra-Comique, was immensely influential. Delsarte believed that the proper motion generated the desired emotion in an actor, rather than vice versa, and to that end he developed an extensive gestural repertoire appropriate for all emotional situations.[23] Émile Jaques-Dalcroze (1865–1950), father of the eurhythmic approach to music education, had studied Delsarte's method, and in 1906 published his own set of rhythmic gymnastic exercises.[24] He, too, was first trained as a musician. His work with the Swiss theatrical designer Adolphe Appia at Hellerau led to a Russian tour in 1912, which included demonstrations and lectures at the state theater in Saint Petersburg. Vsevolod Meyerhold subsequently incorporated eurhythmics into his actor training program, and Brecht's debt to the Russian director, particularly with regard to gestus, is well documented.[25] Daniel Albright has persuasively argued for Dalcroze as a founding father of modernism because he represents a "Modernist urge to restore corporeality to art."[26] That is to say that Dalcroze's work represents the recuperation of a corporeality that had characterized prenaturalist art, as in Delsarte's method, with which Dalcroze was quite familiar.

Brecht's gestus, fundamentally grounded in the body and essential to his epic theater project, is another manifestation of the impulse to recover the body that Albright identifies as endemic to one strand of modernism. The prenaturalist gestural style does not reappear on the epic stage unfiltered; now gests must socially signify and they are designed at least in part to achieve estrangement. They mediate the spectator's experience so that events onstage cannot be viewed as real, or the performer conflated with the character. Nevertheless the appearance of stylized if not outright choreographed gestures was characteristic of earlier nineteenth-century performance practices, against which naturalism had rebelled and to which modernism subsequently returned. In the interim, Cosima Wagner had sought to preserve her husband's legacy at the Festspielhaus by fixing the "Bayreuth style" of acting, ridiculed by George Bernard Shaw as "the intolerably old-fashioned tradition of half rhetorical, half historical-pictorial attitudes and gestures."[27] Shaw's reaction suggests that the Bayreuth acting style was an effective if wholly unintentional means of estrangement, as it shattered the theatrical illusion. Even though Brecht's understanding of gestus eventually extended beyond the actors' bodies to include other elements of production, it never lost the primacy of the corporeal.

Although the course of Wagner's operatic career is typically described as a progression from outer to inner drama, meaning a move away from the primacy of the visual, the physical gesture, and the body around 1870, Mary Ann Smart has shown that these retained an enduring significance for Wagner: by the time Nietzsche wrote that Wagner was "essentially a man of the theater and an actor, the most enthusiastic mimomaniac, perhaps, who ever existed," eighteen years had passed since the inception of the music drama, an operatic genre ostensibly interiorized and unconcerned with the physical exterior—that is, with gestures and the body.[28] Yet even in the music dramas Nietzsche detected and mistrusted "Wagner's continuing attachment to an earlier model of gesture and stage movement, [his] affection for extended pantomime scenes and frequent reliance on small-scale coordination between music and gesture."[29] This is what film scholars today would call "mickey-mousing." In the face of Wagner's claims to a new, superior operatic genre that transcended the physical plane, Nietzsche faulted the music drama for its retention of the literal, choreographic relationship between music and gesture that had animated opera in the first half of the nineteenth century.

Nietzsche's complaints also provide a link to Brecht: "If it was Wagner's theory that 'the drama is the end, the music is always a mere means,' his *practice* was always, from beginning to end, ... a mere occasion for many interesting poses!"[30] Nietzsche's dismissal of Wagnerian drama as nothing more than an excuse for "many interesting poses" connotes a series of discrete, atomized, stylized gestures or actions, which, except for the criterion of social significance, may be understood as analogous to gests. The absence of heat-of-the-moment spontaneity in favor of deliberate stylization is an essential component of Brechtian theatrical performance as well. Wagner considered gesture to be the "generative kernel from which both melody and speech rhythm should grow," in which case the moving, posing bodies on stage can be understood to evince or even create the music, to conjure it forth from the invisible orchestra. Smart notes that the music in the first scene of *Die Walküre* (1856–70) "can be heard as generated by the gestures it accompanies."[31]

According to Brecht in the mid-1930s, music generated gestus, but the primacy given to the performers' visible bodies in motion and stasis remained relevant. His improvisatory rehearsals constituted a lab in which gests were tried on, revised, discarded, perfected; ideally, performances consisted of isolated, socially signifying, stylized physical events that were intended to be read as such. When precomposed music is present (as opposed to improvisatory music), such calculated if not outright choreographed movements are apt to be perceived as mimesis. For Brecht's audiences it may even have had something of the effect of the synchronized film score to it. Amy Wlodarski's chapter in this volume contrasts the effect of such synchronization, as evident in Riefenstahl's *Triumph of the Will*, with the distancing effect Brecht's colleague Hanns Eisler achieved when he broke "the totality of the sound-image relationship" in the 1955 film *Nuit et Brouillard*.[32] This is precisely the context in which "Nietzsche worried that Wagner's emphasis on movement and on music yoked to movement was manipulative," because it exerted an irresistible pull on the unsuspecting audience.[33] As part of the modernist impulse to recover the body, any linking of movement to music in the epic theater would have produced precisely the opposite effect: the overt self-consciousness of such synchronicity was a means of estrangement. A mimetic relationship between music and the performing body would thus tie Brecht to earlier nineteenth-century, pre-Wagnerian opera as an anti-Wagner gesture. Paradoxically, however, if Nietzsche's instincts were correct, it also tied Brecht, almost certainly unwittingly, directly to the contradictions inherent in the music drama.

Brecht's lengthiest general discussion of gestus appears in the 1937 essay "On Gestic Music." The essay is rife with contradictions, however, and it is uncharacteristically abstract, providing no concrete examples from either his own texts or anyone else's. Brecht asserts that the social gest is one that allows conclusions to be drawn from the social circumstances, and that the gest must be very specific to the person and situation in question; otherwise, freed from the restraints of imminent practical application, it is more theoretical, even fanciful, offering numerous memorable images (communists mourning, fascists striding over corpses) but no corresponding gests. "A good way of judging a piece of music with a text is to try out the different attitudes or gests with which the performer ought to deliver the individual sections ... For this the most suitable gests are as common, vulgar, and banal as possible. In this way one can judge the political value of the musical score."[34] This suggests that the music generates the appropriate gests of motion and pose in the actor as a kind of mimesis, and while Brecht does not mention singing explicitly, no discussion of the performance of a song can eliminate the act of vocal production entirely. This ambiguity—is the gest situated in the score or in the performer?—brings us back to the tension Smart identified in Wagner: is gestus more properly the premise (the notated score) or the result (the sounding body) of musical expression?[35]

Perhaps the tension remained unresolved because relocating gestus from the gesturing body to the score required a sounding body to make it audible, and this is the point at which I think Brecht encountered an unexpected problem in calculating the relationship between the body and the music. The modernist fixation on reinstating the corporeal was retained, but now the body was at least as much a sounding one as a showing one. Thus an additional consequence became possible: its realization in the sounding body produces the voice-object, a phenomenon that trumps all else—music, lyrics, drama, staging—and resists control via the gestus (or any other means). Carolyn Abbate describes the voice-object as follows:

> An attraction to opera means an attraction to singers' voices—this goes without saying. But there is also a radical autonomization of the human voice that occurs, in varying degrees, in all vocal music. The sound of the singing voice becomes, as it were, a "voice-object" and the sole center for the listener's attention. That attention is thus drawn away from words, plot, character, and even the music as it resides in the orchestra, or music as formal gestures, or abstract shape.[36]

Brecht attempted to suppress the voice-object through various performance instructions so that audience members would not succumb to its siren song, since opera's narcosis included not only the composer's music but also its manifestation via singers' performances. Efforts to neutralize the voice-object separated the music theater experience from that of the opera house, in which prima donnas continued to peddle the sonic dope Brecht so mistrusted. But, as Abbate points out, the source of the voice-object is not confined to the sounding body of the opera diva; it is present in all vocal music. Perhaps there really was no dosage at which music could be safely administered and consumed in the epic theater.

As an opera composer, Wagner had always contended with the sounding body. His solution was music drama, meaning those operas he wrote after *Lohengrin*—from *Das Rheingold* onward. He resisted that terminology, preferring the rather tongue-in-cheek "acts of music made visible," but their distinguishing feature is that they are all organized according to leitmotifs, and those leitmotifs are presented primarily in the orchestra. In other words, Wagner attempted to thwart the emergence of the voice-object by consistently giving important musical material to the orchestra and not to the singers. As the cult of the Wagnerian singer attests, however, he was no more successful at taming the voice-object than Brecht. In his effort to offset the effects of Wagner's Gesamtkunstwerk, as Brecht received it through Nietzsche, epic theater wound up replicating fundamental aspects of its original incarnation: the totalizing experience, the audience contract, and the problem of mimesis. This brings us back to Martin Puchner's observation that the entire modernist theater project was, at its heart, a rejection of Wagnerian theatricality. Brecht may not have recognized that he was still under the influence of that narcotic when he devised what was supposed to be its antidote.

Notes

1. Vera Stegmann, "Brecht Contra Wagner: The Evolution of the Epic Music Theater," in *A Bertolt Brecht Reference Companion*, ed. Siegfried Mews (Westport, 1997), 249. Regarding opera in Brecht's youth, see particularly Ulrich Weisstein, "Von reitenden Boten und singenden Holzfällern: Bertolt Brecht und die Oper," in *Brechts Dramen: Neue Interpretationen*, ed. Walter Hinderer (Stuttgart, 1984); Werner Frisch and K.W. Obermeier, *Brecht in Augsburg: Erinnerungen, Texte, Fotos* (Frankfurt am Main, 1976), 58–59, 111; and Hans Otto Münsterer, *The Young Brecht*, trans. Tom Kuhn and Karen Leeder (London, 1992), 123. Other major works in which this is discussed include Joachim Lucchesi and Ronald K. Shull, *Musik bei Brecht* (Frankfurt am Main, 1988), 91. See also Albrecht Dümling, *Laßt euch nicht verführen: Brecht und die Musik* (Munich, 1985), 36, 38.
2. See, for example, Mary A. Cicora, *Wagner's Ring and German Drama: Comparative Studies in Mythology and History in Drama* (Westport, 1999). Musicologists have tended to prefer this binary as well; see Stephen Hinton, "The Concept of Epic Opera: Theoretical Anomalies in the Brecht-Weill Partnership," in *Das Musikalische Kunstwerk: Festschrift Carl Dahlhaus*, ed. Stephen Hinton (Laaber, 1988).
3. Christoph Nieder, "Bertolt Brecht und die Oper: Zur Verwandtschaft von epischem Theater und Musiktheater," *Zeitschrift für Deutsche Philologie* 111, no. 3 (1992): 275–76; Ernst Schumacher, *Die Dramatischen Versuche Bertolt Brechts, 1918–1933* (Berlin, 1955), 216–17; Marianne Kesting, "Wagner/Meyerhold/Brecht oder die Erfindung des 'Epischen' Theaters," *Brecht Yearbook/Brecht-Jahrbuch* 7 (1977): 113; Hilda Meldrum Brown, *Leitmotiv and Drama: Wagner, Brecht, and the Limits of "Epic" Theatre* (Oxford, 1991). Timothée Picard takes the opposite position, claiming that Brecht's anti-Aristotelian position is actually anti-Wagnerian, a claim I would refute as opera

was never an Aristotelian genre to begin with. Picard, *L'art total: Grandeur et misère d'une utopie (autour de Wagner)* (Rennes, 2006), 156.

4. Theodor W. Adorno, "Wagner's Relevance for Today," in *Essays on Music*, ed. Richard Leppert (Berkeley, 2002), 596.
5. Matthew Wilson Smith, *The Total Work of Art: From Bayreuth to Cyberspace* (New York, 2007), 78–79.
6. Martin Puchner, *Stage Fright: Modernism, Anti-Theatricality, and Drama* (Baltimore, 2002), 1–58, 139–56. See also Patrick Carnegy, *Wagner and the Art of the Theatre* (New Haven, CT, 2006), 238–39.
7. See Sanna Pederson, "From Gesamtkunstwerk to Music Drama" in this collection.
8. Juliet Koss, *Modernism after Wagner* (Minneapolis, 2010).
9. Lawrence Kramer, *Opera and Modern Culture: Wagner and Strauss* (Berkeley, 2004), 9.
10. Richard Wagner, *Opera and Drama*, trans. William Ashton Ellis (Lincoln, 1995), 46.
11. See, for example, Fredric Jameson, *Brecht and Method* (London, 1998), 63.
12. The concept of the audience contract was developed in Carolyn Abbate's NEH summer seminar entitled "Opera: Interpretations, Stagings, Readings" in the summer of 2002. It emerged from our discussion about Ann Smock, "Don Giovanni, or the Art of Disappointing One's Admirers," in *Enigmas: Essays on Sarah Kofman*, ed. Penelope Deutscher and Kelly Oliver (Ithaca, 1999), 49–66.
13. "Notes on the Opera Mahagonny," in Bertolt Brecht, *Brecht on Theatre: The Development of an Aesthetic*, trans. John Willett (New York, 1992), 35–36.
14. Smith, *Total Work of Art*, 75.
15. Koss, *Modernism after Wagner*, 255.
16. Brecht, *Brecht on Theatre*, 37–38.
17. Ibid., 38.
18. See reviews in Bertolt Brecht, *Die Massnahme: Kritische Ausgabe mit einer Spielanleitung von Reiner Steinweg* (Frankfurt am Main, 1972), 324–26, 333–34, 338–40.
19. Nico Carpentier, *Media and Participation: A Site of Ideological-Democratic Struggle* (Chicago, 2011), 56.
20. Peter Ferran, "The Threepenny Songs: Cabaret and the Lyrical Gestus," *Theater* 30, no. 3 (2000): 7.
21. Mary Ann Smart, *Mimomania: Music and Gesture in Nineteenth-Century Opera* (Berkeley, 2004), 171.
22. See Wayne Heisler, "Reconciling the 'Three Graceful Hellenic Sisters,'" in this collection.
23. *Pastimes at Home and School: A Practical Manual of Delsarte Exercises and Elocution*, (Chicago, 1897).
24. Émile Jaques-Dalcroze, *Eurhythmics: Art and Education*, trans. Frederick Rothwell (London, 1930).
25. Katherine Bliss Eaton, *The Theater of Meyerhold and Brecht* (Westport, 1985).
26. Daniel Albright, *Untwisting the Serpent: Modernism in Music, Literature, and Other Arts* (Chicago, 2000), 102.
27. George Bernard Shaw, *The Perfect Wagnerite* (London, 1898), 135.
28. Smart, *Mimomania*, 167.
29. Ibid., 4.
30. Ibid., 168. Emphasis in original.
31. Ibid., 29.
32. See Amy Wlodarski, "Exposing the Political Gesamtkunstwerk," in this volume.
33. Smart, *Mimomania*, 168.

34. Brecht, *Brecht on Theatre*, 104–5.
35. Smart, *Mimomania*, 171.
36. Carolyn Abbate, *Unsung Voices: Opera and Musical Narrative in the Nineteenth Century* (Princeton, 1991), 10.

Joy H. Calico is Professor of Musicology and Director of the Max Kade Center for European and German Studies at Vanderbilt University. She is the author of *Brecht at the Opera* (2008) and *Arnold Schoenberg's* A Survivor from Warsaw *in Postwar Europe* (2014), both from University of California Press.

CHAPTER 5

Gesamtkunstwerk, Gestaltung, and the Bauhaus Stage

MELISSA TRIMINGHAM

> Artists at the Bauhaus attempted to find an objective common denominator of form—in a way to develop a science of design ... such a foundation of general superpersonal laws provides an organic and unifying background for various talents.
>
> —Walter Gropius[1]

In her book, *Modernism after Wagner*, Juliet Koss acknowledges the Bauhaus theater as an attempt at a Gesamtkunstwerk. She finishes her chapter on the Bauhaus by analyzing a photograph of the stage workshop "in action" as a deliberately posed, and by implication naively self-deceptive, attempt to present the Bauhaus theater stage as the total artwork.[2] She characterizes the "human dolls" in the Bauhaus—dolls in many contexts, primarily but not only on the stage—as sympathetic, infinitely reproducible human figures yet ones devoid of personality and individualism, who were invented to serve an unconscious sanitized vision of modernity, whose characteristic mass spectatorship would prove all too unpalatable in the National Socialist years to come. But her powerful thesis neglects the theatrical reality of these figures. Whilst her art historian's analysis of larger forces at work is very persuasive—Katerina Rüedi Ray says much the same in her closing analysis of the same photograph, which graces the cover of the 1938 MOMA exhibition[3]—I would like to explore here how the uniform and androgynous padded stage figures, with their abstract and uniform full head masks, were also practical research tools used by Schlemmer for investigating the complex nature of theatrical space. This "laboratory" was founded on Gestalt principles and was as romantic and mystical as it was pseudo-scientific. Nonetheless, for all its idealism and utopianism, it was, in retrospect, sinisterly prescient of the future.

A fresh attempt to understand the Bauhaus stage as Gesamtkunstwerk, and the light it throws on the Bauhaus itself as Gesamtkunstwerk, must necessarily be selective. Space will not allow analysis of all the differing aspects of performance that manifested at the Bauhaus, both formally and informally, in Weimar between 1918 and 1925 and in Dessau from 1925 until its move to Berlin in 1933. I concentrate here mainly on the stage work at the Bauhaus under Oskar Schlemmer, who became the official Master of the Bauhaus Stage Workshop in 1924 after the departure of the first Stage Director, Lothar Schreyer, and remained in this position until just before the school moved to the industrial city of Dessau in 1929. It was Schlemmer who took most seriously the connection between architecture (always central to the Bauhaus ideals and present in its very name) and stage space, and subjected it to systematic research. In doing so he reached back into history for his ideas and inspiration, whilst simultaneously trying to keep the Bauhaus true to its original purpose as the "Building House" of contemporary society. Founded as an art school in Weimar in 1918, in the midst of revolution and economic hardship, by the architect Walter Gropius, the "Bauhaus" contained in its name the idea, and the ideal, that the built structure (or architecture) typified society's cultural health, and that, collaboratively realized, it could unite the various art forms. Central to Gropius's problem was maintaining and renewing German cultural and aesthetic values, embodied in the individual talent and creativity of its students, amidst rapid earlier industrialization, the demand for mass production, and the need for the German postwar economy to recover and expand. Despite the name, Gropius never founded an architecture department at the school, caught as he was between the aesthetic ideals of architecture and the hard reality of "the building," which needed to be collaboratively realized.[4] Under him, the Bauhaus instead continued to develop individual creativity in design work in its craft workshops, exploiting new materials, exploring the relationship of form and function, and producing some of the iconic modernist artifacts of the twentieth century.

Walter Gropius spent many years in the United States after leaving the Bauhaus, cleaning up the image of his unruly yet sparklingly creative institution. He was particularly keen to suppress its expressionist period in Weimar, when it was under the sway of Johannes Itten and his mystical, spiritual, and frankly embarrassingly esoteric ideas. Indeed, Gropius's long-running propaganda campaign in the United States to promote modernism as the democratic alternative to fascism, and to present the Bauhaus as its originator, is becoming increasingly recognized; recent literature on the Bauhaus has also started to reassess its myth-making capacities, intentional and unintentional, both at the time of its existence and longer term.[5] For years, Gropius presented a selective history and smoothed over the tensions, disagreements, and downright splits that continually rocked the institution. Much of this was caused by the struggle to assimilate the modern world of technology and industry with artistic and aesthetic values. Later, Gropius stressed his own responsibility for the successful principles underlying the Bauhaus whilst downplaying the influence of prewar ideas that developed in Wilhelmine Germany.[6] Most especially, he consistently failed to acknowledge the influence of the ideas of Henry van de Velde, who had advocated joining industrial crafts with fine art. As an architect, van de Velde was devoted to the Gesamtkunstwerk idea, designing both the interior and exteriors of buildings based on united design principles. Gropius inherited his School of Arts and Crafts (van de Velde was its principal until 1914) along with the School of Fine Art (whose buildings van de Velde designed) in Weimar. James-Chakraborty explores this heritage, and its denial, in particular the fact that Gropius inherited the craft workshops from van de Velde's school.[7]

Gropius's relationship with Oskar Schlemmer was a troubled one. Even from the published letters, it is clear that Schlemmer disapproved of some of Gropius's sexual affairs, and Gropius in turn had at least one spectacular argument with him over the theater ceiling in Jena in 1924.[8] Gropius paid him half a salary when he grudgingly invited him to Dessau as Master of the Stage Workshop; and we can be sure that the letters that Tut Schlemmer and his wife carefully concealed from the world probably contain some unflattering commentaries on Gropius. Nevertheless, Gropius seems to have been a charming if self-aggrandizing personality who had the gift of leadership: able to inspire others whilst getting them to execute, more or less, his ideas. His initial ideas on the need to unite the arts under the banner of the crafts and fine art are contained in the opening manifesto of the Bauhaus, and are expressed in almost visionary language.

On the basis of this declaration, David Roberts observes: "The Bauhaus was itself conceived as a multiple Gesamtkunstwerk: on the level of its guiding idea, the cathedral of the future; on an institutional level, as a collective social and aesthetic synthesis; on the level of the staff and their individual projects."[9] His evidence includes building the "cathedral of the future" through "social and aesthetic synthesis," and the cojoining of individual staff interests including painting, music, photography, dance, theater, printing, ceramics, and weaving. The notion that the Bauhaus intended to unite the art forms persists in contemporary commentaries.[10] We might expect the activities of the Bauhaus theater stage to provide the strongest evidence for it, since Richard Wagner, with whom the notion of Gesamtkunstwerk is most commonly associated, promoted the affective medium of the stage as the means to unite all the arts. The stage, moreover, is always predicated on the presence of an audience who will respond and be moved, even changed, by what they witness. This powerful medium was exploited by Wagner and subsequently developed by the Symbolists[11] and Kandinsky[12] (who later taught at the Bauhaus) among others. Understanding how the notion of Gesamtkunstwerk or "total work of art" played out on Schlemmer's stage and the Bauhaus as a whole requires, I contend, a radical recasting of the idea of *Einheit* or unity in the work of art. This arises from the deeply changed circumstances of art and aesthetics between late nineteenth-century Bayreuth and the Weimar of 1918. It also requires us to recognize, as Nicholas Vazsonyi does in this volume, that the idea of *Einheit* originates in late eighteenth and early nineteenth century Romantic thought.[13] Seen in this way, both Wagner and the Bauhaus are embodied manifestations, peculiar to their time, of what is essentially the same impulse.

Architecture, Theater, and Cultural Crisis

The secular, if not existential, modernist crisis of the arts, identified by the Romantics, addressed by Wagner, and felt as catastrophic by the time of the Bauhaus, had its roots far back in the eighteenth century, with the separation of the arts from religion and state patronage.[14] In the case of architecture the problem was particularly acute in that, as James-Chakraborty demonstrates, grandiose public buildings—museums, art galleries, theaters, opera houses—had largely replaced earlier commissions for princely palaces and cathedrals. German architects of conscience in the early nineteenth century, such as Karl Friedrich Schinkel and his pupil Gottfried Semper, felt their profession had a moral duty not only to exemplify the moral and cultural values that underpinned society, but also actively to promote, indeed create them.[15] In the words of Harry Mallgrave, "Schinkel pursued a vision of architecture as urban theatre: a monumental stage that through its very urbanity appeals to and fosters the highest human instincts."[16] Semper's influence and ideas—none of it acknowledged by Wagner—are central to his former friend's Festspielhaus at Bayreuth, and both Wagner and Semper shared the view that architecture helped "to make the spectator aware of his presence within a larger communal ritual."[17] Wagner's vision of music theater as a transformative aesthetic, social, and political tool insisted upon the whole theater building as an integral and essential part element of this immersive experience. Indeed, the stage and the (theater) building are inextricably linked in the Wagnerian vision of renewal—a notion also echoed in the Bauhaus, not least its name "Building House."[18]

The spiritual remedy that Wagner had offered in the mid nineteenth century to reverse what David Roberts calls the "cultural secularization" of art after the French Revolution was the creation of Gesamtkunstwerk.[19] This work would, he maintained, be realized through the stage, synthesizing the arts in a communal, festive performance that was both manifestation and realization of a revolutionized, utopian society where the spectacle was made complete by the audience's readiness and receptivity to the ideals it promulgated. With hindsight, it is little wonder that Wagner's ideas lent themselves so well to the later totalitarian ideals of Nazi Germany: but I am not here touching on that troubled history. We should emphasize rather that the ideal did not begin as tarnished: on the contrary, potential audience affect or Einfühling in the total work of art remained inspirational within early twentieth-century modernism and the avant-garde to an extent that has been freshly recognized by new and authoritative studies, notably those of David Roberts, Marcella Lista, Juliet Koss, and in the essay collection edited by Anke Finger and Danielle Follett.[20]

The opening manifesto of the Bauhaus art school in Germany in 1918 with its woodcut by Lyonel Feininger (Fig. 5.1) of the "crystalline" cathedral—the ultimate architectural Gesamtkunstwerk[21]—made architecture central to its aesthetic and cultural goals to renew art and society, and declared openly its

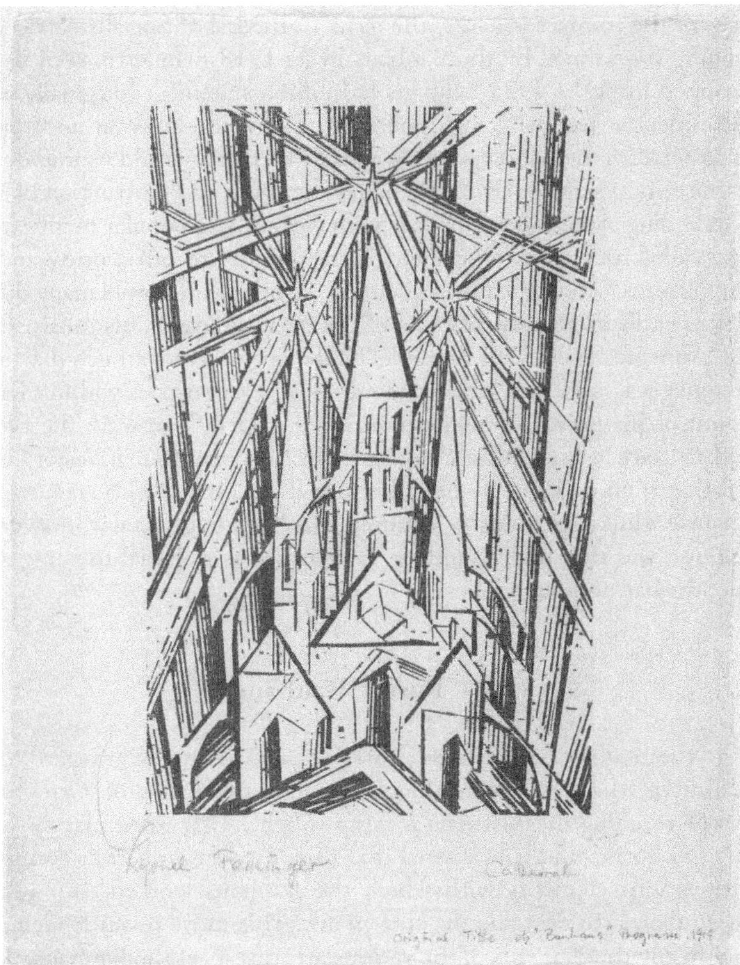

Fig. 5.1. Lyonel Feininger, Cathedral of Socialism for the Program of the State Bauhaus in Weimar, 1919. © 2015 Artists Rights Society (ARS), New York/VG Bild-Kunst, Bonn

allegiance to the idea of the total work of art.[22] Gropius wrote: "Together let us desire, conceive and create the new structure of the future, which will embrace architecture and sculpture and painting in one unity and which will rise one day toward heaven from the hands of a million workers like the crystal symbol of a new faith."[23] Schlemmer likewise declared the aim of the Bauhaus workshops was to "unite and productively stimulate the arts with the aim of combining them in architecture. The concept of the building will restore the unity that perished in debased academicism and in finicky handicraft."[24] Thus far the Bauhaus was a self-declared devotee to the total work of art and was linked, as was Wagner's ideal, to a utopian vision of society to come. Nor did it lack the revolutionary overtones of the younger Wagner: the term "Cathedral of Socialism" was loudly and proudly proclaimed by the Bauhaus in its 1918 manifesto, even if it was later dropped from the 1923 Bauhaus Exhibition statement (originally written by Schlemmer) as too dangerous politically. There was however an important difference between the Bauhaus and Wagner. The Bauhaus and its founder were not, at this critical stage of civilization after the chaos and destruction of World War I, intending to rehearse or engage with current and popular manifestations of the so-called total work of art: and in the late nineteenth century and early twentieth century Wagner was everywhere.[25] "Wagnerism" covers many different attitudes towards and interpretations of the master himself, his music, and his theories. Annegret Fauser, for example, interestingly demonstrates that by this time Wagner was perhaps rather "tainted" or at least suspect within Germany on account of his pervasive influence in French opera.[26] Instead, the Bauhaus intended to start again, with a clean slate. In his opening manifesto, Gropius declared that training in art and architecture should begin with training in the crafts that were linked to industry (ceramics, book binding, metal work, weaving): the intention was that understanding the "parts" was essential to being able to construct the harmonious whole.

The "Purist" Bauhaus

Rarely do the Bauhäusler themselves use Gesamtkunstwerk in regard to their goal of unifying the arts,[27] preferring to summon the notion of "*Gestaltung*" as a means of reaching the aesthetic totality sought. This word may be loosely translated as "form," and it is a word that they used in numerous compounds with the various elements with which the Bauhaus worked—for example, *Bühnengestalung*—to describe the stage work. This move towards *Gestalt* as a means of fusing the elements of the various arts distances the Bauhaus, and the Bauhaus stage in particular, from late nineteenth-century Wagnerian social, cultural, and aesthetic idealism.[28] In his letters, Schlemmer, for example, often vowed his allegiance to a vision of social and aesthetic harmony without ever summoning Wagner's name. Indeed, in their discourse on unity, the Bauhaus and especially its theater appears to have been tapping into a vision of cultural harmony that was manifested strongly in the early nineteenth-century Romantic period and thus preceded Wagner's formulations.

Thomas Schober and Kay Kirchmann point out that much of Schlemmer's stage work at the Dessau Bauhaus after 1925 appears to be the exact opposite to the Wagnerian Gesamtkunstwerk:[29] an abstraction, honing down and synthesizing of elements peculiar to the stage (motion, space, the body, 3D material form, color, light, sound) in order to "work" them at a very minimalist level, rather than a wider inclusive approach.[30] In this way, the Bauhaus stage and the institution as a whole ultimately manifests what Theodore Rippey, following Lutz Koepnick, identifies as a purist rather than synesthetic, or inclusive, modernism.[31] The purist approach in the Bauhaus was a result of the seismic shift in aesthetics in the early twentieth century towards abstraction.[32] In the words of Karin von Maur, "the first decade of our century came to witness almost simultaneous revolutions in music and art," namely, the birth of dissonance in music and abstraction in art, and this had an inevitable effect upon the conception of how the total work of art might be realized.[33]

As Maur points out, both "old" systems of music and art (harmony and mimesis) had been "legitimised for centuries by masterpiece after overwhelming masterpiece," and they needed, in her words, "anarchic energy" to overthrow such systems. The avant-garde provided this energy in its disparate forms: but the will to totality remained stubbornly present even in the most anarchic (and often synesthetic) of these movements, including the Futurists, the Dadaists, the Expressionists and the Surrealists.[34] The means to unity in art were now necessarily different. Connections were sought between disparate art forms, either in violent juxtaposition (Futurism and Dada) or in quasi-scientific, quasi-mystical approaches like those of the Expressionist Blue Rider group. Especially influential were Expressionist inclusive systems of harmony and color correspondences. Whilst the first Bauhaus students preferred Dada, staff at the Bauhaus in its early days eagerly pursued Expressionist ideas, including Johannes Itten, who created and taught the Foundation Course at the school, and Wassily Kandinsky, Russian painter and author of the Expressionist Bible, *The Blue Rider Almanac*. They hoped to expose the metaphysical and mystical truth "underlying" surface appearances. Kandinsky was a synesthete who "heard" colors as sounds. Perhaps as a direct result of this, Kandinsky, along with several others at the Bauhaus, was convinced of the ultimate unity of music and painting, sound and color. Paul Klee was another Bauhaus master committed to this ideal.[35] In 1913, Kandinsky wrote a stage work, *Yellow Sound*, that was Wagnerian (though virtually unstageable) both in its aims of fusing sound, color and action via the stage and its epic scope: but with its Expressionistic tropes, its abstract visual imagery, lack of any poetry or dance, and non-existent plot, it hardly resembled Wagner's music theater, visually or sonically.

Painters using colors and shapes to experiment with pure depth, dynamism, contrasts, and harmonies on the surface of the canvas translated on the Bauhaus stage in Weimar between 1918 and 1923 into moving light shows set to music and "mechanical theaters" of abstract shapes and color, generally speaking more geometric than the images in Kandinsky's 1913 abstract play.[36] Schlemmer created the best known (then and since) experimental pieces in Dessau after 1925, without plot or characters and infused with his painterly ideals of placing the human form in space. Earlier, in *The Triadic Ballet* (1922), he had used elaborate built up, geometrical costumes; the later *Bauhaus Dances* (1927), though pared down and minimal, were similarly geometric and form based.[37] The same minimalist urge is true of other work undertaken in the Bauhaus, especially after the move to Dessau in 1925: ceramics, weaving, wall painting, furniture, and household object design, and even the building of whole houses (the House Am Horn for example created for the 1923 Bauhaus Exhibition in Weimar),[38] all of which honed down "form" into minimalist elements before synthesizing them anew into creative work. It seems that a very different emphasis came to be placed on totality in the Bauhaus, which as its ethos evolved, was realized in terms of an analysis and re-synthesis of basic elements: a "purist" modernism.

Kandinsky's play was never performed at the Bauhaus. The general urge there was in truth both more cynical and more scientific than *Yellow Sound*'s quasi-mystical and spiritual aims, particularly as the school turned away from the openly Expressionistic ethos that dominated the Weimar Bauhaus towards the more purist and Constructivist philosophy driving its second phase of existence at Dessau. The urge to abstraction at the Bauhaus was an urge towards totalizing art, but as they sought after new unity became that of technology and art, it was also an urge towards pulverization, separation, rationalism, minimalism, isolation, simplicity, and analysis.[39] Schlemmer, who led the project on the Bauhaus stage, was aware of the two opposing pulls of analysis and synthesis that abstraction exerted. In "Man and Art Figure" (1925) he writes: "One of the emblems of our time is abstraction. It functions, on the one hand, to disconnect components from an existing and persisting whole, either to lead them individually *ad absurdum* or to elevate them to their greatest potential … abstraction can result in generalization and summation, in the construction *in bold outline of a new totality*"[40] [my emphasis]. This is Gestalt thinking.

Gestalt Thinking on the Bauhaus Stage

In 1961, in the English edition of *The Theater of the Bauhaus*, Arthur Wensinger adds an important note on Gestalt thinking at the Bauhaus. It is one of the few descriptions we have from a Bauhäusler about this fundamental notion within the institution. He added it presumably because what was so self-evident in 1925 Germany was no longer evident in 1960s America, and nor is it obvious to us today. He writes:

> Gestaltung was among the most fundamental terms in the language of the Bauhaus and is used many times by Schlemmer and Moholy-Nagy in their writing, both by itself and in its many compounds, such as Bühnengestaltung.

He goes on to quote T. Lux Feininger:

> If the term "Bauhaus" was a new adaptation of the medieval concept of the "Bauhütte," the headquarters of the cathedral builders, the term "Gestaltung" is old, meaningful and so nearly untranslatable that it has found its way into English usage. Beyond the significance of shaping, forming, thinking through, it has the flavor of underlining *the totality of such fashioning*, whether of an artifact or of an idea. It forbids the nebulous and the diffuse. In its fullest philosophical meaning it expresses the Platonic eidolon, the *Urbild*, the pre-existing form.[41] [my emphasis]

The term Gestaltung represents the particular manifestation of totality in art that emerged in the Bauhaus, which contrasts with the Wagnerian vision of totality. It hinged on developments in philosophy, psychology, and art that revived interest in Goethian idealism. Goethe's ideas chimed precisely with the emerging abstraction in visual art and essentialist thinking in science in early modernism, both of which underpin much neo-Romantic early twentieth-century thinking on unity and totality, particularly via color theory. To Goethe, all organisms demonstrated internal laws of self-organization which ultimately derived from the "Urbild" or ideal form. Goethe prided himself on being able to extract or perceive the underlying form or "Urbild" in all that he saw, whether observing natural forms or works of art.

As described, the "Essences" of form and color in dynamic tension were supposedly realized in abstract canvas compositions and in sculpture from about 1910 onwards. Goethe's "self-actualizing wholeness of organic forms"[42] or "Gestalt" systems were to revolutionize aesthetics and design. The affective medium of theater was part of this revolution.

Certain members of the Bauhaus, even if they never set foot on the stage, dreamed of the stage synthesis of Gestalt form in which motile and immersive stages bristling with action replaced Wagnerian stage machinery with twentieth-century technologies. László Moholy-Nagy laid out his vision of stage totality in his essay "Theater, Circus, Variety" in terms of a multimedia extravaganza. His extraordinary theater of the future has a Wagnerian richness and epic vision with a twentieth-century twist, presenting unified action through several stages and levels, including "complex apparatus such as film, automobile, elevator, airplane and other machinery, as well as optical instruments, reflecting equipment, and so on."[43] Gropius was fascinated by the prospect of designing a "Total Theater" for Piscator in Berlin, a space that would democratically eliminate stalls and boxes, and immerse the audience in the visuals (stage action, film, light) and acoustics. Its fantastic design was never built but the plan reappears years later in Gropius's introduction to the 1961 English version of *The Theater of the Bauhaus*: "Thus the playhouse itself, made to dissolve into the shifting, illusionary space of the imagination, would become the scene of the action itself. Such a theater would stimulate the conception and fantasy of playwright and stage director alike; for if it is true that the mind can transform the body, it is equally true that structure can transform the mind."[44] Beguiling as these artistic plans are—and symptomatic of inclusive modernist thinking—none of them were ever realized. Hopes and aspirations rather than actual achievements permeate the original 1925 *The Theater of the Bauhaus* book in which Moholy-Nagy's design appears. This is also true of Schlemmer's own essay, "Man and Art Figure," in which he too has extravagant technological hopes and visions.[45] In every way, these theater visions subjugated Gestalt analysis in favor of intoxicating synthesis.

In the new building designed by Gropius at Dessau, a tiny frame stage was built. Schlemmer began his "Bühnengestaltung" purist research in 1925/6, in straitened circumstances, complaining of few materials and no trained performers. The removable back wall (or folding doors) linked the intellectual seat of learning (the "aula" or lecture hall, doubling as auditorium) with the canteen, the social heart of the institution. This stage thus symbolized and practically demonstrated in its design the aesthetic and social unity to which the Bauhaus aspired. Schlemmer shared the deeply Germanic belief that the primary means of realizing what Vazsonyi in this volume calls the "bloodless revolution" in society was through the renewal of art and aesthetics.[46] Friedrich Schiller's late eighteenth-century essay, *On the Aesthetic Education of Man*, which espoused this idea, was one of Schlemmer's favorite and inspirational texts for his stage workshop.[47] Importantly, both architecture and the stage are material arts using physical media; moreover, as Wagner himself noted, both are somatically experienced. The touring Bauhaus dances of 1929 consisted chiefly of Schlemmer's plain, abstract moving geometric forms, which were all Bauhaus design fundamentals (poles/lines, hoops/circles and cubes/squares) carried by performers in uniform padded suits that smoothed out their bodily characteristics and heightened their haptic or bodily awareness. The performers also wore expressionless geometric full head masks, which again sensitized their somatic perception of space by forcing them to turn their heads in order to see. Unlike the visually powerful and colorful *Triadic Ballet* of 1922, whose costumes were made up of severe and startling geometric shapes somewhat awkwardly riveted upon the body, Schlemmer now used a minimal color palette of white, black, gray, red, yellow, and blue. The narrative content was pared down, some dances consisting only of movement (literally stepping out the space in shapes painted on the floor as in *Space Dance* and, holding geometric objects, in *Form Dance*); others were humorous comments on the human condition with a few in-jokes about the Bauhaus and its concerns (such as *Gesture Dance* which linked color, movement and emotion, and *Box Play* which showed a community attempting to build an architectonic structure together—with a few comic arguments and mishaps).

Somatic experience brings us to the heart of the stage's power, to Juliet Koss's analysis of the total work of art in terms of Einfühling, or "feeling into" a work of art, and to a different interpretation of the "human dolls," as she characterizes them. Einfühling can be understood as embodied empathy, activated in performance. Wagner said of somatic experience: "Through the employment of every artistic expressional faculty of man, the poet's aim is in drama the most completely carried from the understanding to the feeling—to wit, is artistically imparted to the feeling's most directly receptive organs, the senses."[48] Christiane Heibach has pointed out that Wagner rehabilitated the use of media in the search for a unified work of art, since the Romantics had concentrated on poetry and insisted that "every art ought to direct itself first and foremost to the inner sense of the imagination; structural boundary crossings are possible on this view, but their medial realization disappears into the background."[49] Wagner was committed to Einfühling or affect upon the audience; this is as an essential component of his music theater. The playhouse at Bayreuth was designed to promote the sense of palpable community, absorbing the audience member into the music drama spectacle in front of them by the wide unbroken semicircle of seating, losing the orchestra into a concealed pit, and drawing the eye in to the stage itself by means of a double proscenium. Since Schlemmer literally embodied in somatic experience the abstract ideas that dominated Bauhaus thought, his was more than a "theater of human dolls." Nor was it robotic and mechanical,[50] but rather drama that, in Wagner's words, "carried from the understanding to the feeling," thereby stimulating "feeling's most receptive organs, the senses." In Schlemmer's words, theater was a "powerful force for order" at the Bauhaus, a "Schillerian tribunal"[51] decisively countering disembodied approaches to design and idealist notions of form detached from living, arguing always for the body and the human being as central to any humanist quest.[52]

The definition of Einfühling that Koss traces was articulated in the late nineteenth century by such men as Robert Vischer, Heinrich Wöfflin, Theodor

Lipps, and Adolf von Hildebrand.[53] Hildebrand was a formative influence on Schlemmer during his time in Stuttgart in the 1910s. Schlemmer struggled to reconcile it with his yearning for abstraction, or form: in 1915 he wrote, "I would like to present the most romantic idea in the most austere form."[54] For Schlemmer, the aesthetic experience of a work of art was an experienced reality, strong and efficacious, and his theater was intended as an embodied realization of the formal thinking in the Bauhaus, a living experiment and questioning of certain dogmatic certainties on form that he felt came to dominate the teaching in the Bauhaus.

Music at the Bauhaus

Music played a pivotal role in Wagner's realizations of the Gesamtkunstwerk, even if he declared that the poetry was more important;[55] and music had a central role in everyday life in the Bauhaus, despite its almost complete absence from the stage work. Music's exclusion from *The Bauhaus Dances* that toured Germany in 1929 can be explained entirely by the analytical and Gestalt impulses dominating Schlemmer's work.

Schlemmer was a skilled piano player; music, along with poetry, was an important medium for him. The fact that music did not feature in his pared down Bauhaus Dances, and that he was never satisfied with any of the several scores for *The Triadic Ballet*, indicates not that music was unimportant to him, but rather that it was too complex a medium to accommodate within his minimal Gestalt aesthetic at that time. He says as much in his letters and diaries where he often debates the aesthetics of music, stating it explicitly in the 1927 essay "Bühne" (Stage).[56] Schlemmer had read Nietzsche and was no doubt suspicious of music's capacity to indulge the senses. He refused to use music as a support to the visuals or as "background," and wanted somehow to pare down music, as he did for movement, shape, and color, to its simple elements or most basic Gestalt forms. The truth is, however, that he really had little idea how to do this. He tried to use the natural noises emerging from the materials that he used in his dances (for example, the clinking of glass from the costume in *Glass Dance*) or, less inspiringly, he used simple percussion or even silence. He equated the "word" of poetry (another medium he enjoyed and admired) with the problems presented by sound/music more generally: words/poetry's effect upon the audience was complex and strong, and he preferred to keep it out of his analytical stage completely, though he had hopes (I suggest forlorn hopes, given his aesthetic and the limited time he had for experimentation) that one day he would be able to incorporate both music and poetry in his stage work.[57]

His unwillingness to include music in the official stage work is the more significant and ironic as music flourished within the Bauhaus as a whole. On a day-to-day basis, the walls of both the Weimar and the Dessau Bauhaus echoed with music, as the ability to play an instrument was the norm among Bauhäusler rather than the exception. Gropius viewed the contemporary music performances during the 1923 Bauhaus Exhibition's opening week as an opportunity to declare the Bauhaus's allegiance to cutting-edge art. At Bauhaus parties, the Bauhaus band played into the early hours. Whilst his formal stage work was carefully controlled and intellectually cohesive in terms of his Gestalt thinking, the Bauhaus parties that Schlemmer directed and inspired form an area of theatrical activity that comes remarkably close to a Wagnerian ideal of social community realized through a total artwork. It was at the parties where the discipline of abstraction and form were forgotten and play and pleasure were given free rein. "Tell me how you party," says Schlemmer, "and I will tell you who you are."[58]

At Weimar, there were parties every weekend held in village halls as well as more formal, sometimes outdoor, celebrations involving performance, costumes, and processions. At Dessau, the parties evolved into themed events that knitted together the whole Bauhaus community and involved elaborate preparations for decorating the Bauhaus building and making costumes. These occasions were stage-managed by Oskar Schlemmer, and most fully demonstrated—to quote my earlier description of the Wagnerian ideal—the "communal, festive performance," the "manifestation and realization of a revolutionized, utopian society" and one moreover completed "by the readiness and receptivity of the audience to the ideals it promulgated." A Bauhaus party at Dessau was an immersive and total work of art—albeit ephemeral and conjured from minimal resources.[59] It consisted of students/staff/guests/audience/performers wearing carefully prepared fancy dress costumes made around a pre-declared theme (for example the White Party in March 1926), dancing, games, and food. It was fueled by the music of Wensinger's band, whose music presented a furiously lively blend of jazz and klezmer rhythms, none of which, sadly, was recorded in any way. One of the best descriptions we have of a Bauhaus party comes from Schlemmer's own diary describing the Metal Party in winter 1929: "The unfettered imagination now wrought miracles. A children's slide covered in white sheet metal led one past innumerable gleaming silver balls, lined up and sparkling under spotlights, right into the heart of the party ... The Bauhaus band had dressed festively in coquettish silver top hats, and it launched into the music with great élan, rhythm and verve."[60] He himself acknowledged that "for one night this house of work was transformed into the 'high academy for creative form.'"[61]

The freedom the Bauhäusler found to express themselves at parties and festivals contrasts sharply with the measured outputs of the official Dessau stage, which were carefully controlled "Bühnengestalten," intellectualized and directed by Schlemmer. The parties are arguably closest to the ideal Wagnerian Gesamtkunstwerk, however small and intimate the community that was involved.

The "Active" Audience of Wagner and the Bauhaus

By demonstrating the centrality of Gestalt abstraction in the Bauhaus, I disconnected the purist Bauhaus stage from Wagnerian inclusivity. However, I have also demonstrated that Einfühling was important for all Bauhäusler, whether in official performances or at parties. In a different age and a different mindset, Einfühling or embodied empathy was surely also the source of Wagner's power. I would like to finish by exploring Einfühling further by way of phenomenology and the affective medium of the stage.

Phenomenology emerged from the early researches into "intentionality" by Franz Clemens Brentano in the 1870s, intentionality being the relationship between the perceiving mind and the matter it encountered. Phenomenological "intentionality," like Wagner, focused attention upon the actively receiving and perceiving or "intending" mind. It suggested the importance of the audience reception of the work of art, the part the mind plays in the creation of the totality. The Bauhaus as a whole believed that the actively seeking eye put the artist in touch with an underlying form and order. The "actively seeking eye" is the "eye" demanded by Paul Klee in his teaching, as laid out in the Bauhaus book *Pedagogical Sketchbook*[62] and most fully in his *Notebooks*, especially *The Thinking Eye*.[63] What is most apparent in Klee's design theory is his stress not just on the discovery of unifying form but also its active creation. This idea emerges strongly as a fundamental Bauhaus idea within design, photography, and the stage.

Moholy-Nagy, for example, never considered photography as a medium that reproduced or recorded reality: "Creations are valuable only when they produce new, previously unknown relationships."[64] This process combines both the uncovering of basic form (as in Goethe) with the creation of new form. Creating fresh combinations (or new Gestalt forms) of light, motion, bodies, and objects was central to both photography and stage work at the Bauhaus. Wagner's original vision also depended on the presence of the active audience, watching and in part constituting what Schlemmer describes as the "Weihe Bühne Festspiel" or "consecrated" and "festival stage."[65] Both Wagner and Schlemmer instinctively knew that live performance was a deeply affective medium, the most powerful, potentially, of all art forms: physical, live, and communal.[66] And for both of them, the live audience had an impact upon the total work of art's meaning and significance.

Phenomenological thinking is pervasive within the Bauhaus and should be more widely recognized as an important strand of thought in early twentieth-century Germany, more influential and widespread than that of Freud or Saussure.[67] It underlies Expressionist thought and draws attention to the active spectator completing the work of art. In the Bauhaus, using abstraction to refine the building blocks of art, the stress was then on *Produktion* to create the unified work of art from these fundamental elements, rather than relying upon *Reproduktion*: as Schlemmer remarked, the theater was digging its own grave when it tried for verisimilitude.[68]

In this sense the Bauhaus attempt at the total work of art is both more minimal and more radical than that of Wagner; it attempts a purer realization of the idea as it reaches further back into German idealism. The Bauhaus was both visionary and real, and it still has an impact on us. In various guises, the so-called "Ur-forms" are still handled, tested, and lived today wherever good and useful modernist-inspired design prevails. And in the case of the theater, the Bauhaus helped to free the twentieth-century stage from Wagnerian painted scenery, characters, story, and "verisimilitude"—a legacy that is encountered on virtually every stage today.[69]

This last point is not offered, however, as a value judgment on respective scenographic styles. It is always the cultural vision of our own time in the making that touches us the audience profoundly, whether a full-blown Wagnerian scene of light, painted scenery, poetry, and music, or a scene of Bauhaus minimalism. The timely vision, when we encounter it, as audiences did in Bayreuth and as students and staff did in the Dessau Bauhaus, is not transcendent but it is extremely powerful, for good or for ill. The image is made for us; we "intend" or "make" the image. But most importantly of all, the image profoundly and irreversibly "makes" us. The same could be said for the Gesamtkunstwerk idea itself, continually made and remade. The Gesamtkunstwerk of Wagner and of Schlemmer were embodied forth upon their respective stages, three decades and an aesthetic revolution apart.

Notes

1. "Walter Gropius" in Eckhard Neumann, *Bauhaus and Bauhaus People: Personal Opinions and Recollections of Former Bauhaus Members and their Contemporaries*, trans. Eva Richter and Alba Lorman, rev. ed. (New York, 1993), 21.
2. Juliet Koss, *Modernism after Wagner* (Minneapolis, 2010), 207–44.
3. Katerina Rüedi Ray, *Bauhaus Dream-House: Modernity and Globalisation* (London and New York, 2010).
4. These are the terms in which Wallis Miller describes Gropius's dilemma in "Architecture, Building and the Bauhaus" in *Bauhaus Culture from Weimar to the Cold War*, ed. Kathleen James-Chakraborty (Minneapolis, 2006), 63–89. Schlemmer's dance *Baukastenspiel* or Box Play can be read as a humorous commentary of Gropius's dilemma, a direct joke based on Gropius *Baukasten* building system for prefabricated buildings. Ibid., 71.

5. See Kathleen James-Chakraborty "From Isolationism to Internationalism: American Acceptance of the Bauhaus," in *Bauhaus Culture*, 153–70; and Ray, *Bauhaus Dream-House: Modernity and Globalisation*. Other recent writings have concentrated on the unrecognized role of women in the Bauhaus, but that important reassessment is not so relevant here.
6. See John V. Maciuika, *Before the Bauhaus, Architecture Politics and the German State, 1890–1920* (Cambridge, 2005); and "Wilhelmine Precedents for the Bauhaus: Hermann Muthesius, the Prussian State, and the German *Werkbund*," in *Bauhaus Culture*, 1–25. John Maciuika demonstrates the rich heritage of ideas from before the war that struggled to incorporate art and industry, battles in which Gropius was involved through the Werkbund and his contribution to the Cologne exhibition of 1914. Like many others in the Werkbund, Gropius felt that the exhibition buildings had been largely hijacked by the Prussian government spokesman, the architect Muthesius, imposing his belief in depersonalized architecture that better served the interests of German industry. See Maciuika, "Wilhelmine Precedents," 21–23.
7. James-Chakraborty, "Henry Van de Velde and Walter Gropius: Between Avoidance and Imitation," in *Bauhaus Culture*, 26–42.
8. See Melissa Trimingham, *The Theatre of the Bauhaus: The Modern and Postmodern Stage of Oskar Schlemmer* (London, 2011), 23.
9. David Roberts, *The Total Work of Art in European Modernism* (Ithaca, 2011), 160.
10. For example, Koss, *Modernism*, 236 and 241; Ray, *Bauhaus Dream-House*, 58 and 73; and the exhibition catalogue, Christopher Wilk, ed., *Modernism 1914–1939: Designing a New World* (London, 2006), 59, 62, and 141.
11. Notably Stéphane Mallarmé and Maurice Maeterlinck. See Katherine Kuenzi, "Intimate Modernism: The Nabis, Symbolist Theatre and the Gesamtkunstwerk," in *Art, History and the Senses*, ed. Patricia Di Bello and Gabriel Koureas (Farnham and Burlington, 2010), 67–82.
12. Kandinsky later wrote: "In this isolated world of tension is to be found another isolated world, toward which eyes and ears are turned—the stage./Here is the wish-fulfilling center of the theater, which through its own extreme tension of life is to release the extreme tension that runs through the expectant rows./This center's capacity for absorption is unlimited—by its extreme tensions it is able to communicate all the powers of all the arts to the expectant rows./ This is the inward power of the theater, which only has to be given a new form." Wassily Kandinsky, "Abstract Synthesis on the Stage," in *Kandinsky: Complete Writings in Art*, ed. and trans. Kenneth C. Lindsay and Peter Vergo (Cambridge [1913] 1994), 505.
13. See Nicholas Vazsonyi, "The Play's the Thing: Schiller, Wagner, and Gesamtkunstwerk," in this volume.
14. Harry Francis Mallgrave, *Gottfried Semper: Architect of the Nineteenth Century* (New Haven, 1996), 6; Kathleen James-Chakraborty, *German Architecture for a Mass Audience* (London and New York, 2000).
15. The notion that architecture could save the day was put forward in 1908 by the massively popular aesthetic essay by Wilhelm Worringer, *Abstraction and Empathy: A Contribution to the Psychology of Style*, trans. Michael Bullock (New York, [1908] 1956).
16. Mallgrave, *Semper*, 6.
17. Ibid., 7.

18. *Bauhütten* were the medieval guilds of skilled craftsmen who helped to build the cathedrals: the name Bauhaus (building/house) is a deliberate echo of this ancient German compound.
19. Roberts, *Total Work of Art,* 3.
20. Roberts, *Total Work of Art;* Marcella Lista, *L'Œuvre d'art totale à la naissance des avant-gardes 1908–1914* (Paris, 2006); Koss, *Modernism;* Anke Finger and Danielle Follett, eds., *The Aesthetics of the Total Work of Art: On Borders and Fragments* (Baltimore, 2011).
21. Roberts, *Total Work of Art,* 159–60.
22. In later years Gropius was reluctant to admit how much he owed to van de Velde, but it seems too coincidental that van de Velde (who, again, had led the Schools of Fine Art and Arts and Crafts at Weimar, the immediate predecessors of the Bauhaus) was a devotee of the concept that figured so loudly in the Bauhaus manifesto. See n. 7, above.
23. Hans Wingler, *The Bauhaus, Weimar, Dessau, Berlin, Chicago,* ed. Joseph Stein, and trans. by Wolfgang Jabs and Basil Gilbert, adapted and enlarged edition in English (Cambridge, 1969), 31.
24. Ibid., 65.
25. For a comprehensive survey of Wagnerism as a movement, see David C. Large and William Weber, *Wagnerism in European Culture and Politics* (Ithaca and London, 1984): esp. 15–27. William Weber's chapter, "Wagner, Wagnerism and Musical Modernism," is particularly useful: he mentions Gustav Mahler as coming under the influence of Wagnerian ideas in Vienna; and his widow, Alma Mahler, also later married Walter Gropius (p. 66).
26. Annegret Fauser, "'Wagnerism': Responses to Wagner in Music and the Arts," in *The Cambridge Companion to Wagner,* ed. Thomas S. Grey (Cambridge, 2008), 219–34.
27. Moholy-Nagy characteristically adopted the term *Gesamtwerk* to describe his "total work" as a deliberate statement of the fusion of technology and life, whilst de-emphasizing (traditional notions of) art.
28. There were moreover many different versions of Wagnerism. See n. 25, above.
29. Thomas Schober, "'Man setzt Hoffnungen auf mich': Oskar Schlemmer und das postmoderne Bildtheater," in *Oskar Schlemmer Tanz Theater Bühne,* ed. Eleanora Louis (Vienna, 1997), 124; Kay Kirchmann, "Bühnenkonzepte der Moderne. Aspekte der Theater- und Tanzreformen zur Zeit Oskar Schlemmer," in ibid., 88.
30. Katherine Kuenzli offers an interesting parallel to this in the work of Mallarmé: "While Mallarmé might appear to reject the Gesamtkunstwerk altogether, he in fact viewed the purification of art forms as preliminary to their ultimate unification." Katherine Kuenzli, "Intimate Modernism," 72.
31. See Theodore F. Rippey, "Quiet Audience, Roaring Crowd: The Aesthetics of Sound and the Traces of Bayreuth in *Kuhle Wampe* and *Triumph of the Will,*" in this volume.
32. See also Christiane Heibach, "Avant-Garde Theater as Total Artwork? Media-Theoretical Reflections on the Historical Development of Performance Art Forms," in Finger and Follett, *Aesthetics,* 219–25. Limitations of space prevent discussion of Adolphe Appia's view of Wagnerian staging as utterly unsuited to achieving the effect Wagner wished for; and his advocacy of a more abstract and pared down staging relying on light, neutral backdrops and simple space dividers such as steps and levels. *Adolphe Appia: Texts on Theatre,* ed. Richard C. Beacham (London, 1993), passim but especially 25–28.
33. Karin von Maur, *The Sound of Painting: Music in Modern Art* (Munich, 1999), 41.

34. See Roberts, *Total Work of Art*, 1–2; Lista, *L'Œuvre d'art totale*; and Finger and Follett, *Aesthetics*.
35. See Reto Sorg, "The Drawing as Total Artwork? Image Totality in Carl Einstein and Paul Klee," in Finger and Follett, *Aesthetics*, 227–52.
36. There was in addition much comedy, puppetry, satire, and anarchic good humor, all tending towards the "inclusive" end of the modernist spectrum as identified by Rippey in his contribution to this volume.
37. These were a series of relatively short pieces in which the human figure appeared on a small "framed stage" (i.e. with a proscenium opening) in all-over white or grey padded body suits, with (in the main) full head masks without expression that reduced the human performer to an archetype without character. These figures walked, strode and tripped across the stage, handled 3-D replicas of classic Bauhaus abstract geometric forms (the stick/line; the ball/circle; the cube/square); wore costumes that experimented with materials (glass, metal, wood); and sometimes engaged with simple (gentle slapstick) comedy overlaying moustaches, waistcoats, and glasses onto the neutral padded base costume (such as *Gesture Dance*, *Box Play*, and *Woman's Dance*).
38. Marcia Feuerstein describes how evidence points to Schlemmer's ideas on house design differing markedly from then mainstream Weimar Bauhaus design principles that apparently drove the design of the House Am Horn. Feuerstein sees Schlemmer as emphasizing the integration of the household with the outside community of people, whereas House am Horn had an important enclosed central area or living room into which the family were to "withdraw" together. See Marcia F. Feuerstein, "Body and Building: Inside the Bauhaus's Darker Side," in *Body and Building: Essays on the Changing Relationship of Body and Architecture*, ed. George Dodds and Robert Tavernor (Cambridge, 2002), 226–37.
39. See n. 27, above.
40. Schlemmer, "Man and Art Figure," in *The Theater of the Bauhaus*, ed. Walter Gropius and Arthur Wensinger (Baltimore, [1961] 1996), 17.
41. In Gropius and Wensinger, *The Theater of the Bauhaus*, 50.
42. Mitchell Ash, *Gestalt Psychology in German Culture 1890–1967* (Cambridge, 1995), 85.
43. László Moholy-Nagy, "Theater, Circus, Variety" in *The Theater of the Bauhaus*, ed. Walter Gropius and Arthur Wensinger (Baltimore and London, [1925] 1996), 49–70, here 67.
44. Walter Gropius, "Introduction," in idem and Wensinger, *Theater of the Bauhaus*, 14. Scholars are indebted to Juliet Koss's excellent unpacking of the term "Einfühling" in *Modernism after Wagner* where she demonstrates how pervasive embodied thought (as here manifest in Gropius's sentiment) was in aesthetics, and how it was especially persistent in architectural thinking, 67–94.
45. In *The Total Work of Art: From Bayreuth to Cyberspace* (New York, 2007), esp. 47–70, Matthew Wilson Smith argues that the Bauhaus stage was a disastrous total work of art that ended up as a total machine. While this is an understandable conclusion, given the Bauhaus' writings and grandiose promises, it distorts the reality of the Bauhaus stage. Gropius's theater was never built; nor were Moholy-Nagy's productions ever realized, at least in the form he envisaged (although, as I argue here, the Bauhaus parties came closest to Moholy-Nagy's vision). Finally, for all his lip service in the essay "Man and Art Figure," Schlemmer never employed much technology on his stage. There simply was no money or means to do so, even if he had wanted to. In 1923, at

the opening of the Bauhaus Week in the Theater at Jena, Gropius's new slogan "Art and Technology: A New Unity" was turned into a self-deprecating running joke by the host and master of ceremonies, Andreas Weininger, as the scenery nearly fell down and the evening descended into chaotic good humor. Schlemmer, "Man and Art Figure," 17–32.

46. See Nicholas Vazsonyi's chapter, "The Play's the Thing."
47. Friedrich Schiller, *On the Aesthetic Education of Man in a Series of Letters*, trans. Reginald Snell (London, 1954). Matthew Smith also analyses Schiller's influence on the idea of the total work of art, though he does not connect Schiller with Schlemmer's stage. Smith, *Total Work of Art*.
48. Richard Wagner, *The Artwork of the Future*, in *Wagner on Music and Drama: A Compendium of Richard Wagner's Prose Works*, selected and arranged by Albert Goldman and Evert Sprinchorn, trans. H. Ashton Ellis (New York, 1964), 188.
49. Heibach, "Avant-Garde Theater," 213.
50. Koss does not contend that the "dolls" were mechanical, offering instead a much more subtle argument. Many *do* level this criticism, however, at Schlemmer's figures.
51. Schlemmer, January 1926, *The Letters and Diaries of Oskar Schlemmer*, ed. Tut Schlemmer (Middletown, 1972), 189.
52. Schiller, *Aesthetic Education*, 10.
53. See Koss, *Modernism*, 76–77.
54. Schlemmer, *Letters and Diaries*, September 1915, 29.
55. See Large and Weber, *Wagnerism*, 52–53.
56. "Theater" (Bühne), in Gropius and Wensinger, *Theater of the Bauhaus*, 91.
57. *The House of Pye* was Schlemmer's one attempt at scripted drama with content and characters, and he abandoned it as too difficult to square with his "purist" principles.
58. Schlemmer, *Letters and Diaries*, February 1929, 238.
59. See Adelheid Rasche, "'Freiheit ist nur in dem Reich der träume': Oskar Schlemmer als Festgestalter," in *Oskar Schlemmer Tanz Theatre Bühne*, Austellungkatalog. Kunstsammlung Nordrhein-Westfalen Düsseldorf, ed. Maria Müller (Ostfildern-Ruhl, 1994), 31–39.
60. Schlemmer, *Letters and Diaries*, February 1929, 239.
61. Ibid., 239.
62. Paul Klee, *Pedagogical Sketchbook*, trans. and ed. Sibyl Moholy-Nagy (London, [1925] 1968).
63. Paul Klee, *The Thinking Eye: The Notebooks of Paul Klee*, ed. Jürg Spiller, trans. Ralph Manheim (London and New York, [1956] 1961).
64. Andreas Haus, *Moholy-Nagy, Photographs and Photograms* (London, 1978), 46. Dada's simultaneous poetry was in effect a similar search for what Melzer calls "new previously unknown relationships"; Annabelle Melzer, *Latest Rage the Big Drum Dada and Surrealist Performance* (Ann Arbor, [1976] 1980), 36; and for Moholy-Nagy's experiments with sound and the gramophone, see Haus, *Moholy-Nagy*, 46–47.
65. Schlemmer, without making ostensible reference to Wagner, nevertheless describes this type of stage as closer to a "Religiöse Kulthandlung" or "religious cult activity" in his grid analysis of all types of stage, cult, and popular entertainment ("Bühne, Kult und Volksfest"). See "Man and Art Figure," in Gropius and Wensinger, *Theater of the Bauhaus*, 17–32, esp. 19. With regard to the active audience, see Gary Tomlinson, "Parahuman Wagnerism," *Opera Quarterly* 29, no. 3/4 (2013): 186–202.

66. Schlemmer finishes "Man and Art Figure" by referring to this essential condition: "It depends upon the inner transformation of the spectator—Man as alpha and omega of every artistic creation which, even in its realization, is doomed to remain Utopia so long as it does not find intellectual and spiritual receptivity and response"; "Man and Art Figure," 32.
67. See Leah Dickerman, "Bauhaus Fundaments," in *Bauhaus, 1919–1933: Workshops for Modernity*, ed. Barry Bergdoll and Leah Dickerman (New York, 2009), 14–39, here 27. See also Feuerstein, "Body and Building."
68. Schlemmer, *Letters and Diaries*, September 1922, 126.
69. See n. 32, above.

Melissa Trimingham is a Senior Lecturer in Drama at the University of Kent, UK. Her research and teaching interests are the Bauhaus stage and modernism; contemporary performance; scenography; puppetry; performance art; cognitive studies; and applied theater with a particular interest in autism.

CHAPTER 6

Exposing the Political Gesamtkunstwerk
Hanns Eisler's Nuit et Brouillard

AMY LYNN WLODARSKI

There can't be any doubt about it any longer: the struggle against ideology has become a new ideology.
—Bertolt Brecht, to Walter Benjamin (1934)

Introduction

In 1935, the composer Hanns Eisler delivered a lecture to an American audience in which he outlined how fascist Germany utilized music to further its ideological aims. As Eisler argued, the political climate had negatively transformed the German musical landscape, from the dismissal of Jewish composers under the 1933 Civil Servant Act to the manipulation of music for propagandistic ends. As Albrecht Betz summarizes, "The classics were manipulated by being decoratively inserted into party rituals … demagogy pervaded everything; and finally there was the constant recourse to the 'intoxication music' (*Rauschmusik*) of Richard Wagner, the German 'myth smith.'"[1] The regime's promotion of Wagnerian artworks and aesthetics particularly exasperated Eisler, who was already suspicious of Wagner's "over-worked mythology of the *Germanen*" and the "narcotic effect" of Gesamtkunstwerk.[2] Eisler continued to develop his aesthetic-socialist critiques of Wagner from 1942 to 1948 during his political exile in the émigré community of Los Angeles.[3] In this immediate creative and intellectual sphere, he worked closely with Bertolt Brecht and Theodor W. Adorno, both of whom influenced Eisler's ideas about Wagnerian aesthetics and their mid-century political associations.

As Pamela Potter notes, "The ongoing debates about Wagner's influence over Hitler [and] the Germans … can be traced to suggestions first offered by Germans in exile."[4] Two of Eisler's projects from the 1940s illustrate these suggestions, objecting to Wagnerian music on both political and aesthetic grounds. In *Hangmen Also Die!* (1943), for which he received an Academy Award nomination, Eisler worked with a screenplay that had been adapted from Brecht's original script. Imbued with obvious anti-fascist messaging, the plot pits Czech resistance fighters against the Nazi Gestapo, who come to Prague to investigate the assassination of Reinhard Heydrich. In it, Eisler uses a citation from Wagner's *Tannhäuser* as a leitmotif for Gruber, the Gestapo agent doggedly pursuing the assassin. As Sally Bick argues, Eisler rescores the citation to be mockingly "kitschy"—diminutive, almost cartoonish—and thus "inverts [Wagner] from an example of high art to what Eisler would categorize as popular trash, manifesting his ... disdain for Wagnerian opera."[5] Eisler's marking of Gruber as a Wagnerian also affirmed a political association that was becoming more common in American caricatures of National Socialism.[6]

After the war, Eisler's critique turned to more aesthetic objections to Wagnerian opera. In their co-authored monograph, *Composing for the Films* (1947), Eisler and Adorno accused the total work of art of cultivating an aura of passivity through the use of musical techniques designed for "the delectation of hapless audiences."[7] Not just the audience, but even individual musical aspects of the Gesamtkunstwerk appeared to suffer from the Wagnerian spell, with the leitmotif now described as an uncritical "musical lackey," whose literalism revealed its "extreme [compositional] poverty" and blind acquiescence to the "master," who announces his arrival "with an important air."[8] In contrast, Eisler and Adorno advocated for a more estranged approach to film scoring, a position that borrowed much from the philosophies of Brecht. The promotion of Brechtian *Verfremdungseffekt* as an alternative to Wagnerian largess was not a new revelation; as Joy Calico asserts in this volume, "Wagner and Brecht were frequently arranged as polar opposites in the debates on the fate of German opera in the 1920s," a polemic that continued well into the postwar period.[9]

Recently, however, scholars have begun to question whether the distinction between Wagnerian Gesamtkunstwerk and modernist epic theater was as simple as these narratives suggest. Calico and Matthew Smith contend that the aims of Brecht and Wagner were, in many ways, more related than one might suspect—that Brecht's use of "discontinuity and contradiction" allowed him to create an epic form of Gesamtkunstwerk that achieved its "unity through juxtaposition."[10] Instead, Calico identifies a more subtle divergence between Wagner and Brecht—namely, the preferred role of music within a broader multimedia project. She notes that Brecht remained skeptical of music above all the sister arts, identifying it as the irrational, muddling element of the Gesamtkunstwerk that ultimately lulled the audience into a passive state of suffering. Brecht considered epic theater to be antidotal in its fracture of Wagner's endless melodies; in his productions, music was often confined "exclusively to the song where it was always mediated by Brecht's lyrics," a means of breaking the spell of the continuous soundtrack.[11]

Unlike Brecht, Eisler was less skeptical of music's ability to function as a critical force within multimedia productions, including those that possessed continuous soundtracks; he believed in music's agency and that it could add another active level of intellectual perception to a film. Moreover, his time with the Hollywood studios had helped him to refine his own use of Wagnerian conceits to advance his sociopolitical ideas. By the 1950s, his position vis-à-vis Wagner had matured from his more youthful dismissal to one that recognized the influence of the Gesamtkunstwerk on the modern genre of film music, requiring him to strike some practical compromises in his own work. Indeed, in some cases, Eisler specifically uses Wagnerian compositional devices to generate the aesthetics of discontinuity and contradiction that were at the heart of Brecht's epic theater. This aesthetic flexibility—the ability to borrow from both the "Brechtian" and the "Wagnerian"—made it possible for Eisler to re-employ elements of the Gesamtkunstwerk within modernist projects in order to facilitate the political and critical awakening of the audience.

This chapter considers one of Eisler's postwar political responses to Wagnerian Gesamtkunstwerk: the 1955 documentary *Nuit et Brouillard* (*Night and Fog*) directed by Alain Resnais. In the film, which presents a body of visual evidence to assert the horrific consequences of National Socialism, Resnais deliberately opens with a series of clips from Leni Riefenstahl's 1935 documentary *Triumph des Willens* (*Triumph of the Will*). The celebratory and propagandistic tone of Riefenstahl's imagery quickly gives way to more grave and harrowing images from the Nazi terror: death camps, executions, mass graves. Moreover, Resnais's ensuing montage favors disjunction and juxtaposition in order to reject the unified aesthetic of *Triumph of the Will*. Eisler's score plays a pivotal role in disassembling the synchronicity of Riefenstahl's original, with Eisler simultaneously undermining and embracing Wagnerian conventions in order to dismantle the propagandistic power of the original footage. The result is a political retort to totalitarianism that undercuts Riefenstahl's Gesamtkunstwerk and reveals its illusory facades, all the while consciously acknowledging the continued relevance of Wagnerian techniques to twentieth-century modernist film.

(Re)Defining the Political Gesamtkunstwerk— Wagner, Brecht, and Adorno

Wagner's concept of Gesamtkunstwerk originated around the time of the 1849 Dresden uprising and, consequently, was "imbued with its revolutionary spirit."[12] Albrecht Betz conjectures that Wagner's own involvement in the uprising may have conditioned the young composer to propose an art form in which "music ought not to stand outside of the social interests of mankind. In order to remove the division between art and life, the 'politicization' of music was needed."[13] Such an art–life conception vividly appears in *The Artwork of the Future*, Wagner's seminal treatise in which he posits Gesamtkunstwerk as both an aesthetic and social movement. As Sanna Pederson details in her contribution to this volume, Wagner aesthetically conceived of the Gesamtkunstwerk as the highest form of art, one that could only achieve its possible fullness when each of its separate artistic branches also realized their full potential.[14] And yet, as Nicholas Vazsonyi argues, the Gesamtkunstwerk was "never 'just' about the art work itself"; he writes, "any Gesamtkunstwerk that does not involve performance—meaning the *medium* of human, lived, and live experience—is already a departure from and … a fundamental misunderstanding of the Wagnerian idea."[15] Wagner never intended the Gesamtkunstwerk to be abstract or detached from life—it was to be a reflection and embodiment of a utopian vision of an idealized artistic world.

In light of this observation, it seems appropriate that Wagner would present his aesthetic ideas in quasi-performative terms. Portions of *Artwork of the Future* consciously resemble a stage work, with its heroic protagonist, Artistic Man, freely inhabiting the Gesamtkunstwerk as man does his natural world. Within the treatise, Wagner announces his entrance in bold, mythic terms: "On to the stage, prepared by architect and painter, now steps *Artistic Man*, just as Natural Man steps into a scene of Nature."[16] Artistic Man appears as operatic character, stage actor, creative force, and aesthetic prophet, himself totalized as an amalgam of all parameters of the Gesamtkunstwerk. Wagner tasks him with weighty responsibility and importance, for "Artistic Man can only fully content himself by uniting every branch of art into the collective artwork: in every segregation of his artistic abilities he is not free, not fully that which he can be; whereas in the collective artwork he is free, and fully that which he can be."[17] He is the savior of opera, for "it is in him … that the three sister arts unite their forces in one collective operation."[18] In doing so, he restores their power and artistic integrity, not as individual artistic branches but as a unified life force that allows each to attain an organic sense of completeness.

Wagner portrays his "Artistic Man" not only in dramatic terms—the stage actor, fully subsumed into the Gesamtkunstwerk—but in social terms as well, as the revolutionary agent of an ideal artistic community. This leap was possible for Wagner because he also viewed the Gesamtkunstwerk as a reflection of the needs of a true artistic community: the Volk. For Wagner, the Volk represented "the epitome of all those men who feel a collective need … who concern themselves with that necessity, irresistibly, victoriously, and truly."[19] As Juliet Koss notes, the concept of the Volk provided Wagner with a convenient "conceptual overlap … that covered a range of political [and artistic] meanings";

it could interchangeably refer to the "utopian audiences" that would be united through the experience of a Gesamtkunstwerk, or to "a notion of unified German cultural strength" that carried "an amorphous political significance."[20] Thus, one goal of *Artwork of the Future* was to present an embodied concept of "Artistic Man" as a free, aesthetic representative of the Volk, one who "wished to be unified by a communal experience—an experience that was both aesthetic and political."[21]

By experiencing the Gesamtkunstwerk, Wagner predicted that the Volk would achieve its own awakening to the liberating force of nature, which called it to live according to "the only real necessity, the inner natural necessity."[22] Prompting such an art–social union was the ultimate aim of the Gesamtkunstwerk, as Wagner expounded: "Only by the happy consciousness of his connection with nature will man overcome his dependency and become free; art, too, overcomes its dependency and becomes free only through its connection with actual life."[23] The Gesamtkunstwerk was therefore socially instructive as well as aesthetic; it sought to unleash among its Volk a collective desire that would "teach the world to recognize its own true need."[24] The result was an interdependence between art and the world, for just as it was through the total work of art that its Volk would find unity ("for in this artwork we shall all be one … blissful men"), only "the spirit of fellowship, fulfilled by life can bring this artwork to pass."[25] Thus, as Matthew Smith eloquently realizes, the Gesamtkunstwerk was "as much about collectivity as about unity, about community as about totality."[26] As a collective force, it aimed to transform society into a utopian "Aesthetic State," in which art reflected life and organic artistic expression captured the will of its collective Volk.[27]

During the rise of the Third Reich, Wagner's conception of the Volk was adopted as a model for the totalitarian state, which presented itself with similar aesthetic and political rhetoric. In *Political Aesthetics*, Crispin Sartwell similarly identifies Nazism as an "artpolitical system" given that one of Hitler's aims was "to reshape the world, and conceived in this way, the effort is aesthetic."[28] His point is echoed by Frederic Spotts, who observes in *Hitler and the Power of Aesthetics* that "Hitler held a deep and genuine interest in music, painting, sculpture, and architecture. He regarded politics, not art, as a means to an end, the end of which was art."[29] More specifically, this political approach to art was, at its most idealistic, totalizing; the establishment of the *Reichskulturkammer* (Reich Chamber of Culture, RKK) in 1933 attempted to centralize control of the arts under the auspices of Joseph Goebbels's propaganda ministry. As Betz describes, "everything seemed to be aimed at producing a collective … [and] emotionally welding the masses together into [a] community."[30] Hellmut Lehmann-Haupt concurs, noting that "in order to survive, the totalitarian state must draw the individual away from himself, [and] absorb him into a communal scheme of life that tolerates growth and development of the personality only along narrowly prescribed lines."[31] Total and coordinated control of artistic production, in Goebbels opinion, was one particular means of defining for the individual "what was German," a question that Wagner himself had posed in 1878.[32]

In his policies and speeches, Goebbels described the related process of *Gleichschaltung* (coordination) in distinctly Wagnerian terms, and as David Dennis notes, Wagner's opera *Die Meistersinger von Nürnberg* became one of the most common aesthetic symbols of the new regime. In one of his earliest speeches for the RKK, Goebbels asserted that "culture is the highest expression of the productive forces of a Volk... An art that separates itself from the Volk has no right to complain when the Volk separates itself from it," a statement with obvious resonances to the excerpts from *Artwork of the Future* cited earlier.[33] The association was helped by the fact that the fiftieth anniversary of Wagner's death coincided with the ascension of the Hitlerian regime; thus, public speeches and festivals were designed both to honor the composer and provide a political platform for Goebbels. In one such speech, Goebbels declared *Meistersinger* to be the "incarnation of *Volkstum*," possessing "everything that marked and filled the German soul."[34] Performances of the "Wach auf" chorale from the opera were frequently performed in these contexts, with the *Völkischer Beobachter* describing the opera as "music for marching into the shining future of German culture."[35] Thus began a "close correlation between [Hitler, Wagner, and specifically *Die Meistersinger*] that remained constant."[36]

Despite the fact that the RKK and its subsidiaries did not function perfectly in practical terms—its policies were often initially vague or inconsistently applied—detractors capitalized on its rhetoric and seized the opportunity to criticize both Wagner and the ideology of *Gleichschaltung*.[37] Although the development of Brecht's anti-Wagner discourse preceded the official establishment of the Third Reich, his objections would later directly engage the fascist regime. In the 1930 essay, "The Modern Theater is the Epic Theater," Brecht argued strongly against the dangers that Gesamtkunstwerk potentially posed to both art and society. At the level of aesthetics, Brecht felt that Wagner's specific realization of Gesamtkunstwerk undermined the expressive potency of each separate medium: "So long as the expression Gesamtkunstwerk means that the integration is a muddle, so long as the arts are supposed to be 'fused' together, then the various elements will all be equally degraded."[38] He worried that the manufactured realism of Gesamtkunstwerk—an effect he equated with theatrical "witchcraft"—could only lead to "hypnosis," "sordid intoxication" and the anesthetization of the audience's critical faculty.[39] A radical separation of the individual artistic elements, he argued, was necessary to reassert the social importance of the theater and reawaken those who had been lulled into the seductive "fog" of the total work of art. In the postwar period, Gesamtkunstwerk became an even more potent "anti-model" for Brecht, "a symbol from which postwar generations derived comfort in their perceived distance and difference from it."[40] In his 1948 "Short Organum for the Theater," for example, Brecht explicitly associated the aesthetic Gesamtkunstwerk with political *Gleichschaltung*, suggesting a dangerously close bind between a totalized aesthetic and totalitarianism. Music, he argued, must "strongly resist Gleichschaltung" in order to avoid falling into the "unthinking slavery" of Gesamtkunstwerk.[41]

Similar political associations appear in the writings of Theodor Adorno, albeit more explicitly. As a postwar cultural critic, Adorno's critique focused less on aesthetic parameters and more acutely on the political and social consequences of Wagner's theories. In his 1947 essay "Wagner, Nietzsche, and Hitler," Adorno presented Wagner as "the personification of fascism" and explicitly "link[ed] his work to National Socialism."[42] As Juliet Koss notes, Adorno argued strongly against the Gesamtkunstwerk, declaring that it "rendered spectators the passive recipients of an overwhelming performance, lulling them into appreciation beyond the limits of time itself."[43] His bold equation of Wagner with National Socialism allowed the philosopher to "posit a direct causal link between Bayreuth productions and [fascist cinema]," which then allowed him to implicate Wagner in the "development of the culture industry."[44] This critical framework allowed Adorno the necessary latitude to interpret Wagnerian techniques, such as leitmotif, as aesthetic-political tools for dismantling the critical faculty of the masses. As he averred in *In Search of Wagner*, "The degeneration of the leitmotif … leads directly to cinema music where [its] sole function … is to announce heroes or situations … [It possesses] a commodity-function, rather like that of an advertisement, [and] anticipat[es] the universal practice of mass culture."[45] Adorno feared that such banal literalism had cultivated a passive modern audience, one caught in the phantasmagorical spell of both Gesamtkunstwerk and its modern reiteration, cinema.

In their association of the Gesamtkunstwerk with Hitler's totalitarian model for political art, Brecht and Adorno essentially identified an artistic community to which they wished no admittance. In their mind, the "Artist of the Twentieth Century" should be decidedly anti-Wagnerian, and thus they labored to obscure any potential connections between the Gesamtkunstwerk and modernist dramatic forms. Conversely, Eisler believed in a critical mode of composition that should contend openly with the potential tensions between Wagnerism and modernism, rather than seek to erase them. "A composer has to view a text [as] full of contradictions," he explained, and not be afraid to engage those parts of the text that are difficult. "That is part of musical intelligence."[46] One such example of this approach appears in his score for *Nuit et Brouillard* (1955), in which Eisler utilizes Wagnerian techniques in order to confront a politicized Nazi Gesamtkunstwerk. In the opening scenes, Eisler rescores visual material from Leni Riefenstahl's *Triumph of the Will* in order to break the sonic–visual synchronization of her original, using irony and defamiliarization to deconstruct its convincing naturalism. The result is an open engagement with Wagner, but one with the explicit intent to reveal the seduction of the Riefenstahl's political Gesamtkunstwerk.

(Re)Composing the Political Gesamtkunstwerk— Riefenstahl and Eisler

Hitler's adoration of Wagner and the composer's artpolitical views were not lost on Leni Riefenstahl, one of the Reich's most celebrated film directors. In her memoir, she recalls her first impression of Hitler as imbued with aesthetic discourse, specifically that of Wagner: "He talked about his private life and about things that greatly interested him, especially architecture and music. He spoke about Wagner ... and about Bayreuth."[47] Thus, it seems appropriate that a Nazi-Wagnerian aesthetic of Gesamtkunstwerk would have influenced *Triumph of the Will* (1934), Riefenstahl's majestic political documentary of the 1934 Nuremberg Party Rally which aims at introducing Hitler, in no uncertain terms, as a mythical hero come to save Germany from its shame. Her medium was perhaps best suited to capture a modern-day Wagnerian myth; film had long owed a debt to the tradition of Gesamtkunstwerk, with "words such as *Gesamtkunstwerk, Leitmotif,* and *unendliche Melodie* [endless melody] occasionally employed by film directors, film composers, and film critics to describe the new form."[48]

But, as Matthew Smith asserts, "this indebtedness is even more pronounced in Riefenstahl's creation ... in its utopian evocation of an ecstatic German Volk, a Volk unified not only through a common Will but also through communal participation in a great artwork."[49] David Roberts concurs, describing the process as an aesthetic-political union: "[Riefenstahl's] transformation of politics into the staging of the rapturous communion of the Leader and his people ... tied the goal of transforming the individual into the 'charismatic national community' to the overcoming of the self in the collective experience of the mass."[50] The intent was an "aestheticized image of Germany's cultural past" that sought to create a "sense of collective identity in the present, to inspire the spectator to celebrate the consciousness of being 'German'—a consciousness that [could] be carried beyond the theater."[51] In addition to melding her individual subjects and viewers into the film's collective vision of the Volk, Riefenstahl also strove for self-subjugation by concealing her own subjective presence in the film. Her aesthetic celebrates the invisibility of the mechanical production, resulting in the perception of a realistic organicism. And yet, she presents the mass rally—

and, consequently, its narrative and actors—with total aesthetic control, revealing only a few traces of herself and her crew in the process.[52]

In *Triumph of the Will,* the most overt allusions to Wagnerian aesthetics lay not only in this constructed organicism, but also in the synchronization of the musical score with both the film's visual imagery and political ideology. Herbert Windt composed the score for the film, freely borrowing gestures and harmonic palettes from Wagner's musical language as well as citing politically approved political songs (such as the "Horst Wessel Lied").[53] Although hints of *Tristan* and *Tannhäuser* surface at points in the score, Windt cited only one Wagnerian excerpt at length: the prelude to the third act of *Die Meistersinger von Nürnberg,* which prefigures the opera's "Wach Auf" chorale.[54] As Matthew Smith argues, the choice could hardly have been arbitrary. Originally, the prelude functioned as "daybreak" music in the opera; its placement in Riefenstahl's montage reinforces the visual imagery of the scene, which beautifully captures the spires of Nürnberg as they emerge from a pre-dawn fog on the second day of the rally. At the actual event, *Meistersinger* had been featured in a performance the previous evening, and thus the placement of the prelude reinforces the chronology of the film, allowing the strains of Hitler's favorite opera to linger in Nuremberg the following morning. The choice of this particular chorale melody was also potent with political meaning. As Smith notes, it had long been a custom for Nazi enthusiasts to stand as the chorale was played as a quasi-anthem for the regime, a practice that continued during the Third Reich. "In Party mythology," he writes, "a direct line ran from Hans Sach's '*Wach auf*' to Wagner's '*Wach auf*' to Hitler's '*Wach auf*' … The melody marks the utopian aspirations of the Party Convention itself, aspirations rooted … [in] Wagner's vision of the *Gesamtkunstwerk.*"[55]

Throughout the film, the synchronization of the musical soundtrack to the visual image was paramount to Riefenstahl's aesthetic, and she labored mightily to mask the "cutting-edge techniques of mechanical production … on which [her film] relied."[56] In her memoir, she recalled the herculean effort undertaken to maintain the sense of sonic realism in the parade sequences that conclude the film:

> A special march had been written for the film, but neither [Windt] nor the conductor succeeded in conducting the music so that it synchronized with the images … So I myself took over the task of conducting the eighty-man orchestra. I had every frame down pat, and I knew exactly when the music should be conducted faster and when slower. At last the sound was synchronized precisely.[57]

Such a coordinated presentation of the Nazi Party as a wide-reaching and unified political movement was a central aim of the film, which promoted a totalistic vision of German society—a kind of social vision of Gesamtkunstwerk—in which the separate branches of the nation ideally come together in a unified expression of *völkisch* nationalism.

In one scene involving the consecration of the Labor Service, the utopian premise of Nazi totalitarianism finds one of its most vivid and musical expressions. Roberts describes the scene as "a staging of the identity of the Leader and the nation," a "massive spectacle of regimentation, unity, and loyalty."[58] Although it lacks any musical accompaniment, the scene reaches its apex in a call-and-response exchange that crescendos to a unison choral statement of German *Gesamtheit* (totality):

Leader: Where do you come from, comrade?
Corpsman: I come from Friesland.
Leader: And you, comrade?
Corpsman: From Bavaria ...]
Others: From Königsberg ... from Silesia ... from the Baltic ... from the Black Forest ... from Dresden ... from the Danube ... from the Rhine ... and from the Saar.
All (in unison): One Volk, One Führer, One Reich![59]

This scene functions as the epitome of a totalitarian Gesamtkunstwerk: "The individual German young man [appears] as a monumental object, an emblem, but then [Riefenstahl] pulls back and reveals that the individual body is fundamentally a tiny segment of a huge collective body."[60] Like a Wagnerian artwork, the scene is grand, musically conceived (despite its lack of an accompanying track), and precisely choreographed. As Steven Bach describes, "The faces are carefully lit, intercut with shots of Hitler, Nazi banners, and Speer's wooden eagle, the swastika clutched in its talons ... the rhythm becomes mechanical in its precision, as synthetic as a chorus number in a ... musical ... According to Speer, 'this [scene] was rehearsed—fifty, a hundred times.'"[61] The aesthetic result is indicative of what Joachim Fest describes as the collective "mass desertion [of the individual] to the Nazi camp," a journey aided by an "accompanying fog of nationalistic slogans" that find purpose and resonance through their absorption into Riefenstahl's propagandistic masterpiece.[62]

In 1955, the French director Alain Resnais completed *Nuit et Brouillard* (*Night and Fog*), a documentary project aimed at starkly presenting the horrific dimension of the Nazi terror to a reluctant European audience. In the film, Resnais used visual montages to create a series of alternations between historical archival footage and present-day shots of the abandoned grounds of Auschwitz. The past always appears in black-and-white and often in grainy, static camera shots (e.g., still photography, tripod shots), whereas the 1955 footage is shot in sepia-hued color, often with the camera ceaselessly tracking through the ruins. The result was a filmic memory of Nazi atrocities that considered its moral and historical consequences for the present, with the two temporal periods represented through shifts in media and tone. To lend the project more credibility, Rensais deliberately employed artists whose personal wartime experiences and aesthetics could add further authenticity and rigor to the project.[63] Jean Cayrol, a camp survivor and poet, contributed the text for the documentary while Hanns Eisler composed the film score. As Resnais explained, he felt that working with a "German" composer would dispel the notion that *Nuit et Brouillard* was a piece of anti-German propaganda.[64]

Resnais was determined to avoid the charge of propaganda—an accusation that had been levied against Riefenstahl in the postwar period—in part because he viewed *Nuit et Brouillard* as a retort to Nazi visual culture. To this point, Resnais generously interpolates archival and visual materials produced by the Nazi regime as documentary evidence of the atrocities; from this evidence, he fashions a montage that focuses not on unity and heroism, as Riefenstahl did, but on ethnic conflict and violence. Strategically, his first historical sequence derives from *Triumph of the Will*, specifically clips from scenes that Riefenstahl took the greatest efforts to synchronize in her own version of Gesamtkunstwerk: the labor corps and parade sequences. As Cayrol notes in his accompanying voiceover, the mechanical unity of the Nazi public image was part of the danger ("1933…the machine goes to work"). Resnais's aim was to expose the mechanism of Riefenstahl's total work of propaganda through montage, a technique that "calls attention to [its] fragments; it breaks through the appearance of totality."[65] And yet, his reordering of her scenes fails to break the *Gesamtheit* of her material through visual editing alone; the aesthetic synergy among the smaller separate elements persists. This failure stems from the fact that Riefenstahl was also using montage to structure *Triumph of the Will*; consequently, her individual scenes retain their cohesion and unity in *Nuit et Brouillard*. Despite the differences in their political and aesthetic approaches, their shared editing technique undermines Resnais's resistance of *Triumph of the Will*.

The medium that ultimately creates the necessary critical distance from Riefenstahl's original is Eisler's score. Eisler's approach to film scoring had been directly influenced by his collaborations with Brecht, and yet even before this creative association, Eisler had targeted Wagner as a subject of musical ridicule. Early in his career, Eisler made free references to Wagnerian leitmotifs and melodies, albeit with a sense of irony and critique. In *Zeitungsausschnitte* (Newspaper Clippings), a song cycle written between 1925 and 1927, several of Eisler's satirical techniques emerge with Wagner as their critical target. Eisler uses a leitmotif comprised of a falling chromatic figure to unify the songs in the cycle, thus tying the composition to a Wagnerian technique. And yet, as David Blake observes, the composer's references to Wagner become more tongue-in-cheek as the cycle unfolds. In one setting, Eisler "indulges in the first of his mockings of Wagner by inverting the [leitmotif] to produce a *Tristan* quote to the words 'Am a widower of thirty-four, a wealthy landowner with a child—the child needs a good mother, myself a good wife.'"[66] In a later moment, the *Tristan* chord—famous for its chromatic departure from tonality—is jokingly "followed by a device which was at the very heart of that system—the circle of fifths."[67] After he encountered Brecht, Eisler's jabs continued with Wagner often representing the antihero in their socialist dramas. In 1936, he cited the opening bars from *Tristan und Isolde* to accompany the following lines in Brecht's "Kuppellied": "Money makes you sexy, as experience tells us."[68]

In *Nuit et Brouillard*, Eisler uses similar techniques to create a counterpoint that unsettles the opening clips of Riefenstahl's majestic sequences, and expose the cogs and wheels behind her organic presentation of the Nazi rally. For this sequence, he composes a leitmotif incongruous to the displays of consonant political might in *Triumph of the Will*, imbuing the motive with a critical purpose. The "Nazi Motive," which reappears at the conclusion of the documentary, consists of an ascending scale that traces a diminished fifth or tritone, a highly disharmonious musical interval. Moreover, the leitmotif is performed by pizzicato strings, which provide a delicate accompaniment that clashes with the grand spectacle of the Nazi rally. It also resists development by devolving into a banal ostinato pattern that circles back onto itself, thus never reaching a dramatic climax. The distinction between triumphant visuals and diminutive music undercuts the impact of Riefenstahl's images; they appear more hollow and eerie to the viewer and thus are divested of their original rhetorical power.

Eisler further breaks the Gesamtkunstwerk illusion by departing from two other ideals promoted by Riefenstahl's correlation of musical sound and visual image: those of synchronicity and sonic realism. Just as Riefenstahl personally coordinated the orchestral selections to the speed of her montage, Eisler too conducted his chamber ensemble while viewing the completed version of the film on screen; Eisler, however, intentionally misaligned transitions between musical selections to lag behind the visual sequencing.[69] This miscoordination is clearly visible in the shift to Riefenstahl's footage, where the music from the earlier scene bleeds over into the archival footage of German soldiers marching. In this regard, the music exposes the editorial seams of the documentary and distinguishes it from *Triumph of the Will*, which labors to hide such disjunctions. The sequence ends with an image of the Hitler-Jugend's drum corps, accompanied by an extended snare drum roll. Eisler's aim here is not synchronization, but rather a sly distancing effect. He represents the young drummer with a snare drum roll, a choice in instrumentation that breaks the totality of the sound–image relationship in that the young drummer plays a field drum, which would produce a more muted timbre. In doing so, he asserts a postwar distance from the Riefenstahl original through this revision of its sonic realism, now a retort to its methods of dramatic illusion. Moreover, Eisler again deliberately situates the drum roll after the youth appears in the frame, disrupting the dramatic action and purposefully rejecting Riefenstahl's naturalist interpretation of Gesamtkunstwerk.

Conclusion

When dealing with the Nazi artpolitical system, an analytical danger lies in the absolute equation of Wagnerian aesthetics with those of the totalitarian regime. As Sartwell observes, "We can't understand the specific totalitarian system without understanding its aesthetics. But no specific aesthetic system is identical to totalitarianism in general."[70] And yet, as Pamela Potter suggests, one might come to understand the "historiographic phenomenon [through] a careful scrutiny of the experiences, perceptions, and motives of musical figures driven out of Nazi Germany."[71] A moment from Eisler's 1961 score for Brecht's *Schweyk im zweiten Weltkrieg* demonstrates this point. That year, Eisler composed three scenes for the Paris production. In the first scene, as Hitler, Himmler, Göring, and Goebbels crowd around a globe, Hitler asks Himmler a pointed question: "How does the little man in Europe view me?" As accompaniment, Eisler cites the opening bars of *Tristan und Isolde*, played by four cellos. The musical answer seems clear: the little man [Eisler] views him [Hitler] as a Wagnerite.

Riefenstahl's filmic account of the 1934 Party Rally also seems designed to promote a politicized Wagnerian vision of Nazism and Hitler, with similar musical allusions set in a vastly different aesthetic tone. With its determination to obscure the mechanical labor behind the production and focus on sound–image synchronicity, *Triumph of the Will* was considered one of the monumental artistic achievements of the Nazi era. As Sartwell observes, the ambitious scope of its production linked it to common modes of totalitarian art: the preference for "gigantic works [that are] harbingers of a transformed world [and] ambitious on a world scale."[72] But its filmic emphasis on totalized visions of Nazi culture, along with its recognizable citations of *Die Meistersinger* and presentation of a unified German Volk, also placed it genealogically in the tradition of Wagnerian Gesamtkunstwerk, a lineage strengthened by Hitler's own affection for the composer and his music dramas. Again, whether infallible or not, the wartime perception of Riefenstahl, Hitler, and the Nazi regime was akin to Eisler's postwar insinuation in *Schweyk*: Wagnerism was at the heart of their political aesthetic and, thus, central to the regime's cultural values and expressive modes.

Within the literature, the eerily beautiful Gesamtkunstwerk produced by Riefenstahl has ultimately come to represent the fascist regime and its seductive mythologies; her images and scenes are often reproduced as illustrations of the dangerous aesthetics of the regime. On the other hand, Eisler's musical critique in *Nuit et Brouillard* lodges a postwar response against "Hitler's Wagner" that seeks, at least in part, to deflate the political power of *Triumph of the Will* with a subversion that turns the techniques of the total work of art against itself. In doing so, he seems to promote Brecht's opinion that Gesamtkunstwerk was, at its core, a dangerous aesthetic that required direct confrontation. By musically dismantling the aesthetic work of art, Eisler demanded that the viewer confront the social and moral horrors of the Nazi regime by casting a fresh eye on Riefenstahl's sequences, now deflated of their grandeur and sound–image unity. The result was a rescoring of the footage that sought to pierce the ideological *Nebel* of Wagner and Riefenstahl's *Niebelungen* with a post-Holocaust version of the Nazi *Night and Fog*.

Or is it that simple? Can Eisler's score truly be a rejection of Gesamtkunstwerk if it also recognizes the useful utility of Wagner's dramatic techniques with regard to cinematic scoring? If Eisler's use of the leitmotif provides some measure of unity within *Nuit et Brouillard*, does that film also operate as a political Gesamtkunstwerk with its own dangers? The answer, I believe, lies in taking a less "totalized" hermeneutical approach and embracing the contradictions that these questions suggest. In their quest to differentiate modernism from the Gesamtkunstwerk, Brecht and Adorno denied outright any potential connections between the two, despite certain shared points—what Koss has described as the "invisible specter that haunted modernism."[73] In this vein, they remind me (somewhat uncomfortably) of Riefenstahl, who also labored to keep certain shadows, namely the means of mechanical production, invisibly out of the camera frame in order to advance a perception of the Gesamtkunstwerk and Hitler as mythical and utopian. Also problematic is the fact that both Riefenstahl and Resnais shared a modernist preference for montage. If we accept Olivier Schefer's idea that "what is 'total' in the German expression *Gesamtkunstwerk* is precisely the gathering, the collection of different parts," then both *Triumph of the Will* and *Nuit et Brouillard* might qualify as modernist Gesamtkunstwerke—films that collect together fragments of reality to tell a narrative that seeks to persuade the audience towards a political ideology.[74]

All this seems to support Gerd Rienäcker's contention that the debate is less about Wagner and his theories, and more about "the reception of Wagner-reception"—how various actors have interpreted the nineteenth-century composer and his musico-social intentions.[75] I would suggest that the crucial take-away is more about perception, namely that these works must continue to be "perceived" actively by scholars rather than passively "received" as part of a crystallized reception history. Such critical scrutiny is important given that each of these modernist Gesamtkunstwerke not only have embedded political agenda, but also inherent contradictions that are central to their rich and problematic reception histories—histories that continue today. Where I believe Eisler succeeds, and where the other might be accused of failing, is in his ability not just to perceive these contradictions but to articulate them openly in a way that exposes the disharmonious and unresolved relationships at the core of mid-century modernist film—between sound and image, between generations of composers, between various ideologies of political art. "This is part of musical intelligence," he assures us. It might be that the other part falls to us, as critics and audiences—that is, to listen for them in the unlikeliest of places.

Notes

1. Albrecht Betz, "Music and Politics: Theme and Variation," in *Hanns Eisler: A Miscellany*, ed. David Blake (Luxembourg, 1995), 399.
2. Ibid., 395.
3. Eisler's music had been banned soon after the Nazi takeover in 1933, as part of a general crackdown on German communism enabled by the "Emergency Decree of the Reich President for the Protection of the People and State" of 28 February 1933. During his North American exile, he worked at the New School for Social Research in New York and was also a visiting professor at the Mexico Conservatory. While in Los Angeles, Eisler worked extensively in Hollywood and held a teaching post at the University of Southern California.
4. Pamela Potter, "What is 'Nazi Music'?" *The Musical Quarterly* 88, no. 3 (2005): 447.
5. Sally Bick, "A Double Life in Hollywood: Hanns Eisler's Score for the Film *Hangmen Also Die* and the Covert Expressions of a Marxist Composer," *Musical Quarterly* 93, no. 1 (2010): 124.
6. That same year, Disney released its propagandistic animated short, "Education for Death," which also employed Wagnerian motifs to mark its Nazi characters. See Matthew Wilson Smith, *The Total Work of Art: From Bayreuth to Cyberspace* (New York, 2007), 112–13.
7. Juliet Koss, *Modernism after Wagner* (Minneapolis, 2010), 263.
8. Theodor Adorno and Hanns Eisler, *Composing for the Films* (London, 1994), 6.
9. See Joy Calico, "Epic Gesamtkunstwerk," in this volume.
10. Smith, *Total Work of Art*, 79.
11. Calico, "Epic Gesamtkunstwerk."
12. Smith, *Total Work of Art*, 8.
13. Betz, "Music and Politics," 395.
14. "Das höchste gemeinsame Kunstwerk ist das Drama: nach seiner möglichen Fülle kann es nur vorhanden sein, wenn in ihm jede Kunstart in ihrer höchsten Fülle vorhanden ist." Richard Wagner, *The Art-Work of the Future*, in *The Art-Work of the Future, and Other Works*, trans. William Ashton Ellis (Lincoln, 1993), 184. When I have made alterations to Ellis's translations, the original German passage is included in the footnote for reference.
15. See Nicholas Vazsonyi, "The Play's the Thing: Schiller, Wagner, and Gesamtkunstwerk," in this collection.
16. "Auf die Bühne des Architekten und Malers tritt nun der künstlerische Mensch, wie der natürliche Mensch auf den Schauplaz der Natur." Wagner, *Art-Work of the Future*, 188.

17. "Der künstlerische Mensch kann sich nur in der Vereinigung aller Kunstarten zum gemeinsamen Kunstwerke vollkommen genügen: in jeder Vereinzelung seiner künstlerischen Fähigkeiten ist er unfrei, nicht vollständig Das, was er sein kann; wogegen er im gemeinsamen Kunstwerke frei, und vollständig Das ist, was er sein kann." Ibid., 183.
18. "In ihm, dem unmittelbaren Darsteller, vereinigen sich die drei Schwesterkünste zu einer gemeinsamen Wirksamkeit." Ibid., 189.
19. "Das Volk ist der Inbegriff aller Derjenigen, welche eine gemeinschaftliche Noth empfinden ... und nur das Volk handelt nach Nothwendigkeit, daher unwiderstehlich, siegreich und einzig wahr." Ibid., 74.
20. Koss, *Modernism*, 22.
21. Ibid.
22. Wagner, *Art-Work of the Future*, 71.
23. "Nur im freudigen Bewußtsein seines Zusammenhanges mit der Natur überwindet der Mensch aber seine Abhängigkeit von ihr; ihre Abhängigkeit vom Leben überwindet die Kunst aber nur im Zusammenhange mit dem Leben wahrhafter..." Ibid., 71.
24. Ibid., 77.
25. Ibid., 77, 88.
26. Smith, *Total Work of Art*, 9.
27. Ibid., 14. Smith observes that Wagner's ideas in this regard are heavily indebted to Johann Christoph Friedrich von Schiller's ideas of the "Aesthetic State" in his epistolary treatise, *On the Aesthetic Education of Man in a Series of Letters* (1794).
28. Crispin Sartwell, *Political Aesthetics* (Ithaca, 2010), 18, 19.
29. Frederic Spotts, *Hitler and the Power of Aesthetics* (London, 2002), 20.
30. Betz, "Music and Politics," 398–99.
31. Hellmut Lehmann-Haupt, *Art under a Dictatorship* (New York, 1973), xviii–xix.
32. See Wagner, "What is German," in *Art and Politics*, trans. William Ashton Ellis (Lincoln, 1995), 149–70.
33. David B. Dennis, *Inhumanities: Nazi Interpretations of Western Culture* (Cambridge, 2012), 38.
34. Ibid., 49.
35. Ibid., 377.
36. Ibid., 380.
37. Potter, "What is 'Nazi Music'?," 440, 447.
38. Bertolt Brecht, "The Modern Theater is the Epic Theater," in *Modernism: An Anthology of Sources and Documents*, ed. Vassiliki Kolocotroni, Jane Goldman, and Olga Taxidou (Chicago, 1998), 466.
39. Ibid., 467.
40. Potter, "What is 'Nazi Music'?," 448; and Koss, *Modernism*, 262.
41. Brecht, "A Short Organum for the Theater," in *Playwrights on Playwriting: The Meaning and Making of Modern Drama from Ibsen to Ionesco*, ed. Toby Cole (New York, 1960), 102, 104. See also Finger and Follett, "Introduction," in *The Aesthetic of the Total Artwork: On Borders and Fragments* (Baltimore, 2011), 6, in which they ask, "Does the joining together of the arts compromise their individual integrity or that of the spectator/participant, generating a sort of *Gleichschaltung*, or forced homogenization and participation?"
42. Koss, *Modernism*, 262.
43. Ibid., 254.
44. Ibid., 263.

45. Theodor W. Adorno, *In Search of Wagner*, trans. Rodney Livingstone (New York, 1991), 46.
46. Eisler, as quoted in "Ask me More about Brecht: Conversations with Hans Bunge," in *Hanns Eisler: A Miscellany*, 426–27.
47. Leni Riefenstahl, *Leni Riefenstahl: A Memoir* (New York, 1993), 107.
48. Smith, *Total Work of Art*, 93.
49. Ibid.
50. David Roberts, *The Total Work of Art in European Modernism* (Ithaca, 2011), 250.
51. Linda Schulte-Sasse, "Leni Riefenstahl's Feature Films and the Question of a Fascist Aesthetic," *Cultural Critique* 18 (1991): 143.
52. Smith notes that these glimpses of the workers behind the "total work"—the shadow of a cameraman on a statue; the elevator rising to capture the aerial shot—ultimately reveal the cracks in Riefenstahl's Gesamtkunstwerk. These fissures become evidence of an inherent tension within the total work of art—that between unity and fragmentation; community and individual. As he notes, "No 'organic' artwork, after all, is entirely able to avoid revealing its own mechanical traces." Smith, *Total Work of Art*, 103.
53. As David Dennis notes, the similarities between Windt's score and Wagner's music are so striking that Windt's score has often been misattributed to Wagner throughout its critical reception. See David B. Dennis, "'The Most German of all German Operas': *Die Meistersinger* through the Lens of the Third Reich," in *Wagner's Meistersinger: Performance, History, Representation*, ed. Nicholas Vazsonyi (Rochester, 2003), 98–99.
54. For a discussion of Windt's musical aesthetic, see Michael Walter, "Die Musik des Olympiafilms von 1938," *Acta Musicological* 62, no. 1 (1990): 82–113.
55. Smith, *Total Work of Art*, 102–3.
56. Ibid., 93.
57. Riefenstahl, *A Memoir*, 165.
58. Roberts, *Total Work of Art*, 249, 250.
59. *Triumph of the Will: Triumph des Willens—das Dokument vom Reichsparteitag 1934*, DVD SFD 0115, directed by Leni Riefenstahl (Bloomington, IL: Synapse Films 2001). Translation by the author.
60. Sartwell, *Political Aesthetics*, 28–29. Sartwell is not describing this specific scene, nor is he engaging with Gesamtkunstwerk directly, but his aesthetic conclusions about *Triumph of the Will* resonate well with both.
61. Steven Bach, *Leni: The Life and Work of Leni Riefenstahl* (New York, 2007), 137.
62. Joachim C. Fest, *Hitler* (New York, 2002), 373, 391. Here, Fest describes Hitler's rise to power in 1933 as both a political and symbolic campaign, metaphors perhaps applicable to the political symbolism of *Triumph of the Will*.
63. Richard Raskin, *Nuit et Brouillard: On the Making, Reception, and Functions of a Major Documentary Film* (Aarhus, Denmark, 1987), 28. See also the concept of "symbolic casting" in Julia Goodwin and Margaret Menninger's contribution to this volume.
64. Alain Resnais, "Für Hanns Eisler," in *Sinn und Form*, Sonderheft Hanns Eisler (1964), 374.
65. Peter Bürger, *Theory of the Avant-Garde*, trans. Michael Shaw (Minneapolis, 1999), 72. Also cited in Smith, *Total Work of Art*, 79.
66. David Blake, "The Early Music," in *Hanns Eisler: A Miscellany*, 54–56.
67. Ibid., 57.
68. Ibid., 56n28.
69. Resnais, "Für Hanns Eisler," 373.

70. Sartwell, *Political Aesthetics*, 43.
71. Potter, "What is 'Nazi Music'?", 447.
72. Sartwell, *Political Aesthetics*, 42.
73. Koss, *Modernism*, 263.
74. Olivier Schefer, "Variations on Totality: Romanticism and the Total Work of Art," in Finger and Follett, *Aesthetics*, 32.
75. Gerd Rienäcker, *Musik Theater im Experiment, fünfundzwanzig Aufsätze* (Berlin, 2004), 201.

Amy Lynn Wlodarski is the author of *Musical Witness and Holocaust Representation* (Cambridge, 2015), and co-editor, with Elaine Kelley, of *Art Outside the Lines: New Perspectives on GDR Art Culture* (Rodopi, 2011). Her scholarship has been published in leading musicological journals and received national recognition. She teaches at Dickinson College, Pennsylvania.

CHAPTER 7

Reconciling the "Three Graceful Hellenic Sisters"

Wagner, Dance, and Song-Ballets Set to Richard Strauss's Vier letzte Lieder

WAYNE HEISLER, JR.

It is difficult to imagine that any performed artwork could aspire to "totality" without the inclusion of dance. Indeed, at this juncture in the present collection, it seems fruitful to begin a chapter concerning articulations of Gesamtkunstwerk in twentieth-century dance by considering dance's slippery status in the concept. In the earliest known usage (1827) of the term "Gesamtkunstwerk," Karl Friedrich Eusebius Trahndorff specified four art forms: word-sound (*Wortklang*), music, facial expression (*Mimik*), and dance.[1] This primary status of dance was one aspect of an early-Romantic project that Richard Wagner inherited. Collapsing *Mimik* as a mode of gesture into dance, Wagner theorized a "Kunstwerk der Zukunft" (artwork of the future) with Greek drama as his primary referent. He put forth the metaphor of the arts as "three graceful Hellenic sisters"—Dance, Music, and Poetry—first mentioned in *Die Kunst und die Revolution* (*Art and Revolution*, 1849) and developed further in *Das Kunstwerk der Zukunft* (*The Artwork of the Future*, also 1849). Nevertheless, one might justifiably overlook the important position that Wagner awarded to dance in his early theoretical writings. While Wagner's *Mimik* embraced all stage movement, dance in its own right remained an outlier in his operas and music dramas: a ballet-pantomime for Rienzi's victory pageant in *Rienzi*; the Bacchantes and later reluctantly added Venusberg ballet (for Paris) in *Tannhäuser*; dancing apprentices in the final scene of *Die Meistersinger von Nürnberg*; and the ballet of the Flower Maidens in *Parsifal*.[2]

What exactly is "dance" "in its own right"? By dance, Trahndorff likely meant French and Italian ballet rooted in classical technique. Wagner's point of reference was ballet, too, especially the Romantic ballet in French grand opera. His eventual reclassification of dance as but one form of stage movement reflected his dissatisfaction with ballet in opera, which in practice did not meet the criterion of serving the drama that is implied by *Mimik*. In *Das Kunstwerk der Zukunft*, Wagner identified opera as the "seeming point of reunion" for the arts—*seeming* because "[m]usic claims for herself the supreme right of legislation therein." He then recounted the clash between the "sisters" in opera. Accordingly, Dance

> has only to espy some gap in the breath-taking of the dominating songstress, some chilling of the lava-stream of musical emotion—and in an instant she extends her legs across the entire stage; trounces sister Music off the scene, down to the solitary confinement of the orchestra; and turns, spins, and whirls around, until the public can no longer see the forest for the trees, i.e., the opera for the legs.[3]

Nonetheless, Wagner's ever-evolving conception of music drama progressively limited dance's importance. In the 1851 essay "Eine Mitteilung an meine Freunde" (A Communication to My Friends), for instance, we see that he has transformed the ternary sister-symbol into a binary conception, language versus music, with dance categorized as a function of music due to their shared rhythmic underpinning.[4] In *Oper und Drama* (*Opera and Drama*, also 1851), Wagner declares Beethoven's Seventh Symphony to be the "apotheosis of the dance," but again he aligns dance with gesture, suggesting that dance and spoken language have an analogous relationship to music: "The gesture of dance, like gesture in general, is to orchestral melody what the spoken verse is to the vocal melody that conditions it."[5] To put the gesture–dance–language nexus in terms that Wagner adopted following his immersion in the philosophy of Arthur Schopenhauer: gesture, dance, and language are all phenomenal manifestations of the noumenal intimated by music.

Daniel Albright writes of ballet as "opera's Other," and hones in on the "certain strain or even fracture related to the co-presence of dancing and singing ... where there is little sense of Gesamtkunstwerk but a strong sense of *Zerstückelnkunstwerk* (shattered work of art)."[6] In relation to Wagner specifically, Matthew Smith identifies the body—dance's medium—as "threateningly marginal to idealist totality" and thus the source of "two principal neuroses": "fear of absorption from without" (e.g., "the larger totality of mass spectacle"); and "fear of contamination from within ... by corrupt bodies of the (racial, sexual, ethnic, class-based) Other—or else, more generally, of contamination of the Gesamtkunstwerk by the material body itself."[7] Are dancing bodies, then, too perilous for "total" art? Should sister dance just hang up her slippers?

Whereas Wagner's skepticism about dance's dramatic and symbolic relevance ultimately led him to exclude virtually all dance from his dramas, the years after his death witnessed numerous efforts within the dance community to reclaim the promise Wagner originally saw in dance. Indeed, fueled by goals of totality, unity, integration, and synthesis, choreographers and dancers reimagined ballet as a total theatrical form, in terms that were either deliberately derived from Wagner or that at least exposed affinities with him. This development is especially evident in a subgenre of modern dance and ballet I term "song-ballets"—that is choreographies of texted songs. While song-ballets do not dominate twentieth-century dance history, they occupy a compelling margin. More importantly, through their engagement with dance, music, and poetry (the elements of Wagner's early, tripartite conception), song-ballets attest to Gesamtkunstwerk's continued inspirational power, even absent an effort to replicate Wagner directly.

In particular, this chapter examines choreographies of the most prevalent songs in the song-ballet repertory: the ever-popular *Vier letzte Lieder* (Four Last Songs) for soprano and orchestra by Richard Strauss (1864–1949), composed between 1946 and 1948 and set to three poems by Hermann Hesse—"Frühling" (Spring), "September," and "Beim Schlafengehen" (Going to Sleep)—as well as one by Joseph von Eichendorff, "Im Abendrot" (At Twilight). I explore the ways in which two ballets set to Strauss's songs, Maurice Béjart's *Serait-ce la mort?* (Could this be death?, 1970) and Rudi van Dantzig's *Vier letzte Lieder* (1977) are legible as something akin to dance-centered Gesamtkunstwerke through the interworking of choreography, staging, poetry, and music. I focus on Béjart and Van Dantzig for two reasons: first, despite contrasting techniques, styles, and aesthetics, they produce effects that can be read as operating within the wide bounds of a Gesamtkunstwerk ideal; second, and more practically, both of their *Vier letzte Lieder* ballets are preserved and accessible on video.

In the context of post-Wagnerian dance, I understand the *gesamt* of Gesamtkunstwerk ("total," "unified," "integrated," or "synthesized") above all in terms of reconciliation; song-ballets are thus "reconciled" artworks—a modifier also used by dancer-choreographer Agnes de Mille when describing Martha Graham's creative process.[8] As I discuss, the simultaneity of choreography and words in song-ballets is fraught with conflict in twentieth-century dance; the apparent invocations of Gesamtkunstwerk generally, and at times Wagner specifically, justify the reunion of dance, music, and poetry. Reconciliation is also a theme that is central to Strauss's *Vier letzte Lieder*. Among his most widely performed and lauded compositions, these songs witness the resolution and transcendence of competing aspects of Strauss's oeuvre: Romantic, modern, and avant-garde; dramatic and lyric; and his acknowledged poles of inspiration in Mozart and Wagner.[9] Adoration of the *Vier letzte Lieder* also stems from the circumstances of their composition. Music theorist Timothy Jackson interpreted these songs as an expression of "the *Not* [distress] of the postwar period—both [Strauss's] own personal *Not* and the larger *Not* of Europe," in the context of the elderly composer's spiritual affliction given his complex relationship with the Third Reich and the devastation of war.[10] Strauss died in 1949 at the age of eighty-five, eight months before the *Vier letzte Lieder*'s premiere; consonant with their poems, these songs represent a reckoning of life and death, of body and spirit.[11] A further aspect of the *Vier letzte Lieder* that demands resolution is related to their ontological precariousness, which resonates with the trope of "songs-from-the-deathbed"—of the composer, of German culture, of ethical civilization. These songs were assembled, ordered, and titled posthumously by Strauss's English publisher, Ernst Roth. Were there only four? Were they conceived as a cycle? In what order should they be performed?[12] As this examination of Béjart and Van Dantzig illustrates, both men engage with the themes of conflict, grief, transience, and acceptance that permeate Strauss's work through a medium—song-ballet—that rectifies the historic separation of dance, music, and poetry.

Dance and Song after Wagner

It is a truism that the Gesamtkunstwerk concept waxed and waned with the passage from the late nineteenth century into the twentieth. Of course, many strains of twentieth-century Wagner reception were colored by Nietzsche, whose suspicion of the Wagnerian project is too well known to require discussion here. An oft-cited later example is Bertolt Brecht's rejection of Wagnerian Gesamtkunstwerk as "witchcraft," although as Joy Calico demonstrates in this volume, Brecht's epic theater effectively reconnected with Wagner's earliest conception of Gesamtkunstwerk, even if they worked from divergent aesthetic and socio-political premises.[13] That Strauss himself was entranced by dance at various junctures of his career also reveals Nietzsche's influence and further highlights Strauss's Janus-faced Wagnerism: he remained true to Wagner in terms of compositional technique (harmony, orchestration) but, under Nietzsche's sway, rejected Wagnerian metaphysics. Ultimately, Strauss's two original ballet scores—*Josephslegende* (1914) and *Schlagobers* (1924)—along with a handful of arrangements and orchestrations prepared for choreographers, languished, while his real presence in later ballet and modern dance was through non-dance scores (choreographies of the *Vier letzte Lieder* being the most prominent example).[14]

In dance, ambivalence to the notion of Gesamtkunstwerk predated Strauss and Wagner, rooted in a fear that music would dominate movement. Stephanie Jordan highlights that practitioners and theorists of early twentieth-century dance often espoused modernist values of duality, juxtaposition, disruption, and disjunction between music and movement rather than unity and integration.[15] However, she also emphasizes that a belief in dance-centered syntheses of the arts never disappeared entirely. For instance, that Wagner was on the radar of modernist dance and ballet is attested to by Serge Diaghilev's Ballets Russes, at least early on, in whose historiography a Gesamtkunstwerk ideal (and Wagner) looms large.[16]

Another example is American dancer-choreographer Isadora Duncan, who was, in fact, a crucial inspiration for the Ballets Russes. Duncan's dance aesthetic was an anti-balletic expression of the soul—the body's externalization of sensations and emotions triggered by music—in forms indebted to ancient Greek vase paintings. Having danced Beethoven's Seventh Symphony with the Metropolitan Opera Orchestra under conductor Walter Damrosch, Duncan defaulted to Wagner to describe the experience: "At the first stroke [of the baton] there surges within me the combined symphonic chord of all the instruments in one. The mighty reverberation rushes over me and I become the Medium to condense in unified expression the joy of Brunhilde awakened by Siegfried, or the soul of Isolde seeking in Death her realization."[17] Of course, Duncan also danced Wagner's music, including Isolde's *Liebestod*.

Later, dancer-choreographer Doris Humphrey revealed that Wagner's concerns had outlived Romantic Idealism when she placed herself in the lineage of Duncan and the Ballets Russes. Humphrey's account of the separation of the arts is a gloss on centuries-old narratives that Wagner also voiced:

> Music (the vocal kind especially) and movement have been linked from the very beginning. They were handmaidens ... Roughly by the Middle Ages the two arts seemed to be pulling apart, and they have been pulling apart more and more. They are concerned with their own techniques, with their own theory, with their own procedures. They tend, first of all, not only to drift apart but to forget their heritage ... They not only forget their common origins but also their interdependence.[18]

Like Wagner, Humphrey looked back to distant pasts. Modifying the sisters' metaphor, she intimated the raison d'être of the arts: as handmaidens, music and dance serve each other in serving art itself. Humphrey's diagnosis of their separation targeted technical display and aesthetic self-justification, recalling Wagner's derision of ballet as a spectacle of legs to the peril of drama.

The ideal of the arts serving something greater was recurrent in twentieth-century dance. Composer Wallingford Riegger describes a "well-rounded work of art" in which music and dance are equals, "interwoven to form an organic unit which was neither pure choreography nor pure music, nor their sum, but a fusion into something else for which we have no name."[19] As Riegger acknowledged, though, that "something else" was analogous to music drama. Another example is dancer-choreographer Lester Horton, who expressed a preference for "the making of new music simultaneously with the making of choreography" with the goal of "welding" them "to achieve a homogeneity which is a stronger entity than either separate one"[20]—something of which Wagner dreamed, too.

Clearly, many in twentieth-century dance strove to unite dance with music; composer Vivian Fine regarded them as "two sisters ... [who] create patterns of inter-relatedness that enhance the total work."[21] But what, then, of dance—the arts' third sister, mythologically and historically? In her account of the segregation of the arts, Humphrey reported that in dance "words are rarely used, and movements and music carry all the responsibility of communication."[22] Nevertheless, throughout modern history, dance, music, and words coexisted in various ways, especially in French lyric traditions such as Baroque opéra-ballet as well as the long-standing convention of including ballet numbers at the Paris Opéra, which Wagner confronted (with *Tannhäuser*). Dance could be desirable in opera to decorate the story and/or setting, thus supporting the plot; to embellish opera at symbolic moments in terms unique to dance; and/or to provide respite from "normal" narrative and musical flow.[23] The above instances relate to dance treading on operatic turf; French Romantic ballet offers examples of opera being conjured on dance's terrain. In Romantic ballet of the 1830s and 1840s, sung words were absent, but lexical song was evoked by the orchestra, which referenced excerpts of well-known texted melodies (*airs parlants*) from opera, folk, and popular song. In tandem with narrative pantomime and onstage placards transmitting textual cues, such "singing" verifies the belief in the mutually enriching power of language, dance, and music.[24]

For his part, Wagner claimed an allergy to such eclecticism (although in practice he was immune neither to eclecticism nor to France), eclecticism that would seem antithetical to Gesamtkunstwerk. The subsequent history and historiography of modern dance and ballet attest to a continued insistence on the integrity of the sister arts. Beginning in the late nineteenth century and intensifying into the mid-twentieth, words were resolutely deemed anathema to dance. The path from the nineteenth century proper and Wagner to dance modernism was laid by the symbolists. In his 1886 essay "Ballets," Stéphane Mallarmé portrayed the moving, dancing body as abstract, "a corporeal scripture [that] one would need many paragraphs of dialogue as well as descriptive prose to express ... a poem disengaged from all the apparatus of writing."[25] This view, above all others, drove modern dance and ballet, which generally insisted on freedom from "paragraphs." As Joan Acocella contends, modernism restaged the divide between abstraction and representation, or between classicists and realists, respectively. For realists "the power of dance ... lay in representation: character, incidents, a good story, about life," although it warrants emphasizing that realists ultimately shared with classicists an investment in *dance itself* as the primary medium, whether representational or not. That is, dancers across the abstract–representational divide transposed Gesamtkunstwerk to a dance-centric key and were united in various degrees by the notion that "the only kind of story dance could tell was a dance story, a construction of open symbols created by formal means: rhythm, shape, phrasing, and so on." For classicists, a "literary" ballet "was a contradiction in terms, or at best a bastardization";[26] a ballet that actually incorporated words was a stretch—even for most realists.

As Acocella acknowledges, however, the classicist-realist divide has been permeable, a crucial point for assessing Gesamtkunstwerk's legacy and its value for understanding strains of it in modern dance and ballet. Ballets set to texted music by choreographers of diverse technical and aesthetic stripes exemplify Acocella's point about the continuities in twentieth-century dance. While a comprehensive inventory of song-ballets is not possible here, I offer an overview of the subgenre in Table 7.1.

Table 7.1: Selective Inventory of Song-Ballets

Choreographer	**Ballet Title**	**Music**
Antony Tudor	*Dark Elegies* (1937)	Gustav Mahler, *Kindertotenlieder*
Tudor	*Shadow of the Wind* (1948)	Mahler, *Das Lied von der Erde*
Frederick Ashton	*Illuminations* (1950)	Benjamin Britten, *Les Illuminations*
Tudor	*Hail and Farewell* (1959)	Richard Strauss, Festmarsch, Op. 1; Serenade for Thirteen Wind Instruments, Op. 7; and *Vier letzte Lieder*
Rudi van Dantzig	*Vergezicht* (Distant View, 1960)	Robert Schumann, *Frauenliebe und Leben*
Brian MacDonald	*How Do I Love Thee* (1962)	Strauss, *Vier letzte Lieder*
Maurice Béjart	*Mathilde* (1963)	Richard Wagner, *Fünf Gedichte für eine Frauenstimme*, aka *Wesendonck-Lieder*
Kenneth MacMillan	*Song of the Earth* (1965)	Mahler, *Das Lied von der Erde*
Eliot Feld	*At Midnight* (1967)	Mahler, *Sieben Lieder aus letzter Zeit*, aka *Rückert-Lieder*
Béjart	*Serait-ce la mort?* (1970)	Strauss, *Vier letzte Lieder*
Feld	*Early Songs* (1970)	Strauss, fourteen early songs
Béjart	*Le chant du compagnon errant* (1971)	Mahler, *Lieder eines fahrenden Gesellen*
Lorca Massine	*Four Last Songs* (1971)	Strauss, *Vier letzte Lieder*
Robert Joffrey	*Remembrances* (1973)	Wagner, *Wesendonck-Lieder*
Pina Bausch	*Adagio—Five Songs by Gustav Mahler* (1974)	Mahler, Symphony no. 10 and *Kindertotenlieder*
Van Dantzig	*Vier letzte Lieder* (1977)	Strauss, *Vier letzte Lieder*
Béjart	*Amor di Poeta* (1978)	Schumann, *Dichterliebe*
Van Dantzig	*Antwoord gevend* (Giving Answer, 1980)	Anton Webern, various songs, instrumental and choral works

Song-ballets emerged during the World War II era and became more common by the 1960s at the height of the abstract–representational divide. Although an international phenomenon, most song-ballets have been set to music of Austro-Germanic composers—especially Strauss and Mahler—from the late-Romantic/early-modernist periods, the very era in which the Wagnerian Gesamtkunstwerk reached its pinnacle. The trend of choreographing orchestral Lieder, which given their fuller instrumental resources and presentation on larger, theatrical stages arguably evoke opera, is noteworthy; exceptions include Schumann, early Strauss, and Webern songs with piano. Particularly striking is the popularity of Strauss's *Vier letzte Lieder*, set by more choreographers than any other Strauss score save his ballet-pantomime *Josephslegende* (originally created for the 1914 Ballet Russes season).[27]

Song-ballets across the spectrum raise a number of questions about Gesamtkunstwerk theory and practice. In what ways do text and music shape the forms and meanings of dance, and vice versa? How does dance expand upon the signification of songs (textual, musical), and vice versa? Might singing be regarded as acoustic "movement" analogous to dancing? Might dancing be regarded as a mode of lyricism analogous to singing? Can ballets with words retain abstraction? Are the multiplied interrelationships between the three sisters an evolution of Wagner? Are song-ballets an interstice—not song, not ballet?

Béjart

Maurice Béjart (1927–2007) was infamous for ritualistic, dance-centered spectacles, derivative and pretentious to some (particularly American and British critics) while ultra-modern and socio-politically profound to others.[28] Because Wagner provided explicit inspiration for Béjart, in terms of aesthetics generally and Gesamtkunstwerk specifically, it is fitting to explore how both views of Béjart reveal connections to Wagner. For starters, Béjart choreographed Wagner's music, including the song-ballet *Mathilde* (1965), set to the *Wesendonck-Lieder*; *Les Vainqueurs* (The Conquerors, 1968) to excerpts from *Tristan und Isolde* along with Indo-Tibetan ragas; and *Ring um den Ring* (Ring around the Ring, 1990) to portions of Wagner's tetralogy. That Mathilde began as a Wagner-inspired novel—*Mathilde, ou Le Temps perdu* (Mathilde, or The Lost Time, 1963), reprinted in Béjart's collection *Le Ballet des mots* (The Ballet of Words, 1994), demonstrates that while his main medium was dance, Béjart, like Wagner, was also immersed in music and literature and was preoccupied with bringing the arts together.

Béjart's harshest critics revealed the Wagnerian resonances most plainly. "There is a hint of demagogic appeal here that has no place in art," wrote dance critic Anna Kisselgoff in a review of Béjart's company, the Ballet du XXe siècle (Ballet of the Twentieth Century), during their first American residency at the Brooklyn Academy of Music in 1971.[29] Following the 1971 US premiere of Béjart's seminal *Messe pour le temps présent* (Mass for the Present Time, 1967) with electronic music by Pierre Henry, critic Clive Barnes allowed that "[i]n most of Maurice Béjart's work, even the worst, there is usually a shrewd kind of theatricality." Nonetheless, the *Messe*, "while having the surface appearance of modernity or unsuccessful novelty, is fundamentally provincial in the way in which it is a dim rejection of other work."[30] Demagoguery, theatricality, novelty, provinciality, unoriginality—all refrains in Béjart reception, whose correspondences with Wagner are even more apparent in critic Marcia Siegel's assessment:

> Béjart has created an aura for himself, and a fanatical audience for his work. He panders to them by claiming to have founded a new art form which, naturally, won't be understood by the sophisticated snobs but which the common people in their honest sensitivity can embrace; he stuns them with an eclecticism that borrows successful effects from everywhere and risks no inventions of its own; and he disarms them by bravado with which he reduces tremendous ideas to their least common denominator.[31]

By implication Siegel evoked phantasmagoria, which, in Theodor W. Adorno's view, Wagner mastered. On the one hand, Béjart's populism might be viewed as paralleling Wagnerian Gesamtkunstwerk's roots in the Volk; that is to say, what takes place in the theater both reflects and constitutes the masses. But whereas Wagner imagined an audience with shared myths and bloodlines, Béjart envisioned more sincere inclusiveness, at once crossing the line into commercial "art" (hence Siegel's connotation of kitsch) and offering something of a politicized revision to circumvent Wagner's conservative politics and their effects.

By occasionally taking dance out of the theater to sports arenas, circus tents, and outdoor spaces, Béjart was guided by his self-stated philosophy of "giving dance to everyone"—a conscious reinterpretation of Wagner's belief (after philosopher Ludwig Feuerbach) in redemption through love.[32] Related to Béjart's communal embrace are his choreographies for public spaces: for example, *Nijinski, Clown de dieu* (Nijinsky, Clown of God, 1971) was created for the Forest National Auditorium in Brussels and landed at Madison Square Garden in 1972; and *Il Trionfi di Petrarca* (The Triumphs of Petrarch, 1974) was conceived for Florence's Boboli Gardens. Analogous to Wagner's insistence on the centrality of the festival theater at Bayreuth for music drama, Béjart treated environment and architecture as supportive of dramatic art in what Pamela Gay-White termed the choreographer's "total stage form": an aesthetic, dance-centered offshoot of Wagnerian music drama, but again, with contrasting socio-political aspirations.[33]

Premiered in 1970 by Ballet du XXe siècle in Marseilles, Béjart's *Serait-ce la mort?* (Could This Be Death?) occupies a small subgroup of his work: "straight ballets," or choreographies rooted in ballet classicism, with linear narrative eschewed in favor of symbolic meaning that is channeled through dance.[34] Thus, while this ballet seems at first glance to be technically atypical of Béjart's trademark spectacles, *Serait-ce la mort?* is consistent with his oeuvre in its indebtedness to post-Wagnerian symbolist Gesamtkunstwerk dramaturgy. As Jean-Louis Rousseau notes, in Béjart's works

> dance is a total means of expression, a vehicle for the whole being, for all emotions and thoughts, the rival of music and poetry … Béjart demands that the various artistic disciplines blend into a single expressive whole, mingling words and music, basing movement on the rhythms of a sacred text as easily as on the ticking of a metronome, breaking down the barriers between different kinds of stage spectacle in order to arrive at one limitless spectacle.[35]

For Wagner, opera's integrity as drama was sacrificed in the poetry–music–dance sisterhood-*cum*-rivalry. While movement was an important element of music drama, dance arguably became its greatest casualty. By contrast, Béjart's work is dance centered: dance is his principal medium, and as the foundation for a total experience—feeling and thinking, body and mind, music and poetry—dance brokers reconciliation of distinct ways of being and knowing. The keyword is "limitless": dance for Béjart is synthesis itself and the vehicle to achieve everything for which the arts—indeed, everything for which *we*—strive.

Serait-ce la mort? stages a dying man's encounters with women he has loved.[36] The curtain rises before the orchestra begins playing to reveal a whited-out landscape. To the sound of stormy winds, a man approaches center stage; one by one, a woman emerges from each of the four corners, executes an arabesque, and poses with arms crossed. In turn, the women reach for him and then follow his lead, forming a diagonal chain with the man at the center. When "Frühling," the first of the *Vier letzte Lieder*, begins, the whole group dances a pas de cinq. While the music-less introduction charted the passage of recollection, the first song takes place in the realm of memory, marked by the orchestra's initial strains. When conceiving *Serait-ce la mort?*, Béjart approached the *Vier letzte Lieder* with an eye towards their total context: poetic, musical, and cultural-historical. By investing Strauss's music with the power to evoke the past, Béjart symbolically connected his ballet's argument to the composer's "past-ness": à propos of the dying man's recollections, these autumnal songs also represent Strauss's journey back, in a belated Romantic musical idiom with texts from and reflective of that bygone era.

In "Frühling," winter exalts in the memory of trees, breezes, scents, and birdsong. Spring returns and winter welcomes spring bodily: "Your presence quivers through all my limbs" (*es zittert durch alle meine Glieder*). That spring possesses and is embodied by winter in the poem has its correlate in Béjart's choreography. Linguistic and musical evocations of spring effect physical reverberations in the form of invigorated lyrical dancing to increasingly longer vocal phrases (two beats in 6/8 time on "trees," nearly four on "breezes," nine on "birdsong"). The bodily seductiveness of "Frühling" was surely a magnet for Béjart, whose exploration of the interrelationships among words, music, voice, and body was further guided by Antonin Artaud. Artaud celebrated "pure theatre," characterized by "a new use of gesture and voice ... a new physical language ... that sort of theatrical language foreign to every *spoken tongue*."[37] Recall Rousseau's description of how Béjart "bas[ed] movement on the rhythms of a sacred text as easily as on the ticking of a metronome," which registers Artaud's relativized lexicality.[38] Artaud regarded "pure theater" as an "intense stage poetry" and "many-hued spatial language." Actor-dancers are "animated hieroglyphs," the meaning of which is received intuitively and results from syntheses of media—for example, "the musical quality of a physical movement." Béjart's Gesamtkunstwerk was, it seems, as much Artaudian as it was Wagnerian, for Béjart conceived of the body, in Gay-White's words, as "a resonator of sound, and as a locus from which is also directed a particular movement."[39] While not totally discounting the meaning of song texts, Béjart regarded language as but one bodily utterance: voices, words, and movements all issue from bodies and are materialized by dance.

Although known for spectacular theatricality, Béjart rarely indulged in traditional ballet garb such as tutus or pointe shoes.[40] In *Serait-ce la mort?* the dancer-lovers wear simple leotards and tights, which showcase the dancing body as the central(izing) medium. Scenery in the painterly, realist sense is also absent. Instead, the performance space is drowned with what Béjart described as "pools of light whose varying color and intensity create an atmosphere that is both calm and mysterious," drawing on Adolphe Appia's downgrading of scene painting and his appeal for an active use of stage lighting.[41] I infer another layer of Wagnerian influence vis-à-vis Béjart's lighting, that of Wagner's grandson, opera director Wieland Wagner. The post–World War II Gesamtkunstwerk was the one on which Béjart cut his teeth and, along with Artaud and Appia, Wieland provided a lens through which Béjart interpreted Gesamtkunstwerk. Wieland's aesthetic of abstraction informed his (Appian) declaration that, "Illuminated space has replaced the lighted canvas,"[42] which corresponds to Béjart's description of the staging of *Serait-ce la mort?* This song-ballet is "mysterious" because it is symbolic of a psychic space: a man's memory. On one level, the colors and lighting of Béjart's "pools" are icons for "Frühling" (green), "September" (orange and red), and "Beim Schlafengehen" (darkness and shadow). Nevertheless, in these poems and Strauss's songs, spring and autumn are not just seasons, nor is *Schlafengehen* bedtime. Developing the symbolism, Béjart stages a series of pas de deux between the man and each woman: in an interlude between "Frühling" and "September" (man and first woman, to the wind sounds from the prelude), in "September" (second woman), and in "Beim Schlafengehen" (third woman). Their duets represent memories of life stages; more specifically, they are kinesthetic memories of body states, for which green, orange, red, darkness, and shadow are no more direct than the temporal signifiers with which they are associated.

That fact that Strauss's posthumously assembled *Vier letzte Lieder* are somewhat precarious as a unified group or cycle seems moot to Béjart. In *Serait-ce la mort?* he merges and fuses the individual songs; he treats them as an extended dance-musico-poetic utterance, a dying man's memory journey in the presence of all three sisters. That the choreography begins before the music and words is remarkable: dance has the effect of conjuring music and poetry-in-song, and acts as the arbiter of their reconciliation. Significantly, the dancers continue to move in the non-sung, non-orchestral interludes between each song, too, as the man passes from one memory to the next.

In the fourth and final song, "Im Abendrot," an old couple (voiced by the soprano soloist) wearily reflects on their lives together. Gazing over the countryside, they embrace dusky solitude and ask, "Is this perchance death" (*ist dies etwa der Tod*)? The octogenarian Strauss famously recast Eichendorff's final line—"is that [*das*] perchance death?"—and colored the more pressing question ("is this?") as autobiographical by punctuating "death" with a self-quotation from his own earlier orchestral work *Tod und Verklärung* (Death and Transfiguration, 1890). In *Serait-ce la mort?*, "Im Abendrot" is marked in terms of the choreography, too. From a pas de quatre of the women during the song's orchestral introduction, Béjart transitions to a pas de deux between the man and the fourth and final woman. Yet she is different than the others, as he has loved but only ever "glimpsed" her.[43] Their dance is further distinguished from the three that preceded it in that it is fractured: the man and woman break away from one another, and rather than drowning in a moment together she seems to be leading him—somewhere.[44]

Might the first three women be a stand-in for the triumvirate of sisters (dance, music, and poetry—but in what order?), with the fourth representing their reconciliation? To pursue such a fanciful allegory would be to miss the message and effect of *Serait-ce la mort?*, in which the sisters' separation is impossible. The man gestures towards the enigmatic fourth woman while gazing beyond the audience, trying to reconcile her with his past, present, and future. This woman aligns *Serait-ce la mort?* with what Gay-White identified as Béjart's throwback to late nineteenth-century symbolist theater, itself indebted to Wagner: "A total staging reliant on movement to create a particular mood or dominant symbol."[45] That symbol is the fourth woman, as evidenced by the dying man's attempt to decode her. His moment of recognition, then, is one not just of death incarnate, but of death as a process incarnate in the entire ballet. Experienced through Béjart's trademark "fusion of performance symbols,"[46] dance assumes a transcendent attitude, is greater than the sum of its parts and bearer of a self-reflexive, universal moral: this is death, everyone will dance with her someday.

Van Dantzig

Mortality, the nagging preoccupation in Strauss's *Vier letzte Lieder* and Béjart's *Serait-ce la mort?*, is a theme that also runs through Rudi van Dantzig's (1933–2012) oeuvre.[47] Along with Hans van Manen and their younger contemporary Jiří Kylián, Van Dantzig secured a place for the Netherlands in the international spotlight of ballet and modern dance, first as a dancer with Sonia Gaskell and Netherlands Dance Theater, and later with the Dutch National Ballet, for which Van Dantzig served as an artistic director from 1969–1991. The axis of death, Strauss, and the *Vier letzte Lieder* links Van Dantzig with his contemporary Béjart as well. In 1975, a decade after choreographing his seminal *Monument voor een gestorven jongen* (Monument for a Dead Boy), Van Dantzig set Strauss's *Tod und Verklärung* for the ballet *Blown in the Gentle Wind*, in which a dying man, accompanied by two angels of death, experiences flashbacks from his life.[48] *Blown in a Gentle Wind* is one of Van Dantzig's "death ballets," a subset of his oeuvre Luuk Utrecht has characterized as works "concerned with the spiritual struggle to accept death as the natural solution to all life's problems."[49]

Van Dantzig and Béjart are on some levels worlds apart. Béjart's occasional classicism is but one ingredient of a choreographic-theatrical *métissage*, or seemingly indiscriminate crossbreeding.[50] Van Dantzig's works are generally rooted in classicism, which he synthesized with psychodramatic expressionism in the vein of Martha Graham and Pina Bausch.[51] But distinct movement vocabularies aside, Van Dantzig's approach to ballet as a total theatrical experience reveals an aesthetic that is compatible with Béjart, beginning with the conviction that dance is the agent that reunites the sister arts. While Van Dantzig had less explicit ties to Wagner than Béjart, the symbolism of Van Dantzig's narrative and non-narrative ballets can likewise be understood as a dance-centered articulation of Gesamtkunstwerk. In Utrecht's interpretation:

> A characteristic feature of [Van Dantzig's] dance idiom is the quality of profuse movement which with its passionate dynamic—proverbially convulsive bodies, contorted lines of dancers and explosive movements—is charged with intimations of the soul's deeper layers: that realm where the powers of reason no longer

> prevail and judgment is utterly out of true [*sic*], and where emotions are given free rein to rush headlong on an overwhelming tide.[52]

Putting Utrecht's exegesis in Schopenhauerian terms, ballet is of the order of the Will, with dance being a shadow of the noumenal. Thus, much like that of Béjart, Van Dantzig's work reveals aesthetic resonances with Wagner but diverges from him in terms of socio-political beliefs. Moreover, Van Dantzig's socially conscious ballets such as *Geverfde vogels* (Painted Birds, 1971) and *Life* (1979, a collaboration with designer and choreographer Toer van Schayk) bring together dance, music, and words in a way that is pointedly more drastic than the song-ballets outlined in Table 7.1. In *Geverfde vogels*, the dancers themselves sing "Wir setzen uns mit Tränen nieder" (We sit down in tears) from Johann Sebastian Bach's *St. Matthew Passion*, while the collage score of *Life* includes the dancers' own vocal rendition of the socialist anthem "The Internationale."[53]

Effectively a companion to both his own *Blown in a Gentle Wind* and Béjart's *Serait-ce la mort?*, Van Dantzig's *Vier letzte Lieder* was premiered by the Dutch National Ballet in 1977. This ballet is documented via several films housed at the Dance Division of the New York Public Library for the Performing Arts; I rely most heavily here on a video recording of the premiere production that was broadcast on television (produced by Nederlandse Omroep Stichting and Hessischer Rundfunk). Set against the backdrop of a stormy, hilly landscape, Van Dantzig's *Vier letzte Lieder* is prefaced by a quotation from "September," indicating that the choreographer regarded this song as the ballet's essence: "Summer smiles amazed and exhausted at the dying dream that was this garden. He lingers by the roses, yearns for rest. Slowly he closes his great weary eyes" [*Sommer lächelt erstaunt und matt/in den sterbenden Gartentraum./ Lange noch bei den Rosen/bleibt er stehen, sehnt sich nach Ruh./ Langsam tut er die großen/ müdgewordnen Augen zu*]. Unsurprising from a choreographer who also makes his dancers sing, Van Dantzig's foregrounding of poetic text—in the printed program for live performances and as an epigraph on film—is notable for its embrace of language as a vital component of a dance-centered work.

Parallel to the intermittent wind sounds in Béjart's *Serait-ce la mort?*, Van Dantzig's choreography is not restricted to Strauss's score. The start of the first song, "Frühling," is delayed by the slow, silent procession of four couples from stage left towards a lone figure, an Angel of Death. The angel is to revisit a concept introduced above in relation to Béjart, Van Dantzig's "dominant symbol." In the Vier letzte Lieder and works across Van Dantzig's oeuvre, death is "an interloper … interrupt[ing] the game by removing a loved one and leaving the world colder and emptier for those left behind … forever forcing his way into the relationship between two people."[54] By foregrounding the metaphor of "September"—mature summer facing fall as the living must face death, represented by the lording angel as an externalization of the songs' central theme—

and by filling in the spaces before and in between Strauss's songs with dance, Van Dantzig, like Béjart, tightened the bonds between the four songs. Moreover, it is striking that both ballets are built around four pas de deux. Their considerable differences notwithstanding, the degree of aesthetic consonance between Béjart's and Van Dantzig's *Vier letzte Lieder* ballets calls to mind the Gesamtkunstwerk conceit of an organic unity among the arts. Working with the same poems and music, and grounded in a shared movement idiom (classical ballet), Béjart's *Serait-ce la mort?* and Van Dantzig's *Vier letzte Lieder* are on an abstract level the same "work," albeit with different external appearances.

The interrelationships between dance, poems, and score in Van Dantzig's *Vier letzte Lieder* suggest that he was committed on a fundamental level to the Gesamtkunstwerk concept, which in turn helps to make his work legible. One reviewer put it, "[The ballet] combines text, music and choreography into a perfect unity."[55] Exiting as the music for "Frühling" begins and remaining absent for the first couple's pas de deux during that song, the Angel of Death returns only at the end of the second couple's dance in "September," where he creeps up behind them.[56] Following the last line of this song's text—"slowly [summer] closes his great weary eyes"—a solo horn recalls the vocal melody from the poem's second strophe on "summer smiles amazed," after which couple number two had parted ways temporarily. When re-voiced from soprano to horn, this melody is punctuated by the reappearance of Death, who becomes the woman's porter. One might, however, only experience the horn song at the end of "September" as nostalgic in a traditional, non-danced performance. In its initial, vocal rendering, the line "summer smiles amazed" is danced tenderly, sensually by the second couple. That the woman touches the Angel of Death at the song's end and he porters her back to her beloved, corresponding with the horn's version of the melody, suggests that the vocal line is not being simply recalled. Rather, it had been a premonition, treated by Van Dantzig as a leitmotif for an eventual meeting with Death that compelled intimacy, whether or not the lovers fully understood why.

In another review of Van Dantzig's *Vier letzte Lieder*, a critic expressed awe at how "the choreography clings skintight to the music" (*sich hauteng der Musik anschmiegt*), particularly the vocal line.[57] Van Dantzig's fusion of song and movement also mirrored Béjart's in that it drew inspiration from a particular voice and performance. Whereas Béjart channeled Elisabeth Schwarzkopf, in her classic 1965 interpretation of Strauss songs (with George Szell and the Berlin Radio Symphony), Van Dantzig turned to Gundula Janowitz's 1974 recording with the Berlin Philharmonic under Herbert von Karajan, for the Dutch National Ballet's 1977 premiere.[58] From the very first pas in "Frühling," it is striking how long and lyrical the dance phrases are. For instance, the first two dance phrases with text (the poem's inaugural stanza) last nine and eight bars, respectively. Like Strauss's melody and Janowitz's voice, Van Dantzig's choreography is lyrical. The phrases of voice and dance are enmeshed: movement intensifies as a response to vocal intensity—in pitch, dynamic, articulation, rhythm—rather than merely responding to, much less miming, the words. This intense fusion creates a chicken-and-egg situation: it is as if the singing is propelled or "breathed" by the movement onstage, which models physicality the voice cannot resist.

For the first two strophes of the third song, "Beim Schlafengehen," only couple number three appears on stage. The second strophe is followed by an instrumental interlude featuring solo violin during which the other three couples re-enter; everyone is on stage together for the first time since the ballet's silent introduction, and the additional couples function as an ensemble backdrop to the third couple's pas de deux. But the Angel of Death also reappears and takes a turn as the third woman's porter, just as he had with the second woman at the end of "September." The instrumental interlude in "Beim Schlafengehen" lies at the heart of Van Dantzig's ballet, illustrating both the reconciliation and the conjoined identity of voice and choreography. Having escaped the Angel of Death's clutches, the third woman is lifted by her partner in conjunction with the opening text of the final strophe of "Beim Schlafengehen": "And the unguarded spirit wants to soar on free wings" [*Und die Seele unbewacht/will in freien Flügen schweben*]. An obvious interpretation of this lift is as choreographic "text painting"—an illumination of the text, that visually and kinesthetically doubles the melody's high, sustained A-flat (the apex of this song so far in terms of pitch) on "spirit." Text aside, and more importantly, the lift also coexists with the re-entry of the voice. Recalling Béjart's location of the body as the common source for movement as well as singing, the instrumental interlude in Van Dantzig's "Beim Schlafengehen" is its own integrated strophe—one without words but not without song in the sense of a physical resonance, with the high note voicing movement, and acting as an agent of physical escape.

This escape is, however, only temporary, as Van Dantzig's "Im Abendrot" marks the final, inevitable passage from mortality to immortality.[59] At the song's ultimate question, "Is this perchance death?", the angel joins the willing assemblage in a movement choir. Similar to the climax of Béjart's *Serait-ce la mort?*, there is gazing into the beyond. In Van Dantzig's ballet, however, the question has already been answered. The dance continues after the final cadence has faded, with all stretching upwards, ready.

Conclusion

Alongside music and poetry, dance was a vital component in romantic theories of Gesamtkunstwerk. Dance might even be regarded as the most fitting metaphor for bringing the arts together in the first place. Although Wagner by and large jettisoned dance, he expressed the relationship of the "sisters" in *Das Kunstwerk der Zukunft* in terms of a "united chain" that gives them "life and motion"—that is, in terms of dancers *dancing*.[60] In the twentieth century, song-ballets reunited dance, music, and poetry, thereby offering diverse visions for reconciling the aesthetic, philosophical, and practical issues that had broken the sisters' chain.

Neither Béjart nor Van Dantzig was committed to revitalizing Wagnerian Gesamtkunstwerk as such. Rather, through their song-ballets and those of other twentieth-century choreographers, Gesamtkunstwerk emerged in reimagined, mediated forms. For Wagner, dance threatened to compromise dramatic integration and was blatantly phenomenal, as was mere language, while music (in the forms and idioms of opera) had metaphysical privilege as a bearer of the drama's essence. Post-Wagnerian dancers and choreographers of songs essentially returned to what Wagner had rejected: Romantic ballet, with its unashamed embrace of dance, music, and words. In song-ballets, both words *and* music are phenomenal, while bodies that dance and sing offer glimpses—visual, aural, kinesthetic—of the noumenal. Song-ballets and music dramas alike have textual narratives that interact with music and movement; but song-ballets claim the voice for the body, effectively translating Gesamtkunstwerk into a danced drama. As quintessential song-ballets, choreographies of Strauss's *Vier letzte Lieder* display solidarity in their embrace of these revered songs as a unified expression of universal phenomena—life and death, dance, music, and poetry—through embodied theatrical performances. The Gesamtkunstwerk did not go as gently as the Strauss of the *Vier letzte Lieder*, and these song-ballets reveal the persistence and malleability of an ideal, or at least a belief in the possibility of a dance-centered unity, in which words, like death, must be embraced.

Notes

1. Karl Friedrich Eusebius Trahndorff, *Aesthetik oder Lehre von der Weltanschauung und Kunst* (Berlin, 1827), trans. in Juliet Koss, *Modernism after Wagner* (Minneapolis, 2010), 13. For an archaeology of pre-nineteenth-century thought regarding gesture–word–music relations, see Mary Ann Smart, *Mimomania: Music and Gesture in Nineteenth-Century Opera* (Berkeley, 2004).
2. The Venusberg ballet in Tannhäuser represented Wagner's compromise, but also a compromise on the part of the Paris Opéra's requirements, according to which the obligatory ballet occurred in Act 2. See esp. Carolyn Abbate, "The Parisian 'Vénus' and the 'Paris' Tannhäuser," *Journal of the American Musicological Society* 36, no. 1 (1983): 80n11.
3. My translation is modified from Wagner, "The Art-Work of the Future," in *Richard Wagner's Prose Works*, trans. William Ashton Ellis (1892; reprint, New York, 1966), 1:152. On the three sisters and the necessity of "loving self-sacrifice that mirrors the

truth and necessity of the tragic action," see David Roberts, *The Total Work of Art in European Modernism* (Ithaca, 2011), 74–75.

4. Jean-Jacques Nattiez, *Wagner Androgyne: A Study in Interpretation*, trans. Stewart Spencer (Princeton, 1993), 16. See also Sanna Pederson, "From Gesamtkunstwerk to Music Drama," in this collection.
5. Trans. in Nattiez, *Wagner Androgyne*, 35.
6. Daniel Albright, "Golden Calves: The Role of Dance in Opera," *The Opera Quarterly: Performance, Theory, History* 22, no. 1 (2006): 29, 22.
7. Matthew Wilson Smith, *The Total Work of Art: From Bayreuth to Cyberspace* (New York, 2007), 5. See also Smart, "Mimomania: Allegory and Embodiment in Wagner's Music Dramas," in *Mimomania*, 163–204.
8. Agnes de Mille, *Martha: The Life and Work of Martha Graham* (1991), excerpted in Katherine Teck, comp. and ed., *Making Music for Modern Dance: Collaboration in the Formative Years of a New American Art* (New York, 2011), 149.
9. Strauss scholars regard the *Vier letzte Lieder* as his "finest in any genre" (Bryan Gilliam, *The Life of Richard Strauss* [New York, 1999], 180), and as evidence of "a genius of the highest rank" (Norman Del Mar, *Richard Strauss: A Critical Commentary on His Life and Works* [Ithaca, 1986], 3:466–67). A counterexample is Hesse (again, the poet of three of Strauss's songs), letter to Herbert Schulze dated 23 June 1957, in Hermann Hesse, *Musik: Betrachtungen, Gedichte, Rezensionen und Briefe*, ed. Volker Michels (Frankfurt, 1986), 208.
10. Timothy L. Jackson, "Ruhe, meine Seele! and the Letzte Orchesterlieder," in *Richard Strauss and His World*, ed. Bryan Gilliam (Princeton, 1992), 94.
11. On the premiere of the *Vier letzte Lieder*, see Del Mar, *Richard Strauss*, 3:466; Jackson, "Ruhe, meine Seele," 92.
12. On the *Vier letzte Lieder* as a cycle, see Alan Frank, "Strauss's Last Songs," *Music and Letters* 31 (1950): 305–6; Alan Jefferson, *The Life of Richard Strauss* (Newton Abbot, 1973), 224; Georg Balanchine and Francis Mason, *Balanchine's Complete Stories of the Great Ballets*, rev. and enlarged edn. (Garden City, 1977), 268. While the *Vier letzte Lieder* were among Strauss's last works, his song *Malven* was the *last*, completed 23 November 1948 for soprano Maria Jeritza. Jackson's argument (*"Ruhe, meine Seele"*) that Strauss's "Ruhe, meine Seele" in an orchestrated version of his own earlier (1894) Lied setting of a poem by Karl Henckell should be included in what he dubs the "letzte Orchesterlieder" (i.e., not just four), is in many respects convincing. Still, it does not explain why Strauss, who chose the singer (Kirsten Flagstad) for the premiere, did not specify the order of the songs, much less the inclusion of "Ruhe, meine Seele."
13. Bertolt Brecht, "Notes on the Opera *Aufstieg und Fall der Stadt Mahagonny*," in *Brecht on Theatre: The Development of an Aesthetic*, ed. and trans. John Willett (New York, 1964), 37–38. Precedents for Calico's argument for viewing the Gesamtkunstwerk and modernism as polarities "bound together by the current flowing between them" include Anke Finger and Danielle Follett, eds, *The Aesthetics of the Total Artwork: On Borders and Fragments* (Baltimore, 2011); Roberts, *Total Work of Art*; Koss, *Modernism after Wagner*; Smith, *Total Work of Art*.
14. See Wayne Heisler, Jr., *The Ballet Collaborations of Richard Strauss* (Rochester, 2009). The most recent and authoritative exploration of Strauss's Nietzscheism is in Charles Youmans, *Richard Strauss's Orchestral Music and the German Intellectual Tradition: The Philosophical Roots of Musical Modernism* (Bloomington, 2005). Monika Woitas also made the point that Strauss's non-dance scores are the ones that became relevant to

twentieth-century dance. Woitas, "Richard Strauss und das Tanztheater seiner Zeit," in *Richard Strauss und die Moderne*, ed. Bernd Edelmann, Birgit Lodes, and Reinhold Schlötterer (Berlin, 2001), 411–21.

15. Stephanie Jordan, *Moving Music: Dialogues with Music in Twentieth-Century Ballet* (London, 2000), 7.
16. See "Ballets Russes" in *Grove Art Online. Oxford Art Online*, http://www.oxfordartonline.com/subscriber/article/grove/art/T005959; Jean-Louis Rousseau, "From Wagner to Fellini," intro. to Maurice Béjart, *Béjart by Béjart*, trans. Richard Miller (New York, 1980), 6–7; and Hélène Lanternier, "Petrouchka: Le ballet comme art total?" in Danielle Cohen-Levinas, ed., *Le Renouveau de l'art total* (Paris, 2004), 155–70.
17. Isadora Duncan, *My Life* (1927), in Teck, Making Music, 14. On Duncan as a "rebellious disciple of Wagner" and her mediation of him for American modernism, see Mary Simonson, "Dancing the Future, Performing the Past: Isadora Duncan and Wagnerism in the American Imagination," *Journal of the American Musicological Society* 65, no. 2 (2012): 511–55.
18. Doris Humphrey, from a speech at Juilliard (7 November 1956), in *Teck, Making Music*, 73.
19. Wallingford Riegger, "Synthesizing Music and Dance" (1934), in *Teck, Making Music*, 61.
20. Lester Horton (interview, 1936), in *Teck, Making Music*, 165.
21. Vivian Fine, untitled essay (1983), in *Teck, Making Music*, 66.
22. Humphrey, "Music for an American Dance" (1958), in *Teck, Making Music*, 71.
23. Albright, "Golden Calves," 24, 27.
24. See Marian Smith, *Ballet and Opera in the Age of Giselle* (Princeton, 2000).
25. Trans. Albright, in "Golden Calves," 30. Cf. Roberts, *The Total Work of Art*, 133.
26. Joan Acocella, *Mark Morris* (New York, 1993), 156–57.
27. Omissions from Table 1 include examples of non-"art" music—traditional, folk, and popular songs—the latter of which eclipsed Lieder in postmodern dance. Table 7.1 ends at 1980 and excludes dancer-choreographer Mark Morris, whose challenge to modernist binaries includes his prolificacy at choreographing songs. See Acocella, *Mark Morris*, Chapter 7 and "Chronology of Works by Mark Morris," 267–86. Morris was also a pioneering choreographer of opera, e.g., Henry Purcell's *Dido and Aeneas* (1989). Involving the setting in dance of an entire opera, "choreographer's opera" (a term coined by David Levin) disperses and multiplies the signifying practices of conventional and Regieoper staging practices, and suggests parallels to choreographies of song. I am grateful to Levin for sharing with me his unpublished paper "Choreographer's Opera? Bodies, Voices, and Meaning in Pina Bausch's Production of C.W. Gluck's *Orpheus and Eurydice*." Levin's earlier work, including *Unsettling Opera: Staging Mozart, Verdi, Wagner, and Zemlinsky* (Chicago, 2007) and *Richard Wagner, Fritz Lang, and the Nibelungen: The Dramaturgy of Disavowal* (Princeton, 1999) is also attentive to movement, dance, and Wagner's legacy in operatic staging.
28. Two reviews summarize the controversy: Anna Kisselgoff, "Bejart and His Ballet of the 20th Century," *New York Times*, 28 January 1971; Clive Barnes, "Dance: A Century Short. Béjart's Ballet Appears Far Behind the Times," *New York Times*, 29 January 1971. A recent reassessment is Pamela Gay-White, *Béjart and Modernism: Case Studies in the Archetype of Dance* (New Orleans, 2006).
29. Kisselgoff, "Bejart and His Ballet of the 20th Century."

30. Barnes, "Dance: A Century Short."
31. Marcia Siegel, "Maurice Béjart's Ballets," *Boston Herald*, 21 February 1971.
32. Béjart, in Gay-White, Béjart and Modernism, 7. See also Marie-Françoise Christout, "Béjart, Maurice," in *International Encyclopedia of Dance*, ed. Selma Jeanne Cohen et al. (New York, 1998), 1:405.
33. Gay-White, *Béjart and Modernism*, viii.
34. On classicism in *Serait-ce la mort?*, see Hugh McDonagh, "'Four Last Songs' Is Given Premiere By Bejart Troupe," *New York Times*, 11 February 1971.
35. Rousseau, "From Wagner to Fellini," 7–8.
36. The following draws extensively on the Australian Ballet's filmed studio performance of *Serait-ce la mort?*, available on YouTube, "The Australian Ballet—Four Last Songs," in three parts (Part I may be found here: https://www.youtube.com/watch?v=88C_qYfD5wE, accessed 24 February 2015). Significantly, this production also used the same Berlin Radio Symphony Orchestra 1965 recording of Strauss's *Vier letzte Lieder* employed for the Béjart's 1971 premiere. Nonetheless, since choreography and staging often change subtly (or not so subtly) from dancer to dancer and theater to studio, my interpretation of this ballet also relies on photographs and reviews of earlier performances, as well as exegeses by Béjart himself.
37. Antonin Artaud, "On the Balinese Theatre," in *The Theater and Its Double*, trans. M. Richards, reprinted in *Total Theatre: A Critical Anthology*, ed. E.T. Kirby (New York, 1969), 212–14, 220, 222. Artaud also served as filter for the influence of Eastern cultures on Béjart (e.g., his Mudra Academy); see Gay-White, *Béjart and Modernism*, 8, 68, 74–75.
38. Rousseau, "From Wagner to Fellini," 8.
39. Gay-White, *Béjart and Modernism*, 8.
40. On Béjart's costumes for *Messe*, see René Julliard, "Béjart, Maurice," *Current Biography Yearbook 1971* (New York, 1955–[n.d.]), 32; for *Actus Tragicus* (1969), see Anna Kisselgoff, "Ballet by Béjart Makes U.S. Debut," *New York Times*, 31 January 1971.
41. Béjart, *Béjart by Béjart*, 62; Adolphe Appia, "The Scenic Form," in *Staging Wagnerian Drama*, trans. Peter Loeffler (Basel, 1982), 48–57. For a color photograph by Colette Masson that supports my comments on Béjart's simple, body-focused costumery and symbolic staging, see Béjart, *Béjart by Béjart*, 63.
42. Wieland Wagner, in Roger Savage, "The Staging of Opera," in *The Oxford Illustrated History of Opera*, ed. Roger Parker (New York, 1994), 400.
43. Béjart, *Béjart by Béjart*, 62.
44. See Colette Masson's photo in ibid., 64.
45. Gay-White, *Béjart and Modernism*, 43.
46. Ibid., 59.
47. Luuk Utrecht, *Rudi van Dantzig: A Controversial Idealist in Ballet*, trans. Nicoline Gatehouse (Zutphen, 1992), 50, 53; Utrecht, "Dantzig, Rudi Van," *International Encyclopedia of Dance*, 2:347.
48. Helmut Scheier, "Verklärte Resignation. Ein Richard-Strauss-Ballett für Nurejew von Rudi van Dantzig," *Das Tanzarchiv* 23, no. 12 (1975): 397–98; Utrecht, *Rudi van Dantzig*, 170–72.
49. Utrecht, *Rudi van Dantzig*, 53.
50. Gay-White, *Béjart and Modernism*, viii, ix, 11, 29; Rousseau, "From Wagner to Fellini," 10–11.

51. On Van Dantzig's classicism, see [O.E.], "'Vier letzte Lieder', Ein Meisterwerk van Dantzigs (TV)," *Das Tanzarchiv* 4, no. 26 (1978): 140–41. For a discussion of the influence of Graham technique on Van Dantzig's early ballets, see Utrecht, *Rudi van Dantzig*, 119–24.
52. Utrecht, *Rudi van Dantzig*, 43.
53. Ibid., 90–96. On the resonances between Van Dantzig and Bausch vis-à-vis these ballets, see ibid., 49. Albright addresses the taboo of singing dancers in "Golden Calves," 22.
54. Utrecht, *Rudi van Dantzig*, 50, 173.
55. Uncredited review from *De Volkskrant*, in ibid., 178.
56. Jorge Fatauros's photo of couple two (Robert Machherndl, Valerie Valentine) with the looming Angel of Death (Clint Farha) is reproduced in ibid., 176.
57. [O.E.], "Vier letzte Lieder," 141.
58. Janowitz sang live, though, for the work's 1979 Viennese premiere. While originally inspired by Janowitz's voice, other productions of Van Dantzig's ballet relied on different singers. The 1987 Paris premiere by the Opéra Ballet, for instance, featured soprano Michèle Lagrange. On the troubled circumstances leading up to the Paris premiere, see Rudi van Dantzig, *Remembering Nureyev: The Trail of a Comet*, trans. Katie de Haan (Gainesville, FL, 2008), 187–98.
59. See Jorge Fatauros's photo of this scene in Utrecht, *Rudi van Dantzig*, 175.
60. Smith also refers to the sisters' dancing and employs the metaphor of a pas de deux to describe the dialectic of high art and mass culture. Smith, *Total Work of Art*, 9, 11.

Wayne Heisler, Jr. is Associate Professor of Historical and Cultural Studies in Music at The College of New Jersey. He authored *The Ballet Collaborations of Richard Strauss* (Rochester, 2009) and recent essays in *Dance Chronicle* and the *Journal of the American Musicological Society*. He is also the guest editor of *Opera Quarterly*'s recent issue devoted to Richard Strauss vol. 31 no. 4 (2015).

III

Inspirations

CHAPTER 8

The "Translucent (Not: Transparent)" *Gesamtglaswerk*

JENNY ANGER

Bruno Taut's Glashaus (Glass house, 1914, Figure 8.1) stood on the eastern bank of the Rhine River, across from the monumental cathedral of Cologne, for just two years. It was accessible to the public for shorter still: a few weeks in the summer of 1914. The outbreak of war—and the need to garrison soldiers on the German Werkbund's exhibition grounds—might have darkened this temple of light forever.[1] Despite its brief existence, however, the Glashaus contributed to an ideal that aspired to be as enduring and inspirational as those of its sister temple on the far shore. Following the German tradition of constructing utopian neologisms out of constitutive parts—the Glashaus, for example, or Richard Wagner's Gesamtkunstwerk (total work of art)—I call this ideal the *Gesamtglaswerk* (total work of glass). As one might expect, the *Gesamtglaswerk* is a sort of Gesamtkunstwerk made of glass. Its less obvious, though more significant feature is that its glass is translucent. Yet its purview extends far beyond that which the eye can see.

Wait; should that not read *transparency*? That would seem to make more sense. Transparency, after all, is highly valued in modernist discourse; even its meaning is thought to be clear—that is, transparent. One sees straight through glass and gains complete "insight" into everything visible on the other side. The value and meaning of translucence, however, are less immediately clear, perhaps even opaque. Light filters through, but translucent glass halts the gaze, even as it engages it. Therein may lie the power of translucence, but we cannot know this right away. Translucence makes us pause.

So let us approach the *Gesamtglaswerk* from another direction. Transparency—not translucence—and the Gesamtkunstwerk are more ubiquitous associations with modernism. The former surfaces most commonly in architectural discourse; the latter appears in all of the splintered discourses of the various art forms that the Gesamtkunstwerk had sought to unite. The

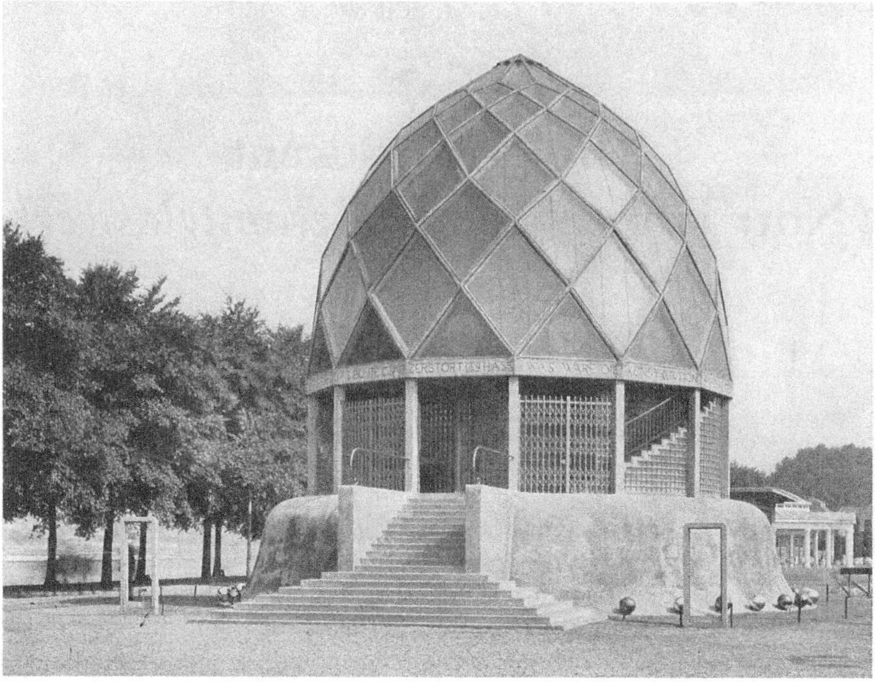

Fig. 8.1. Bruno Taut. Glashaus (Glass house), Cologne, 1914. Photograph from *Jahrbuch des deutschen Werkbunds* (1915): 77. Photograph in public domain

Bauhaus (Weimar, then Dessau, then Berlin, 1919–33) may be the prime example of both ideals. Walter Gropius's building at the Bauhaus school in Dessau (1926) epitomizes the transparency of glass, its revelation of structure, and its metaphoric clarity of purpose. In 1941, Siegfried Giedion famously pointed to such buildings of Gropius as illustrative of "space-time," of which a primary characteristic is "the extensive transparency that permits interior and exterior to be seen simultaneously."[2] The Bauhaus's goal was to turn this visual union into a material union of the arts and a social union of their makers, in order to build a more united society for all. Lyonel Feininger's aptly titled woodcut, *The Cathedral of Socialism* (1919, see Figure 5.1), which graced the institution's published manifesto, symbolizes this synthesis with its interlocking facets ascending to the sky, and simultaneously spreading across the whole page.

Taking the example of the Bauhaus, one might legitimately consider transparency and the Gesamtkunstwerk to be complementary. Indeed, such a pairing applies to utopian modernisms as well as it does to dystopian ones. As Andre Schuetze recently observed, "Glass is a building material not only for utopias, promising clarity, openness, and candour; at the same time, its transparency offers the possibility of observation and surveillance."[3] Analyzing a case in point,

Boris Groys memorably linked modernist aesthetics and infinite control in his provocatively titled book, *The Total Art of Stalinism*.[4]

Schuetze, however, gestures toward the characteristic that preserves the utopian spirit of the *Gesamtglaswerk*: translucence. Regarding the writing of architectural fabulist, Paul Scheerbart—to whom we will return and to whom Taut dedicated the Glashaus[5]—Schuetze declares: "One cannot compare Scheerbart's glass world with contemporary architecture, not even with modernist buildings that were constructed immediately after the First World War, because glass is not the same as *glass*. With Scheerbart, the invisible was not yet to be revealed, the transparent was not yet to be seen all the way through."[6] Schuetze does not explain how the "transparent was not yet to be seen all the way through"; the statement, in fact, appears contradictory. Yet there was a metaphorical transparency, I contend, that Scheerbart and Taut embraced, and it was, in fact, "not ... to be seen all the way through"; literally, translucence produced the *effect* of transparency.

The attentive reader will notice that I dropped "yet" in the previous sentence, a reformulation of Schuetze's text. The implication is not that Schuetze's "not yet" is incorrect, for transparency did largely eclipse translucence in the history of architecture, even in its textual records. In 1929, for example, architect Ludwig Hilbersheimer already recognized a difference between glass and *glass*, identifying one as "romantic" and the other as "constructive," but he also declared, matter-of-factly, that the "characteristic effects" of glass are "lightness and transparency."[7] In this essay, however, I avoid Schuetze's "not yet," because the phrase assumes an inevitable development. Instead, I want to recover the moment when Hilbersheimer recognized that different glass effects were in play (even though he neglected to mention translucence). I want to restore translucence to the history of architecture, and, more ambitiously, to consider the *Gesamtglaswerk* in relation to the utopian and dystopian Gesamtkunstwerk. The dystopian one, it seems, is marked by transparency. What does translucence do to or for utopia? In what follows, we will begin with the Glashaus, but we then venture well beyond its limited material existence. The essential medium of the *Gesamtglaswerk* is glass, but, true to the spirit of the Gesamtkunstwerk, its practice brings many media and people together, far across time and space. The example of the *Gesamtglaswerk* teaches us that the Gesamtkunstwerk is not limited to or dependent on a prescribed set of participants or material forms; there need not even be music, it seems, for many to experience the comprehensive thrill of the total work of art.

The Glashaus entry for the Werkbund exhibition in Cologne had been accepted so late in the planning stages that it was not included in the area reserved for buildings by master architects.[8] Indeed, it was not ready when the exhibition opened in June 1914, so its construction became part of the exhibition; it was, literally, a work in progress. It gradually took shape just beyond the entrance of the park. If a surviving plan of the exhibit is reliable, one entered and saw the stepped entrance to Taut's pavilion directly ahead.[9] Looking left (west), one would see the Rhine, which flows south to north and, at that time, paralleled the axial orientation of Taut's pavilion. As noted above, Cologne's great cathedral rose considerably higher just across the river. But the Glashaus's more immediate neighbor, just to the right of the exhibition's entrance, was the amusement park, which offered the latest electric rides and thrills.[10] It is tempting to read the Glashaus as the union of these two worlds, the sacred and profane, the ancient and the modern, the solid and the electric. The flow of the river and the flows within and between the structures—water, electricity, people, even cash—brought them into an ever rushing and shifting counterpoint.[11]

What did the Glashaus look like?[12] According to photographic and written records, Taut's pavilion gleamed at night, as any glass structure might, but its glow emanated through two layers of glass: the outer, larger panes, which by day reflected the surrounding atmosphere, and an inner layer of small, colorful "Luxfer prisms." The latter were semi-translucent, colored tiles whose interior ridges increased illumination through refraction.[13] Visiting by day, one climbed the steps that rose in the direction of (and parallel to) the neighboring Rhine's current. After paying a nominal fee, one was directed due right or left, up one of two sets of gracefully curving, glass brick steps rising to the cupola. Daylight filtered through its blue, green, and yellow prismatic ceiling. As darkness began to fall, multicolored, electric bulbs radiated man-made light. Thus, both natural and artificial light entered from beyond the structure, yet from within one could not see outside.

After soaking in the atmosphere of the dome, one could look down through the oculus to a somewhat darker, mysterious space below. Following another set of stairs down to this room, one discovered a glass tile atrium with a cascade of water streaming still further down. It flowed south, reversing and symbolically counterbalancing the great stream of the Rhine just beyond. Now one joined the flow of the water (metaphorically); the carefully orchestrated itinerary led one down steps alongside the waterfall.[14] Then one came, finally, to the darkest space, a niche lined in purple velvet. Perhaps most surprising of all, one heard the whirring and clicking of a machine behind a translucent glass screen. It was a kaleidoscope. According to the prospectus, artists Adolf Hoelzel, Franz Mutzenbecher, and "others" had selected the colored glass fragments that appeared in an infinite number of random, yet symmetrical, combinations over time.[15] The viewer perceived this ever-changing and blending symphony of colors both in its projection on the two-dimensional screen that separated him from the machine, and in his own (metaphorical) melting and mixing with the colors as they enveloped him in this space. After this rich, sensory experience, one ascended to the light of day and the everyday.

It seems that when visitors left the Glashaus, their recollections lost the specificity that I have just endeavored to provide. Nonetheless, their accounts are striking not only for their jubilation but also for their collectively *imprecise* descriptions. "The sight that opens above you is overwhelmingly beautiful ... The warm, mild waves of light surge through the dome and spread an indescribable fantasy mood throughout the space," reads one of many similar accounts.[16] Architecture critic Adolf Behne gives more descriptive detail, but even his more sober account includes the following: "Anyone who enters the cupola and has any receptivity for beauty at all will be excited by this wonderful impression. That is a space that has never existed before: in its purity and ease and in this glorious unity of light."[17] Taut himself, years later, offered a telling sociological impression: "For the most part the puzzled men tried to find crutches for their understanding, but women and children, without exception, gave themselves over to the effect."[18]

Whether the gendered interpretation holds or not, these quotations, taken together, suggest that experiencing the Glashaus was something like the oft-reported experience of the Gesamtkunstwerk: an overwhelming flow and mixture of colors and sensations all resolving in perfect unity. Critically, such an experience requires that one give oneself over to it. (This, of course, is one of Theodor Adorno's objections to Wagner.[19]) To be fair, however, there is no reliable record of actual music played or sung at the Glashaus, so does it make any sense to consider it in the context of the Gesamtkunstwerk?[20] I contend that evidence requires us to do so.

For starters, the flyer circulated on site recorded Taut's (and Scheerbart's) conviction that "The Gothic cathedral is the prelude to *glass architecture*."[21] Not only did the cathedral across the river literally precede the Glashaus's construction, but it preceded it in visitors' consciousness, its soaring rhythms remaining with them as a prelude or an overture does while experiencing an opera. The musical allusion is reinforced in a text Taut published in the Berlin journal, *Der Sturm* (The Storm), in February 1914, mere months before the Werkbund exhibition opened. In "Eine Notwendigkeit" (A Necessity), he wrote:

> The Gothic cathedral is the sum of all of its artists; filled with a wondrous sense of union, they achieved an all-encompassing rhythm that rang through the architecture of the building ... Let us [today] work on a magnificent building! One that is not architecture alone but in which everything—painting, sculpture, all together—forms a greater architecture, and in which architecture is once more subsumed into the other arts ... The whole will ring with a single, magnificent harmony.[22]

Architecture, in this representation, makes music.

Although Taut did not publish his theatrical production, *Der Weltbaumeister* (Builder of the World), until 1920, its subtitle alone affirms the direction that I am attributing to his work: "Architektur-Schauspiel für symphonische Musik" (Architecture-Play for Symphonic Music).[23] Indeed, Angelika Thiekötter has identified many parallels between the guided tour of the Glashaus and the development of the very abstract "plot" of *Der Weltbaumeister*.[24] The Glashaus may have inspired this visual opera, the central figure of which was, as we might now expect, a cathedral.[25]

Thus, although the Glashaus was in all likelihood silent—aside from the murmurs of delight and the whir of the hidden kaleidoscope—it calls out to be understood as a Gesamtkunstwerk. Other historians have already heard this call.[26] Perhaps most significantly, architectural historian Kai Gutschow recognizes that a close "antecedent of Taut's work can be found in the wide array of Gesamtkunstwerk theory and experiments that blossomed amidst eighteenth- and nineteenth-century Romanticism, as well as the turn-of-the-century applied arts movements that influenced Taut's early training."[27] He foregrounds the "immersive, theatrical, and experiential" aspects of the exhibition building; these, he argues, render it a forerunner of today's "installations." Gutschow concentrates on the Glashaus as "among the first exhibition buildings designed primarily as a mechanism to create vivid experiences throughout, from exclusively optic to partly haptic." Finally, he, too, cites visitors who "frequently remarked on the profound emotions they encountered, not merely the experiences of the five senses, but of the psychic and often visceral reactions they had."[28]

Gutschow's research contributes to our understanding of visitors' metaphysical, if not spiritual, responses to this aesthetic environment. In their recent anthology on the aesthetics of the Gesamtkunstwerk, Anke Finger and Danielle Follett argue that the total work of art usually fulfills three purposes: aesthetic, metaphysical, and political.[29] I want to build on Gutschow's scholarship to argue that the Glashaus fulfills not only the aesthetic and metaphysical but also the political purpose of a Gesamtkunstwerk. The Glashaus did not wear its politics on its sleeve, so to speak, but it materialized a radical utopian vision to improve humankind. Receptive visitors experienced a glorious aesthetic unity together; since Wagner's *Art and Revolution* (1849), a Wagnerian hope had been that such shared aesthetic pleasure would translate into a harmonious people. Much more concretely, this structure provided a ring of sayings around its architrave to help visitors make the connection between the structure and its politics. Scheerbart, a committed pacifist, provided the witty aphorisms, including "*Das bunte Glas zerstört den Haß*" (colored glass destroys hatred), which one read overhead upon entering the pavilion.[30] This mixture of language, color, and architecture underscores the Gesamtkunstwerk ideal of unifying the arts for a whole greater than the sum of its parts.

Translucence is essential here. Pondering the utopian potential of glass while traversing the space of the pavilion might lead one to think expansively about the world. Precisely because one could not see outside, the visitor might be more likely to relinquish control of time and space, to allow the charged atmosphere to work its magic. (Taut's statement notwithstanding, women and children were not the only ones to submit to this marvelous effect.) Thus, the Glashaus activated a power traditionally attributed to theater, a darkened space explicitly shut off from the outside world. Here one might engage in the fantasy of people the world over coming together in peaceful harmony, just as the colorful light pervaded the space and the lovely rush of the cascade. It would remain a fantasy, of course, but it could be far more profound than an experience with clear glass might have been. Imagine the Glashaus with transparent glass: from within one could have watched the people lining up outside, wondered why this particular pavilion was so close to the front gate, considered whether to go to the amusement park before or after attending to the more serious architecture in the distance—that is, one could have remained anchored in daily life. Even more, if the glass had been transparent, the controlling personality might not just look around, but, rather, survey all of the territory—the people, their movements, the layout of the grounds, the quickest route from the entrance to the river or the railroad—and might have experienced the powerful fantasy of surveillance. Translucence, it appears, lends itself better to utopia.

Scheerbart's pacifist aphorisms introduce yet another critical aspect of the Gesamtkunstwerk: collaboration. Once we bring collaboration into the mix, this *Gesamtglaswerk* opens far beyond its temporary site in Cologne to Berlin; to other participants; and to other moments of synthesis. Its realization far exceeded the summer of 1914. The nexus of this expanded network is Herwarth Walden (1878–1941), the director of *Der Sturm* enterprise, a journal, a gallery, a performance space, an art school, and a press in Berlin from 1910 to 1932. Walden's world of mixed media also opens the *Gesamtglaswerk* to projects that are not literally made of glass.[31]

Walden wanted so much for the Glashaus to succeed that he sent the Swedish painter Gösta Adrian-Nilsson to Cologne to give guided tours of the pavilion, as well as to sell copies of Scheerbart's book, *Glasarchitektur* (*Glass Architecture*), which was fresh off *Der Sturm*'s own press.[32] We will return to that book below, but first we must trace the long-standing creative bond between Scheerbart and Walden; it provides another prelude to the collaborative *Gesamtglaswerk* in Cologne.

Scheerbart (1863–1915), fifteen years Walden's senior, nevertheless belonged to the latter's longest-standing set of artistic friends in Berlin. Although earlier meetings have been postulated, the earliest surviving correspondence between them dates to 1903.[33] The very first letter, from Scheerbart and writer Erich Mühsam to Walden, is an invitation to collaborate with them on a proposed pacifist journal with an ironic title, *Das Vaterland* (The Fatherland).[34] The journal did not come to pass, but that gesture opened a rich vein of collaborative possibilities over the following years. In early 1904, Walden wrote that he was so taken by Scheerbart's play, *Dschinnenschlacht* (Genie Battle), that he planned to compose music for it.[35] The writer, in turn, was so enthusiastic about the possibility that he referred to the work as "*our*" *Dschinnenschlacht* in subsequent correspondence.[36] Neither the *Dschinnenschlacht* collaboration nor another potential journal came to fruition, but Scheerbart became one of the first speakers at Walden's newly founded *Verein für Kunst* (Society for Art) in 1904. That lecture, too, became an opportunity to blend the arts: Walden and Scheerbart conferred back and forth by mail before they decided on the proper timing, type, and amount of music to complement the verbal presentation.[37] Their working together was always a mixed-media affair.

The subject of glass appears in the correspondence for the first time in 1905. Scheerbart wrote to Walden to consult about the stage set the latter was preparing for a production of Scheerbart's: "The *shiny* paper seems just too dangerous to me. Simple walls are supposed to be the 'background' behind the actors; for that reason they can't be too intense—otherwise they don't stay in the background. I might experiment with a shiny backdrop (maybe with glass) at some later date."[38] Scheerbart objected to Walden's apparent suggestion that the stage backdrop shine; if it did so, the writer feared, it would overwhelm the play. Scheerbart indicated that he did want to consider a shiny set, perhaps even, specifically, a glass set, sometime in the future, but only if it could provide the total effect that he desired.[39] He did not want glass for its own sake but rather for its potential to contribute to a total work.

Walden and Scheerbart must have had passionate discussions about the possibilities of modern theater. In the spring of 1908 they dreamed of founding their own theater (along with Rudolf Bluemner, an acting coach and another long-time friend of Walden's).[40] That vision remained just that, but Scheerbart recorded a possible version of it—or, at least, of his own vision—in 1910 in a short story titled, simply, "Das Glas-Theater" (The Glass Theater). In the tale, the theater director muses:

> Just imagine so-called shadow plays with transparent and opaque glass sheets. On to these glass sheets, which can be in all colors, shadows from colored glass can be projected ... Cannot extraordinary moods be achieved with these colored shadows? Will this not give a whole new direction to theater art in which glass plays the dominant role?[41]

Architectural historian Rosemary Haag Bletter recognized that Scheerbart's "proposed nonobjective color play" dates to the same period in which artists such as Wassily Kandinsky were discovering pure color in painting, and that it also foreshadows the kaleidoscopic display in Taut's Glashaus of 1914 and

László Moholy-Nagy's light experiments at the Bauhaus and beyond.[42] All of these experiments, I contend, contribute to the *Gesamtglaswerk*, but there are more unexpected connections still to draw.

In 1910, Walden founded *Der Sturm* journal, and in 1912, to celebrate the hundredth issue, he began to host exhibitions of modern art. In a fortuitous crossing of paths, Bruno Taut purportedly worked on a site at the very same address (Tiergartenstraße 34A) as Walden's first two shows. But it is likely that Walden exhibited works in a villa that was scheduled for demolition or that Taut was associated with a replacement project.[43] After that, Walden opened a permanent gallery at Potsdamerstraße 134A, near Potsdamer Platz. In the fall of 1913, though, he rented another space large enough to hold the 366 works that he included in the "Erster Deutscher Herbstsalon" (First German Autumn Salon) exhibition.[44] Taut may have missed the first two shows, but he gained familiarity with the new, regular gallery during 1913, and this extraordinary, international exhibition appears to have crystallized his ideas about architecture.

The Herbstsalon—ostensibly not about architecture—consisted predominantly of painting and sculpture. Taut recorded his response in the essay, "Eine Notwendigkeit," introduced above. Here I quote at greater length from what scholars have called the "first manifesto of Expressionist architecture." This essay appeared, appropriately, in *Der Sturm*. It is a call for the *Gesamtglaswerk*:

> The Gothic cathedral too is the sum of all of its artists; filled with a wondrous sense of union, they achieved an all-encompassing rhythm that rang through the architecture of the building … Let us [today] work on a magnificent building! One that is not architecture alone but in which everything—painting, sculpture, all together—forms a greater architecture, and in which architecture is once more subsumed into the other arts … The building must contain rooms that incorporate the characteristic manifestations of the new art: the luminous compositions of [Robert] Delaunay in great stained-glass windows; on the walls Cubist rhythms, the painting of a Franz Marc, and the art of Kandinsky. The piers without and within must await the constructive sculptures of [Alexander] Archipenko; the ornament will be provided by [Heinrich] Campendonk … The whole will ring with a single, magnificent harmony.[46]

Taut aspires to combine all of the arts in a construction that would achieve the social and aesthetic union that he, like many of his contemporaries, projects onto the Gothic past and into the utopian future.[47] Each of the artists he names figured in the recently closed Erster Deutscher Herbstsalon. Robert Delaunay, in fact, was represented there by the second largest collection of any other living artist (his wife, Sonia, whose collection included decorative arts objects, was the only one to have more).[48]

Turning to these artists' non-architectural works brings us, surprisingly, still closer to the *Gesamtglaswerk* ideal. Earlier in 1913, Delaunay had enjoyed his first solo exhibition at *Der Sturm*. The paintings that won him wide acclaim belong to his colorful, abstract, Window series. The most famous of these, *Simultaneous Windows (1st Part, 2nd Motif, 1st Replica)* (1912, Figure 8.2), features as the only color reproduction in the Album that Robert and Sonia conceived together and that served as the catalogue for that show. Art historian Gordon Hughes has recently paid close attention to this long-admired, yet never well understood, painting.[49] He argues persuasively that the work replicates the process by which we learn to see—that is, to make sense cognitively of the flat color on our retinas (as nineteenth-century science had explained the process). Although other Cubists prioritized form over color, inferring from modern optical theory that vision cannot be trusted, Delaunay prioritized color, building on the "realization that infantile vision is initially experienced as pure optical sensation prior to the learned perception of form and space," a learning process that depends on memory of other things seen and touched in the past.[50]

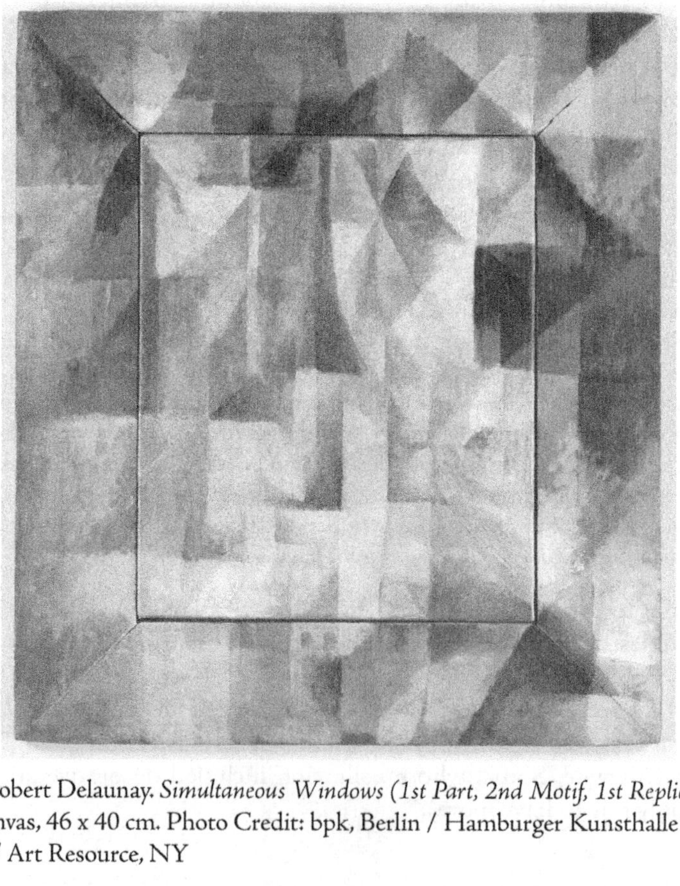

Fig 8.2. Robert Delaunay. *Simultaneous Windows (1st Part, 2nd Motif, 1st Replica)*, 1912. Oil on canvas, 46 x 40 cm. Photo Credit: bpk, Berlin / Hamburger Kunsthalle / Elke Walford / Art Resource, NY

From this perspective, Hughes opens up what is otherwise a very flat, opaque painting, despite its titular claim to represent a window. If one looks closely, though, opacity becomes translucence, and our eyes accustom themselves to the depth that Delaunay sought to achieve in this *Gesamtglaswerk* without glass.[51] As Hughes explains, Delaunay's title, *Simultaneous Windows*, foregrounds simultaneity, so we know that the prismatic colors that we see are what they appear to be precisely because of their placement adjacent to each other, their "simultaneity." The colors painted on the canvas and the attached wooden frame read at first as flat pattern, yet they awaken our tactile sensitivity as we recognize their different texture on the separate, though contiguous, supports. Surmising from the title that we are supposed to be seeing through a window, despite the obvious materiality of the actual work, we most easily identify the elongated green triangle in the center of the painting as a view of the Eiffel Tower in the distance.[52]

Viewers typically stop there, but Hughes encourages us to keep looking. He identifies two broadly brushed, intentional marks in the center of the bottom of the frame as other "windows" seen in the distance. Then he points out something that has long gone unnoticed—miraculously so, because it is one of those things that you cannot not see after you have seen it once. Hughes identifies "a face in the yellow field of the viewer's right-hand side of the painting. The dark green patch of paint, two-thirds of the way down the right-hand side, functions as lips, while the quarter-circle of yellow beneath it forms the chin. The ear nestles in the right-hand corner of the base of the tower."[53] It represents a reflection, of course: vague enough to be our own, which we know from experience, and vague enough also to be a record of Delaunay's own view of the "window" long ago, as Hughes suggests.

With remarkable acuity, Hughes proceeds to identify an overlay of an aerial view of the Eiffel Tower as well as intersecting support beams that one might see from beneath and within the tower.[54] His invitation to look closely at the painting, though, leads me to another startling revelation: there is a second face. It materializes out of the orange facets near the top of the viewer's left-hand side of the painted canvas. Just as the right side of Robert's face is nearly contiguous with one side of the Eiffel Tower, the curve of the left side of the second face echoes the slope of the other side of the tower, with the important difference that the second profile, however parallel to the tower's curve it may be, is an inch or two removed from it. Thus, this "face" is higher on the canvas and smaller, too, than his, suggesting that "she" stands a bit behind "him" and off to the side. A horizontal bar of deep orange, overlapping strokes, parallel to the frame just above it, forms her left eye; her nose emanates from the lighter orange that descends close to the vertical edge of the frame (on the viewer's left-hand side); the suggestion of her dark orange lips seems to emerge from behind some otherwise inexplicable green marks (below and to the right of which her chin gently curves). I have used "she," for who is this if not a specter of Sonia Delaunay, looking over the painter's shoulder, while "her" colors and shapes simultaneously provide the colorful sweep of curtain drawn to the (viewer's) left side of the painting? And is it not, after all, double vision; does she appear again, a little higher? What had been "eye" in the first Sonia "face" suddenly transforms itself into her "mouth" in the second, overlapping face. Is she simultaneously in two places, or is one or both a memory? She is certainly "there"—wherever that is—and as soon as one looks at and for her.

Sonia and Robert both identified with their work.[55] Analyzing a photo of Robert in front of another painting, the *First Disk*—the photo is inscribed, in part, "Exposé à Berlin 1914 [sic] au Herbstsalon" (exhibited in Berlin 1914 [sic] at the Herbstsalon)—Hughes argues convincingly for its simultaneous representation of the artist and his work, both of which were "exposed" at the Herbstsalon.[56] Following that logic, it makes good sense that in the window painting, the edge of the orange face is contiguous with what can only refer to a drawn curtain, for Sonia also made "simultaneous curtains," some of which were also shown at the Herbstsalon. They were titled *Profondeur Mouvement Vorhänge* (Depth Movement Curtains, 1912).[57] The title's combination of French and German, the source of which could be either Sonia or Walden, combines the languages of two countries as the words appear simultaneously together.[58] Walden's exhibits have always been known for their internationalism; the potential to unite peoples across a border is achieved here, if only metaphorically.

After learning to see all of these layers, prompted by Hughes, I wonder why he did not recognize Sonia in the painting. Presumably he was not looking for her, because in his text he emphasizes Robert's "increasingly evident individualism."[59] In this sense, Hughes follows the traditional, modernist narrative of the solitary, male, genius artist. But we opened our analysis here with the fact of collaboration: Sonia and Robert designed the *Album* together, and, as Whitney Chadwick has shown, their lives and their work from the period are closely intertwined. Now, with their simultaneous creativity in mind, something else in the painting suddenly appears, light as day. Those two daubs of paint on the bottom of the frame—the ones that Hughes identifies as "windows" in the distance—transform themselves into the backs of Sonia's and Robert's heads as they stand at ground level gazing together at the Eiffel Tower in the distance. That is, now they "stand" not in the space of the "window" and their own "reflections," but out of doors, on the Champs de Mars, in the area around the tower itself. Memory, we recall, shapes the many layers of visual perception in this simultaneously singular and retrospectively collective work. Expectations do as well. This painting is a *Gesamtglaswerk* in that sustained attention to its initial non-transparency leads us forward and backward in time to a simultaneously multi-layered and clear vision of a world and a life of collaborative production.

It is impossible to know how much of this Taut might have recognized, but the fact remains that conscientious, carefully considered vision—what might seem like a clear, metaphorically "transparent" view of our perception of the world—emerges here from the most opaque of "windows." Taut's words do not register the collaborative nature of this or any work by Delaunay, but it is this sort of simultaneously flat and deep, visually arresting and cognitively challenging painting that he proposes as the model for the actual windows in his utopian building. Indeed, scholars believe that Taut chose the yellows, blues, and greens of the interior prisms of the Glashaus in overt emulation of Delaunay's paintings of windows.[61] His decision to do so would have been reinforced by the critical reception of these paintings as *musical*. For example, the critic Behne wrote the following in late 1913: "With a determination like that of no other artist before, Delaunay has turned color into the expressive means of his art, and he has achieved results that one can compare only with musical effects!"[62]

Whatever Taut actually saw at the *Sturm* gallery and at the Erster Deutscher Herbstsalon, he was enmeshed in its network during the early months of 1914, during which he planned and executed the Glashaus in Cologne. Behne, who had identified the musicality of Delaunay's Window paintings earlier that winter, published a glowing review of Taut's building projects in the *Sturm* issue immediately following the one with his own essay, "Eine Notwendigkeit."[63] Taut and Scheerbart were introduced and they built a fast friendship. Taut much admired Scheerbart's architectural fantasies, which appeared regularly in *Der Sturm*, and Scheerbart recognized the man who might bring his glass dreams to fruition. Taut invited Scheerbart to write the aphorisms for the Glashaus, and Scheerbart gladly complied. Walden wanted to publish all of the maxims in *Der Sturm* but for some reason Scheerbart said no. The older man may have disappointed Walden with this refusal. If so, it was tempered by the offer of a different opportunity: Scheerbart asked Walden if *Der Sturm* might publish his book, *Glasarchitektur*.[64] Within a week, their correspondence reveals that Walden said yes; the two old friends would collaborate again. It was March 1914; Scheerbart was eager for the book to appear in May 1914, when the Werkbund exhibition would open. With remarkable speed, the team nearly made its deadline, such that Walden could dispatch Adrian-Nilsson to peddle the book at the exhibition in Cologne in July 1914.[65]

However, before we look closely at that book, there is another exhibition at *Der Sturm* that warrants our attention. As Hodonyi has reported, the exhibit at the gallery in April 1914 included a model (1:15) of Taut's Glashaus.[66] He also notes that the headline show at the time was Paul Klee's first solo show at this Berlin venue. Presumably because Klee was not widely known, Walden printed only a flyer for the show, rather than a longer catalogue. Previous scholars had missed this record, likely due to its flimsy and transitory nature.[67] But as Hodonyi discovered, the flyer's list of Klee's works faces a one-page description of Taut's Glashaus.[68]

This juxtaposition expands the reach of the *Gesamtglaswerk* still further. Taut's description is useful, in that it confirms what scholars have been able to glean from photographs and descriptions of the actual Glashaus in Cologne. However, its proximity to Klee's list of drawings and paintings, together with the context that we have been reconstructing, leads to a more significant recognition: Klee's works were shown together with Taut's model in what we can only assume was a purposeful combination. Their "simultaneous" exhibition, if I may, encourages a consideration of Klee's paintings in terms of glass. It is easy to do so; it is also one of those things, like the Delaunays' reflections, that is obvious once you see it. In my book, *Paul Klee and the Decorative in Modern Art,* I argue that the order of listed works reveals the artist's slow assimilation of decorative color and drawing. This mixture of means, if not media, reaches its then current apogee in a group of five watercolors from early 1914: *Ansteigende Villen* (*Houses Rising,* 1914, 1), *Stadt mit den drei Kuppeln* (*Town with the Three Domes,* 1914, 2), *Das Fenster* (*The Window,* 1914, 5), *Park* (*Park,* 1914, 6), and *Erinnerung an einen Park* (*Memory of a Garden,* 1914, 7).[69] No other group of Klee's at this time could be more window-like.

Park's current location is unknown; in fact, the last data that the Klee *Catalogue Raisonné* includes is Klee's message to himself in his private Oeuvre Catalogue: "Walden-Sturm Nov[.] [19]19 notified as sold and not yet paid."[70] Unfortunately, there are no known reproductions. We do glean one piece of information from this paltry evidence, however; for five years Walden showed this painting, in rotation, in Berlin and presumably in traveling shows as well. Thus it likely sustained the accessibility and longevity of the *Gesamtglaswerk.*

The Window and *Houses Rising* are also missing today, although we are fortunate to have reproductions, which reveal networks of abstract facets that build uniformly across the picture plane. From Klee's records, we also know that Walden either bought or sold them in 1916, so they stayed with *Der Sturm* for two years of at least occasional viewing.[71] It is hard to tell from black-and-white reproductions, but the watercolor of *The Window* appears to be somewhat transparent, as watercolor often is, but the medium of *Houses Rising* appears to be less so. Klee records that he used *chalk* along with watercolor here, and a look even at a small, black-and-white reproduction reveals the chalky substance on the page; therefore, this is no transparent vision, but one that is difficult to make out beyond the nearly crusty surface of the cardboard support.

The two remaining works, *Town with the Three Domes and Memory of a Garden*—the first of which Walden bought, the second of which Klee gave to Walden—remain in all their prismatic, colorful glory.[72] *Memory of a Garden* is the more translucent of the two, although a knot of graphic marks with a ponderous dark area below it in the middle of the painting blocks any illusion of transparency. Perhaps the titular memory blocks a clear view. *Town with the Three Domes* is a magical checkerboard of light, with three half circles becoming the suggested "domes" in the viewer's mind. Klee uses gouache here, and the opacity across the entire picture reflects that choice. He also specially mounted it on green-gray cardboard, which immediately ties the greens in the painting to this flat base and heightens the intensity of the contrasting reds.[73] There is a visible "horizon" far in the distance. The angled facets above it suggest colored searchlights, yet their larger shapes emphasize the materiality of the work as a whole.

Klee, we know, admired Delaunay; he had visited Robert and Sonia in Paris in 1913. Elsewhere I have written about the likely influence of Sonia's quilting on Klee's visual imagination.[74] Here I underscore the fact that Klee clearly admired Robert's painting, too. In 1912, Klee reviewed Robert's recent work and likened it to "a fugue by Bach."[75] The Frenchman was so pleased with the description that he chose Klee to translate his own essay, "Sur la lumière" (On Light), for *Der Sturm* in 1913.[76] It is a loose translation, one that emphasizes the musicality of Robert's principles (or the reception thereof). In a striking example, the French "l'harmonie" (harmony), which might have appeared in the German simply as "die Harmonie," transforms instead on two occasions into "der Zusammenklang."[77] The latter also means harmony, but it has a distinctively more aural connotation than the former; literally, it is a "sounding together." Together these artists all contributed to the larger project of the *Gesamtglaswerk*.

Surely these works, then—Klee's window-like paintings and Taut's model of the Glashaus—were together by design. They were in any case complemented by the appearance of Scheerbart's book, *Glasarchitektur*, to which we finally turn. In honor of their mutual respect, Scheerbart dedicated the volume to Bruno Taut. Scheerbart's collection of 101 "chapters" opens with the following:[78]

> We live for the most part in closed rooms. These form the environment from which our culture grows. Our culture is to a certain extent the product of our architecture. If we want our culture to rise to a higher level, we are obliged, for better or for worse, to change our architecture. And this only becomes possible if we take away the closed character from the rooms in which we live. We can only do that by introducing glass architecture, which lets in the light of the sun, the moon, and the stars, not merely through a few windows, but through every possible wall, which will be made entirely of glass—of colored glass. The new environment, which we thus create, must bring us a new culture.[79]

Let us open up our dark rooms, Scheerbart says, and the light will make us better people. In Chapter Seventy-Three, he writes: "our hope is that glass architecture will also improve mankind in ethical respects. It seems to me that this is a principal merit of lustrous, colorful, mystical and noble glass walls."[80]

Scheerbart's *Glasarchitektur* speaks to the aesthetic, metaphysical, and political aspects of the *Gesamtglaswerk*. This is the dream of the "Cathedral of Socialism" in its incipient form.

But what about transparency? Here I must ask for the reader's patience, because an early reference appears to contradict my claim for translucence over transparency. We need to remember, however, that the proper apprehension of translucence takes time. To begin: in Chapter Fifteen, Scheerbart writes, "Reinforced concrete is a building material which is very strong and weather-resistant. It has been rightly acclaimed by architects as the ideal material. A pity that it is not transparent: only glass is."[81] Clearly, Scheerbart approves of the use of reinforced concrete, but he values the propensity of glass to be transparent.

But is transparency *literal* transparency? The philosopher Salomo Friedländer, known as Mynona, also belonged to the Walden–Scheerbart circle. In a tribute to Scheerbart from 1913, Friedländer connected his friend's "adventurous predilection for glass in all lights and colors" to an "ardent need for purity, clarity, transparency, penetration." Scheerbart's ideal, Friedländer believed, represents the "the most radical banishment of all possibilities of darkening."[82] What Friedländer does not say, and what scholars to date have missed, is that this metaphorical transparency is not dependent on actually transparent glass—even if glass *can* have that remarkable quality.

A closer reading of *Glasarchitektur* supports this claim. Scheerbart, we discover, has utopian hopes for the possibilities of translucent glass. He writes, in Chapter Thirty-Five, "It will seem very natural that ventilators should have a principal part to play in a glass house, and will supplant everything window-like. When I am in my glass room, I shall hear and see nothing of the outside world. If I long for the sky, the clouds, woods and meadows, I can go out or repair to an extra-veranda with transparent glass panes."[83] He reinforces this idea in Chapter Forty-Seven: "the word 'window' will disappear from the dictionaries. Whoever wants to look at nature can go on to his balcony or into his loggia, which of course can be arranged for enjoying nature as before."[84]

Is it possible that the widely claimed literary impetus for modernist glass architecture envisioned not only colored glass, which already differs from most expectations, but also *non*-transparent, colored glass?[85] Scheerbart has no problem with the continuation of human pleasure in viewing nature. We simply will have to go outside to see it (or go to a transitional space that Scheerbart concedes may have transparent glass). We will *not* be able to see outside from inside the ideal *Glasarchitektur*. Scheerbart confirms these conclusions when he writes about Taut's Glashaus in a technical journal: "Glass, in its translucent (not: transparent) state, has in fact not [yet] fulfilled its potential as material for walls, because there is no other building material with which one could achieve similarly magnificent effects."[86] Scheerbart's specific formulation, "translucent (not: transparent)," is surely an effort to highlight the distinction that many others gloss over. Addressing building professionals, Scheerbart stresses the practicality of his promotion of translucent glass, declaring: "It is by no means a utopian claim."[87] Yet he does not abandon what, in hindsight, we would have to consider a utopian dream: "Due to its nature, glass architecture strives toward cathedral-like effects, because of which, in my opinion, ethical effects might also be derived from it."[88]

Finally, although Scheerbart was primarily a writer, in the context of the *Gesamtglaswerk*, it is vital to explore some of his work's visual aspects.[89] Of particular importance in this context is the special edition of *Glasarchitektur*.[90] Advertisements in *Der Sturm* reveal that the regular edition cost two marks, but this luxury edition cost twenty-five marks. It was clearly very special; it was available in "twenty numbered and signed copies on Van Gelder paper, cover and endpaper by Anna Scheerbart."[91]

So this, too, was a collaborative project (beyond Walden's editing of Scheerbart's prose). With blue swirls, accented by streaks of red and green, Scheerbart's wife Anna's cover attains a glorious marbleized effect.[92] It calls to mind the wonderful world of color that Scheerbart prophesies within the pages of the book. The surprise comes, though, when one opens the cover, front or back, and looks closely at the pasted paper endpapers. Let us start at the front (Figure 8.3). Color is missing; the dirty gray does not invite the eye to luxuriate in it. But if we spend a little time gazing at the endpaper inside the front cover, we begin to believe that this gray is not abstract for abstraction's sake (or not only for that); rather, we think that we are looking at water streaking down a pane of glass.[93] The lower left corner, especially, has this dripping effect; the darkest spots on the right make us think of some actual smudge that the water might collect and then wash away. In *Glasarchitektur*, Scheerbart writes that water's reflective properties make it a natural partner with glass.[94] Taut echoes that call with his cascade in the Glashaus.[95] Here, the paper itself appears as if it were a pane of glass. But we cannot see through it. The patterns of dripping water preclude that. Not to mention the fact that we cannot actually see through the paper; it, too, is not transparent, especially as it is permanently affixed to the cover and first page of the book. The image of translucence emerges through an opaque medium.

The viewer is in for another delight when he/she reaches the other end of the book. That endpaper (Figure 8.4) shares the gray tones of the front endpaper, but it looks like something altogether different. It appears to be a hard surface from which parts have crumbled away; or perhaps it was never smooth and even. It does not look like paper, though. It recalls, in fact, an uneven plane of concrete—that other building material that Scheerbart highly recommends.[96] In the book, Scheerbart appears to regret that concrete is not transparent, but here, in Anna Scheerbart's paper, we enjoy a translucent vision of the strength and beauty of its opacity. Scheerbart's published letters to his

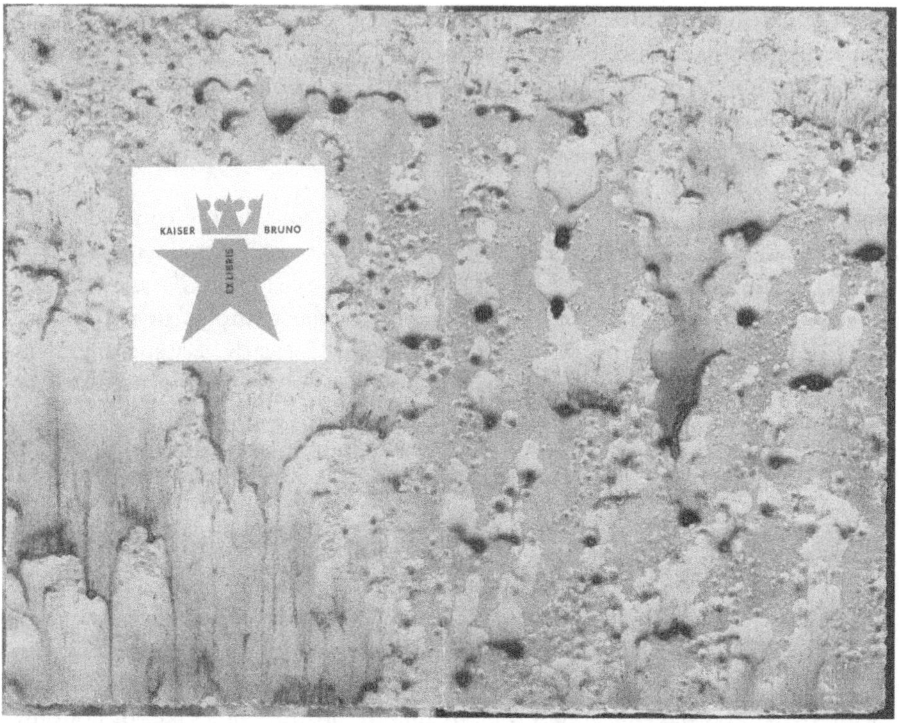

Fig. 8.3. Anna Scheerbart. Front endpapers to Paul Scheerbart, *Glasarchitektur* (Berlin: *Der Sturm*, 1914). Photo Credit: bpk, Berlin/Staatsbibliothek zu Berlin–PK/Art Resource, NY

wife demonstrate that he found her handmade paper "exquisite" (*köstlich*).[97] He dedicated *Glasarchitektur* to Taut, but his contemporary novel about glass architecture, *Das Graue Tuch und Zehn Prozent Weiss* (*The Gray Cloth and Ten Percent White*, 1914), reveals his debt to his wife's inspiration, in art and life: "To my dear bear, Frau Anna Scheerbart."[98]

If the *Gesamtglaswerk* is translucent, as I have argued, we may wonder why modernist architecture largely came to fetishize transparency.[99] The *Gesamtglaswerk* promises transformation or transcendence; in that way it provides metaphorical transparency. But part of its point seems not to position the viewer as omniscient and omnipotent. The way to greater spiritual and intellectual growth—and potential communion with humankind, if not the universe—appears to call for very close looking and experience of something that we cannot see through. Adolf Behne, finally, may have tried to communicate this principle when he reflected, after the Werkbund exhibition had closed, on the Glashaus that he had personally experienced. After declaring, as we have seen, that the Glashaus would appeal to anyone who had any receptivity to beauty at all, he continued:

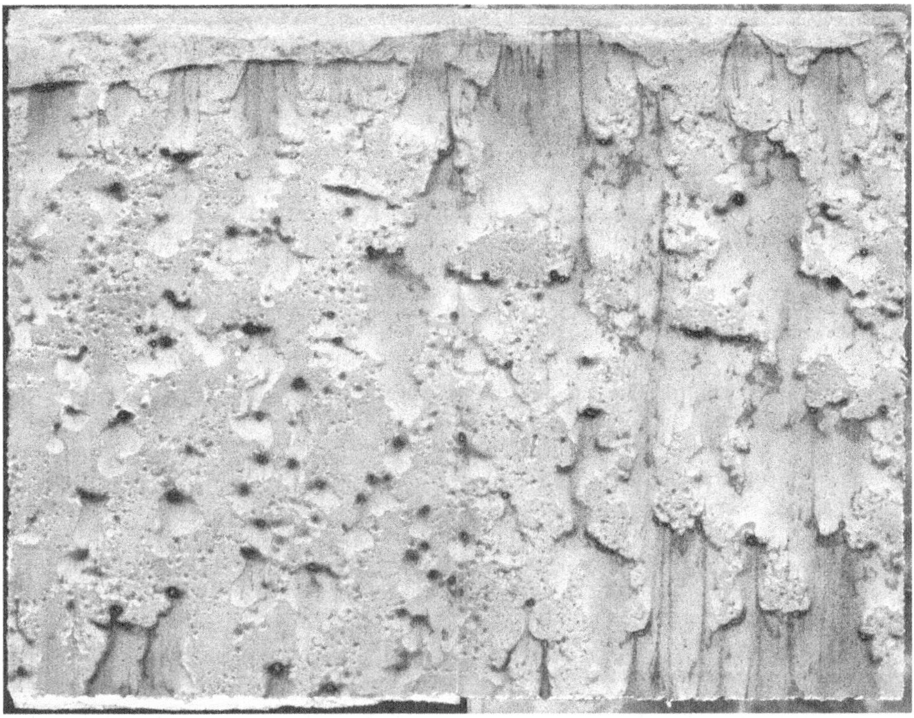

Fig. 8.4. Anna Scheerbart. Back endpapers to Paul Scheerbart, *Glasarchitektur* (Berlin: *Der Sturm*, 1914). Photo Credit: bpk, Berlin/Staatsbibliothek zu Berlin–PK/Art Resource, NY

> That is a space that has never existed before: in its purity and ease and in this glorious unity of light. This hall is radiant and shining like a jewel, yet full of gentleness and expanse. Of course it is not meant to be a lookout or observation room! The appeal is not that we can now see everything that goes by outside; the walls, rather, are non-transparent. So why doesn't one just stick with brick, and what is glass for, if it is in fact not transparent? Yes, the value of glass is not exhausted by the fact that one can see through it. That is just one, purely practical quality of glass, the one that we have put to our service. But over and above that, glass is in and of itself a material of unique beauty, and even when we cannot see through it, it has an inestimable significance as wall, as enclosure of a space.[100]

Reminding us of the musical model with which we began, Behne then builds on a quotation from the Glashaus brochure: "'The Gothic cathedral is the prelude to glass architecture.' A *glorious* prelude!"[101] However, the "inestimable significance" that Behne ascribes to the *Gesamtglaswerk*—its potential for cognitive and spiritual clarity and transcendence thanks in part to the "translucent (not: transparent)" quality of its glass—has remained opaque for some time. If we attend more closely, more patiently, to that translucence, might we not envision more utopian potential for the Gesamtkunstwerk?

Notes

I am grateful to the editors of this volume and to colleagues Jay Clarke, Sandy Isenstadt, Vanessa Lyon, Daniel Reynolds, and Susan Strauber for their insightful comments on previous drafts of this chapter.

1. The most exhaustive source is Angelika Thiekötter et al., *Kristallisationen, Splitterungen. Bruno Tauts Glashaus* (Basel, 1993). Birgit Schulte records that the German government required Taut himself to pay for the building's destruction in 1916. Karl Ernst Osthaus tried to intervene, suggesting that the building be used for demolition practice or that its glass be salvaged, but to no avail. See Schulte, "Dekonstruktion," in Thiekötter, *Kristallisationen*, 158–59.
2. Siegfried Giedion, *Space, Time and Architecture: The Growth of a New Tradition* (Cambridge, 2008), 493.
3. Andre Schuetze, "Der gläserne Raum: Paul Scheerbarts Utopie einer Glasarchitektur," *Seminar: A Journal of Germanic Studies* 48, no. 1 (February 2012): 31. Unless otherwise noted, translations are mine.
4. Boris Groys, *The Total Art of Stalinism: Avant-Garde, Aesthetic Dictatorship, and Beyond* (Princeton, 1992).
5. Above all, Paul Scheerbart, *Glasarchitektur*, ed. Herwarth Walden (Berlin, 1914). Unless otherwise indicated, however, all references in this essay are to this text's English translation: *Glass Architecture by Paul Scheerbart and Alpine Architecture by Bruno Taut*, ed. Dennis Sharp (New York, 1972).
6. Schuetze, "Der gläserne Raum," 45, emphasis added.
7. Ludwig Hilbersheimer, "Glasarchitektur," *Die Form* 4, no. 19 (1929): 521–22.
8. Thiekötter, *Kristallisationen*, 15–16. The Werkbund exhibition opened on 16 May 1914, but Taut's pavilion was not ready until July. Also see Kai Konstanty Gutschow, "The Culture of Criticism: Adolf Behne and the Development of Modern Architecture in Germany, 1910–1914" (PhD diss., Columbia University, 2006), 260.
9. The plan of the exhibition in relation to the river and city is reproduced in Thiekötter, *Kristallisationen*, 10.
10. See Thiekötter, *Kristallisationen*, 19–20, for a suggestive account of the significance of the amusement park's proximity.
11. Taut was initially dismayed by the placement, but in the end found it "versöhnlich" (conciliatory). Bruno Taut, "Glaserzeugung und Glasbau," *Qualität* 1, no. 1–2 (1920): 10, in Thiekötter, *Kristallisationen*, 25n6.
12. See Thiekötter, *Kristallisationen*, 26–28, for a more extensive, imaginary tour of the Glashaus. Plans of the structure appear in Thiekötter, *Kristallisationen*, 163.
13. According to Dietrich Neumann, the original patent application claimed that the "window glass with prismatic ridges inside … would 'double the quantity of reflection or illumination of the plain window-glass of the same size.'" Dietrich Neumann, "'The Century's Triumph in Lighting': The Luxfer Prism Companies and their Contribution

to Early Modern Architecture," *Journal of the Society of Architectural Historians* 54, no. 1 (March 1995): 24.

14. Taut, in fact, specified that the path through the building was "componiert" (composed). See Taut, "Erläuterungsbericht zur Errichtung des Glashauses," 7 February 1914, in Thiekötter, *Kristallisationen*, 28n1.
15. See Jan Torsten Ahlstrand, "Der 'künstlerischer Erklärer' im Glashaus. Gösta Adrian-Nilsson," in Thiekötter, *Kristallisationen*, 153. Hoelzel was a well-known professor at the Art Academy in Stuttgart. Hoelzel scholar Sharon Reeber notes that Hoelzel expanded his painting practice to stained glass around 1915. See Sharon Reeber, "Finding Harmony: What Adolf Hoelzel Learned from European Sacred Art," *Zeitschrift für Kunstgeschichte* 76 (2013): 255. One wonders if there was a connection with the kaleidoscope venture. I am grateful to Reeber for sharing her research with me. Mutzenbecher, for his part, was a friend of Taut's and a former student of Hoelzel's. He also designed the largest and centermost stained-glass "picture" for the wall surrounding the top of the Glashaus's waterfall. For reproductions, see Thiekötter, *Kristallisationen*, 68–69.
16. Felix Linke, "Die neue Architektur," *Sozialistische Monatshefte* 2, no. 18 (October 1914): 1134–35, in Thiekötter, *Kristallisationen*, 26.
17. Adolf Behne, "Das Glashaus," *Die Umschau* 18 (1914): 712–16, in Behne, *Architekturkritik in der Zeit und über die Zeit hinaus*, ed. Haila Ochs (Basel, 1994), 27–28.
18. Bruno Taut, "Farbenwirkungen aus meiner Praxis," *Das Hohe Ufer* 1, no. 11 (November 1919): 266.
19. Regarding Wagner's projected audience member, for example, Adorno writes, "The monad is 'sick.' It is too impotent to enable its principle, that of isolated singularity, to prevail and to endure. It therefore surrenders itself." Theodor Adorno, *In Search of Wagner*, trans. Rodney Livingstone (London, 2005), 143.
20. In the literature about the Glashaus, one encounters claims such as the following: "In addition to the play with light the designer also introduced a continuously flowing cascade of water at the base of the pavilion, as well as an aural background of piped music." In the more explicit, technical reports, however, I have not been able to locate evidence of such "piped music," the technical possibility of which is also doubtful for the period. Thus, I am inclined to ascribe excess enthusiasm to such sources. See Dennis Sharp, "Paul Scheerbart's Glass World," in *Glass Architecture*, 12.
21. The program page with this quotation is reproduced in Sharp, "Paul Scheerbart's Glass World," 10. A similar expression appears in Scheerbart's book: "It ought to be stressed here that the whole of glass architecture stems from the Gothic cathedrals. Without them it would be unthinkable; the gothic cathedral is the prelude." Scheerbart, *Glass Architecture*, 61.
22. Here we recognize a critical source of the Bauhaus as "Cathedral of Socialism." I borrow Benson's translation in Timothy Benson, ed., *Expressionist Utopias: Paradise, Metropolis, Architectural Fantasy* (Los Angeles, 1993), 282–83.
23. Bruno Taut, *Der Weltbaumeister. Architektur-Schauspiel für symphonische Musik*, ed. Manfred Speidel (Berlin, 1999).
24. Thiekötter, *Kristallisationen*, 67–70.
25. In Taut's accompanying drawings, the first thing one sees after the curtain rises is a cathedral, also rising. See Taut, *Weltbaumeister*, n.p.
26. Iain Boyd White writes, for example, "This small pavilion gave tangible form to Taut's vision, which was simultaneously published as text in Herwarth Walden's journal *Der*

Sturm, of a *Gesamtkunstwerk* in which architecture would join with abstract painting and sculpture to produce an inspirational alternative to the grey façades of the city." Iain Boyd White, "The Expressionist Utopia," in *Tracing Modernity: Manifestations of the Modern in Architecture and the City*, ed. Mari Hvattum and Christian Hermansen (London, 2004), 260–62.

27. Kai Konstanty Gutschow, "From Object to Installation in Bruno Taut's Exhibition Pavilions," *Journal of Architectural Education* 59, no. 4 (May 2006): 63–64.
28. Ibid., 66.
29. Finger and Follett provide this tripartite definition in their anthology, *The Aesthetics of the Total Artwork: On Borders and Fragments* (Baltimore, 2011), 4–5.
30. Taut published the aphorisms along with Scheerbart's letters to him in his journal Frühlicht, reproduced in Bruno Taut, Frühlicht. *Eine Folge für die Verwirklichung des neuen Baugedankens, 1920–1922* (Berlin, 1963), 19.
31. Architectural histories of the period register the significance of Taut's Glashaus but, to the best of my knowledge, have thus far missed its position within the network of *Der Sturm*. For example, Wolfgang Pehnt devotes four pages to the Glashaus in his encyclopedic study, *Die Architektur des Expressionismus*, and some of his sources originally appeared in *Der Sturm* journal or were published by *Der Sturm* press, but he mentions neither Walden nor *Der Sturm* in this section of his book. See Wolfgang Pehnt, *Die Architektur des Expressionismus* (Ostfildern, 1998), 103–6.
32. In Hodonyi's excellent book, *Herwarth Waldens "Sturm" und die Architektur. Eine Analyse zur Konvergenz der Künste in der Berliner Moderne* (Bielefeld, 2010), see especially "Dialog der Künste. Glasarchitektur," 168–220. For a more complete assessment of Adrian-Nilsson's role, see Ahlstrand, "Der 'künstlerischer Erklärer,'" and Ahlstrand, "GAN, Berlin und der Sturm," in *Svenskt Avant-garde och Der Sturm i Berlin. Schwedische Avantgarde und Der Sturm in Berlin*, ed. Jan Torsten Ahlstrand et al. (Osnabrück, 2000), 29–49.
33. All of the known letters from Scheerbart to Walden are located in the Sturm-Archiv, Handschriftenabteilung, Staatsbibliothek zu Berlin, and appear in Scheerbart, *Paul Scheerbart: 70 Trillionen Weltgrüsse—Eine Biographie in Briefen 1889–1915*, ed. Mechthild Rausch (Berlin, 1991). Unfortunately, the other half of the correspondence is not known to be extant. Hodonyi reviews the possibilities of earlier meetings in Hodonyi, *Herwarth Waldens "Sturm,"* 170–71.
34. Mühsam and Scheerbart to Walden, 25 August 1903, in Scheerbart, *Paul Scheerbart*, 221.
35. Mechthild Rausch surmises that the play has been lost. Mechthild Rausch, *Von Danzig ins Weltall. Paul Scheerbarts Anfangsjahre (1863–1895)* (Munich, 1997), 72.
36. Scheerbart to Walden, 18 March 1904 and 7 April 1904, emphasis added, in Scheerbart, *Paul Scheerbart*, 234–35.
37. Scheerbart to Walden, 23 August 1904 and 25 August 1904, in ibid., 244–45.
38. Scheerbart to Walden, 17 November 1905, emphasis original, in ibid., 303.
39. Scheerbart's play, *Herr Kammerdiener Kneetschke: Eine Kammerdiener Tragödie*, premiered at the *Verein für Kunst* on 1 December 1905. Scheerbart, *Paul Scheerbart*, 544. Hodonyi notes that the play was published in 1904 and republished for a new audience in *Der Sturm* 4, no. 156–57 (April 1913): 10–14. See Hodonyi, *Herwarth Waldens "Sturm,"* 174–75. The play itself is a parody of social mores in the eighteenth century, and has nothing literally to do with glass.
40. Scheerbart to Walden, 12 March 1908, in Scheerbart, *Paul Scheerbart*, 348.

41. Scheerbart, "Das Glas-Theater," *Gegenwart* 78 (12 November 1910): 913–14. I borrow the translation from Rosemary Haag Bletter, "Paul Scheerbart's Architectural Fantasies," *Journal of the Society of Architectural Historians* 34, no. 2 (May 1975): 91.
42. Bletter, "Paul Scheerbart's," 91. All of these artists were eventually connected with *Der Sturm*. Kandinsky and Moholy-Nagy each enjoyed three solo exhibits at the Berlin gallery. See Georg Brühl, *Herwarth Walden und "Der Sturm"* (Leipzig, 1983), 242, 256.
43. See Gutschow, *Culture of Criticism*, 235–36.
44. Herwarth Walden, *Erster Deutscher Herbstsalon* (Berlin, 1913).
45. Rosemary Haag Bletter, "Expressionist Architecture," in *German Expressionism: Documents from the End of the Wilhelmine Empire to the Rise of National Socialism*, ed. Rose-Carol Washton Long (Berkeley, 1993), 124; Gutschow, "From Object to Installation," 66.
46. The issue of *Der Sturm* in which this article appears is not otherwise about architecture. I borrow David Britt's translation from Benson, *Expressionist Utopias*, 282–83.
47. See Magdalena Bushart, *Der Geist der Gotik und die expressionistische Kunst: Kunstgeschichte und Kunsttheorie, 1911–1925* (Munich, 1990).
48. Robert had twenty-one; Sonia had twenty-seven. See Walden, *Erster Deutscher*, 15–17; and Brühl, *Herwarth Walden*, 227–28.
49. Gordon Hughes, "Envisioning Abstraction: The Simultaneity of Robert Delaunay's First Disk," *Art Bulletin* 89, no. 2 (June 2007): 306–32.
50. Hughes, "Envisioning Abstraction," 313. As is well known, infants see first in black and white. Current research suggests that their color perception is well developed by month four, whereas their depth perception develops between months four and six. R. Aslin, "Development of Binocular Fixation in Human Infants," *Journal of Experimental Child Psychology* 123 (1977): 133–50. I am grateful to Dr. David Jensen for this source. Hughes also foregrounds the role of memory in the development of visual perception, 311.
51. As Delaunay wrote in a letter to Franz Marc, "I am not talking about a mechanical movement, but rather about a harmonic one, because it has to do with simultaneity, that is, depth." Delaunay to Marc, after 14 December 1912, in Peter-Klaus Schuster, ed., *Delaunay und Deutschland* (Cologne, 1985), 498.
52. Hughes, "Envisioning Abstraction," 314.
53. Ibid.
54. Ibid.
55. In the aforementioned letter to Marc, Delaunay wrote, "I exist only in my work and cannot separate my means from my end." Delaunay to Marc, 1912.
56. Hughes, "Envisioning Abstraction," 326.
57. Walden, *Erster Deutscher*, 17.
58. Both Sonia Delaunay and Herwarth Walden were polyglots.
59. Hughes, "Envisioning Abstraction," 309.
60. Whitney Chadwick, "Living Simultaneously: Sonia and Robert Delaunay," in *Significant Others: Creativity and Intimate Partnership*, ed. Chadwick and Isabelle de Courtivron (London, 1993), 31–49.
61. Thiekötter, *Kristallisationen*, 43–47; Gutschow, *Culture of Criticism*, 261.
62. Adolf Behne, "Der erste Deutsche Herbstsalon," *Die neue Kunst* (December 1913): 223f., and *Die Tat* 8 (1913): 841–43, both in Schuster, *Delaunay*, 510.
63. Adolf Behne, "Bruno Taut," *Der Sturm* 4, no. 198–99 (February 1914): 182–83.

64. According to Scheerbart's letters to Taut, he had already (unsuccessfully) sought out some other publishers, so Walden was not his first choice. A possible reason for Scheerbart's reluctance was Walden's continual failure to pay him in a timely manner.
65. Gutschow, *Culture of Criticism*, 260.
66. Front and side views of the model, by Emil Weinert, are reproduced in Scheerbart, "Glashäuser. Bruno Tauts Glaspalast auf der Werkbund-Ausstellung in Cöln," *Technische Monatshefte. Technik für Alle* 4, no. 4 (28 March 1914): 105, 107. The first is reproduced in Hodonyi, *Herwarth Waldens "Sturm,"* 211; and Thiekötter, *Kristallisationen*, 160.
67. I, for one, surmised that there was no contemporary publication in Jenny Anger, *Paul Klee and the Decorative in Modern Art* (Cambridge, 2004), 62–69.
68. The brief essay is titled "Das Glashaus von Bruno Taut," in *Der Sturm. Vierundzwanzigste Ausstellung: Paul Klee*, ed. Walden (Berlin, 1914), n.p. The Taut–Klee relationship is explored in Regine Prange, *Das Kristalline als Kunstsymbol. Bruno Taut und Paul Klee. Zur Reflexion des Abstrakten in Kunst und Kunsttheorie der Moderne* (Hildesheim, 1991).
69. See Paul-Klee-Stiftung (Paul Klee Foundation), ed., Paul Klee. *Catalogue Raisonné*, vol. 2, 1913–1918 (Bern, 2000), 119–21 for available reproductions and pertinent sources, and a stunning color reproduction of *Town with the Three Domes* (133).
70. Paul-Klee-Stiftung, *Paul Klee*, 120.
71. Ibid., 119–20.
72. Ibid., 119, 121.
73. I attribute some degree of specialness to the mount because Klee noted it in his Oeuvre Catalogue.
74. Anger, *Paul Klee*, 48–49.
75. Paul Klee, "Die Ausstellungen des Modernen Bundes im Kunsthaus Zürich," *Die Alpen* 4, no. 12 (July 1912): 696–704, in Schuster, *Delaunay*, 494.
76. Robert Delaunay, "Über das Licht," trans. Paul Klee, *Der Sturm* 3, no. 144–45 (January 1913): 255–56, in Schuster, *Delaunay*, 146–47 (original French and translated German).
77. One might assume that Klee sought to Germanify the language, but there are other instances in the essay in which he keeps the original French, so *Zusammenklang* is likely intentional.
78. Scheerbart refers to them as chapters, but they are more akin to paragraphs.
79. I use the translation in Paul Scheerbart, *Glass Architecture*, trans. James Palmes, in Sharp, *Glass Architecture*, 41.
80. Ibid., 63.
81. Ibid., 45.
82. Salomo Friedländer, "Paul Scheerbart. Ein Medaillon," *Die neue Kunst* 1, no. 2 (December 1913): 203–11, in Salomo Friedländer/Mynona, *Philosophische Abhandlungen und Kritiken 1896–1946*, ed. Detlef Thiel (Herrsching, 2005), 377–78.
83. Scheerbart, *Glass Architecture*, 52.
84. Ibid., 55.
85. Architectural historian Sandy Isenstadt assures me that architects today are well aware of the divide between more expressionist and more constructivist, modernist architecture, just as Hilbersheimer was already in 1929. However, it remains noteworthy that "translucence" drops out of the discourse, *and* that major architectural critics, such as Reyner Banham, long accorded Scheerbart's book a pivotal position in the develop-

ment of modernist architecture *understood* as *transparent*. Banham wrote in 1970 that "of all the visionary writings of that period, this book has the greatest impact nowadays as the concrete and tangible vision of the future environment of man." Banham in Sharp, "Paul Scheerbart's," 8.

86. Paul Scheerbart, "Glashäuser. Bruno Tauts Glaspalast auf der Werkbund-Ausstellung in Cöln," *Technische Monatshefte. Technik für Alle* 4, no. 4 (28 March 1914): 105.
87. Ibid., 106.
88. Ibid., 107.
89. *Glasarchitektur*, unlike some of his other publications, does not include his drawings.
90. The one I have examined, No. 10, is in the collection of the Staatsbibliothek zu Berlin.
91. The book is first advertised in *Der Sturm* 5, no. 4 (May 1914): 32, and its publication is announced in *Der Sturm* 5, no. 6 (June 1914): 48. Both issues advertise the exhibit of Chagall, whose work supplemented and then supplanted the exhibit space shared by Klee's paintings and Taut's architectural model. The latter issue inaugurates a long-standing advertisement for Anna Scheerbart's hand-colored papers.
92. Colored paper experts Susanne Krause and Julia Rinck surmise from my photographs of the paper on the cover that it is technically not "marbleized" paper but probably *Kleisterpapier* (pasted paper), a technique by which one brushes colored glue on paper. I am grateful for their technical expertise. Correspondence with the author, 30 November 2012.
93. Krause and Rinck do not believe that Anna Scheerbart possessed the technical skill to achieve these effects purposefully. Although neither of them had the opportunity to examine this paper in person, Rinck has seen other examples of Anna Scheerbart's paper at the Deutsches Buch- und Schriftmuseum der deutschen Nationalbibliothek in Leipzig. For comparisons, see www.hamburgerbuntpapier.de and www.buntpapier.org (accessed 24 April 2016). Correspondence with the author, 30 November 2012.
94. "Water, because of its intrinsic capacity to reflect, belongs to glass architecture; the two are almost inseparable, so that in the future water will be introduced wherever there is none at the moment." Scheerbart, *Glass Architecture*, 58.
95. Bletter has shown that the association of water with glass goes back to the earliest known models: representations of King Solomon's temple, for example, the Revelation of St. John, and certain Islamic legends. Bletter, "The Interpretation of the Glass Dream—Expressionist Architecture and the History of the Crystal Metaphor," *Journal of the Society of Architectural Historians* 40, no. 1 (March 1981): 20–43.
96. Again, Krause and Rinck do not believe that Anna Scheerbart possessed the requisite skill to achieve these effects purposefully. At the same time, I cannot dismiss either the strength of the effects, purposeful or not, or the (purposeful) selection of the papers for this edition of *Glasarchitektur*.
97. Paul Scheerbart, *Von Zimmer zu Zimmer: 70 Schmoll- und Liebesbriefe des Dichters an seine Frau* (Erlangen, 1977), 19, 38, 44.
98. Paul Scheerbart, *The Gray Cloth: Paul Scheerbart's Novel on Glass Architecture*, trans. and intro. John A. Stuart (Cambridge, 2001), 2.
99. A preliminary answer is that transparency is linked to the fetishization of industrial, technological progress that made the huge expanse in transparent glass manufacture possible to begin with. See Ufuk Ersoy, "The Fictive Quality of Glass," *Architectural Research Quarterly* 11, no. 3–4 (2007): 237.
100. Behne, "Glashaus," 28, emphasis original.

101. Behne mistakenly attributes the quotation to Scheerbart's *Glasarchitektur*, in which a similar formulation can be found (*Glass Architecture*, 61). To my mind, the mistake highlights the collaborative nature of the entire project. Behne, "Glashaus," 28, emphasis original.

Jenny Anger is professor of art history at Grinnell College in Grinnell, Iowa. She has published widely on Paul Klee, abstraction, the decorative, gender, and modern art. Anger's second book, tentatively titled "Metaphors of Modernism: *Der Sturm* and the *Société Anonyme*," is expected to appear in 2016.

CHAPTER 9

Quiet Audience, Roaring Crowd

The Aesthetics of Sound and the Traces of Bayreuth in Kuhle Wampe *and* Triumph of the Will

THEODORE F. RIPPEY

In the Zurich essays of 1849–50, Richard Wagner formed an amorphous concept of an aesthetic event that would unify the three sister arts of poetry, music, and dance and form an organic link between artist, artwork, and audience. This Wagnerian notion of Gesamtkunstwerk was a utopian idea: its value lay in the fact that it was impossible yet imaginable as an artwork of the future. Yet, Wagner kept imagining and aspiring to realize the idea in some form. Some twenty-eight years later at Bayreuth, the inaugural performances of the *Ring* cycle presented an unprecedented audiovisual artwork whose creative impulses were manifestly rooted in Wagner's mid-century dream of an artwork that would transform art itself and all who experienced it.

Wagner did not originate the notion of Gesamtkunstwerk, but as Juliet Koss argues, his idea represented a "complete and mutual overlap of aesthetic and political radicalism" that was absent from earlier conceptualizations. Radicalism, in the literal sense of a return to the roots, was a large part of Wagner's project: taking a (highly stylized) vision of the audience of ancient Greek drama as his ideal, he sought an artwork that, in performance and reception, would not only serve but create an audience, returning a fragmented, distracted public to a more attentive, self-aware state of unity, and generating creative communion between audience and artist. In Wagner's thought, this new art was thus not merely a symptom but a critical vehicle for transforming German society, of its re-becoming a Volk.[1] This aesthetic radicalism involved a melting at the peripheries of the individual arts, coupled with a drive to their respective cores. Above all, Wagner's fusion of the arts sought not to dissolve those components but to set them in a relation that would foster their natural interactivity and amplify each art's individual essence as well.[2]

These two dimensions of Gesamtkunstwerk—as an audiovisual work that combines distinct forms of art and as an object for and maker of an audience—connect Wagner's aesthetic undertakings with two of the most ardently political films of the interwar era: Slatan Dudov's *Kuhle Wampe* (1930) and Leni Riefenstahl's *Triumph of the Will* (1935). Their art form, sound cinema, was made of the confluence of image, words, sound, and motion that Wagner pioneered. Like him, they forged aesthetic objects that joined individual recipients in a collective, inherently political aesthetic experience. Unlike Wagnerian music drama, though, these interwar films depicted the historical present and featured masses of German citizens such that their respective audiences could envision themselves in action as audiences on screen. Moreover, these films featured the *noise* of the roaring crowd: the stadium, the city, the street. This introduction of noise into the work of art meant that the sounds of industrial modernity permeated the films far more than in any work of Wagner's.

In addition, the two films underscore and build on the radical implications of Wagner's ideas on Gesamtkunstwerk, especially as they relate to the relationship between artwork and audience. To grasp this point, we must focus on the centrality of sound in music drama and film. For as waves of sound propagate through an auditorium and permeate the bodies of the listeners, each audience member becomes physically connected to all others. In other words, Gesamtkunstwerk's sonic field is a crucial means of audience unification. When Wagner visualized the Bayreuth festival house and oversaw the specification of its configuration, dimensions, and materials, he sought to design a precisely controlled experience of sound. The actual experience that coalesced at each performance was a product of that design; indeed, it provided an opportunity for his audiences to process the sensory data of his music dramas under aesthetic conditions that he had either authorized or himself devised. Appropriating a key term from sound studies, we can view such a linkage of aesthetic environs and events as a "soundscape", something that Emily Thompson calls "simultaneously a physical environment and a way of perceiving that environment."[3] In Wagner's case, designing and realizing the tightly delineated soundscapes of Bayreuth meant connecting technical and musical processes with the aim of generating revolutionary audiovisual works of art that would guide the audience to achieve awareness of itself as Volk, chiefly through patterns of sensation and perception that are not tied to words. Wagner's proto-cinematic signification, moreover, joined soundscape with kinetic, framed images, and that experience brought together his radical aesthetics and radical politics.[4]

To understand how soundscapes function with respect to audiences and artwork, we need also to reflect on auditory experience itself, on the act of listening. Lutz Koepnick's work on the "modernization of listening" is especially important in this context.[5] Opposing the critical narrative of the "disintegration of perceptual synthesis in the face of the distractions of industrial culture" that pitted "purist" against "synesthetic" modernists, Koepnick reminds us that it "is virtually impossible to conceptualize forms of hearing independent from our faculty of touch or our mental operations of visualizing space."[6] To understand the modernization of listening, he contends, "we need to leave hearing not to the ear alone and instead ask how the advent of modern culture changed the way in which listeners ... came to experience the relationship of acoustical to other sensory stimulation as something structured by contingency, chance, and mutability."[7] Koepnick thus distinguishes pointedly between acoustic modernisms (be they purist or synesthetic) and the modernization of listening, the process by which "modern culture caused the individual to develop ever more provisional maps to navigate the landscapes of both abundant and deterritorialized stimulation."[8]

Wagner's own writings identify him as a synesthetic modernist, particularly in the second chapter of *The Artwork of the Future*, where he discusses the outer and inner human being and the distinct senses to which each presents itself. Here he writes, "The bodily [i.e., outer—TFR] human being, and its involuntary display of the pleasurable or painful impressions that result from external contact, present themselves directly to the eye."[9] Conversely, the inner human being "conveys itself directly to the ear, specifically through the sound of the voice."[10] It is through "the sense of hearing that sound propels itself out of [and] then back to the feelings of the heart."[11] Here Wagner frames the optical system as a register of the pleasure and pain that writes itself on the body and the ear as the processor of innermost human feeling. Over the balance of the treatise, he elaborates a model of the artwork, which, in construction, performance, and reception, conjoins these registers, emphasizing the voice as both a medium of speech and, more pertinent here, non-verbal sonic material. As I will examine below, both Dudov and Riefenstahl continue this audiovisual conjoining, exploiting the non-verbal sound of the voice in particular, as they pursue their distinct aesthetic-political agendas.

Wagner's attempt to realize the Gesamtkunstwerk idea at Bayreuth had to confront the modernization of listening, as did Dudov and Riefenstahl in their films. All three recognized the deterritorialization of aural sensation that came with the increasing noise of modernity. Nonetheless, their respective responses to the sheer intensity and the sound/source riddles of the modern soundscape differed significantly. At Bayreuth, first with the *Ring*, then with *Parsifal*, Wagner created a soundstream that seemed both to emanate and not emanate from specifiable sources, fostering a sense of oneness between audience, artwork, and artists that shielded all from modern din. Dudov exploited the cinema to demonstrate how his audience could work within fields of noise to generate its own soundscapes beyond the movie theater. Like Dudov, Riefenstahl used noise and crowds as material, but her manipulations yielded strictly cinematic versions of both, irreproducible in the street. The two films thus represent a strange bifurcation in the Gesamtkunstwerk's line of descent. *Kuhle Wampe* ruptured the boundary between art and everyday life, but even as it moved aesthetic activity from the sacred to the profane, it maintained a vibrant relationship with the audience. By contrast, *Triumph of the Will* kept the tradition of sacrosanct aesthetic event, but it left the audience in the limited role of beholder.

The Quiet Audience and the Festspielhaus as Medium

More than any venue before it, the Bayreuth Festspielhaus was designed as a generator and conveyor of elaborate audio and visual impressions. There were no box seats, and as Smith notes, the "narrowed, steeply raked" amphitheater-style seating rows made Bayreuth the "first proscenium theater since ancient Rome designed with the explicit purpose of giving all spectators a clear view of the stage."[12] The importance placed on seeing, and seeing a similar object in a similar manner, set Wagner's auditorium design apart from those of theaters and opera houses constructed with the express purpose of providing different levels of visual access for different strata of society.[13] Music drama is made for the eye as well as the ear, and the eyes of the audience, to the extent that it is spatially and architectonically possible, were supposed to see (as one collective eye). The characteristic emphasis on collective sensory processing on reception as an aesthetic as well as social act, distinguishes Wagner's Gesamtkunstwerk concept from that of his forerunner, Carl Friedrich Trahndorff. In his two-volume treatise on aesthetics, Trahndorff extensively categorized the sound-based temporal arts and the vision-based spatial arts, tying the inner nature of each form to a specific set of perceptual and epistemological processes. He posited that the four main artistic enterprises—word-sound (*Wortklang*), music, expressive gesture (*Mimik*), and dance—might flow together in one artwork, following a core "aspiration toward a Gesamt-Kunstwerk" that was common to all arts.[14] Trahndorff's concerns are clearly Wagner's as well, but the latter's conceptualization of the audience is more socially and historically specific than Trahndorff's abstract figure of the perceiving and understanding human being.

What the audience's collective eye sees was framed at Bayreuth in an unprecedented manner. Wagner and Brandt countersank the pit beneath the stage, removing the orchestra from sight and creating what Wagner called a "mystic gulf" (*mystischer Abgrund*), from which the music would seem magically to emanate. Before this pit they placed a second proscenium, which had the dual effect of further obscuring the gulf and of making the actors on stage seem larger and more distant through forced perspective.[15] This double framing distorted the audience's traditional visual image of the stage, reinforcing the impression of the stage-space and its contents as an integral moving image, not simply as an area where people interact and things happen. Smith notes Wagner's fascination with making the Bayreuth music drama performances into "landscape painting in sight, sound, and motion,"[16] a stream of kinetic visual information, intricately bound to an aural sister strand. The audience's visual concentration on this stream was fostered by one final innovation, a practical measure that has now become so common as to escape notice: "[F]or the first time in theater history, house lights were darkened during all performances, forcing spectators to direct their entire attention on the work. This last innovation, perhaps Bayreuth's most famous, anticipates not only later theatrical practice but twentieth-century cinemas as well."[17] James H. Johnson has documented the practice of darkening in Paris concert halls of the late 1800s.[18] But it is accurate to view Wagner's Bayreuth performance model as the first to make full darkening of the house a consistent practice, integral to the design of the audiovisual experience.

The repercussions of this practice were significant. As a range of scholars have demonstrated, a fundamental transformation of listening and spectating in European theaters and opera houses took place between roughly the last quarter of the eighteenth century and the last quarter of the nineteenth. These places of entertainment and edification, which began this period with fully illuminated auditoriums that frequently teemed with mobile and vocal occupants, eventually came to be places of quiet concentration.[19] During much of the nineteenth century, Sven Oliver Müller observes, audiences went to the opera to be seen and heard as much as performers did. Neither visual representations of class status nor oral communication among audience members or between audience and artists halted during the performance. Thundering applause could mean a demand for an immediate encore of an aria, while performers deemed substandard could be whistled from the stage. Weber goes so far as to argue that if we anachronistically apply today's standards of audience behavior to the audiences of the eighteenth century, we could easily conclude that those audiences did not even listen to music at performances at all.[20]

Müller argues convincingly that Wagner's paradigm was pivotal in the transition from the vocal, physically dynamic audience to its quiet, still successor. It was thus a decisive factor in a continent-wide quieting of the listening public, which had once brought all the noise of society into the auditorium.[21] This change was due both to the architectural and acoustic features of the Bayreuth house and to the music itself, the structure of which left the audience few if any opportunities to inject applause or cheers. This disciplining of the audience during the long nineteenth century did not proceed in a smooth, linear fashion, and it reflected the interests of different groups: the state (which, until the late eighteenth century, literally policed the public sphere by posting guards in theaters[22]), artists, critics, and those sectors of the audiences themselves who came to deem quiet appreciation the mark of personal erudition and good taste. The theater became a noise-reduction machine and the spectator-auditor's attention was directed squarely on the sights and sounds of art.

The audiences of Bayreuth attended to something unprecedented. Opera before Wagner, as Friedrich Kittler argues, "was based upon a separation between verbal and acoustic data, recitatives and arias, which in final analysis may have simply duplicated the division of labor between libretto and score, between text supplier and composer."[23] As Gesamtkunstwerk, Wagner's music drama generated a relationship between the aural, the visual, and the kinetic that was more important than any referential relationship that reached beyond the bounds of the work: the "reciprocal motivation of different sensory fields" was his prime aesthetic objective, not context-dependent meaning.[24] This reciprocal motivation generated a new kind of aesthetic information that could evince significance without accumulating historically contingent meaning.

In Kittler's analysis, breathing assumes a central place as both a bearer of this information and a thing that can be seen, heard, and touched. He makes much, for example, of Isolde's lament over Tristan, in which the hero's dead body begins to breathe again: "*Is it only I who hear / this air, / so wondrous and quiet, / sweetly lamenting, / telling all, / mildly reconciling, / sounding from him, / penetrating into me, / rising upward, / sweetly resounding, / ringing around me?*"[25] Kittler observes that in this passage, a "crescendo in both the text and the score … enables a … body no longer capable of breathing and singing to be brought back to life. Tristan's extinguished breath returns as orchestral melody: the sounds he emits penetrate the listener."[26] For Kittler, the orchestra has "the exact function of an amplifier." Taking signals from the body of the singer and making them greater in size, scope, and intensity, it fills the space of the auditorium with the virtual breath of the singers. This process creates a positive feedback loop, in which the original vocal signal, fed into and amplified by the orchestra, is then picked up again by the voice—either the original singer's or a new singer's. "The voice in Wagner is so unindividuated," argues Kittler, "his acoustics so ecstatic, that to the ear of a woman singing, her own voice appears essentially as the voice of the other."[27]

In a journalistic piece on the Bayreuth experience, Simon Williams noted, "I have never felt, as some do, that the sound of the orchestra from the sunken pit is more muffled than it would be in a conventional theater, but the music does emerge more blended and, as it rebounds off the wooden walls of the auditorium, sounds as if it emanates from the whole space, rather than from a particular spot in the theater."[28] Processed through the unseen orchestral amplifier, the voice remains with and moves outside the singer, blending synergistically with the instrumental music to generate a soundstream that emanates from the whole space and penetrates the listener in the dark: for Kittler, this all makes the Bayreuth confluence of music and architecture "the first artistic machine capable of reproducing sensuous data as such."[29] And in the collective, simultaneous processing of this sensuous data, audience and performers link in an aural community.

The sensuous data of the Gesamtkunstwerk that Kittler theorizes were not totally abstract. For as much as the Wagnerian total work of art worked outside conventional verbal meanings, its creator nonetheless desired something very specific to be sensed by the occupants of the auditorium. In essence, the point of quieting and concentrating the audience, of enveloping and permeating it with all those waves of sound, was to grant the audience, as distillate of the Volk, a visceral, mental and spiritual experience of its ideal state. The inclination and capacity of the artist to express that ideality, and the inclination and capacity of the audience to feel and recognize it as such, both come from the same place: "Only out of shared life," writes Wagner in *The Artwork of the Future*, "can the impulse to form life into a comprehensible object in art emerge; only the community of artists can express this impulse; only communally can they satisfy it."[30] In practice, Wagner's tendency to assert control over all dimensions of a performance may have put him at cross-purposes with his principle; the emphasis on collectivity here is striking nonetheless.

But if the community of art producers envisioned in 1849 was difficult to realize in 1876, then the stakes were even higher for assembling the audience, whose participation formed the second, essential condition of the Gesamtkunstwerk. Dramatic action, for Wagner, was "that which makes participation possible for all; that which makes participation necessary; that which, *without this participation, could never emerge*."[31] In other words, the creative force flows from the Volk, through the artist, and into the drama. But the Volk's experience of drama is what gives drama life. As Joy Calico argues in Chapter 4 of this volume, "Wagner was focused on what an audience member saw, heard, felt, and thought during a performance." In a community of sensation, thoughts and feelings out of sync with the design would disrupt the feedback loop, bringing the entire aesthetic undertaking to the point of collapse.

For Wagner, the audience's reception of the total work of art was both a new aesthetic experience and an act through which the Volk rediscovered and reinvigorated itself. As Smith argues, the Festspielhaus "would serve as a common destination for a larger Volk, a Volk currently lost in the hurly-burly of industrialized culture."[32] Again here, one encounters the aesthetic-political overlap that marks Wagner's particular understanding of Gesamtkunstwerk. Constructing Bayreuth as a place of art pilgrimage was an "attempt to return society to an antique form of marking the landscape." That form of marking was inherently collective and the pilgrims who made the journey "became essentially visitor-actors, participants in a single, great drama of collective reawakening."[33] The festival experience became a means of putting the audience aurally and visually back in touch with what Wagner imagined as its premodern self. The new experience of sound—made possible only by great technical innovation and the newly quiet audience—was a product of architectural design and cultural engineering, both of which filtered the noise of the world out of the aesthetic aural experience. The generation and reception of a clean sensory data stream became a means of experiencing primal, ideal unity.

Wagner's modernism thus demonstrates acute awareness of the deterritorialization of sensation, the conundrums with which the modernization of listening confronts the modern listener. But the Bayreuth model brackets those conundrums, manipulating aural and visual perception in ways intended to induce a sense of magical oneness, rather than jarring fragmentation. That means that the audiovisual experience of the festival performance runs against the current of the modernization of listening that Koepnick theorizes. This perspective is a logical consequence of Wagner's aim to work against what he deemed the deleterious effects of modern culture on the Volk, even as he oversaw an unprecedented technical modernization of his art. For the filmmakers of the interwar era, dominated as it was by mass politics and permeated with mass media, it was critical to work with, not against, the noise of the modern crowd.

Aural Demonstration—*Kuhle Wampe*

On 30 May 1932, some eighty-three years into the future that Wagner wrote of in 1849, a large audience sat quietly in the Atrium Theater in Berlin-Wilmersdorf and saw and heard a rare experiment in left-independent cinema: Slatan Dudov's *Kuhle Wampe oder Wem gehört die Welt?* (Kuhle Wampe or Who Owns the World?).[34] The crowds in Kuhle Wampe were no customary extras marshaled to a set: they were Berlin's young workers themselves, in their swimsuits and sweaters, astride roaring motorcycles, packed into grandstands and cheering in unison. The audience applauded loudly at the end,[35] and reviews confirm that the interaction between film and audience was a conscious mix of aesthetics and politics. Referring to the film's emphasis on collectives, one critic noted, "Private lives have become insignificant and uninteresting; the struggles over the fate of masses have begun. This contention is more than many people can take, and for once, one notes its presence in film. Otherwise, this tone is unknown in cinema auditoriums, where the flicker of operetta love stories has reigned to date and will continue to reign."[36] That tone was supposed to resonate with the modern mass, accelerating its transition to a self-aware revolutionary collective. In this section, I compare how *Kuhle Wampe* established a relationship between audience, art, and sound that both corresponds to and departs from Wagner's model. My analysis of the film focuses more on the aurality of the audiovisual texts themselves than on the auditorium. The matter of soundscape remains central, however. In the Wagnerian soundscape, the modern collective listenership is present only in the seats. In Dudov's soundscapes, that listenership is both on and before the screen.

Kuhle Wampe begins as a silent film would, with only images and score. In the first montage, we rush from the Brandenburg Gate down the broad streets and through the back alleys of Berlin, jostle with the unemployed on a dreary corner, and flash rapidly through the unemployment-crisis headlines of the day. As the camera propels us along these interwoven trajectories through actual street-space and virtual news-space, a physical sensation of tension increases. The editing establishes a pulsating visual rhythm; Eisler's shrill, driving musical score raises the intensity. In this opening, a curious paradox develops in which we achieve multiperspectival command of the city's spaces, people, and problems, yet remain acutely aware of the fragmentary, limited quality of that command. *Kuhle Wampe* illustrates how the tools of cinema can introduce a profusion of information and then remind audiences that they have only a tenuous grasp of those data.

The segment concludes with eight seconds of silence: sound mix reduced to zero. Then, as the unemployed young man Bönike (Alfred Schäfer) enters the courtyard of his family's tenement, harmonium and bowed-saw music fill the space of the frame and the ears of the audience. Bönike pauses to listen, and we have an image that could be a *Neue Sachlichkeit* painting of city life. Seconds later, we are in the family apartment. As father Bönike (Max Sablotzki) sits up to write something down, we hear the first ambient sounds of the film: a slight creaking of sofa frame and wooden floor, a knife clanking against the breadbasket. Mrs. Bönike (Lilli Schoenborn) is setting the table for lunch, and we hear the soft clinking of porcelain and flatware. This is also the moment at which we hear a human voice for the first time, Herr Bönike, observing in monotone, "Now the boy will no longer get any support, whatsoever." Herr Bönike looks to his wife for a reply, not recognizing that his remark is more of a notice than an initiation of dialog.

During this non-exchange, we hear something else: the saw and harmonium music, muted to signal the vertical distance between courtyard and apartment but clear and present throughout. This is a technique that Dudov and sound editor Peter Meyrowitz employ throughout the film: using off-screen sound associable to a previously established space in order to link it to the space established in the current frame. This is not a classic sound bridge, employed to link a chain of actions across disparate spaces or preserve the sensation of narrative continuity across a temporal or spatial break that would otherwise register as jarring. Here, the bridge enables a cinematic perception of distinct yet contiguous spaces, thereby illustrating how aural range can extend beyond the tightly demarcated location of the body and the visually specifiable field of perception.

This delimited expansion of the sensory field is directly connected to the modernization of listening. As Koepnick maintains, the principal question raised by the loss of perceptible connection between a sound and its source is how the listening subject will solve the ensuing riddles and come to terms with that new contingency. In this scene, no such riddles are posed. The aural configuration of apartment, window, and courtyard generate an auditory field that is perfectly territorialized, not deterritorialized, as Koepnick describes modernized aural sensation. The auditory field is larger than the visual field, but it is still a small soundscape in which connections between sound and source are clear, even if not seen. At the same time, the impression of the perceptually unwieldy city persists from the opening montage. That impression triggers an awareness that the small soundscape is enveloped in something far greater, a sonic sea that must be structured by cinematic, architectural, or social-political means. The courtyard is a buffer zone between the dynamic spaces of the city and the static space of the apartment, and it is in this buffer zone that diegetic sound (that is, sound originating within the story-world of the film) enters our aural picture. That sound is soothing, not probing; it provides a moment of respite for young Bönike by detaching him aurally from the desperation of the work-search cycle, just as stepping into the courtyard puts physical distance between himself and the street.

There is a strange echo of Wagner in this sheltering space of sound. But unlike at Bayreuth, where the sound-field was designed to hold all thought of modern society at bay, the sonic scene in the film demonstrates how precarious such shelter is. Having passed through the frontier of the courtyard, young Bönike faces a withering, myopic critique at home. Although the father is reading a newspaper, his speech offers no evidence that he comprehends the complexity beyond the buffer zone, to which the domestic space is linked. The sonically established, dual-space enclosure of the tenement has a dual edge; its protection is not genuine. The courtyard is not a passage to a place of greater security but a tidal zone between threatening sea and merciless land. As the sound of the music reaches up from the street-level courtyard, it charts for young Bönike the path that he will soon take back down, ending his life in the only place that he can find shelter. He faces propulsive, kinetic dehumanization in the streets and sits immobilized by parental castigation at the lunch table, compelled to absorb verbal blows. The courtyard permits him the privilege of choosing where he stands, listens, and rests.

The climactic sports festival provides a contrasting case of how *Kuhle Wampe* establishes these politically charged relationships between sound, space, and image. The festival has a prelude that is similar to the opening of the film: a montage of images (this time, motorcycle, swimming, and rowing races, and the anthem "Learn to Triumph!"). The balance of the sequence features multiple sources and layers of sound, on- and off-screen, creating a set of contours that lend form to the relationship between the sonorous collective of worker-athletes depicted on the screen and the listening spaces in which that collective comes together.

As, for example, the crowd and camera switch locations from the finish line of the motorcycle race to an open-air stage and its surrounding grandstands, we hear steady applause and low-intensity cheers. A whistle and a shout rupture this layer of sound, and the beat of the snare drums and the cadences of the agitprop troupe The Red Megaphone (*Das rote Sprachrohr*) follow. As the troupe performs vocal snapshots of their audience's everyday life, there is a smattering of murmurs, which, like the troupe's shouts and declarations, float suspended in or shoot through a matrix of ambient sound. This creates a mixture of the purposeful and the incidental, illustrating the formation of a designed soundscape within an ambient soundscape.

The agitprop performance concludes with a collective rendition of the film's anthemic "Solidarity Song," and the next twenty-four shots track the dispersal of the crowd and its departure from the festival site. Nearly four minutes of screen time elapse, a striking amount for a departure sequence in any film. Only four shots in the sequence contain dialogue, two of which I will treat briefly here. In the thirteenth shot, Kurt (Adolf Fischer) and Gerda (Marta Wolter), a politically and athletically active pair, briefly discuss the evolution of their friend Fritz's flawed thinking on the concept of freedom and conclude that he ought to reunite with his estranged fiancée, Anni. In the fourteenth, Fritz (Ernst Busch) admits to Anni (Hertha Thiele), "You may be right." As the couple has dealt with relationship strife and an unplanned pregnancy, Anni has pushed for them to strengthen their commitment to one another, while Fritz has withdrawn. In addition, she has gravitated to the young workers' movement, while he has resisted joining. In both instances, he has insisted on maintaining his freedom, and his admission to her is a concession that he was wrong on both counts. In the bulk of the sequence (twenty of the twenty-four shots), there is no dialogue whatsoever. The sound track is composed principally of human voices, but no words are intelligible. This is a non-verbal layer of vocal sound that by turns interferes with, encases, or enhances the sequence's other sonic constructs. In the Kurt and Gerda exchange, the sound mix grants the non-verbal layer a relatively high intensity, but it does not overpower the featured characters' speech. The Fritz and Anni shot strikes the same balance between the characters' articulate words and the inarticulate collective vocalization, but the source track switches as a visual edit signals change of location. In each case, the filmmakers subtly manipulate the sonic raw material to produce concentrated sound formations of limited scope within encompassing fields of noise and ambient sound. And the non-verbal layer fills the background in both cases: the collective vocalization surrounds the pairs as far as the ear can hear, but it does not threaten their individual voices. These scenes take the sheltering dynamics of Wagner's soundscapes and repurpose them for street-level use. There is a basic, common desire to unify bodies through fields of sound, but unlike at Bayreuth, where those fields were to be integral and sustained, the film simultaneously demonstrates their viability and their ephemerality.

The audience hears the "Solidarity Song" throughout the last nine shots of the departure sequence, but always at a distance. It enters the aural scene as the rowers put their boats back in the water for the return trip, and this connection recalls the aural contiguity of the Bönike apartment sequence. Here Dudov uses shots not only of athletes (thus drawing an association between those not singing in the frame and those singing beyond it) but also of objects, showing how the sound waves that the worker-athletes produce permeate the atmosphere, even when human figures are absent. A shot of departing motorcycles follows the shots of the boats, and the rumbling motors counterbalance the song, which intensifies slightly as the motorcycles recede spatially from the camera location and the marchers approach it. As the last athletes enter the S-Bahn station, the last refrain of the song weaves itself into the chatter and bustle.

In the winding down of the mass event, scripted dialogue is combined with semi-audible bits of background conversations, whistling, and singing, all held together both by post-production processing and by the ambient sound captured during shooting. In narrative terms, Dudov is intentionally inefficient here, intermixing images of people and objects, and lingering over the sounds in a display of cinema's audio configuration. Dudov and Meyrowitz establish a basic sonic texture, then insert or overlay intelligible utterances at strategic points, thus counterposing voice-as-speech and voice-as-noise. But they also let a talking picture stop talking without going silent, matching ambient, spatially captured sound to the objects that occupy that space.

Among these sound forms, those in which the *Kuhle Wampe* filmmakers visually displace the sounds of the collective are especially paradigmatic. The collective voice filling the background demonstrates how the worker-athletes have dispersed themselves throughout the auditory field and generated enough sonic material to achieve sonic hegemony within that space. The individual listener does not become one with the Volk in the sacred hall. Rather, he or she resonates with the collective in this expanse of sound, receiving an impression of its scope and power. The collective's sonic hegemony counteracts to the point of near inversion the deterritorialization that Koepnick has identified. One can trace this effect throughout the progression toward and dispersal from the festival. Marchers, bicyclists, and motorcyclists proceed out of the city in columns, and the vocalization of their songs combines with the sound of their motors to generate a mobile field of sound that they control en route and expand once they reach the event site. Just as the mobile sound field builds toward the intensity and density of the festival itself, it dissipates upon conclusion, and the lessening intensity of organized sonic event displays the transitory character of any hegemony—sensory, political, or otherwise. Implicit in this model of audiovisual assembly and disassembly is the idea that sound agents and political agents alike (individual or collective) must achieve their hegemonies through direct engagement with a sensory and political here and now that can never be dominated completely. The always-returning ambient sound field serves as the nagging but encouraging reminder of those dimensions of human experience that will resist any aesthetic and ideological assimilation.

As the collective sound agents within *Kuhle Wampe* generate their local and mobile sound fields, the specific traits of each and the ambient matrices within which they cohere reveal not only the complexity of their sonic environs but also the variety of aesthetic manipulations that cinematic intervention into those soundscapes makes possible. The film's tendency to display its workings signals that each technique is one among many, implying that myriad paradigms of sound manipulation can hold sway within and outside cinematic bounds. Noise as material and modern technologies of sound recording and amplification are critical as both instruments and content of this presentation. Unlike the Wagnerian Gesamtkunstwerk paradigm, in which modern technology's achievements are exploited to construct a field of sound against the noise of industrial, urban modernity, that same noise here becomes productive material for the self-generation of soundscapes that have a progressive aesthetic and political charge. *Kuhle Wampe* lets noise in, takes it up, and fashions from it a sound-art that displays its own construction and thus provides a blueprint for how such construction might relocate from the cinema auditorium to the streets. Following the convention cemented in Bayreuth, the cinema audience sat quietly. But as it did, it saw and heard itself in action, as captured by recording devices, not the expression of its essence, as channeled through mythical characters. And as it saw and heard the exhortation that concluded the film—"Who *will* change the world?" / "Those who it does not please!"—it could contemplate a cinematic experience that had shown how making purposeful noise could forge the revolutionary collective. The *Kuhle Wampe* team directed its audience into the heart of a noisy aural and political modernity, even as the film shared the Wagnerian Gesamtkunstwerk's impulse to make the artwork a medium through which artists and audience would join in a larger cause.

In his work on nationalistic singing and cheering as "acoustic mass mobilization"[37] on the brink of World War I, Daniel Morat has analyzed a resonant collective with an altogether different political charge. What he describes on the Berlin street in 1914, however, shares aesthetic and physical traits with what unfolds in *Kuhle Wampe*. Morat's approach emphasizes how acoustic communication creates shared affective states, how "sound brings bodies in relation with one another and sets them in collective motion."[38] This mode of acoustic communication calls into being a new mode of "feeling and moving together" that will proliferate, Morat argues, in the interwar years.[39] *Kuhle Wampe* proves this point. And to an extent, Bayreuth anticipates it. In my discussion above, I stressed the critical status of quiet in the festival hall. And yet the concept of the resonant collective is indispensable to Wagner's idea of how the audience, through the experience of music drama, is to achieve oneness with itself as Volk.

Sound Sculpture—*Triumph of the Will*

In Riefenstahl's cinematic territorialization of sound, even the ambient sound field is synthesized in the studio whenever possible. The sound-images offered are therefore documents of product, not process. They do not re-present the extracinematic soundscape in detail. Rather, they pare that soundscape down, substituting studio synthesis for virtual aural reality. In this respect, Riefenstahl's project is even more radical than either Wagner's or Dudov's, for it is not at all "live."

Triumph of the Will waits twenty-five minutes to become a *talking* picture. Consider what one does not hear during that interval. Hitler's Junkers Ju-52 had three BMW 132T radial engines that produced a combined 2,145 horsepower. They are silent. As are all the automobiles—eighteen in one shot. As is the woman, who comes out into the street with her daughter, bearing a personal gift of flowers for the Führer. The children singled out for close-up are silent, and so are all the individual Germans who line the route, mouthing phantom words. What one hears is music and the rolling waves of cheers, which, upon close review, are diegetic, in the sense that they can be logically linked to a source within the narrative world of the film. This crowd noise, however, was joined to the images through post-shoot audio dubbing, creating a superimposition of sound onto image. As with many mechanisms of filmmaking, it is unlikely that this dubbing registered consciously with audiences who saw the film a single time. Even at first hearing, though, it triggers a momentary sensation of strangeness, akin to that caused by slight imperfections in post-synced dialogue.

Sound travels far more slowly than light. When we hear, the physical fusion of sound and visible source is already a thing of the past, but our sensing and neural processing equipment makes the match as a means of orientation. The apparent union of sound and image enhances our sense of security in the dual flows of time and space, and this perceptual habit of audiovisual matching is hard to break. As Michel Chion argues, "[a] sound that falls at the same time a visual movement will stick to it, even if the sound's consistency, color, and timbre are hardly even coherent with the visual phenomenon it accompanies. This is what I call *synchresis*."[40] Chion posits that the everyday processing of related aural and visual stimuli prepares us to resolve perceptual quandaries by creating synchretic associations where physical links do not exist. These quandaries arise most frequently when we are confronted with acousmatic sounds—that is, sounds without specifiable sources—that proliferate in modern aurality. At Bayreuth, Wagner built acousmatic sound into the design of the space by countersinking the pit and creating the mystical gulf, but this had the effect of enhancing, not disturbing the aesthetic experience. In *Kuhle Wampe*, acousmatic sound (crowd noise) abounds, but its association to situations on and beyond the screen made it a means of linking cinematic and social reality. In *Triumph of the Will*, Riefenstahl frequently inverts the acousmatic effect: her sculpting of sound increasingly dissolves the ties between artist, art, and audience that both Wagner and Dudov sought to create.

As Chion notes, Warner Brothers' early interest in Vitaphone sound-on-disc recording technology was spurred not by the desire to create a *talking* picture but to institute a means of synchronizing image and music that would make expensive orchestras redundant. In *Triumph of the Will*, we hear an approximation of this approach. As Amy Wlodarski details elsewhere in this volume, Riefenstahl herself directed a concert band in post-shoot studio sessions to generate the musical track for most of the marching sequences in the film.[41] Like the crowd noise, the processed soundstream of the march music is matched to the visual information-stream post-event. The match is nearly perfect, but the absence of ambient sound and random background noise generates a note of artifice. Again and again, Riefenstahl reverses the acousmatic process: sound sources abound in our visual field, but many are silenced in the final sound mix. We also perceive a carefully engineered synchresis in which, for example, the crowd's sonic cascades adhere not only to the cheering mass but to the Führer's face. Similarly, the martial music and orchestral setting of the "Horst Wessel Lied" form a bond with the black-enameled steel of the motorcade and the corrugated contours of the Ju-52. Here we see and hear a response to the dilemma of modern aurality that Koepnick describes. Sounds and sources are decoupled, signaling the contingent and arbitrary relationship between the visual and the aural. But Riefenstahl's aesthetic interventions transform that decoupling into a coherent audiovisual image, which works within established cinematic convention and thus eliminates the disorientation that the audience might feel.

In Riefenstahl's film, synchresis forms an aesthetic symbiosis with the visual technique of freeze-dissolve. The segue between the matinal scenes of the city and the raucous images of morning at the SA and youth camps, for instance, is a freeze-dissolve of the spires of Nuremberg's St. Sebaldus Church and the rows of tents on the camp field. As the church towers fade and the tents materialize, an instrumental facsimile of the church bell tolls. The depicted structures melt into one another visually, and the sound adheres to both. Such moments present a purely cinematic audiovisual image, one impossible for a human being to perceive in the sensory environs beyond the screen, and it is in this kind of formal innovation that Riefenstahl comes closest to Wagner's proto-cinematic fusion of the arts.

A similar moment occurs when Hitler concludes his address to the Reich Labor Service men. In this case, Riefenstahl freezes the leader's medium-shot profile image with his arm defiantly thrust toward the upper-right corner of the frame, as the last word of his speech lingers a moment, then blends in with the lyrics and music of the marching hymn. The dynamic image that fades in is a low-angle shot of a marching column. They pass the camera's eye in half-profile, moving in a slightly upward direction from frame-right to frame-left. Thus they literally move within and through the Führer, creating a half-kinetic canted cross, linking the fluid motion of their corps to the iron constancy of the frozen face and stiff arm, and coating both with the associational audio lacquer of the hymn. This example also merits note because in a single frame it makes explicit the visual associations that persist across edits—for example, when Riefenstahl cuts from the orating Führer to the listening crowd without interrupting the audio track. Such cuts take the sound of the leader's voice off-screen and make his image an after-image, allowing the sound of his voice to adhere both to his own (momentarily absent) visage and to the on-screen image of the mass of corpsmen.

This superimposition illustrates an encompassing aesthetic strategy that, in strict visual terms, entails a split-second de-evolution of cinematography into photography and thus a temporary cohabitation of the older and the younger medium within the film frame.[42] This models a visual practice of conjoined perception and recall that ameliorates the formal and medial friction inherent in the forced coexistence of the static and the kinetic; the spectator experiences the presence of the frozen past moment not as a disturbance but as an enhancement of the present-in-motion. On a sonic level, the logic of the audio sculpture is simple: pare the soundscape down in order to form a critical mass of sonic connective tissue among visual images, and encase those images in a synchretic aural membrane. Here Riefenstahl is a sonic minimalist who places tight reins on sound so that it magnifies the impact of the audiovisual construct without palpably splitting the audience's attention.

The last two words of Hitler's speech to the Labor Corps men are *marschieren* (to march) and *seh'n* (to see). Riefenstahl freezes the close-up image of his face and arm at the end of marschieren, and the freeze persists for approximately 105 frames (just over four seconds, at the standard rate of 24 frames per second). For the first twelve of those frames (a half-second or so), the audio track contains the word *seh'n,* creating a moment of aural continuity that carries the spectator-auditor across the threshold of visual arrest by providing concrete sensory evidence of the continuing flow of time. The sense of an abrupt halt is further resolved by the almost immediate visual introduction of the kinetic marching column. But the "almost" here is critical: in order for Riefenstahl's cinematic aesthetic to hold, the static image must not rupture the narrative flow or the formal unity of the film, but stasis must be clearly articulated nonetheless. The twelve frames are just long enough to provide an impression of coexistence of stasis and kinesis that is striking but not jarring.

In the way that it gradually decomposes one image and composes another, the freeze-dissolve also gives screen time and visual expression to the compression of space that any cut entails. The voice-bridge works in concert with the dissolve, not to erase the temporal and spatial disfigurations that the edit constitutes but to harmonize them, to foster the audience's achievement of a stable relationship with them. Such audiovisual constructs train a mode of perception comfortable with a strange combination of temporal suspension and temporal flow, of frozen posture and dynamic action.

Scholarly interpretations of this precarious balance of stasis and motion tend to unfold within the framework of psychoanalytic theory, media genealogy, or text-based critiques of fascism's aesthetic antipathy toward language. Brigitte Peucker's analysis of Riefenstahl's "tableaux" draws on all three trajectories, expanding the psychoanalytic reading through careful attention to the intertextual and intermedial dimensions of the tableaux.[43] Russell Berman has characterized "fascist rhetoric as the displacement of the verbal by the visual,"[44] and Peucker's analysis qualifies but essentially shares this position. Like Berman, Peucker finds that "fascist artistic practice favors the respatialization that occurs when the temporality of language is abandoned in favor of the image."[45]

But the striking thing about these examples is that they do not abandon the temporality of language (or sound generally), even as Riefenstahl constructs an image that momentarily suspends kinetic temporality. Language here is speech, however. It thus affords the opportunity to use verbal material as sonic material. Riefenstahl constructs and melds two images: one visual, one sonic. The sonic element of this cinematic fusion is both language and image: it registers with listeners who sense themselves as receivers of an intelligible message and beholders of an encompassing, resonant form.

Triumph of the Will introduces audiovisual images that cannot exist in the perceptual field outside cinema. As Georg Seeßlen argues, "Modernity is present in Riefenstahl's films, in the conspicuousness of their technical devices and in the very direct manner in which the power of the medium itself is represented."[46] Riefenstahl's technical achievement is to make these thoroughly modern, medium-specific convergences of visual and aural information something comfortable, not jarring, for the audience. When kinesis and stasis coexist within the frame, the film openly reveals its cinematographic, photographic, and phonographic construction, but the effect of that revelation is pleasurable beholding. Recognition of artifice easily coexists with sensory rapture.

These images condition a level of comfort with perceptual paradox and a habit of accommodating the perceiving self to the conundrum without resolving it. This perceptual comfort is structurally analogous to the comfort that the rational self must develop with the ideological contradictions of fascism. But a sensate awareness of the conundrum persists, leading the spectator-auditor to regard the audiovisual image as something that can be witnessed but not entered. As Seeßlen puts it, "Coldness is not an error, but rather the essence of Riefenstahl films. They are perfect, but they are uninhabitable."[47] By contrast, with Gesamtkunstwerk, Wagner endeavors to make art a process of emerging consciousness: hence, in the music drama, the Volk awakens to itself. *Kuhle Wampe* has no use for a mythical Volk, but it, too, seeks to promote a process of revolutionary becoming. *Triumph of the Will* takes Germany's history-altering rebirth as a fait accompli, and simply presents the Volk with its ideal image, now realized in the historical present. It does not foster a process; it presents a product.

Conclusion

Dudov and Riefenstahl share an awareness of the modernization of listening that Koepnick analyzes, and both of their films capitalize on cinematography and analog recording technology to respond to the perceptual problems that modern aurality presents. Central among those problems is a strange paradox: the relationship between sonic stimuli and sensory impressions is arbitrary, contingent, and mutable; seeing, hearing, and touching, however, are not split but linked. Wagner's synesthetic modernism rejects this paradox in two ways. First, it assumes the split of the senses. Second, it responds to that split with a Gesamtkunstwerk that deterritorializes aural sensation—the sound emanates from everywhere—but does so in such a way that the encompassing aesthetic experience registers as organically unified, not arbitrary or contingent.

The basic approaches of working with or against the modernization of listening mark a distinction between Wagner and the filmmakers. Nonetheless, Gesamtkunstwerk's theorist is linked to the artists of the moving image. The most fundamental connection is the establishment at Bayreuth of the conditions of perception that define the interwar cinema auditorium. Beyond that, the purification of soundstreams in the music drama and the sealed auditory space in the Festspielhaus signal a desire to control the soundscape that informs Riefenstahl's audio-sculpture. At the same time, the soundscapes within soundscapes that take form throughout *Kuhle Wampe* demonstrate an aesthetic and political reluctance to give up on the idea of forging integral, interactive experiences of sound within the din of modernity, even as they show that the deterritorialization of sensation and the modernization of listening make it impossible for such experiences to achieve durability.

Matthew Smith stresses the distance between the Bayreuth audience and the Bayreuth spectacle, and Simon Williams remarks on the way that the double proscenium makes the figures on stage seem both closer and farther away. Still, the music dramas Wagner presented at Bayreuth are not uninhabitable by design in the same way as in Riefenstahl's film. In Wagner's imagination, premodern perfection originates with the genius of the Volk, the sounds of the music drama permeate and link everybody present, and the existence of the music drama as art hinges both on modern technology and on a participatory audience. Wagner envisioned an audience that, in its awakened processing of the aesthetic effects of the Festspielhaus, achieved communion with its mythical self through the artwork. In the Dudov film, habitability is built in, in the displays of the human figures that populate the everyday of life of the audience, the demarcation of the spaces of that life, and the demonstration of how mobile, temporary soundscapes that are generated and dissipate within those spaces can be a product of the revolutionary collective's action and a process of the revolutionary collective's construction. In Riefenstahl's film, however, habitability is obliterated by coldness, but it is also simply obsolete: once the perfect image of the Volk has been struck, the original (real or imagined) is no longer required. As I have argued above, not forming the participatory bond with the audience means a major break with the Wagnerian Gesamtkunstwerk. Riefenstahl's film displays the aesthetic dimensions that one would expect—indeed, she even extends the formal bounds described by Trahndorff and Wagner when she integrates the still image—but deactivating the audience runs counter to the tendency that connects Wagner and Dudov.

To close, I will take one more look at the still image in *Triumph of the Will*. I argued earlier that, when Riefenstahl carries the sounds of speech across the divide between static and moving image, she works against what Berman and Peucker identify as the respatialization of experience in fascist aesthetics. Because I make use of the static image, however, my argument must accept theirs in order to work. Riefenstahl does in fact repeatedly force her art of motion to a standstill, and this puts her in direct opposition to Wagner, who sought to make Romantic painting move on the Bayreuth stage. This opposition raises a critical question about the Gesamtkunstwerk's conceptual genealogy, a question pertinent to Wagner's and even Trahndorff's formulation: Why the antipathy toward stasis? Whether one takes Trahndorff's four foundational arts or Wagner's three sisters, one notes that all involve *movement* and its inherent quality of *change* over time. A static image, in itself, will not change except by deterioration. If it can be shielded from deterioration (by virtue of its technical reproducibility, for example), it will achieve permanence. Trahndorff posits that there is something inherent in all arts, even those that generate static products, that drive each one toward the Gesamt-Kunstwerk. But his selection of four candidates inherently suggests that the static image does not belong, and Wagner's quest to make painting unfold in time and space only amplifies that suggestion. The Wagnerian Gesamtkunstwerk is about process, about becoming, about a mutually constitutive movement toward awareness and participation in an aesthetic event—and this sense of movement is inherent in Trahndorff's concept as well. The total work of art would appear to resist a total embrace of all arts.

Structurally and formally, Dudov's film follows this pattern of emphasis on motion at the expense of stasis. There is certainly no simple, linear model of progress: situations recur in variation, and though the dynamism of the festival overcomes the paralysis embodied by young Bönike in the early part of the film, it is clear that the process of revolution is nowhere near complete. With each sonic and narrative cycle, however, there is change, and the combined streams of aural and visual information are organized to involve the audience in that process. Riefenstahl's repeated resistance to kinesis forces her out of synch with this basic program. There is a linear progression, but the film's opening explains that the progression has already reached its conclusion. Movement abounds, but nothing ever changes.

This is not to suggest that it was Riefenstahl's intent to call out Wagner, Trahndorff, or anyone else on the inability of their total work of art to achieve true totality. Nor do I suggest that the Gesamtkunstwerk concepts of Trahndorff, Wagner, and all who followed them should now be considered illegitimate due to the restrictive tendencies lurking in their rhetoric of totality. It must be, though, that the coexistence of the kinetic and the static, felt most forcefully when one contemplates a static image at a distance while sensing the dimensionality and intensity of the sound forms associated with that image, has aesthetic and political potential that outstrips that of Riefenstahl's film. In that unspecified potential lies new territory for the creative, receptive eye and ear. It is inadvisable if not perilous to explore that territory as if it exists in a political vacuum, losing oneself in audiovisual sensation for its own sake. At the same time, the effort to understand the evolving relationship of sound, vision, media, and audience from the late nineteenth century through to the interwar period stands to gain from sensitivity to aesthetic traits shared across political divides.

Notes

With thanks to the volume editors for their constructive criticism.

1. Juliet Koss, *Modernism after Wagner* (Minneapolis, 2010), xxvii.
2. Matthew Wilson Smith, *The Total Work of Art: From Bayreuth to Cyberspace* (New York, 2007), 27, proposes that landscape painting be added to the traditional Wagnerian artistic trinity of music, poetry, and dance.
3. Emily Thompson, *The Soundscape of Modernity: Architectural Acoustics and the Culture of Listening in America, 1900–1933* (Cambridge, 2004), 1; other seminal works on sound studies include R. Murray Schafer, *The Soundscape: Our Sonic Environment and the Tuning of the World* (Rochester, 1994); and Alain Corbin, *Village Bells: Sound and Meaning in the 19th-Century French Countryside*, trans. Martin Thom (New York, 1998).
4. As Koss and Smith show, the intricacy with which image and movement were interlinked in the festival performance designs demonstrates their conceptualization as a kinetic stream of visual impressions, not just a series of set pieces; and the double proscenium at Bayreuth had the effect of magnifying the contents of the stage space and making its seem to float in the air as a framed, moving picture. Friedrich Kittler argues that Wagner did not just push the bounds of art at Bayreuth; he also created a new medium. See Kittler, "World-Breath: On Wagner's Media Technology," in *Opera Through Other Eyes*, ed. David J. Levin (Stanford, 1994), 215–35.
5. Lutz Koepnick, "Rilke's Rumblings and Lang's Bang," *Monatshefte* 98, no. 2 (2006): 198.
6. "Purist" modernists focused on single senses (especially vision) and sought to exploit the splitting of the senses as a catalyst of innovative expression; whereas "synesthetic" modernists strove to "reunify what was experienced as a painful differentiation of the senses." Koepnick, "Rilke's Rumblings," 200.
7. Ibid., 202.
8. Ibid.
9. Richard Wagner, *Das Kunstwerk der Zukunft* (Leipzig, 1850), 38. Although I have consulted the classic William Ashton Ellis translation, for the purposes of my argument, I have used more literal translations of the passages I cite from Wagner's prose writings.
10. Ibid.
11. Ibid.
12. Smith, *Total Work of Art*, 30.
13. See Hermann Korte, "Historische Theaterpublikumsforschung," in *Das Theater glich einem Irrenhause: Das Publikum im Theater des 18. und 19. Jahrhunderts*, ed. Hermann Korte and Hans-Joachim Jakob (Heidelberg, 2012), 9–54; and Jeffrey S. Ravel, *The Contested Parterre: Public Theater and French Political Culture* (Ithaca, 1999).
14. Carl Friedrich Trahndorff, *Aesthetik, oder Lehre von der Weltanschauung und Kunst* (Berlin, 1827), 2:212. See also Koss, *Modernism after Wagner*, 13.
15. Smith, *Total Work of Art*, 30–31.
16. Ibid., 27.
17. Ibid., 30–31.
18. James H. Johnson, *Listening in Paris: A Cultural History* (Berkeley and Los Angeles, 1995).

19. See Johnson, *Listening in Paris*; Korte, "Historische Theaterpublikumsforschung"; Sven Oliver Müller, "Distinktion, Demonstration und Disziplinierung: Veränderungen im Publikumsverhalten in Londoner und Berliner Opernhäusern im 19. Jahrhundert," *International Review of the Aesthetics and Sociology of Music* 37, no. 2 (2006): 167–87, and "The Invention of Silence: Audience Behavior in Berlin and London in the Nineteenth Century," in *Sounds of Modern History: Auditory Cultures in 19th- and 20th-Century Europe*, ed. Daniel Morat (New York and Oxford, 2014), 153–174; Ravel, *Contested Parterre*; and William Weber, "Did People Listen in the Eighteenth Century?" *Early Music* 25, no. 4 (1997): 678–91.
20. Weber, "Did People Listen?" 678.
21. Müller, "Distinktion," 179–84.
22. Peter Heßelmann, "Der Ruf nach der 'Policey' im Tempel der Kunst: Das Theaterpublikum des 18. Jahrhunderts zwischen Andacht und Vergnügen," in Korte, ed., *Das Theater glich einem Irrenhause*, 85–87.
23. Kittler, "World-Breath," 217–18.
24. Ibid., 218.
25. Wagner, *Tristan und Isolde*, Act 3, quoted in Kittler, "World-Breath," 230.
26. Kittler, "World-Breath," 230–31.
27. Ibid., 231.
28. Simon Williams, "Bayreuth: Summer Pilgrimage," *Opera News* (May 2001): 26.
29. Kittler, "World-Breath," 216.
30. Wagner, *Das Kunstwerk der Zukunft*, 208.
31. Ibid., 207, my emphasis.
32. Smith, *Total Work of Art*, 25.
33. Ibid.
34. Georg Herzberg, "Film-Kritik: Kuhle Wampe," *Film Kurier* (31 May 1932). The tag *Who Owns the World* was not originally used in international distribution, though it is now used in the DEFA Amherst/Icestorm edition. The 1932 English title was *To Whom Does the World Belong?*
35. Betz, "Kuhle Wampe oder Wem gehört die Welt?" *Der Film* (4 June 1932).
36. Felix Henseleit, "Kuhle Wampe," *Reichsfilmblatt* (4 June 1932).
37. Daniel Morat, "Cheers, Songs, and Marching Sounds: Acoustic Mobilization and Collective Affects at the Beginning of World War I," in idem, ed., *Sounds of Modern History: Auditory Cultures in 19th and 20th Century Europe* (Oxford, 2014), 177–200.
38. Morat, "Cheers, Songs," 181.
39. Ibid., 192.
40. Michael Chion, *Film: A Sound Art* (New York, 2009), 37–38.
41. See Amy Wlodarski, "Exposing the Political Gesamtkunstwerk: Hanns Eisler's *Nuit et Brouillard*," in this volume.
42. Using other examples, Brigitte Peucker discusses the relationship between Riefenstahl's cinematography and photography. See Peucker, "The Fascist Choreography: Riefenstahl's Tableaux," *Modernism/Modernity* 11, no. 2 (2004): 279–97.
43. Peucker, "Fascist Choreography," 280.
44. Russell Berman, "Written Right Across Their Faces: Ernst Jünger's Fascist Modernism," in *Modernity and the Text: Revisions of German Modernism*, ed. Andreas Huyssen and David Bathrick (New York, 1989), 61.
45. Peucker, "Fascist Choreography," 281.

46. Georg Seeßlen, "Blood and Glamour," in *Riefenstahl Screened: An Anthology of New Criticism*, ed. Neil Christian Pages, Mary Rhiel, and Ingeborg Majer O'Sickey (New York, 2008), 19.
47. Seeßlen, "Blood and Glamour," 23.

Theodore F. Rippey is an associate dean of Arts and Sciences and associate professor of German at Bowling Green State University, Ohio. He has published on Weimar and exile film, literature, and culture. His current research focuses on sound and media in interwar Germany.

CHAPTER 10

The Will to Heal

Gesamtkunstwerk and Memorial Music since 1945

JULIA GOODWIN AND MARGARET ELEANOR MENNINGER

Less than a month after the German army's surrender to the Allies, composers, conductors, and musicians began staging concerts within occupied Germany that featured music and musicians banned during the Nazi regime. A hastily reconstituted Berlin Philharmonic led by Leo Borchard, who had actively sheltered Jewish musicians from harm during the National Socialist years, gave a concert featuring Felix Mendelssohn's *Overture to a Midsummer Night's Dream* for nearly a thousand people on 16 May 1945.[1] Then, in late July, violinist Yehudi Menuhin gave twenty to thirty concerts accompanied by composer and pianist Benjamin Britten. Among these was one for the liberated prisoners at Bergen-Belsen. A shattering experience, the lasting impressions of this particular concert inspired both men to use music for purposes that extended beyond musical performance itself.[2] Menuhin, notably, emerged as a self-proclaimed musical ambassador, devoting his life to political as well as musical concerns. In 1947, he also became the first Jewish musician to perform after the war under the baton of the politically suspect German conductor, Wilhelm Furtwängler.[3] For his part, Britten channeled his energies into writing pieces and planning musical events that explicitly aimed to promote reconciliation among peoples.

The dedication of musicians like Leo Borchard, Yehudi Menuhin, and Benjamin Britten to restoring Jewish music and musicians to places from which they had been banned and to using music as a means of bringing together former enemies invested their many performances with a clear message of reconciliation. But Britten took these activities a step further, creating a novel form of memorial music, which melded older traditions of commemoration with a new focus on healing, bringing back together that which had been split apart. Critically, in the years after World War II, such memorial music took as a prerequisite the full participation of its listening audience. That is, as musical act and as form of musically mediated reconciliation, it encompassed not simply the score, but also choice of performers, performance dates, and even performance venues. It also expected that the audience invest their listening with an active awareness of both the performance and their own experiences. It is precisely this mix of strategies linked to performance as well as reception that suggests reading postwar memorial music in terms of Gesamtkunstwerk. Doing so offers us a potent means of exploring the complex and dialectical ways in which audiences experienced memorial music.

To understand how these musical performances may be read as experiments in Gesamtkunstwerk requires, first, that we return to basic definitions of the total work of art. The words making up the term Gesamtkunstwerk may be parsed to mean a "total art" work *and* a "total art-work." But, as has been observed elsewhere in this volume, the term "total" may also mean "communal," or "collective," even "integrated."[4] Matthew Wilson Smith, too, reminds us that "the concept includes all of these ideas, for it is an art-form as much about collectivity as about unity, about community as about totality."[5] This vision of community particularly describes what Borchard, Menuhin, and especially Britten hoped would come from their performances, namely, the bringing together of a human community torn asunder by conflict.

Aesthetic and political considerations also help us to see how memorial music fits within the rubric of a total work of art.[6] Smith has noted that the many works conventionally designated as Gesamtkunstwerk are imbued with an aesthetic sense of "earnestness," a quality that also strongly marks the works under analysis here.[7] Similarly, postwar composers and performers viewed their art as capable of promoting such political goals as societal transformation and reconciliation. To that end, they articulated visions of artistic responsibility and engagement that echoed the artistic-*cum*-social programs of Wagner, the Bauhaus, and Brecht, among others.[8] In the introduction to their edited volume, Anke Finger and Danielle Follett emphasize that Gesamtkunstwerk involves a metaphysical construction of totality that "aspires to the spiritual or redemptive."[9] In this sense, postwar memorial music can be set within an intellectual heritage that stretches back to the early Romantics, particularly Friedrich Schiller. As Nicholas Vazsonyi argues, Schiller saw the theater as an "institution that could undertake humanity's re-education and moral redemption."[10] Drama was thus a critical vehicle of spiritual renewal, individual redemption, and ultimately cultural reconciliation. Moreover, as Vazsonyi and others in this collection point out, redemptive art requires an audience. In memorial musical performance, though, an engaged audience does more than just help realize the work's reconciliatory aspirations. Through the device of symbolic casting, composers like Britten actually anticipate audience expectations and incorporate them into the performance of the work itself.

In this chapter we contend that this dual conception of audience/reception simultaneously marks postwar memorial music as an experiment in Gesamtkunstwerk and as a major interrogation of the very Gesamtkunstwerk ideal, especially during the period following the collapse of National Socialism. Thus understood, memorial music draws upon notions of audience and reception in two (if also overlapping) ways. First, these works treat the audience as both a traditional passive consumer and an active listener with some stake in the ideals of the performance. Second, composers actually lay the groundwork for the audience's "mental state" (or receptivity) during the performance, chiefly by casting performers who evoke (or should evoke) certain sentiments within the targeted audience. With this approach to audience and reception, the musical pieces and performances discussed below, principally Benjamin Britten's 1962 *War Requiem*, subvert the poisonous element in National Socialist aspirations toward total works of art that Walter Benjamin identified, namely the transformation of spectator to participant. Benjamin regarded this change as inherently dangerous.[11] Likewise, Frederic Spotts and David Roberts have stressed that Nazi political rallies, infused as they were with a specific aesthetic sensibility, aimed to seduce and enthrall their spectator-participants.[12] The works analyzed here also require the listeners' active participation, but with a crucial difference. Rather than anticipating an externalized, active, and politically inflected response from the listeners, memorial music aims to prompt inward transformation on the part of each individual listener, and of the audience as a whole. We contend that these acts must themselves be read as part of a total work of art, a Gesamtkunstwerk in which the ideal of unity has been extended to include an ideal of open and welcoming community, a community including the performers, the place, and the audience.

Ritual Acts of Reconciliation: Benjamin Britten's *War Requiem*

Any discussion of postwar memorial music as Gesamtkunstwerk begins, of necessity, with Britten's *War Requiem*. The work's genesis, its textual and musical realizations, and the circumstances of its initial presentation have all contributed significantly to its enduring resonance as a piece of memorial music. In it, Britten pioneered a set of practices that attracted, gathered, and enhanced the composition's meaning for the audience that went beyond the aesthetic features of the music itself. Moreover, the success of its première and subsequent first performance in Germany created a powerful legacy that shaped not just the *War Requiem*'s further reception, but also expectations for other pieces of memorial music that strove to achieve intercultural understanding and harmony.

The *War Requiem* emerged out of a commission Britten had received to compose a work for the rededication of Coventry Cathedral. Largely destroyed during the 1940 Blitz, its bombed-out shell became a postwar symbol of the horrors of total war. As the new St. Michael's Cathedral neared completion in the late 1950s, its administrators made reconciliation the cathedral's mission and watchword. In 1958, the city had already been "twinned" with Dresden, victim of the notorious fire-bombing of February 1945. As construction on the new cathedral was finished, its officers sponsored a "Cross of Nails" project, using nails from the ruined Gothic cathedral to create crosses that were then sent to churches abroad, among them the Frauenkirche in Dresden and the Gedächtniskirche in Berlin, which—like the cathedral—had been heavily damaged during the war.[13] For the rededication ceremony, scheduled for 30 May 1962, the Coventry Festival Arts Committee turned to Benjamin Britten, asking him to compose a work fitting for the exceptional occasion.[14] Britten's response, the *War Requiem,* became an extension of the new cathedral's mission of international reconciliation, and eventually a new kind of Gesamtkunstwerk. A look at its key features reveals how it succeeded.

As part of the planning for the *War Requiem,* Britten pioneered the practice of symbolic casting, which has had a lasting impact on the way composers and even organizations commissioning pieces have approached commemorative works. Symbolic casting also lies at the heart of how these pieces functioned in terms of Gesamtkunstwerk.[15] Britten always preferred to write for specific voices, such as fellow Britons contralto Kathleen Ferrier and tenor Peter Pears, but prior to the *War Requiem* his choices had not carried any particular representative weight. For this new piece Britten consciously sought to politicize the work by having each of the work's three soloists represent one of World War II's major belligerent nations: Great Britain, (West) Germany, and the Soviet Union. Peter Pears took the tenor part, and the baritone Dietrich Fischer-Dieskau represented "Germany." Soprano Galina Vishnevskaya was Britten's choice to complete the trio, but the Soviet government, determined to block her from sharing the stage with a West German citizen, refused to allow her to perform in the Coventry première. At the last minute British soprano Heather Harper stepped in to replace Vishnevskaya.

The uproar that Britten's initial casting choices caused, at least in Soviet circles, showed that his political message had been received. Of course, Vishnevskaya's withdrawal foiled the composer's effort to invest each soloist with the burden of national association, a strategy that also aimed to enact a ritual of reconciliation and give voice to the composer's unmistakably pacifist message. It seems, though, that the significance of Britten's symbolic casting was so overwhelmingly clear that the Soviets quickly recognized their non-participation as a grave error; with an abrupt and unexplained volte-face, the

Soviet government allowed Vishnevskaya to participate in the recording that followed the first live performances.

Symbolic casting proved only one means through which Britten advanced the message of reconciliation, which was so important to him and to the cathedral's mission. Reconciliation was inherent in the dramatic action of the piece itself. Consisting of six movements, the *War Requiem* follows the order of the Proper and Ordinary of the Latin Requiem Mass. However, in order to develop his message further, Britten interpolates into this structure nine poems by the British poet Wilfred Owen, one of the leading poets of World War I.[16] Significantly, the composer set all of these poems for the two male soloists. The words serve as bitter commentary on the carnage of war and frustrate any chance that the audience might be easily comforted by familiarity with the requiem or organized religion of any sort. In the process, Britten forces his audience to deal directly with the horror of war in the presence of the enemy—as represented by the singers. In short, the *War Requiem*'s construction and very performance requires more from its listeners than simple participation in a religious form of healing.

Just as this piece demands that the audience participate, via Owen's poems, in the same types of confrontations that occurred on the front, the work also directly involves the audience in the process of reconciliation. Herein lies a major source of the *War Requiem*'s exceptional power and resonance. The moment of reconciliation itself comes in the setting of the poem, "Strange Meeting," which Britten embeds in the "Libera me" section at the requiem's climax. In this poem, one soldier encounters a soldier he has killed. Owen did not assign either soldier a particular nationality. Through the act of symbolic casting, however, Britten eliminates this ambiguity and provokes a more emotional response from the audiences. In the performance the British tenor soloist/soldier meets the German baritone soloist, who represents the fallen soldier. The larger context of the requiem adds political significance to Owen's poem, just as the World War I lament enriches the piece's religious meaning. Perhaps more significantly, Britten's casting choices turned the German soldier into a victim, killed by his British counterpart. That reversal of the aggressor–victim narrative, so common after World War II, forced the audience to confront the reality that both sides kill and were killed. Britten's innovation added great poignancy to this moment, especially for the British audience, the overwhelming majority of whom would have remembered the Battle of Britain and, specifically, the bombing of Coventry. It is worth noting too that, through this act of symbolic casting, Britten's inclusion of the former "other," the German soldier, in the *War Requiem* shifts attention to the British and German soldiers' humanity, which Britten intends the audience to understand as representing all of humankind.

Indeed, the specific choices of singers and their parts in Britten's opus required the audience to think about both who the singers were and whom they represented. This casting move thus overcame the abstract idea of singers' disembodied voices, what Carolyn Abbate calls the "voice-object."[17] Britten did not see as problematic the voice's complicity in the mind-numbing Gesamtkunstwerk that Brecht and others were determined to avoid. In fact, Britten pushed the idea of embodiment further. With the *War Requiem*, he charged the audience to engage in active listening, and he expected them to respond to the music in terms of their own war experiences. That is, he realized the ideals of reconciliation and inclusion via the "performed" confrontation with the former enemy, the wartime "other." Of course, Britten set up the conditions for such a political reading of the *War Requiem* in advance, through his compositional and textual choices. But only in its performance and reception, in its anticipation of audience responses and its direct interpellation of the audience in the work's dramatic unfolding, does his vision became a total work of art.

The *War Requiem*'s emotional effectiveness was clear to many who experienced the performance, whether in person or via the live radio broadcast. Although reviews of the world première were uniformly laudatory, they tended to focus on the music's perceived greatness, not an unusual occurrence in the music world but one that, given the première's context and the piece's message, seems shortsighted. Other witnesses, though, grasped and talked about the work's emotional impact and its larger significance. Among the many letters the composer received was one from William Plomer, Britten's occasional librettist, who wrote: "If only one could think that music, that even your music, could influence the world in the direction of peace and reconciliation and imagination."[18] Britten's characteristically restrained replies also reveal his own sense of having accomplished his objective: "I've had lots of nice letters so perhaps the idea *has* got over—the main point really."[19]

Fischer-Dieskau's biographer, Kenneth S. Whitton, gleaned something beyond musical excellence and even the piece's general pacifist message: "This performance, the token of reconciliation for the destruction of Coventry by German bombers in 1940, could be said to have brought to an end the postwar Anglo-German estrangement, and I am sure that it was no coincidence that Fischer-Dieskau was chosen as the artistic ambassador of the new bond in friendship."[20] The significance of Whitton's statement is twofold. First, it acknowledges how the performance itself, not the physical rebuilding of the cathedral or any official political statement, promoted reconciliation. Such an insight elevates a musical performance, and especially its reception, to a ritual act endowed with the power to soften the enmity between nations. Second, because this sort of response to the *War Requiem* happened at each of its performances, it suggests that the work's ability to advance reconciliation—its status as a "total work of reconciliation"—could be duplicated. Its power was not limited to a single festival performance.

With this piece of memorial music, Britten may be said to have achieved a new form of Gesamtkunstwerk: a powerful, massive intertwining of words, music, theater, and venue that verged on the operatic, further intensified through symbolic casting and the allusions to ritual. Notable too was the exponential widening of the première's audience via mass media. At the same time that the radio broadcast expanded the audience, it also altered what we normally think about the relationship between the audience and Gesamtkunstwerk. The radio audience was neither physically present, nor consequently was it able to respond to the spectacle's visual dimensions. But, as contemporary sources suggest, the message was received all the same. Britten successfully used his music and a musical event to redeem humanity, not by absolving members of the audience, but by allowing them to witness or at least hear the reconciliation of the British and German soldiers. In short, he gave them a glimpse of a new reality, one that showed that inner peace could only come through the cessation of warfare.

The *War Requiem*'s German première, set for later in 1962, further underscored the work's political valences, both in its planning and initial reception. Britten agreed that the piece's second performance should take place in Germany, a geopolitical choice that could be read as extending the hand of friendship to the former enemy and meeting the "other" on his home ground. Critically, he opted to hold the event in West Berlin, a move rife with political overtones.[21] Berlin was Germany's capital during both the world wars, and after the construction of a wall between the city's Soviet and Western zones the previous year, Berlin epitomized the perilous divisions in postwar Germany and across Europe. Britten's proposals for the performance date and venue added further layers of significance to the occasion. To begin with, the first German performance of the *War Requiem* was scheduled to take place on 18 November 1962, Memorial Day (*Volkstrauertag*). The holiday itself had a controversial past. Initiated during the Weimar Republic to honor the Great War's dead, in 1934 the Nazis transformed it into Heroes Remembrance Day (*Heldengedenkentag*), which normally fell in late March. The holiday was revived in 1948 as Memorial Day, but to distinguish it more firmly from the Nazi past, in 1952 the West German government decided to move the feast to the end of the liturgical year (November). Notable too is the fact that the concert took place at the Hochschule für Musik as part of the Memorial Day activities organized by the German War Graves Commission (Volksbund deutsche Kriegsgräbefürsorge), the very group that had initiated Memorial Day in Germany in 1919.

Berlin's critics responded warmly and expansively to the concert. Whereas British reviewers had tended to concentrate on the piece's musical merits, German reviewers and audiences embraced it as the bridge between peoples that Britten intended. One reviewer hailed it saying that it was in West Berlin that the *War Requiem* was given in its "full European context."[22] West Berlin's reviewers also tended to acclaim the *War Requiem* as "Versöhnungsmusik" (music of reconciliation).[23] Writing for *Der Tagesspiegel,* for instance, Werner Oehlmann claimed: "[With this work] Britten has fulfilled the great mission to make connections between peoples with and through music."[24] Oehlmann's response demonstrates the degree to which he and others understood music's important potential for facilitating conflict resolution and reconciliation. Moreover, he recognized the special power the *War Requiem* had to transform the performers and the audience into a single, politically minded community.

Recapitulation and Reconciliation: The *War Requiem* in 1980s Berlin

The successful premières in Coventry and West Berlin coupled with the work's patently pacifist and reconciliatory message rapidly ensured worldwide acceptance for the *War Requiem.* In November 1964, for instance, it was performed in Münster to commemorate the bombing of that city's cathedral during World War II. The first East German performance was organized at the Martin Luther Church in Dresden a few months later, on 13 February 1965, twenty-one years after Allied bombing raids had destroyed much of the city. Japanese audiences had their chance to hear Britten's masterpiece days afterwards, when David Willcocks directed a performance at Tokyo's Metropolitan Festival Hall.[25] The timing and contexts of these and many subsequent performances helped cement the *War Requiem*'s status as a pre-eminent work of memorial music. But, as events in Berlin during the 1980s later showed, the masterpiece's capacity for encouraging reconciliation and pushing the bounds of Gesamtkunstwerk were far from exhausted.

In 1987, the divided city of Berlin celebrated its 750th anniversary. Tellingly, organizers on both sides of the Wall programmed the *War Requiem* as part of the festivities.[26] Most analyses of the 1987 anniversary year have focused on political discourse and building projects, overlooking entirely the important role that music played in the events.[27] Indeed, assessments of Berlin's celebrations have tended to emphasize the strong element of competition between East and West Berlin, concluding that there was "no cooperation between East and West in staging this anniversary."[28] "Actually, East and West celebrated separately," as Jeffrey M. Diefendorf has noted. Along the same lines, Mary Fulbrook concludes that the celebrations acted as a world-class venue in which to stage German–German competition emphasizing the political and economic disparities between the two halves of the city.[29]

By thus limiting their assessments, scholars have overlooked musicians' agency and music's deployment in breaking down or at least undermining the barriers—physical, social, and cultural—that divided Berliners. If this episode appears to have eluded mention by the historical community, participants, audience members, and even critics were fully cognizant at the time of the *War Requiem* concerts' historical significance. Attempts by political officials from East and West Berlin to coordinate aspects of the anniversary celebrations may have failed, but the musical organizers pulled off their goal of staging concerts of the *War Requiem* on both sides of the Wall. What is more, these concerts were made accessible to television audiences in both East and West Berlin, an unprecedented achievement in the divided city's history.

In 1962, the choice of soloists had figured prominently in the political message Britten wished to send. Twenty-five years later, in Berlin, that honor fell mainly to the orchestra. Rather than name one of the city's leading ensembles to play the concerts (for instance, the Berlin Philharmonic or the Berliner Sinfonie), organizers sought out the World Youth Orchestra. This group was an especially fitting choice to perform Britten's "reparation" work, as it was itself the product of conciliatory desires and goals. Conceived in 1940 by Marcel Cuvilier, the director general of the Brussels Philharmonic Orchestra, the Jeunesses Musicales movement sought to promote international understanding through music.[30] After the war, it spread to other countries, including West Germany with the founding of the German affiliate, Musikalische Jugend Deutschlands (MJD) in 1951.[31] From the outset, the MJD asserted its desire to use music to promote social progress and cultural understanding. Two years later, the MJD expanded on this vision by issuing the so-called "Kitzinger manifesto." The text pledges the group's support for the "joint endeavor of the whole of mankind through art," arguing that music is the only true universal language.[32] The manifesto further declares the MJD's commitment to promoting contemporary music and emphasizes the young musicians' individual responsibility to be socially engaged citizens.[33] In short, by inviting the Jeunesses Musicales to perform in Berlin for the 1987 *War Requiem* concerts, organizers directly linked the orchestra—with its mission of serving mankind through art and insistence that musicians act responsibly towards society—with the *War Requiem* and its performance history, thereby heightening the symbolic claims they had for the Berlin events.

The idea for the Jeunesses Musicales to perform the *War Requiem* as part of Berlin's 750th anniversary celebrations originated in 1985 with Alan Fluck and Michael Jenne, the joint chairmen of the Orchestra of the International Federation of the Jeunesses Musicales. The two men then developed this idea into an opportunity to "stage a publicly pacifist gesture" by programming performances in both parts of the divided city.[34] Fluck and Jenne secured the cooperation of the East Berlin authorities by offering them the right to broadcast the Schauspielhaus concert live. The opportunity to display the Gendarmenmarkt, the square in which the newly restored Schauspielhaus was located,[35] and the opportunity to make a grandiose gesture proved too great a temptation for the DDR.[36] Hence, on Sunday afternoon, 16 August, young musicians representing thirty-one nations played the first of two back-to-back performances of the *War Requiem*. Michael Jenne himself introduced the East German television broadcast, which one critic later saluted as a "model example of diplomacy." Indeed, in his remarks Jenne carefully refrained from pairing the words "East" and "West" with "Berlin," referring only to the locales of the two concerts.[37] That same evening, the second of the two concerts duly began at 8:00 p.m. in West Berlin's Philharmonie.

Casting decisions for the concerts were made without explanation or comment. The American Carol Vaness sang the soprano solo for the two performances, suggesting that the soprano's national identity had already become less essential to the work. But for the male soloists, whose casting was critical for Britten's message of reconciliation, the organizers followed the composer's example: British tenor Robert Tear assumed the one role, and West German baritone Andreas Schmidt the other. For the Berlin concerts, the message of international understanding even extended to the choice of choral forces, as the organizers enlisted the collaboration of two groups: the Vienna Youth Choir and the Boys' Choir of Harlem. Great Britain's Jeffrey Tate conducted. Curiously, none of the reviews commented on the lack of Soviet participation or the inclusion of Americans, but they made repeated reference to youth and the "radiantly youthful hope" projected by the ensemble.[38]

Audience response to the Berlin *War Requiem* performances in 1987 followed patterns similar to the reception in the 1960s. Commentators noted "the public's unusually high level of listening concentration" during the Schauspielhaus television broadcast.[39] The sequence of "stunned silence" followed by "thunderous applause" that marked audience response to the dual premières in 1962 were repeated in both of the 1987 concerts, even though the evening performance lacked the "edge" of the earlier offering. Writing for *The Times*, Stephen Pettitt reported the applause to have been "rapturous and prolonged."[40]

Critical reaction to the concerts was passionate and deeply, but not divisively, political. That these were the only joint events of the entire 750th anniversary celebration was not lost on either the local Berlin critics or their foreign counterparts. Regina Leister of the *Berliner Morgenpost*, for instance, contended that the dual concerts comprised a "total Berlin experience" (*gesamtberliner Ereignis*), the only one of its kind during the anniversary year.[41] The *Tagesspiegel*'s critic, Martin Wilkening, reached an even more emotional conclusion regarding the concerts' significance: "With the World Orchestra 'Jeunesses Musicale' performances of Benjamin Britten's 'War Requiem,'" he stated, "appeared the entire, single collective reason to have anniversary celebrations in West and East Berlin."[42] Although Hansjürgen Schaefer, the critic for East Berlin's *Neues Deutsch-*

land, was reticent on the subject of East–West reconciliation, he did profess that, within the framework of Berlin's 750th anniversary events, Britten's intentions were especially well fulfilled, calling it "one of the century's most profound anti-war and pro-peace musical messages."[43]

Schaefer's observation about the successful realization of Britten's intentions is significant here, not least for underscoring how effective Britten had been in defining the spectacle's extra-musical elements as fundamental to the work itself and its reception. Schaefer highlights, for example, the international cast, especially one that included and represented world youth. He also draws a parallel between the Schauspielhaus that "arose from the rubble" (restoration on the house had only finished in 1984) and the site of the *War Requiem*'s première, Coventry Cathedral. Moreover, as per the original, the work was transmitted live, this time on both television and radio. Over and above any aesthetic consideration, he emphasized that these performances' virtues lay in their context, calling the dual event a "great night in our artistic life and an avowal of the musical art's humanitarian peace mission in our day." Indeed, for Schaefer, this memorable event was significant not just for Germany but for the entire world.[44]

Regina Leistner appeared overwhelmed by the performance and its significance for the city. She called it a "rare birthday gift" that was also a small cultural-political sensation. Indeed, she notes, the audience sat breathless for a minute and a half after the "gray music of war and the poet's words of reconciliation" had ended. She also called attention to the work's central event, the "Strange Meeting," and the choice of the male soloists, acknowledging that "Britten wanted English and German singers [to act] as a symbol of reconciliation." In a closed Senate reception after the Philharmonie performance, West Berlin mayor Eberhard Diepgen was heard congratulating all the performers on "an interpretation that anyone could understand as anti-war and in support of making connections and fostering understanding among peoples."[45]

The foreign critics in attendance were no less appreciative of the performances' historical significance, especially their fulfilment of the *War Requiem*'s political program. In a review entitled "Symbolic Sounds," the *Financial Times*'s Paul Driver tellingly refers to the Jeunesses Musicales as a "resonantly symbolic entity." Driver, however, does not equate this symbolism with triumph or redemption. What he sees is tragedy. This becomes clear in the following passage, where he expands on his characterization of the youthful, international orchestra:

> Never will its symbolic status have been felt so acutely, however, as this year when its rehearsals and all but one of its six concerts took place in that most tragically symbolic of cities—Berlin. Symbolic sound is created by a symbolic orchestra through a symbolic musical work performed in a highly symbolic venue

> for an all too tragically divided people, who understand the *War Requiem*'s conciliatory message and their own powerlessness to fulfill its goal.[46]

The Times' correspondent, Stephen Pettitt, also called attention to the particular poignancy of the East Berlin performance, noting, "Schmidt's singing in the tragic, reconciliatory 'Strange Meeting' had of course a special significance here." He concludes his review by expressing the hope that "those responsible for the perpetuation of the divide had been among the people so obviously moved by these musicians and by this music." That is, he wished that participation in this musical spectacle would prompt political leaders on both sides of the wall to work for the desperately needed reconciliation between East and West.[47]

As the critics variously noted, programming this work of memorial music created a rare cultural bridge across Berlin's wall. It also injected a serious note of remembrance into the city's anniversary celebrations: remembrance of the two world wars for which Germany was responsible; remembrance of the tremendous personal losses suffered on all sides; remembrance of the city's postwar division. In 1987, those who experienced the *War Requiem* performances immediately grasped their significance as the sole point of common experience in an otherwise bifurcated "celebration." But perhaps they also acknowledged and appreciated how the two concerts adroitly combined commemoration and celebration. For by intermingling two potentially inimical public modes, memorial ritual and anniversary festival, the concerts provided the German people with a potent formula for incorporating *Vergangenheitsbewältigung* (coming to terms with the past) into a vibrant and even celebratory present.

In the years following the Berlin Wall's collapse (1989) and German unification (1990), Germans have further expanded the *War Requiem*'s capacity for promoting peace and reconciliation by placing it at the center of a program of educational outreach. The chief actor in this endeavor has been the Berlin Philharmonic's educational division, which in 2003 launched "Projekt 10," an initiative designed to educate young Germans about the two world wars via Britten's masterpiece. Students began by studying both Wilfred Owen's wartime poetry and the ethical concerns that war presents. Then, using the *War Requiem* as a model, participants were asked to collaborate in the composition of their own anti-war requiem. In December 2003, the students organized performances of their work in the Philharmonie and the Kaiser Wilhelm Gedächtniskirche.[48] As this example demonstrates, the *War Requiem* has become deeply embedded in German musical culture and public life since its première in 1962. Without question, part of its attraction and staying power reflects the genius of Britten's composition, specifically his success in creating a piece of memorial music that develops through performance into a ritual of reconciliation. But, from the West Berlin première in 1962 and the Berlin anniversary concerts of 1987 to the Philharmonic's Projekt 10, the *War Requiem*'s history in Germany underscores not just the importance of audience and performer engagement with the work, but the centrality of this active involvement and reception to the work. They are essential parts of both the artistic medium and the political message.

Variations of Reconciliation

As powerful as the *War Requiem* remains as an example of memorial music, not all musical efforts at promoting conflict resolution exactly follow the pattern Britten laid down. But even in the cases where Britten's work does not serve as the inspiration, some of the basic ideals in the *War Requiem*—the audience investing the work with a particular message of reconciliation, and the intent to read the work politically—remain crucial. Indeed, in some cases, the audience may engage thusly with the piece despite the composer's initial wishes. Take the case of the Polish composer and conductor, Krzysztof Penderecki. His output is filled with works that are frequently interpreted as conveying sociopolitical messages of reconciliation. Nonetheless, he has insisted that he does not "write political music," which, he has said, "is immediately obsolete."[49] Such statements, however, have not prevented Penderecki's work from entering the established repertoire of memorial music. The example of the *Threnody for the Victims of Hiroshima* (1960) is especially telling. Listeners, rather than the composer, invested the piece with its political meaning, marking it indelibly as a work commemorating the tragic events of 6 August 1945. In this case, early audiences asserted agency that goes beyond Wagner's and even Britten's expectations of audience participation.

At first glance, Penderecki seems an even less likely candidate than Britten to discuss in terms of the total work of art, and particularly in terms of music of reconciliation. Yet if Penderecki remains mum on the subject, others have drawn the parallel. The critic Louise F. Kenngott, for one, pointed out the common taste for epic drama that Penderecki and Wagner share (cf. Penderecki's opera, *Paradise Lost*, 1978) and audiences' enthusiasm for their respective compositions.[50] Still, Penderecki has always shied away from such claims, fearing that an overly close association with political events would quickly make his music passé. In 1998, for instance, he remarked: "I cannot be sure that I have not sinned too much, especially towards the free 'I,' in yielding to the imperatives of power and the national ethos. Works like the *Polish Requiem* and *Threnody for the Victims of Hiroshima*, while they may possess an autonomous existence, are likely to be read as journalism."[51]

Penderecki's original title for *Threnody*, *8'37"*, a nod to John Cage's *4'33"* (1952), announces neither an underlying program nor a desire to create extra-musical associations. Rather, like Cage, it simply states the piece's projected length, thereby allowing audience members to make their own speculations as to its meaning. Shortly after the work's 1960 première, however, discussions began that rapidly transformed it into memorial music: a threnody to the victims of the first atomic bombing at Hiroshima. The actual process by which this occurred remains shrouded in mystery. Penderecki's biographer and friend, Wolfram Schwinger, for instance, merely observes: "This work," he states, "subsequently dedicated by Penderecki to 'the victims of Hiroshima,' won an almost symbolic esteem for new Polish music, and was ranked as a milestone in its most recent development."[52] In his acclaimed survey of twentieth-century music, *All the Rest is Noise*, Alex Ross likewise can only comment on the initial consequences of the new name: "[Polish] Officialdom took a favorable view [of the piece] only when someone [alas, Ross does not identify this person] suggested that the work be renamed *Threnody for the Victims of Hiroshima*."[53]

Whatever his original intentions and whatever his early protestations, with *Threnody* Penderecki too contributed to a growing body of memorial music in which listeners' experience outside the performance helped create a community of experience and reconciliation during the performance. Moreover, there is considerable evidence that critics and other composers accepted the transformation of *8'37"* into *Threnody*. In his work on early Penderecki reception, the musicologist Ray Robinson concludes that American critics and composers fully endorsed the *Threnody* title as authentically evocative of the Hiroshima bombing experience. The composer Elliott Carter, for instance, thought the "new" subject matter fully justified both the compositional techniques Penderecki employed (for example, the frequent recourse to microtonality to heighten the sense of dissonance) and the music's "violence" (it opens, for example, with a high, shrill note from the violins, resembling a scream).[54]

Even if we cannot definitively name the party responsible for calling the piece *Threnody for the Victims of Hiroshima*, we still have the result. And if we accept Alexander Rehding's claim that "the monument is meant to *mean*," then Penderecki relinquished any claim to absolute music as soon as he embraced the new title.[55] Rehding's assertion, however, also requires us to dismiss Penderecki's contention that the piece's value rests on the music's abstract quality. Instead, the work's association with Hiroshima and the dropping of the first atomic bomb have served to organize the work's reception and understandings of its broader meaning, precisely because of the new title. In other words, it is not as an abstract work with an open, or at least highly ambiguous, sense of meaning that Penderecki's composition thrives, but rather as a piece with very specific, accumulated meanings—a piece whose political content (at least seen as such) is capable of fostering cross-cultural connections and understanding. Although unable to attend the piece's Japanese première in Hiroshima on 1 December 1964, Penderecki did send a letter to the city's mayor in which he described the bombing as a "tragedy of mankind."[56] This correspondence also makes it clear that Penderecki had fully accepted the notion that *Threnody* indeed reflected the work's subject matter. There is also no mystery about the piece's subsequent, positive reputation. The musicologist Glenn Watkins, for example, concludes: "The popularity the piece achieved was undoubtedly due to the imagery [that] audiences drew from its title, though the composer denied explicit reference to airplane drones, whistling bombs in freefall, or catastrophic explosions."[57]

Of course, the annals of classical music abound with examples of works receiving their titles, or at least their prevailing appellations, after the fact and quite independently of the composer (Beethoven's *Moonlight Sonata,* for instance). As we have suggested here, though, the rebaptism of *8'37"* as the *Threnody* was not just a name change; it was itself a transformative act that thrust greatness upon Penderecki's short work. What started out as abstract was invested with concrete meaning. The title literally remade the piece into an instance of memorial music, and provided audiences with an emotional framework for hearing and responding to it. Thus, like Britten's *War Requiem,* the effectiveness of Penderecki's *Threnody* owes as much to the audience—its mindset, its experiences, its expectations—as it does to the music itself and its actual performance. In short, while Penderecki had little intention of composing a piece of memorial music, much less something in the spirit of Gesamtkunstwerk, thanks to the audience's reception and engagement his *8'37"* became both.

In other instances of memorial music, Britten's *War Requiem* does seem to provide a clearer template for works that hope to inspire ideals of international reconciliation and lasting peace. A case in point is the *Requiem of Conciliation* (*Requiem der Versöhnung*), which the Internationale Bachakademie Stuttgart commissioned for the 1995 European Music Festival to commemorate the fiftieth anniversary of the end of World War II. That work took Britten's idea of symbolic casting one step further by promoting a symbolic collaboration of composers.[58] The Bachakademie commissioned movements from fourteen noted composers who would represent each of the war's major belligerent nations (e.g., Luciano Berio, Italy; John Harbison, the United States; Wolfgang Rihm, Germany) as well as many of the occupied nations (e.g., Penderecki, Poland; Arne Nordheim, Norway). To perform the collaborative work, German conductor and Bachakademie founder Helmuth Rilling assembled an international ensemble including the Gächinger Kantorei Stuttgart, the Krakow Chamber Choir, the Israel Philharmonic, and a group of six soloists (three Germans, one American, one Briton, and one Canadian). In its composition and performance, the *Requiem of Conciliation* offers ongoing endorsement of the effectiveness of Britten's idea of symbolic casting. Indeed, Rilling's project depends almost exclusively on the associations people could make with the individual composers and the performers to realize the message of reconciliation and world peace. For unlike Britten's *War Requiem,* the *Requiem of Conciliation* serves the pieces of the traditional requiem mass straight up:

there is no interpolation of other texts into the structure. (Rilling did, though, allow Luciano Berio to base his prologue on a non-liturgical text borrowed from the writings of the Jewish Romanian poet Paul Celan.[59]) Moreover, the work's political and symbolic intentions—reflected in the casting, the performance date (16 August 1995, the day after the fiftieth anniversary of VJ day), and the work's very monumentality—served a critical functional, integrating purpose. As Harry Draschke noted in his review for *Die Welt*, "None of the composers would have thought about composing a work together. They are of varying styles and approach the central subject in different ways. Pieces were composed that became a [coherent] symbol only in their combination."[60] This collective composition also represents a significant rethinking of Gesamtkunstwerk that hearkens back to discussions prominent at the beginning of the twentieth century. While the *Requiem of Conciliation* eschews the creation of a single, "total" aesthetic vision, it relies on its political, extra-musical (even extra-dramatic) aims to integrate the parts into a meaningful whole.[61]

Lera Auerbach's 2012 *Requiem*, subtitled "Dresden: Ode to Peace," further demonstrates how Britten's overall package—composition, casting, and performance venue—coalesced into a recognizable form that engages, even if unintentionally, with ongoing discourse about Gesamtkunstwerk. The Saxon Staatskapelle Dresden and the Frauenkirche Foundation jointly commissioned the work from the Jewish Russian-American Auerbach, and it enjoyed its world première at the Frauenkirche in Dresden on 11 February 2012, in commemoration of the anniversary of its destruction in 1945. The work was performed again as the central piece in the official annual remembrance concerts held on the thirteenth and fourteenth of the same month. The Frauenkirche was officially reconsecrated on 30 October 1995. Like its sister institution in Coventry, one of its main missions has been to promote peace and reconciliation. Using the church for the première of Auerbach's "Ode" therefore hearkened back to the circumstances of the *War Requiem*'s première, and offered Auerbach's piece similar potential to invest the musical event with symbolism.[62]

"Dresden: Ode to Peace" contains all the elements of a musical act of reconciliation that made *War Requiem* so powerful. Auerbach herself cites Britten's casting choices as a major inspiration.[63] She, too, uses boy sopranos and male soloists (including a countertenor), but no female voices, reasoning that only males took part as combatants in the war. Auerbach's choice of title and text follow Britten's example, but also add vital elements that further demonstrate how it works as an essay on Gesamtkunstwerk. For instance, the title itself invokes Schiller's "Ode to Joy," who also happened to write part of this poem in Dresden. Musicians—and governments—seem to be perpetually fixated on Schiller's "Ode" and, by association, Beethoven.[64] But the trope of international brotherhood ("Alle Menschen werden Brüder") in the poem is not really what interests Auerbach. Rather, it is Schiller's belief in art's redemptive power, as mentioned earlier in this volume (and in this essay).

Auerbach makes the theme of peace and reconciliation explicit in her requiem by scoring the "Kyrie" in over twenty languages, and incorporating several other extra elements including a prayer by the Franciscan Mychal Judge, the chaplain to the New York City Fire Department who perished in the attacks of 11 September 2001. In addition, she incorporates the traditional Jewish prayer "Sh'ma Yisrael," the Twenty-Third Psalm as it appears in the *Tehillim* (Mizmor l'David, Adonai Ro'i, lo echsar), and a Kabbalistic prayer (Ana B'koach).[65] The use of Jewish texts is significant on two levels. First, it brings particular poignancy to the work both by expressing the composer's own religious identity and by recalling the German government's horrific treatment of Jews during the war that also caused the Frauenkirche's destruction. Second, the inclusion of Jewish liturgical music in the Catholic requiem mass symbolically includes and integrates a community excluded and branded as "other" in National Socialist Germany. This process is particularly apparent in Auerbach's handling of the *Requiem*'s "Libere me" section. Following Britten's example, Auerbach opts to insert a non-canonical text into this part of the mass, namely the Jewish prayer "Ana B'koach." Her choice does not force the audience to relive the confrontation that occurred on the battlefield, as in the case of Britten's interpolation of "Strange Meeting." But her decision is no less provocative: it introduces a clear Jewish presence into a work explicitly composed to commemorate the bombing of a German city at the height of both the war and the *Shoah*.

Auerbach's work does not shy away from the word "reconciliation" or the mission of those directing the rebuilt Frauenkirche. Her requiem demands more than a facile response from her audience; it requires that they process not only feelings of loss and suffering for the destruction of a church and indeed a city, but that they also engage in reflection about those who died in Dresden in 1945 and their complicity in a larger slaughter. It clearly stands in the tradition of Britten's *War Requiem*, particularly in its dependence on extra-musical factors to realize the work's political and social goals. In so doing, it highlights the ways in which postwar memorial music engaged, extended, and perhaps even rewrote central ways of thinking about Gesamtkunstwerk.

Conclusion

Resolution of conflict begins with rupture, fracture, and suffering. Its reconciliation through music demands political awareness and conscious political activity on the part of musicians and audiences alike. Peace activists recognize what musicians perhaps knew first: music can create an emotional space where both listeners *and* performers can confront their perceptions about the "other" and, to some extent, resolve them. This approach echoes the 1945 concerts of Borchard and Menuhin–Britten where the special circumstances invested particular musical events with ritual designed to begin the work of social change. These performers staged acts of conflict resolution and reconciliation through acknowledgement and inclusion. They set a path still followed to this day. For example, Daniel Barenboim and Edward Said created the West–Eastern Divan Orchestra in 1999, a youth orchestra designed to bring together young musicians from around the Middle East. The Israeli, Palestinian, and other musicians of the Divan have even performed Wagner in Israel under Barenboim's baton, allowing that audience to confront *its* difficulties with a composer whose own muddled politics and anti-Semitism made him such an attractive tool for the Nazis.

The World Orchestra for Peace, founded by Sir Georg Solti, debuted in Geneva in 1995 for the United Nations' fiftieth anniversary. Musicians from forty countries participate in special events "to use the unique power of music as an ambassador of peace." The orchestra even commissions new works in addition to performing standard repertoire. One such commission, Penderecki's *Prelude for Peace*, premièred on 1 September 2009 at a concert in Krakow marking the sixtieth anniversary of the Wehrmacht's invasion of Poland.[66] A 2008 commission went to Roxanna Panufnik, whose offering links the Jewish, Christian, and Muslim traditions in a work she called *Three Paths to Peace*.[67]

In all these cases, Britten has proven to be an inspiration. In 1964, two years after the *War Requiem* premièred in Coventry and Berlin, Britten aired his thoughts on composers and social responsibility: "It is the composer's duty, as a member of society, to speak to and for his fellow human beings."[68] While Britten was not the first composer to pour his hopes for conflict resolution into his music, he was perhaps the first to develop a recognizable means of presenting memorial music, perfectly capturing the goals of reconciliation through casting and performance, and its demands on the audience. Now musicians, composers, and performers, many of whom have been personally affected by the upheavals of the twentieth and now the twenty-first century, create works that made the "other" visible, that place him, her, or them on center stage. This inclusive and "borderless" music is invested with a creative rather than a destructive force. And, rather than simply addressing mass suffering, this memorial music requires more of its listeners. It demands that members of the audience consider both the present experience of the performance and their own memories of suffering, anger, and loss. These pieces attempt to create a new, intentionally inclusive unity that bridges these two conflicting feelings, transforming an act of commemoration into Gesamtkunstwerk.

Notes

1. Ruth Andreas-Friedrich, *Battleground Berlin: Diaries 1945–1948*, trans. Anna Boerrensen (New York, 1990), 34–35. See also Dirk Nabering, "Out of the Shadows: Dirk Nabering Recalls Leo Borchard," *The Musical Times* (August 1995), 411; and Matthias Sträßner, *Der Dirigent Leo Borchard: Eine unvollendete Karriere* (Berlin, 1999), 215, 269.
2. Benjamin Britten, *Letters from a Life, Volume Two 1939–45* (Rochester, 2010), 1273. Also see Humphrey Carpenter, *Benjamin Britten: A Biography* (London, 1992), 226–27.
3. The Nazis had banned Jewish performers as well as Jewish music from German concert halls; musicians worldwide also refused to perform on those formerly revered stages.
4. Anke Finger, *Das Gesamtkunstwerk der Moderne* (Gottingen, 2006), 80; Marcella Lista, *L'Œuvre d'art totale à la naissance des avant-gardes, 1908–1918* (Paris, 2006), particularly 5–20. See also Anthony J. Steinhoff, "Richard Wagner, *Parsifal*, and the Pursuit of Gesamtkunstwerk," in this volume.
5. Matthew Wilson Smith, *The Total Work of Art: From Bayreuth to Cyberspace* (New York, 2007), 9.
6. Ibid.; Anke Finger and Danielle Follett, eds. *The Aesthetics of the Total Artwork: On Borders and Fragments* (Baltimore, 2011), 6.
7. Smith, *Total Work of Art*, 115.
8. On the political dimensions of the Bauhaus project, see also Éric Michaud, "Oeuvre d'art totale et totalitarisme," in *L'œuvre d'art totale*, ed. Jean Galard and Julian Zugazagottia (Paris, 2003), 35–65.
9. Finger and Follett, *Aesthetics of the Total Artwork*, 4 and 6.
10. See Nicholas Vazsonyi, "The Play's the Thing: Schiller, Wagner, and Gesamtkunstwerk," in this collection.
11. Walter Benjamin, "The Work of Art in the Age of Mechanical Reproduction," in *Illuminations*, ed. Hannah Arendt, trans. Harry Zohn (New York, 1968), 241.
12. Frederic Spotts, *Hitler and the Power of Aesthetics* (Woodstock and New York, 2002), xi; David Roberts, *The Total Work of Art in European Modernism* (Ithaca, 2011), 238–44.
13. Julia Anne Goodwin, "Breaking Down Barriers: Music and the Culture of Reconciliation in West Berlin, 1961–1989," PhD diss. (University of Rochester, 2007), 77–79. See also Frauenkirche Dresden, http://www.frauenkirche-dresden.de/nagelkreuzzentrum/ (accessed 24 April 2016). The frequent use of cathedrals as venues for memorial music strengthens the connections between such performances and Gesamtkunstwerk, as the cathedral is a symbol much discussed in the literature of the total work of art. See, in addition to the scholars mentioned above, Roger Fornoff, *Die Sehnsucht nach dem Gesamtkunstwerk: Studien zu einer ästhetischen Konzeption der Moderne* (Hildesheim, 2004); also Melissa Trimingham, "Gesamtkunstwerk, Gestaltung and the Bauhaus Stage," and Jenny Anger, "The 'Translucent (Not: Transparent)' Gesamtglaswerk," both in this volume.
14. Mervyn Cooke, *Britten: War Requiem* (Cambridge and New York, 1996), 21. Coverage of the *War Requiem* world première can be found in any of the biographies including Carpenter, *Benjamin Britten*; Michael Kennedy, *Britten*, revised edn. (Oxford, 1993); and Michael Oliver, *Benjamin Britten* (London, 1996). See also Wilbur R. Maust,

"Benjamin Britten's Music of Conscience and Compassion," *The Conrad Grebel Review* 5, no. 2 (1987): 103–16.

15. Goodwin, "Breaking Down Barriers," 80.
16. Cooke, *Britten: War Requiem*, 59.
17. Carolyn Abbate, *Unsung Voices: Opera and Musical Narrative in the Nineteenth Century* (Princeton, 1991), 10. See also Joy Calico, "Epic Gesamtkunstwerk," in this volume.
18. Britten, *Letters from a Life, Volume 5: 1958–1965*, 402.
19. Ibid., 407.
20. Kenneth S. Whitton, *Dietrich Fischer-Dieskau Mastersinger* (London, 1981), 53, 91.
21. Wolfgang Stresemann, the then director of the Berlin Philharmonic, was also instrumental in this decision. Helge Grünewald, liner notes, *Sir John Barbirolli—Brahms Symphony No. 2*, Testament SBT1469, 2011, compact disc.
22. "Benjamin Brittens Versöhnungsmusik," *Der Kurier*, 20 November 1962.
23. For a more complete account of the *War Requiem*'s German reception, see Goodwin, "Breaking Down Barriers," 84–97.
24. Werner Oehlmann, "Der Requiem von Coventry: Benjamin Brittens Chorwerk im Philharmoniker-Konzert unter Colin Davis," *Der Tagesspiegel*, 21 November 1962.
25. Cooke, *Britten: War Requiem*, 82.
26. Goodwin, "Breaking Down Barriers," 160–67.
27. Cf. Krijn Thijs, *Drei Geschichten, eine Stadt: Die Berliner Stadtjubiläen von 1937 und 1987* (Cologne, Weimar, and Vienna, 2008); Gottfried Korff, "Zweimal 750 Jahre Berlin. Das Stadtjubiläum 1987 im Vergleich," in *DDR Heute: Wandlungstendenzen und Widersprüche einer sozialistischen Industriegesellschaft*, ed. Gerd Meyer and Jürgen Schröder (Tübingen, 1988), 130–54.
28. Jonathan Osmond, review of "Felix Escherm, Berlin und sein Umland: Zur Genese der Berliner Stadtlandschaft bis zum Beginn des 20. Jahrhunderts," *The Journal of Modern History* 60, no. 3 (1988): 603. This volume was one example of the series of scholarly studies sponsored by the Historische Komission zu Berlin for the 750th anniversary of the city.
29. Jeffrey M. Diefendorf, review of Wolfgang Ribbe and Jürgen Schmädeke, eds, "Berlin im Europa der Neuzeit: Ein Tagungsbericht," *The Journal of Modern History* 66, no. 4 (1994), 848. Fulbrook's brief account lays out a stark dichotomy of East German rants and West German riches with an amalgam of unplanned but nevertheless reawakened shared cultural consciousness across the political divide. The mechanism of this reconnection remains unexplained, although culture is suggested as the means. See Mary Fulbrook, *German National Identity after the Holocaust* (Malden, 1999), 91.
30. For the early history of the organization see Jeunesses Musicales de Belgique, "What is Junior Music? Its Growth, its Aims, its Organisation, its Achievement, its Future" (Brussels, 1948).
31. The organization's website puts the date of formation at the "end of December, 1950." Jeunesses Musicales Deutschland: Chronik, https://www.jmd.info/jmd/ueber-die-jmd/chronik (accessed 24 April 2016).
32. "...sieht sie ihr Endziel im Zusammenwirken der ganzen Menschheit durch die Kunst, insbesondere durch die Musik, als der einzigen allen Menschen gemeinsamen Sprache..." "Kitzinger Manifest der MJD, 1953," in *Zeitschrift für Musik* 114 (1953): 156–57.
33. Ibid. See also Goodwin, "Breaking Down Barriers," 161.

34. Goodwin, "Breaking Down Barriers," 162.
35. On the 750th anniversary's contribution to the rebuilding of historic sectors of East Berlin, see David Clay Large, *Berlin* (New York, 2000): 481, 500–1.
36. Stephen Pettitt, "Peace Leaps the Wall: Review of an Historic Music Occasion," *The Times*, 19 August 1987.
37. Martin Wilkening, "Ein west-östliches Ereignis: Das 'War Requiem' von Benjamin Britten in der Philharmonie," *Der Tagesspiegel*, 18 August 1987.
38. Regina Leistner, "Ovationen in Ost und West für ein sensationelles Gastspiel zum Stadtjubiläum: Brittens 'War Requiem' voll jugendlich glühender Hoffnung," *Berliner Morgenpost*, 18 August 1987.
39. Wilkening, "Ein west-östliches Ereignis."
40. Pettitt, "Peace Leaps the Wall."
41. Leistner, "Ovationen in Ost."
42. Wilkening, "Ein west-östliches Ereignis."
43. Hansjürgen Schaefer, "Brittens Friedensbotschaft von jungen Musikern verkündet: 'War'-Requiem in internationaler Besetzung im Berliner Schauspielhaus," *Neues Deutschland*, 17 August 1987.
44. Schaefer, "Brittens Friedensbotschaft."
45. The original German reads: "Britten wünschte als Symbol der Versöhnung einen englischen und einen deutschen Sänger." Leistner, "Ovationen in Ost und West."
46. Paul Driver, "Symbolic Sounds," *Financial Times*, 22 August 1987.
47. Pettitt, "Peace Leaps the Wall."
48. *Projekt 10: Britten's War Requiem* http://www.berliner-philharmoniker.de/en/education/archive/education/ptitel/war-requiem/ (accessed 28 September 2013). See also Zukunft@BPhil, *Projekt 10: Britten's War Requiem*, Program 21, 2003–2004 Season (Berlin, 2003) http://www.berliner-philharmoniker.de/fileadmin/education/0304/projekt_010_ph21_01.pdf (accessed 28 September 2013).
49. Philip Anson, "Krystof Penderecki Talks about the Polish Requiem," in *La Scena Musicale*, 1 April 1998.
50. Louise F. Kenngott, "Penderecki: He's Today's Wagner," in *The Milwaukee Journal* (10 December 1978), 40.
51. Krzysztof Penderecki, *Labyrinth of Time: Five Addresses for the End of the Millennium* (Chapel Hill, 1998), 18. The composer himself remains obdurate: as late as 2010, he was convinced that the significance of his music lay outside its ability to convey specific meaning, which contradicts critical and audience response. "My *Threnody for the Victims of Hiroshima*," he claims, "remains important because it is abstract music." See also, Anson, "Krystof Penderecki."
52. Wolfram Schwinger, *Krzysztof Penderecki: His Life and Work: Encounters, Biography, and Musical Commentary*, trans. William Mann (London, 1989), 28. Schwinger is clearly interested in the prestige the piece has accorded the composer and Polish music without concern over the key to its political acceptance or popular success: the title.
53. Alex Ross, *The Rest is Noise: Listening to the Twentieth Century* (New York, 2007), 459–60.
54. Ray Robinson, "Recapitulation through Synthesis: Penderecki's Reception in the United States," in *Krzysztof Penderecki: Musik im Kontext, Konferenzbericht Leipzig 2003*, ed. Helmut Loos and Stefan Keym (Leipzig, 2006), 330–63, here 311.
55. Alexander Rehding, *Music and Monumentality: Commemoration and Wonderment in Nineteenth-Century Germany* (New York, 2009), 26.

56. Schwinger, *Krzysztof Penderecki*, 35.
57. Glenn Watkins, *Soundings: Music in the Twentieth Century* (New York, 1995), 498.
58. Goodwin, "Breaking Down Barriers," 186.
59. Harry Draschke, "Im Gedenken an die Toten, als ein Gespräch mit Gott," *Die Welt*, 17 August 1995.
60. Ibid.
61. See, for example, Didier Plassard, "Approches de l'art monumental: Kandinsky et la synthèse des arts," in *L'œuvre d'art totale*, ed. Denis Bablet and Élie Konigson (Paris, 1995), 111–28.
62. Frauenkirche Dresden, "Ort des Friedens und der Versöhnung." http://www.frauenkirche-dresden.de/leitgedanken/ (accessed 18 May 2016).
63. Säschsisches Staatskapelle Dresden, "Ode to Peace: Lera Auerbachs Requiem 'Dresden' to be premiered by the Staatskapelle" (19 January 2012) http://www.staatskapelle-dresden.de/en/news/article/ode-an-den-frieden-urauffuehrung-von-lera-auerbachs-requiem-dresden/34/ (accessed 18 May 2016).
64. See, for example, David B. Dennis, *Beethoven in German Politics, 1870–1989* (New Haven, 1996), 26, 61.
65. Our thanks to Rabbi Justin S. Kerber for his assistance.
66. World Orchestra for Peace, http://www.worldorchestraforpeace.com/ (accessed 10 September 2013). A statement by the current director Charles Kaye may be found at http://www.worldorchestraforpeace.com/content/media/gigmag-article-14-11-08.pdf (accessed 29 September 2013).
67. Hilary Whiteman, "A message from the composer," 24 October 2008, CNN http://edition.cnn.com/2008/WORLD/europe/10/24/panufnik.orchestra.peace/index.html?iref=allsearch (accessed 4 February 2015).
68. Benjamin Britten, "On Winning the First Aspen Award," in *Composers on Modern Musical Culture: An Anthology on Twentieth-Century Music*, ed. Bryan R. Simms (New York, 1999), 177.

Julia Goodwin is an instructor at Oregon State University where she teaches music, history, and music history. She holds a PhD in modern European history from the University of Rochester and a BMus in piano performance from Oberlin College.

Margaret Eleanor Menninger is NEH Distinguished Teaching Professor in the Humanities and Associate Professor of History at Texas State University. She has published articles on the history of cultural philanthropy in both the United States and Germany, and was a contributor to *The Cambridge Wagner Encyclopedia*. She is completing a book entitled *A Serious Matter and True Joy: Philanthropy, the Arts, and the State in Nineteenth-Century Leipzig*.

CHAPTER 11

Consuming Voices

Musical Film and the Gesamtkunstwerk of Mass Culture

DAVID IMHOOF

A spotlight and a song: that's what Lola Lola uses to entrance Immanuel Rath in Josef von Sternberg's 1930 film *The Blue Angel* (*Der blaue Engel*). Lola growls that she seeks "a man, a real man," while shining a spotlight on the feckless high school teacher who stumbles into The Blue Angel nightclub. Visual and musical synthesis sets up Rath's ultimate defeat, too: the final scene contrasts Lola's singing triumph on stage with Rath's death in his former classroom, as the soundtrack plays a children's tune about moral rectitude. This film's ability to meld music and image prompted many German critics at the time to call it the first artful sound film.[1] Twenty-two years later, *The White Horse Inn* (*Im weißen Rössl*) did something similar. Early in this filmed operetta set in 1910, director Willi Forst introduces, by a clever blend of song and action, the romantic interest that will throw everyone's plans into hilarious upheaval yet produce happy endings all around. The scene shows the appeal of the well-known operetta theme song and its subject matter of broken hearts mending at the White Horse Inn in Austria's picturesque *Salzkammergut*. The unity of music and image also determines the thrust of the Third Reich melodrama, *La Habanera* (1937). Music marks that film's racial poles, and shapes the main narrative turning points. Indeed, director Detlev Sierk—later and better known in Hollywood as Douglas Sirk—built the film's structure around music, capitalizing on Zarah Leander's voice. The theme song "La Habanera" represents the dangerous appeal of the exotic that is at the heart of this Nazi cautionary tale.

In each of these three films, music functions in various important ways. Diegetic music helps define main characters and directs crucial story lines. Nondiegetic music tells viewers what is at stake on the screen and contextualizes the film's meaning. Cinema has always wed sight and sound, even in the silent era.[2]

In these musical films, the weave of audio and visual especially signifies meaning. Like Gesamtkunstwerk, musical film draws its value from a synthesis of various aesthetic forms. Indeed, Adorno argues in *In Search of Wagner* that leitmotifs in Wagner's own attempted Gesamtkunstwerk led directly to cinema, serving as orientation tools for audiences. Adorno also challenges the supposedly anti-commercial aim of Gesamtkunstwerk. He calls Wagner's music the essence of commodity fetish, something that disguises its commercial roots even as it relies upon consumption. This consumerism dooms Gesamtkunstwerk's purported goal of unifying and controlling all elements, because listeners signify the piece through their own associative experience of consumption.[3] My analysis begins with this unmasking of Gesamtkunstwerk.

I explore here how consumption helped promote a sense of unity *outside* musical films. Rather than labeling the movies studied here as Adorno-approved examples of commercial Gesamtkunstwerk, this chapter focuses on how we may better understand the function of consumer culture by using Gesamtkunstwerk as an analytical concept. Consumption habits helped viewers create connections between the elements of these movies. In particular, previous iterations of their stories, soundtracks, and careers of stars all worked to integrate discrete experiences of watching the film into viewers' general habits of cultural consumption. These three instances demonstrate that broad experiences of cultural consumption may have in fact determined audiences' views on specific musical films as much as their viewing of an individual film did.

Musical film makes especially evident mass culture's iterative and connective functions. Since *The Jazz Singer* debuted in 1927, musical film has united major forms of mass consumer culture: cinema, recorded music, sheet music, and the lives of celebrity performers. New sound film immediately made clear around the world the reinforcing commercial relationship between popular songs and popular film.[4] I use these three mid-century German films to explore this relationship, specifically the degree to which consumption generally helped connect viewers' experience of these films with other mass cultural products. Whereas other chapters in this collection have studied perceptions of unity and their construction vis-à-vis specific artistic works,[5] here I employ Gesamtkunstwerk's yearning for unity as a conceptual tool to interrogate the social dimensions of a specific work's apparent unity. Indeed, Adorno's recognition that Gesamtkunstwerk relied upon consumption, even as it sought to cover those capitalist roots, encourages us to examine that tension inherent in Gesamtkunstwerk to explain cultural experience. Studying Gesamtkunstwerk thusly can illuminate how consumption generally helped viewers imagine a broad, synthetic vision of cultural activity.[6] Unlike the various would-be Gesamtkunstwerk creators discussed in this volume and elsewhere, audience members watching musical films may have imagined a total work of art in their heads by uniting the connections offered in musical film to their broader consumption habits.

Scholars of modern mass media have unpacked mass consumer culture's important functions in twentieth-century Germany. Walter Benjamin's seminal study on reproducibility demonstrates that mass culture, removed from the context of its original experience, can become a vessel for significance.[7] Friedrich Kittler has theorized more specifically that records and film capture time and thus turn it into a portable sign.[8] Sound studies scholars have explored this idea further.[9] Nora Alter and Lutz Koepnick, for example, maintain that recorded sound's transmutable, consumable nature in the twentieth century helped manufacture a sense of unity in listeners' minds.[10] Other scholars point out the interconnectedness of mass media and its impact on the development of twentieth-century German states.[11] The fluidity of mass consumer culture, in other words, shaped Germans' perceptions about culture as much as discrete cultural experiences did. Because musical film functions as various forms of mass culture—film, recorded music, theater, and vehicle for stars' multiple careers—it highlights especially well this complex process of diachronic and synchronic consumption. Moviegoers experienced these films synchronically as singular moments of consumption and diachronically as part of their larger habits of cultural consumption. Employing Gesamtkunstwerk as an analytical concept forces us to ask how these two modes of cultural consumption helped unify moviegoers' experiences.

The Blue Angel, *La Habanera*, and *The White Horse Inn* are not necessarily emblematic of all German musical film. But these three movies reveal the changing role of sound in cinema and film's connection to other forms of culture. Their stretch from 1930 to 1952 captures an important era in sound cinema, from the first talkies through the maturity of filmed musicals during the "golden age" of cinema before television's real impact on viewing habits. Likewise these movies offer a glimpse of how mass culture evolved over the course of three very different German regimes. I focus here on the story, sound/track, and stars—three important nexuses between the films themselves and broader trends of cultural consumption. I will close by returning to the larger question of how the concept of Gesamtkunstwerk helps to illuminate the linkages between musical film and mass culture more generally.

The Story

Previous iterations of each film's story shaped the way moviegoers responded to these three works.[12] Most dramatically, Josef von Sternberg radically altered Heinrich Mann's 1905 novel *Professor Unrat* to make *The Blue Angel*. Both narratives center on the fall the tyrannical Immanuel Rath, who humiliates his students and revels in his small-town authority as professor. Seeking to control their private lives too, Rath follows his students to the seedy Blue Angel nightclub to stop their visits. But the chanteuse Lola enchants Rath there with her visual and aural power on stage and sexual innuendo in the dressing room, and they sleep together. Afterwards, his morals compel him to marry the singer, at which point his peers force him to surrender his prestigious position. In Mann's novel, Rath continues his cruelty by opening a casino and brothel with Lola to smite the town citizens who stripped him of his authority. That story critiques Germans' obsession with social status at the turn of the twentieth century. Sternberg's 1930 film, however, makes Rath (played by Emil Jannings) into a tragic character, who slowly falls apart, loses Lola (Marlene Dietrich), and dies broken-hearted clinging to the desk of his old classroom. Lola uses her looks and her voice to destroy Rath. By the end of the film, we have forgotten his previous tyranny or even what took him to the Blue Angel in the first place, and instead lament his sad demise.

Heinrich Mann approved of the film's alterations; reviews also noted the changes from book to film.[13] Mann's fame in 1930 ensured that his novel *Professor Unrat* (literally "Professor Trash") shaped viewers' perceptions of Sternberg's film. Most critics celebrated the film as a cautionary tale about dangerous female sexuality. Some right-wing writers faulted Sternberg's focus on "sex appeal" (a new, popular English-language term), while some leftist critics decried the film's weakening of Mann's social critique.[14] Nevertheless, because of Mann's novel, reviewers and moviegoers in 1930 connected the experience of watching *The Blue Angel* with popular literature. Sternberg also crafted Lola from characters in well-known theater, namely, Frank Wedekind's 1895 *Earth Spirit* and his 1904 *Pandora's Box*.[15] These backstories placed The Blue Angel between literature, theater, and cinema, conjoining different forms of culture in 1930. Since World War II (if not the late 1930s), the film has become an icon of cool Weimar sexuality. Its meaning has grown in association with the fame of Marlene Dietrich and the film's music, topics to which I return later in the chapter.

Detlev Sierk, an early auteur filmmaker, created the story for *La Habanera*, one of the biggest hits of the Third Reich. Unlike *The Blue Angel*, Sierk's melodrama did not reprise an existing tale. But the film's narrative, success, and implications all drew directly on previous music and well-known tropes. The entire plot is wrapped around the appeal of "La Habanera," a song in the movie derived from a dance and musical pattern epitomizing colonialism and exoticism. If German moviegoers in 1937 did not identify "La Habanera" as the most famous aria from Georges Bizet's well-known 1875 opera *Carmen*, they almost certainly knew the ostinato rhythm that defined the song and dance. That aria's opening lyrics—"Love is a rebellious bird"—parallel the major tension in the film between passion and order. We also hear the famous

"Toreador Song" from the same Bizet opera at two pivotal moments in Sierk's story: to introduce a bloody bullfight that contrasts "civil" North Europeans and "barbaric" Latinos, and to presage the final climax over similar issues at the film's end. Visually, *La Habanera* matches this racialized sonic tension by contrasting the pale Astrée Sternhjelm (played by Zarah Leander) and the dark Don Pedro de Avila (Ferdinand Marian). Familiar opera music thus helped frame the film's basic narrative tension. Like Bizet, other classical composers (e.g., Camille Saint-Saëns, Claude Debussy, and Maurice Ravel) had also helped popularize the "Habanera" theme song, which fused elements of African, French, and Spanish Caribbean culture.[16] This rich backstory in classical and popular music, in other words, embedded the film's music and story in a broad European context about the exotic Other.

In 1937 viewers may also have known about French composer Raoul Laparra's successful 1908 opera *La Habanera,* which addressed the same themes of Latin romance, longing, and exoticism.[17] In Sierk's movie, the sensual Swedish Astrée falls in love with the "savage ... paradise" of Puerto Rico. Drawn by the *Habanera* song and the dark, mysterious, powerful Don Pedro de Avila, she runs from her planned trip back to Sweden, and into his arms. They marry and have a very blonde, very Swedish-looking son. Ten years go by. Her aunt in Sweden, who had first brought Astrée to Puerto Rico a decade earlier and watched her flee into the Don's arms, continues to hope that Astrée will return to her rightful place in her cool, bourgeois homeland. She funds the medical research trip to Puerto Rico of Dr. Sven Nagel (Karl Martell), who is also an old flame of Astrée's, in the hope he will bring Astrée and her son back to Sweden. In fact, Astrée now considers life in the tropics with Avila to be "hell." Longing to show her son the snow, beauty, and order of Sweden, she schemes to leave. Yet even when she and the boy do escape with her old Swedish love, she pines for "La Habanera."

Sierk's film thus uses the *Habanera* song's "going and returning" tropes to warn against sensual, overly emotional connections. Music, dance, and plot from Bizet, Laparra, and others establish the tension in the film between cool Nordic civilization and sweaty Latin barbarism. But like the "rebellious bird" in Bizet's *Carmen,* a sensual woman may fall prey to the romance of the latter. Female characters in fact played such roles in many Third Reich films.[18] Familiar music thus previewed and deepened the story in Sierk's film, further signifying the movie by placing it within a web of cultural consumption.

The backstories that informed viewers' experiences of Forst's 1952 *White Horse Inn* are more concrete. Oskar Blumenthal and Gustav Kadelburg first debuted a theatrical comedy in Berlin in 1897 with that name about a headwaiter in the Austrian lake district who woos his boss, the widowed owner and manager of an inn. Then in 1926, Austrian director Richard Oswald made it into a silent movie featuring the celebrated actress Liane Haid. In 1930, the popular Austrian composer Ralph Benatzky wrote this story into a highly successful operetta that fared well across Europe.[19] Five years later, Austrian filmmaker Carl Lamac turned that version into a movie. Forst's 1952 *White Horse Inn* essentially reprised the music and story from Benatzky's operetta, still well known at that time.[20] In the play/operetta/film, the entire lake district town of St. Wolfgang, and especially the White Horse Inn, is in an uproar in 1910, because Kaiser Franz Josef is coming to visit. Various stereotyped characters—a blustery and all-business Berliner, emotional Italians, a romantic French couple, and super-friendly Austrians—all interact in humorously conflicting stories of love. Above all, the two main characters, the inn owner Josepha (played by Johanna Matz in Forst's film) and her head waiter Leopold (Walter Müller), find themselves so wrapped up in the preparations that they cannot appreciate how close they have grown. Josepha believes she loves the dashing Dr. Siedler (Johannes Heesters), while Siedler has fallen for someone more appropriate for his station, the daughter of the rich Berliner, with whom he has a business conflict. When the Kaiser finally arrives, the old monarch puts everything right. A surprisingly insightful matchmaker, he helps the two main characters see that their work conflicts should not come between what is really love.

Viewers in 1952 would have known the nostalgic story, since it had already served as a filmic and operetta paean to a bygone era. Blumenthal and Kadelburg's original 1897 play had celebrated the contemporary culture of imperial Austria. The films of the turbulent interwar period, as well as Benatzky's highly successful operetta, then constructed a mythical world that idealized imperial Austria. After the Second World War, *Heimat* films often constructed the years before the Great War as being free of the intense, unpleasant political conflicts that had determined Germany and Austria's fates after 1918.[21] Forst himself claimed in his autobiography that his nostalgic films mythologized an Austria free from ugly politics, and defined instead by light-heartedness, music, and humor.[22] Forst made this assertion specifically about the "Viennese trilogy" of films he made late in the Third Reich, so he had definite reasons to describe his work as "apolitical." Nevertheless, the fact that he imagined his movies about imperial Austria as antidotes to political conflict fits well with the general function of *Heimat* films, which often used music to evoke "tradition," in post–World War II West Germany and Austria. Moreover, this claim indicates that *The White Horse Inn* was in fact referring directly to his own movies of some fifteen years earlier. In short, this 1952 film drew its meaning from several well-established stories on stage and screen, as well as broader nostalgia in the 1950s.[23] Even more than *The Blue Angel* and *La Habanera*, Forst's *White Horse Inn* encoded its meaning with references to previous versions and thus to consumer culture broadly.

In all three of these cases, previous stories or tropes informed the moviegoer's trip to see one of these films. Related consumer culture—music, fiction, operetta, dance, theater, and other movies—mean that diachronic consumption directly influenced viewers' possible interpretations of the synchronic experience of seeing one of these movies. These musical films could create a semblance of aesthetic unity by uniting stories from consumer culture generally with the specific narratives of these movies. The music and sound of these films serve this conjunctive function even more explicitly. It is to these connections that I now turn.

The Sound/track

Audio in these three films especially linked them to other forms of contemporary culture. The songs in *The Blue Angel* and the nightclub setting served as important vehicles for the modifications to Heinrich Mann's original novel. Sierk used well-known opera motifs in *La Habanera* to define characters, narrative tension, and action. And Forst's *White Horse Inn* was, of course, a filmed version of a famous operetta. The movies themselves turned these multivalent stories into mass cultural products. Their soundtracks made the recorded music a free-floating cultural product only partly signified by its original context. Indeed, all three movies spawned popular songs that played on the radio and sold many records. The biggest hits from *The Blue Angel* and *La Habanera*, in fact, shaped Dietrich's and Leander's respective careers for the rest of their lives. The sound and soundtrack from each film could most easily be disassociated from the films by being played on the radio or phonographs, thus making essential pieces of the films a part of Germans' larger consumption of mass culture.

Music helps direct the plot in each movie. In *La Habanera*, music demarcates the film's polarities: hot and cold, entrapment and escape. The title song entices Astrée to flee her cold, planned life back in Stockholm. Zarah Leander was already a popular diva in Nazi Germany by 1937, but we have to wait for half the movie for her to sing at all. She sings "You Just Can't Know" ("Du kannst es nicht wissen") to her son, Juan, as a way to explain her feelings at that point in the narrative: her now acute longing for the North, especially its snowy Christmas, and the importance of her Nordic-looking son vs. the dark-skinned, tyrannical Puerto Rican father/husband. Lothar Brühne wrote the music, but Sierk penned the lyrics. Sierk likewise wrote the words for a whimsical "A-B-C Children's Song" that actually does a lot of the film's plot work by describing Astrée's feelings for Sweden, the fantastic world she inhabits as an inner escape from Puerto Rico, and even her plans for escape. In each case, the songs serve as more than vehicles for the star's voice. They actually propel the story forward. For instance, Astrée uses her climactic performance of "La Habanera" ("Cheated by the Wind" or "Der Wind hat mir ein Lied erzählt") to enchant her jealous, sweating, dying husband and to buy time for Dr. Nagel to escape the authorities who would stop his work on the very disease that is killing the Don. Astrée thus turns the song that ten years before had entrapped her into a vehicle for escape, revealing that a clever Nordic woman could exploit the attraction of the exotic Other. Yet even as she leaves Puerto Rico for good, the song beckons to her. Until that closing scene, we only hear "La Habanera" in German. Finally, as Astrée listens from the departing ship, we hear it in Spanish, which drives home its alien quality. Sierk consciously placed music in the center of this film. He sought to emulate Bertolt Brecht and Kurt Weill's synthesis of music and drama in *The Three-Penny Opera* (1928) and G.W. Pabst's 1931 filmed version of it, in which music is part of the narrative, rather than a pause in the action for characters to stop and sing.[24] Reviews noted the "strong factor" that Brühne's music played in this film.[25]

In *The Blue Angel*, Sternberg similarly utilizes music to drive home the film's larger cautionary tale about powerful female sexuality. Lola may have seduced Rath with her looks and coquettish behavior, but she employs sound to dominate her environment. She entrances Rath during his first visit to The Blue Angel with her theme song, "Head to Toe I'm Ready for Love" ("Ich bin von Kopf bis Fuß auf Liebe eingestellt"), which later became the jazz standard "Falling in Love Again." And in her dressing room, the constant opening and closing of her door to the stage disturbs Rath, as it probably did viewers in 1930, who were still unaccustomed to dramatic volume shifts in new sound films. But Lola calmly works within this noisy environment, in marked contrast to Rath's efforts to control all sound in his classroom or the whistling songbird in his apartment. Unlike *La Habanera* or *White Horse Inn*, *The Blue Angel* makes only limited use of non-diegetic music, which was still quite new in 1930. Composer Friedrich Holländer's film music featured the traditional song "Always Practice Truth and Honesty" ("Üb immer Treu und Redlichkeit"), in contrast to the potentially destructive sexuality in Lola's siren song.[26] Music makes the film's final point, too. After Rath's ultimate humiliation on the Blue Angel stage, Lola sings "Falling in Love Again" alone. She looks contemptuously at the audience, adding visual power to her lines, "Men flock around me like moths to a flame / And if their wings burn, I know I'm not to blame." After stumbling back to his old classroom desk and former source of sonic authority, Rath dies while chimes play "Always Practice Truth and Honesty" to conclude the film. The contrast between the two songs—female "sex appeal" vs. traditional patriarchal morality—determines *The Blue Angel*'s narrative.

As a filmed operetta, *The White Horse Inn* naturally uses music differently. More ubiquitous yet crafted as specific pauses in the narrative, diegetic music nevertheless shapes important narrative elements of Forst's film. All three male leads announce their affection for the women they are not supposed to love through song. A little singing in the mountains even loosens up the gruff Berlin businessman Giesecke. And when his one-time business rival, Dr. Siedler, adds his voice to the alpine echo chamber, their duet prompts Giesecke to forgive him, an opening that begins a chain of events that eventually allows Siedler to propose marriage to Giesecke's daughter. Siedler's radiant charm is matched by his mellifluous voice, both of which he employs at key moments in the film. Just as his opening singing of the operetta's theme song signals the social inevitability of his winning Giesecke's daughter, Ottillie (Marianne Wischmann), so too does his drunken performance of the song later start the process of reconciliation with head waiter Leopold, who envies Josepha's interest in Siedler.

The film's rendering of this love triangle among Leopold, Josepha, and Siedler in fact underscores well how musical film could build upon and even play with the original operetta. Soon after Siedler arrives at the White Horse Inn, Leopold spies Josehpa in Siedler's room. Watching from the street below, Leopold sees shadows on the curtains that convince him that the two are embracing, when in fact they are across the room from each other. We hear him singing in his head one of the operetta's major hits, "I Can't Look" ("Zuschau'n kann i net"). The medium of film makes it especially easy to let the audience hear a song in someone's head. The popularity of this song made this trick of cinema more meaningful, especially for a song about not being able to watch something. Leopold's singing in Austrian dialect also points to the way that aural cues help define the Austrian lake district as distinctive from other parts of the German-speaking world. At the start of the film, the Berliners remark on the "cute" Austrian accent, and the first conversations we hear between Austrians come in dialect, though most of the main characters otherwise use *Hochdeutsch*. Finally, the abundance of music and dance at the climactic small-town sharpshooting festival (*Schützenfest*) brings all plot lines to a head and, like the repeated theme song, demonstrates the mythical healing power of the inn, the location, and, at least for viewers, the memory of 1910.

These three films form an important arc in the historical relationship between diegetic and non-diegetic music in film. Between *The Blue Angel* (1930) and *The White Horse Inn* (1952), some of the most important improvements in cinema came in the arena of sound. Sternberg only used non-diegetic music to introduce and conclude his film, whereas twenty-two years later Forst cleverly wove together diegetic and non-diegetic music in his creation. This evolution likewise highlights the changing role that movie music played in popular culture. Like *The Jazz Singer*, *The Blue Angel* features a musical performer as lead in order to showcase singing. Sternberg employs a non-diegetic soundtrack only at the beginning and end to frame the film's narrative. Only in the final scene, when the school night watchman discovers Rath dead at his desk, does the soundtrack accompany any action on the screen. The halting ascending chords with high string tremolo match the watchman's anxious search for Rath, culminating in a cadence on a big major chord, before chimes ring out "Always Practice Truth and Honesty," the refrain that signals the film's morale. Here Sternberg cleverly reprises the synthesis of sight and sound. Just as Lola initially captured Rath with a spotlight and a song, the movie closes on the expired Rath with the night watchman's single lamplight and song that should have inspired him.

A mere seven years later, *La Habanera* boasted a more integrated soundtrack that underscores the narrative by working closely with music in the film. During the short span between these two movies, filmmakers found more ways to employ non-diegetic music in cinema. Indeed, until the introduction of color in the late 1930s and early 1940s, it was advances in sound technology that changed movies most during this decade.[27] The soundtrack's use of "March of the Toreadors" from Carmen firmly ties Sierk's film to that opera, still popular in the 1930s. The film score also marks shifts in action between snowy, bourgeois Sweden and sweltering, feudal Puerto Rico, demonstrating for the viewer the emotional power that music has on the characters. Rosita, a longtime servant in Don Avila's house, blames the weakness of Avila and Astrée's son on "a mother who sings foreign songs full of tears." A fade between the dark, angry Rosita and the pale, smiling Astrée emphasizes this point. And as tensions rise between Astrée and the Don, the Habanera song finally pushes their relationship to breaking point. She tells him that she hates that song most about Puerto Rico, prompting Avila to inform her that he and Rosita will take over their son's rearing. When the Don leaves, Astrée again hears the strains of "La Habanera" coming through her window, which she has opened due to the oppressive heat. After this final straw, Astrée hurries to a travel agent to book one-way tickets to Sweden for her and Juan. Although the *Habanera* soundtrack is more robust than that of *The Blue Angel*, Sierk's film still draws heavily from diegetic music. Given that Astrée refuses throughout the film to sing the ubiquitous *Habanera* song for Avila, Leander's performance at the end takes on greater significance. Both diegetic and non-diegetic music, in other words, shape *La Habanera*.

The White Horse Inn merges diegetic and non-diegetic music seamlessly, showing how far film scores developed in the 1930s and 1940s. Important pieces, such as the overture, remind viewers of music they likely already knew as well as previous incarnations of the story. The setting (and story) also affords Forst many opportunities to use diegetic music. Some music seems natural in this setting, like the yodelers at the sharpshooting festival performance. Others seem more contrived, like the yodeling postal worker walking through the hills. Yet the multiple examples of happy singing help advance the film's point to cast and audience alike: this place offers emotional respite and a chance to assess what matters most. At several points the soundtrack completes music begun by characters. During the opening scene, for example, Siedler first whistles and then sings the theme song. After his encounter with Ottillie Giesecke, the non-diegetic soundtrack joins his song, as do all the villagers, merging diegetic and non-diegetic music.

The movies' soundtracks also pointed toward each film's potential political implications. Although their rationales differed, commentators on the left and right objected to *The Blue Angel's* emphasis on Lola's sexual power. Dietrich's beauty may have dominated discussions about the film, but her use of music—especially "Falling in Love Again"—best articulated the tension at the heart of this film between empowered female sexuality and patriarchal control. *La Habanera* was a well-supported Ufa film that came out when Goebbels held considerable authority over the cinema industry in Nazi Germany. It lays out the Nazi Party line about racial difference. In the film, music, especially the title song, repeatedly makes the point that good Nordic types (especially women) must beware of the appeal of the exotic Other. Significantly, Bizet's own opera similarly warns of the dangers represented by attractive, sensual Gypsies like Carmen. Ironically, Forst's happy-go-lucky *White Horse Inn* ran into the most direct political resistance at the time of its release. Austrian Social Democrats even required Forst in one important scene to replace the old imperial Austrian national anthem, Haydn's "Imperial Hymm," with Franz von Suppé's 1849 "My Austria," which had long been considered Austria's second national song.[28] Thus, music's emotive power crystalizes some of the more powerful ideas implicit in all these films: fear about sexual liberation, challenges to social hierarchy, and even nationalism. The fact that these songs could also be consumed apart from the films only increased their power.

The recorded soundtrack in fact served important purposes outside all three films. Benatzky's operetta has been recorded often. Since the operetta's debut in 1930, various labels across the West have released certain songs or the entire production, and in multiple languages.[29] Even viewers who had never attended a stage performance would have heard this music on phonographs or the radio. Ufa Studios consciously promoted *La Habanera* as a vehicle for Zarah Leander as singer and actor. The two songs her character sings to her son were minor hits. The theme song "La Habanera" became Leander's most popular song ever.[30]

The Blue Angel's soundtrack, perhaps most significantly, helped define that film's meaning in 1930, and ever since. Friedrich Holländer's hit songs, especially "Falling in Love Again," imprinted this 1930 film onto the history of popular music. English lyrics by Sammy Lerner turned the sexually aggressive original German, "Ich bin von Kopf bis Fuß auf Liebe eingestellt," into a romantic, melodic jazz standard. Next to Brecht and Weill's "Mack the Knife" from *The Three-Penny Opera,* Holländer's song ranks as one of the most lastingly popular from Weimar Germany. The soundtrack for *The Blue Angel* helped market the movie when it was released, too. Outside Berlin, where the film premièred in April 1930, most Germans heard the music on the radio or phonograph before the film arrived in their local theaters. In Göttingen, for example, one reviewer compared the recording with the sound film.[31] Holländer's group, the Weintraub Syncopaters, was a popular jazz combo in Germany at the time, and its presence in the film lent musical credibility to *The Blue Angel*, and popularized the vibrant jazz scene of Weimar Germany.

These movies exemplify the development of the soundtrack into an increasingly integrated and sophisticated part of film. Music in these films creates a sense of unity in two ways. First, it directs the storylines and articulates the films' moral, social, and political implications. Even more than visual cues, music holds these films together. Second, the songs, soundtrack, and sounds refer to previous forms of culture: opera, operetta, traditional songs, recordings, and other films. In fact, the films draw meaning from those predecessors. Music therefore linked the experience of watching those films with German viewers' other consumption habits. In each of these films, music and sound forged a number of temporal connections between viewers' experiences of watching the movie and other forms of consumer culture. Indeed, their music enabled viewers to link their synchronic experience of moviegoing with their diachronic consumption of culture. This tendency to signify the movies themselves through their associative links to other culture echoes Adorno's discovery of consumerism at the heart of Wagner's Gesamtkunstwerk.

The Stars

The stars of *The Blue Angel*, *La Habanera*, and *The White Horse Inn* all sang, and not just in these films. The voices and personas of Marlene Dietrich, Zarah Leander, and Johannes Heesters especially offer a third vehicle to connect these individual films with larger habits of consumer culture in mid twentieth-century Germany. Movie stars and movies have shared a symbiotic relationship since the early twentieth century. By the 1930s, movie stars were playing even more important roles in Western society. "They had," Samantha Barbas writes in *Movie Crazy*, "become models of modern selfhood."[32] Stars with longer careers connected for viewers at the time (and ever since) the discrete experience of watching a specific movie with the larger discourses about their career. Stars were meant to function both inside and outside the movie: they helped create the film's diegetic fiction and attract viewers because of their non-diegetic persona built upon previous work.

The Blue Angel highlights the intersection between Marlene Dietrich's rise to stardom and the function of sex in cinema.[33] Just as Lola conquered Rath in *The Blue Angel*, Dietrich superseded Emil Jannings as star. At the time Jannings had notched a successful career in German and American cinema, capped by winning the first Academy Award for Acting in 1928 (for *The Last Command*, also directed by Sternberg). The fact that sound film hastened his departure from Hollywood helps explain why Dietrich eclipsed his status. For *The Blue Angel* she was paid only 25,000 marks, while he received 200,000.[34] But the film made her career. As soon as *The Blue Angel* debuted in Germany, Dietrich left with Sternberg for Hollywood and began her meteoric rise. Many of Dietrich's subsequent characters exhibited the cool sexuality that Sternberg's imagery and Holländer's music had crafted in *The Blue Angel*. Dietrich's roles in 1930s Hollywood films like *Morocco, Blonde Venus, Devil is a Woman*, and *Desire* wedded established tropes of vamp and exotic foreigner with her portrayal of a bold chanteuse in Blue Angel. When *The Blue Angel* premièred in Berlin in April 1930, reviewers were almost universally taken with Dietrich as a new kind of movie star.[35] By the time German viewers outside Berlin saw the film later that year, they already knew about Dietrich's defection to the United States. Some reviews noted that she was following Greta Garbo to Hollywood stardom.[36] Writers continued to cite the movie well into the 1930s as a standard for effective sound film and the appeal of a movie star.[37] And scholars since have used Dietrich's image and voice to evoke "Weimar culture."[38] When *The Blue Angel* came out, Jannings defined a successful movie star in Germany, but it was Dietrich's career thereafter that has subsequently shaped the film's meanings. Dietrich's voice had as much to do with the film's impact as her much-touted legs. Beginning in the 1920s, she made nearly 180 recordings in her long career, and by the 1950s singing had become her principle occupation. Ernest Hemmingway purportedly claimed, "If she had nothing more than her voice she could break your heart with it." Contemporary Kenneth Tynam called Dietrich's voice her "third dimension" that helped her develop from 1930s sex symbol into twentieth-century icon.[39]

Zarah Leander followed a similar if slightly more limited path. She was already a star when *La Habanera* came out in 1937, albeit just barely. After a successful career in her native Sweden, she got her German-language start with a 1936 Benatzky stage comedy in Vienna. That year, Ufa and Goebbels cast her in *To New Shores* (*Zu neuen Ufern*), Sierk's first musical melodramatic vehicle for Leander. They even hired Benatzky, by then famous, to write some of her music. (Benatzky in fact wrote for Leander well into the 1950s.) *La Habanera* followed quickly and demonstrated why Leander had become Germany's biggest movie star and vocalist.[40] Her recording and film careers reinforced each other, epitomizing the combined publicity campaigns typical of German and American studios in the 1930s. Like Dietrich, her cool, sophisticated appeal, on screen and off, blended image and music. Leander's career is necessarily bound up with her position as Third Reich diva. *La Habanera* makes a clear statement about the superiority of Nordic culture. Yet her character's emotional attraction to the Latin Other (especially manifested in music), right up to the final scene of the movie, marks her as more of a pawn than principal in this ideological tale. Leander played a similarly ambiguous role in the Third Reich. Her character in various films, recording career, and function as movie star all succeeded partly because she was an outsider who exhibited mixed feelings about her place. For example, she clearly benefitted from Goebbels' patronage and from government-sponsored radio events (as did *White Horse Inn* star Johannes Heesters).[41] But she also negotiated contracts that paid her partly in Swedish crowns. Brian Currid points to Leander's 1938 *Heimat* as an example of her ability to employ her own position in the "*audiovisual* star system" of Nazi Germany in ways that could both reinforce and challenge the regime.[42]

David Lee concludes that Leander, as female lead, is able to render *La Habanera* potentially oppositional to the Nazi regime by engendering alienation from the film's ideology, what he identifies as "Brechtian" moments.[43] Her singing in the film reveals her character's psychological tension and ambivalence about the film's message. And the successful sale of resultant hit songs helped expand, through consumer culture, the film's potential opposition to Nazi ideas. After all, in her biggest hit, "La Habanera," Leander sings in German as a sultry Swede longing for Latin America. Like "Falling in Love Again," this song could mean many things to listeners. Both songs shaped their stars' careers and the films' legacies for years thereafter. And by foregrounding female sexuality, both "La Habanera" and "Falling in Love Again" defined and challenged the films' basic ideologies.[44]

Both Dietrich's and Leander's voices helped express their authority, ambiguity, and long-term resonance as stars. Each used singing to enhance their "sex appeal" and their value as cultural product throughout their careers. In these two films, which employ music narratively, the female lead can, through singing, take a scene "outside time and space," as Laura Mulvey puts it, and make that scene potentially more significant.[45] By looking at these performances as part of stars' longer careers in cinema and music, viewers at the time likewise could have experienced this music as liminal moments, rendered all the more potent by the fact that these hit songs were the most reproducible parts of a film. Movie stars made these songs simultaneously symbols of these films and free-floating cultural products. Viewers' overall cultural consumption habits helped bridge this gap.

The stars in *The White Horse Inn* were not as iconic, although Johannes Heesters enjoyed an astounding ninety-year career on stage and screen. Born in Holland, he began acting in 1921 at the age of eighteen and appeared in his first film in 1924. He excelled in romantic comedies during the Third Reich, a fact that both enhanced and slightly tainted his image after 1945. These "safe" movies were among the few cultural products Germans could reclaim from the Third Reich, although they also reminded viewers of how well Heesters had fared during that era. His long-burning fame shaped views of Forst's 1952 film, before its release and since. Viennese-born Johanna Matz made a name for herself in 1950s *Heimat* and musical films, often playing the "Vienna girl." *The White Horse Inn* helped define this role and worked well because Matz had already played prominent "Austrian" roles. Otto Preminger even cast her, with Heesters, in a German version of *The Moon is Full* (1953), and she starred in the English-language version of the 1954 *They Were So Young*. She spent most of her career after 1960 in German or Austrian television and theater. While she sang in *The White Horse Inn* and other films, she did not pursue a significant recording career. By playing a part for which she was known, Matz helped cement *The White Horse Inn* as familiar *Heimat* film.

The dramatic career of Viennese director Willi Forst highlights *The White Horse Inn*'s function as nostalgia and even source of political tension. Forst had directed and acted in German and Austrian films since the early 1920s. In the 1930s he made films that idealized pre–World War I Austria. After the *Anschluß*, Third Reich officials encouraged his making such light entertainment. Forst later called these movies, which conjured a considerate, witty, musical Austria that no longer existed, a form of "silent protest."[46] That kind of nostalgia, a way of looking past Nazi-era events, held great appeal in 1952. Forst could thus craft *The White Horse Inn* as myth on two levels. First, he evoked the halcyon pre–World War I era of Imperial Austria as a prosperous time free of ideological conflict. Second, he could actually salvage his own work under the Nazi regime by making a film that reprised some of the same themes featured in those movies in the late 1930s and early 1940s. The substantial genealogy of Benatzky's operetta reinforced this multivalent function of nostalgia.[47] In addition, Forst had experienced the cultural strictures of 1950s West Germany. Only the year before he had prompted a major scandal with *The Sinner* (starring Hildegard Knef), a racy film about a woman's resorting to prostitution and eventually suicide for the sake of love.[48] This trouble surely reinforced Forst's previous experience that pleasant comedies set in "safe" eras fared better in the anxious years after World War II. While the popularity of the ensemble's "Austrian" credentials most directly shaped perceptions about *The White Horse Inn*, Forst's varied, politically charged career helped make the film's dripping nostalgia an antidote to the challenges facing Germans and Austrians in 1952.

In short, movie stars and directors served as individual connection points between Germans' ongoing (diachronic) consumption of cinema and specific (synchronic) attendance of individual films, before television provided another vehicle for consuming films and stars. Stars like Marlene Dietrich, Zarah Leander, Johannes Heesters, and Johanna Matz used body, voice, and persona to situate specific films within a larger context of cultural consumption. Stars appeared to unite viewers' consumption of film, music, and theater. These individuals, in fact, helped make each of these three films a nexus for cultural consumption. This semblance of unity was not the same kind imagined by Wagner, Schiller, or others in the nineteenth century. But musical film seemed nonetheless to "solve" an important tension in Gesamtkunstwerk, namely that between audience members' discrete cultural experiences and broader habits of cultural consumption. Similarly, movie stars' different roles in these films—commodities defined both inside and outside the films—helped unify viewers' experiences as consumers. Previous careers like those of Heesters and Forst informed viewers' perceptions of *The White Horse Inn*. A consciously created diva, Leander's singing and acting reinforced each other in the 1930s and 1940s. And Dietrich's performance in *The Blue Angel* defined her career for the rest of her life and continues to embody the view of "Weimar culture" many scholars have created. Movie stars helped connect for moviegoers important elements in and related to these films, uniting viewers' consumption habits and thus, to some degree, their views on the world.

Conclusion—Locating Gesamtkunstwerk

The present essay collection chiefly explores the various ways composers, artists, philosophers, architects, choreographers, filmmakers, and others have imagined total works of art, especially as attempted expressions of unity. Yet one finding to emerge is the ongoing nebulousness of the concept itself. It seems thus that we have been looking in the wrong heads for manifestations of Gesamtkunstwerk, which as an idea may work better as a tool for articulating a project's purpose and relationship to aesthetic and social structures than as a strict definition of some work of art or another. Indeed, my exploration of musical film indicates that we can understand these movies better by analyzing them through the lens of Gesamtkunstwerk, rather than as essays *in* Gesamtkunstwerk. Likewise, these examples urge us to loosen our ideas about Gesamtkunstwerk, especially its promotion of certain notions of unity. This idea of unity occurs—or may occur—in viewers' heads. As such, it is nearly impossible to access. Rather than take that conclusion to mean we cannot understand Gesamtkunstwerk, I maintain that using it as a way to analyze real and imagined connections in German cultural life can instruct us about specific cultural products and activities, as well as possible ways consumers used them in their daily lives. Let me close by detailing three levels of implications from my analysis.

What can we learn, first, from the films themselves? The previous articulations of these films' stories shaped viewers' perceptions, and music was usually critical to how these backstories functioned. *The Blue Angel* focused more on the singer Lola than on Professor Rath, marking the greatest alteration to Mann's original novel. By citing existing, familiar musical material, the music in *La Habanera* created the tension between characters that personalized the movie's racialist story. *The White Horse Inn* functioned as an updated version of Benatzky's operetta, using the cinematic medium, especially the combination of diegetic and non-diegetic music, to enhance a familiar story.

The sound, music, and soundtrack help unify aspects of the films' narratives and their meanings as consumer products. Within each one, sound and music create and resolve major tensions: Rath's meticulous life vs. losing control over Lola; the song that entraps and liberates in *La Habanera*; and the issue of who loves whom in White Horse. The stars of these productions also illustrate the broad consumer appeal of such musical films. *White Horse Inn* was part of a long line of performances of Benatzky's operetta from 1930 to today; the film's stars and the operetta's fame shaped recordings made from the movie in 1952. Leading divas Dietrich and Leander used their roles to create exotic personas, as much with their voices as their physical appearance. The music of these films helped make them famous singing stars. Their voices also defined Dietrich's and Leander's ambivalent representation of various political and gender ideologies. Musical film thus helps to establish and maintain a different way of "consuming" works like film—less ephemeral, more interconnected, and this discursive fabric is larger than the individual works themselves.

Second, my broader definition of Gesamtkunstwerk highlights the links between these specific cultural products and mass culture generally. This perspective asks us to consider how mass culture fulfilled some yearning for unity that many proponents—from Schiller to Wagner to scholars in this collection—identify as central to Gesamtkunstwerk *qua* concept. Such a view enables us to ask better questions, though without necessarily offering clearer answers. Treating mass culture as individual products engaged in dialectical discourse with consumption generally helps explain the meaning of individual films or recordings or other cultural products, as well as the larger history of mass culture. My analysis also illustrates that consumers ascribed meaning to cultural products dialogically.[49]

Finally, using Gesamtkunstwerk as a concept to consider broader implications of mass culture begs some important questions about the function of culture generally in modern Germany and beyond. How did political organizations attempt to direct the vague sense of unity we have seen here toward their own ideological purposes? Brian Currid calls the musical film a "new organ of experience," uniting consumption and ideology.[50] How has this process worked in other media and in other places? How have individual consumers used this total work of consumption to their own ends, perhaps in opposition to the expectations of cultural producers or politicians? The importance of culture in modern German history enriches the analytical possibilities of these questions, and makes them essential to study. Matthew Smith points out that examples of Gesamtkunstwerk provide means for understanding disparate connections in the modern world. Recorded sound in particular can disrupt the flow of time or experience in the modern world.[51] Considering how consumption can "solve" that disruption enhances our view of how Germans used mass culture in the tumultuous twentieth century.[52]

Notes

I appreciate the helpful comments from my co-editors Margaret Menninger and Tony Steinhoff, as well as from members of the Philadelphia Area Modern Germany workshop, especially Paul Steege, Greg Eghigian, Julia Sneeringer, Pieter Judson, and Jeffrey Johnson.

1. Reviews in Werner Sudendorf, *Marlene Dietrich: Dokumente, Essays, Filme* (Berlin and Vienna, 1980), 117–32.
2. Russell Lack, *Twenty-Four Frames Under: A Buried History of Film Music* (London, 1997); Mervyn Cooke, *A History of Film Music* (Cambridge, 2008); Kathryn Marie Kalinak, *Film Music: A Very Short Introduction* (Oxford, 2010).
3. Theodor Adorno, *In Search of Wagner*, trans. Rodney Livingstone (London, 2005), 21–36, 74–84, 92–93. Carolyn Birdsall discusses the connection between Gesamtkunstwerk and cinema in Chapter 4 of *Nazi Soundscapes: Sound, Technology and Urban Space in Germany, 1933–1945* (Amsterdam, 2012).
4. Kalinak, *Film Music*, 51–56.
5. Further, see Matthew Wilson Smith, *The Total Work of Art: From Bayreuth to Cyberspace* (New York, 2007); David Roberts, *The Total Work of Art in European Modernism* (Ithaca, 2011); Juliet Koss, *Modernism after Wagner* (Minneapolis, 2010).
6. George Williamson argues similarly in *The Longing for Myth in Germany: Religion and Aesthetic Culture from Romanticism to Nietzsche* (Chicago, 2004).
7. Walter Benjamin, "The Work of Art in the Age of Mechanical Reproduction," in *Illuminations*, ed. Hannah Arendt, trans. Harry Zohn (New York, 1968), 217–51.
8. Friedrich A. Kittler, *Grammophon Film Typewriter* (Berlin, 1986).
9. Emily Thompson, *The Soundscape of Modernity: Architectural Acoustics and the Culture of Listening in America, 1900–1933* (Cambridge, 2002); Holger Schulze, ed., *Sound Studies: Traditionen—Methoden—Desiderate: Eine Einführung* (Bielefeld, 2008); Florence Feiereisen and Alexandra Merley Hill, eds, *Germany in the Loud Twentieth Century: An Introduction* (Oxford, 2011); Jonathan Sterne, ed., *The Sound Studies Reader* (London, 2012).
10. Nora Alter and Lutz Koepnick's Introduction to *Sound Matters: Essays on the Acoustics of Modern German Culture* (New York, 2004), 14.
11. Corey Ross, *Media and the Making of Modern Germany: Mass Communications, Society and Politics from the Empire to the Third Reich* (Oxford, 2008); Karl Christian Führer and Ross, eds, *Mass Media, Culture and Society in Twentieth-Century Germany* (New York, 2007); Ross, "Writing the Media into History: Recent Works on the History of Mass Communications in Germany," *German History* 26, no. 2 (2008): 299–313.
12. More generally, see Anton Kaes, *Kino-Debatte: Texte zum Verhältnis von Literatur und Film 1909–1929* (Munich, 1978).

13. Heinrich Mann, "Der Blaue Engel wird mir vorgeführt," *Berliner Börsen-Courier*, 30 March 1930.
14. See positive reviews in Sudendorf, *Dietrich*, 117–32; Siegfried Kracauer, *Die Neue Rundschau*, June 1930, 861–63.
15. Josef von Sternberg, *Fun in a Chinese Laundry* (New York, 1965), 230.
16. Frances Barulich and Jan Fairley, "Habanera," in Grove Music Online. Oxford Music Online, http://www.oxfordmusiconline.com/subscriber/article/grove/music/12116 (accessed 22 July 2014); Wendy Thomson and Christopher Webber, "Iradier, Sebastián"; Irene Weiss Peery, "Boyle, George Frederick"; Steven Huebner, "Chabrier, Emmanuel"; Barbara L. Kelly, "Ravel, Maurice," *The Oxford Dictionary of Music*, 2nd edn. rev. *Oxford Music Online*, Oxford University Press, http://www.oxfordmusiconline.com/subscriber/article/grove/music/12116; http://www.oxfordmusiconline.com/subscriber/article/opr/t237/e11201; http://www.oxfordmusiconline.com/subscriber/article/grove/music/03781; http://www.oxfordmusiconline.com/subscriber/article/grove/music/05351; http://www.oxfordmusiconline.com/subscriber/article/grove/music/52145 (accessed 22 July 2014).
17. Richard Langham Smith, "Laparra, Raoul," in *Grove Music Online*. Oxford Music Online, http://www.oxfordmusiconline.com/subscriber/article/grove/music/16011 (accessed 22 July 2014).
18. Jo Fox, *Filming Women in the Third Reich* (Oxford, 2000).
19. Andrew Lamb, "Benatzky, Ralph" and "Im weissen Rössl," in *The New Grove Dictionary of Opera*, edited by Stanley Sadie. *Grove Music Online. Oxford Music Online*, http://www.oxfordmusiconline.com/subscriber/article/grove/music/02632 and http://www.oxfordmusiconline.com/subscriber/article/grove/music/O003479 (accessed 22 July 2014); Richard Traubner calls it "one of the greatest hits of its day" in *Operetta: A Theatrical History* (Garden City, NY, 1983), 309.
20. And the iterations have kept coming. Werner Jacobs remade the movie in 1960, and additional versions appeared on television in 1967, 1971, and 2013.
21. Willi Höfig, *Der deutsche Heimatfilm, 1947–1960* (Stuttgart, 1973); Heide Fehrenbach, *Cinema in Democratizing Germany: Reconstructing National Identity after Hitler* (Chapel Hill, 1995).
22. Cited in Gertrud Steiner Daviau, "Willi Forst: Bel Ami in the Third Reich," *Modern Austrian Literature* 32, no. 3 (1999): 150–51.
23. Fehrenbach, *Cinema*, 150–66; Johannes von Moltke, "Evergreens: The Heimat Genre," in *The German Cinema Book*, ed. Tim Bergfelder, Erica Carter, and Deniz Göktürk (London, 2002), 15–28; Gertraud Steiner, *Die Heimat-Macher: Kino in Österreich 1946–1966* (Vienna, 1987).
24. Thomas R. Nadar, "The Director and the Diva: The Film Musicals of Detlef Sierck and Zarah Leander: *Zu neuen Ufern* and *La Habanera*," in *Cultural History through a National Socialist Lens: Essays on the Cinema of the Third Reich*, ed. Robert C. Reimer (Rochester, 2000), 66–74.
25. E.g., *Freiburger Zeitung*, 4 February 1938.
26. Friedrich Holländer, "Die Musik in Tonfilm," *Reichsfilmblatt*, 10 May 1930. Mozart had used the melody in *The Magic Flute* (1791) to signify Papageno's innocence in that character's famous aria, "The Bird Catcher." Simon Richter, "The Return of the Queen of the Night: Joseph von Sternberg's *Der blaue Engel* and *Die Zauberflöte*," *German Life and Letters* 61, no. 1 (2008): 171–85.
27. Kalinak, *Film Music*, 58–67.

28. Paul Hühnerfeld, "Nur ein gerechter Mann," *Die Zeit* (22 January 1953); Peter Branscombe and Dorothea Link, "Suppé, Franz," *Grove Music Online, Oxford Music Online*, Oxford University Press, http://www.oxfordmusiconline.com/subscriber/article/grove/music/27130 (accessed 1 August 2014). Germany had taken Haydn's anthem as its own after World War I, which may explain Austrian Social Democrats' sensitivity to the subject in 1952.
29. Kurt Gänzl, *The Blackwell Guide to the Musical Theater on Record* (Oxford, 1990), 290–94.
30. Nadar, "Director," 72–73.
31. *Göttinger Volksblatt*, 19 June 1930.
32. Samantha Barbas, *Movie Crazy: Fans, Stars, and the Cult of Celebrity* (New York, 2001), 36.
33. David Davidson, "From Virgin to Dynamo: The 'Amoral Woman' in European Cinema," *Cinema Journal* 21, no. 1 (Autumn 1981): 31–49; Richard McCormick, "From 'Caligari' to Dietrich: Sexual, Social, and Cinematic Discourses in Weimar Film," *Signs* 18, no. 3 (Spring 1993): 640–68.
34. Sudendorf, *Dietrich*, 68, 71–72.
35. See reviews in Sudendorf, *Marlene Dietrich*.
36. *Göttinger Tageblatt*, 7 April 1930.
37. E.g., *Göttinger Zeitung*, 21 July 1932; *Göttinger Tageblat*, 17 January 1935.
38. Peter Gay does so most notably in the introduction to his seminal *Weimar Culture: The Outsider as Insider* (New York, 1968), xiii.
39. Steven Bach, *Marlene Dietrich: Life and Legend* (Minneapolis, 2011), 361–62 and 521–28.
40. Nadar, "Director."
41. Hans-Jörg Koch, *Das Wunschkonzert im NS-Rundfunk* (Cologne, 2003), 247.
42. Brian Currid, *A National Acoustics: Music and Mass Publicity in Weimar and Nazi Germany* (Minneapolis, 2006), 148–55, quote on 153.
43. David Lee, "A Flash of Enlightenment: A Brechtian Moment in Douglas Sirk's 'La Habanera,'" *Monatshefte* 100, no. 3 (Fall 2008): 400–14.
44. The career of *La Habanera*'s male lead, Ferdinand Marian, on the other hand, marks him as a symbol of the Nazi film industry (even if his personal life did not). Marian made his first movie in 1933, more or less stopped in 1945, and is best known for the fantastic color film *The Adventures of Baron von Munchausen* (1943), and especially the anti-Semitic *Jud Süß* (1940).
45. Cited in Adrienne L. McLean, "'It's Only That I Do What I Love and Love What I Do': 'Film Noir' and the Musical Woman," *Cinema Journal* 33, no. 1 (Autumn 1993): 3.
46. Daviau, "Willi Forst," 149–51.
47. Kevin Clark, "Zurück in die Zukunft: Aspekte der Aufführungspraxis des *Weisen Rössl*," in *Im weißen Rössl: zwischen Kunst und Kommerz*, ed. Ulrich Tadday (Munich, 2006), 116–23.
48. Heide Fehrenbach maintains that the outcry against this film served to justify conservative social policies in *Cinema*, 93–117.
49. Joy Calico's contribution to this collection argues similarly that Brecht's *Lehrstücke* of the 1920s sought to unite consumer and producer.
50. Currid, *National Acoustics*, 65–118, quote on 115.
51. Smith, *Total Work of Art*, 187–88.

52. Kittler, *Grammophon*; Alter and Koepnick, Introduction to *Sound Matters*; Führer and Ross, Introduction to *Mass Media*.

David Imhoof is Associate Professor of History at Susquehanna University in Selinsgrove, Pennsylvania. His book, *Becoming a Nazi Town: Culture and Politics in Göttingen between the World Wars*, appeared with University of Michigan Press in 2013. He has published on sports, film, and sharpshooting in interwar Germany and is co-editing a forthcoming edition of *Colloquia Germanica* on sound studies. He directs the Music and Sound Studies Network for the German Studies Association.

AFTERWORD

Gesamtkunstwerk as Epistemic Space

KEVIN S. AMIDON

In the annals of German academic discipline formation, the year 1910 can claim a position of some significance. Most memorably, Ferdinand Tönnies called the initial conference (*Soziologentag*) of the German Sociological Society (Deutsche Gesellschaft für Soziologie) in Frankfurt am Main, at which Max Weber spoke vigorously for the separation of sociological study from race theory, race hygiene, and eugenics.[1] Now largely forgotten, but nearly as academically star-studded, was the founding of the journal *Logos: Internationale Zeitschrift für Philosophie der Kultur* by a group of major Neo-Kantian academic philosophers. The journal is probably best understood as a significant but ultimately unsuccessful attempt to retain the disciplinarily synthetic ambitions of German academic philosophy in the face of the inexorable rise of the social scientific disciplines like psychology, sociology, and ethnology/anthropology, as well as the powerful fashion for biological argument in all of the human sciences of the day.[2] In the inaugural issue of the journal, surrounded by shining luminaries including Heinrich Rickert, Georg Simmel, Benedetto Croce, Ernst Troeltsch, Wilhelm Windelband, Edmund Husserl, Hans Cornelius, and Hermann Graf Keyserling, the ambitious young philosopher Leopold Ziegler (1881–1958) published an article with the provocative title "Wagner. Die Tyrannis des Gesamtkunstwerks (The Tyranny of Gesamtkunstwerk)."[3] It is revealing enough that the most prestigious figures in German academic philosophy would feel it necessary to feature an obviously polemically charged article about Wagner in their brand-new journal of the philosophy of culture. Certainly some these men saw the culture of their day as too often synonymous with Wagner and Wagnerism(s), and perceived that despite the near-flood of commentary on Wagner at the time, his legacy required further discussion, justification, and critique at the highest academic level. What Ziegler's title further reveals is another achievement of the present volume: it does not just clarify Wagner's position as the figure to whom the Gesamtkunstwerk concept sticks most fast, it also explores the ways in which Wagner is to be understood with respect to the contested history of the concept both before and after his engagement with it.

The *Logos* scholars' concern also prefigures what this collection of essays strives to map out across many historical and contemporary moments of cultural activity: that Wagner, and the unstable Gesamtkunstwerk concept that adheres variously to him and his works, have become inescapable moments of any Western artistic-cultural epistemology. To know art is to hear, and perhaps to resist, the siren song of totality. To know art is to see a work conceived intellectually and conceptually, but also instantiated as (embodied) performance, and thereby capable of becoming more than any text or score can notate. To know art is to know that every work fails to contain all its possible performances, but at the same time to acknowledge that every performance fails to exhaust the scope of the work or its conception. Gesamtkunstwerk is thus ultimately a category of knowledge, a conceptual network that reveals the potential boundary conditions of all art in the very impossibility of their clear delimitation. The ironically exasperated title of one of Thomas Mann's last comments on Wagner, coming after innumerable and sometimes politically risky attempts to capture the Wagnerian legacy in essays, lectures, and narratives, might reasonably therefore stand, yet again, as an epigraph for this volume: "Wagner und kein Ende" (Wagner without End).[4] At the same time, Mann's expression of Wagner's "bombast, endless peroration, hogging the spotlight, having the last word…"—and statement of their likeness to Hitler's—cannot undermine his own sense that "I simply become young again when things begin with Wagner."[5] This volume attests, once more, that Mann's characteristically layered juxtaposition of emotions when facing Wagner and Gesamtkunstwerk represents no vacillation or contradiction or empty ambivalence, but the marker of a search for meaning so ceaseless as to achieve the status of the epistemological.

When considered as a whole across the periods, forms, and genres they analyze, the chapters in this volume resolve Gesamtkunstwerk's epistemological significance through, paradoxically, its dialectical partner: particularity. This particularity can have many aspects, and the essays explore them, sometimes in multiple ways in the same essay, both conceptually and interpretively. The volume's editors have proposed one scheme for analyzing these particularities, namely that of foundations, articulations, and inspirations. But, to give the kaleidoscope a few more turns and promote further reflection on the total work of art (a Gesamtkunstwerk without end?), I propose here a different framework for examining the essays and their epistemological significance. There are, for instance, essays that map the more abstractly conceived conceptual space of the Gesamtkunstwerk's significance, and do so in two ways: by exploring the historical and ideological particularity of the term itself and by demonstrating the constitutive tension between performance and work in the musical and theatrical arts, and in those, like film and architecture, that incorporate performative elements. There are also essays that take more concrete interpretive approaches, highlighting three elements of particularity that accrete productively to the Gesamtkunstwerk: the moment of resistance to totality that all art can reveal through its production and consumption; the nature of performance as an embodied act carried out by particular artists and performers and experienced by spectators and audiences; and the ways in which the bodies that carry out those performances evince and bear an ineradicable mark of particularity, namely gender.

Three essays emphasize the ways in which totality is essentially inconceivable without the particularity of individual artistic manifestations. Steinhoff's essay mines Cosima Wagner's cryptic assertions that link arguments about Germans' racial superiority with *Parsifal*'s artistic mission. Out of this material he pursues an argument that while Wagner himself remained ambivalent about the conceptual utility of Gesamtkunstwerk in his own artistic and ideological vision, because he himself neither invented nor deployed it particularly broadly—a point made persuasively by both Vazsonyi and Pederson in this volume—the totalizing concept of Gesamtkunstwerk has the differentiated power to do justice to *Parsifal* as *Bühnenweihfestspiel*: a work so megalomaniacal in its particularity that it and only it has the power to consecrate the stage for other works. In Steinhoff's reading of *Parsifal* as Gesamtkunstwerk, the particular is revealed as a sublation of the general in Wagner's vision: by transcending the commercialism of lesser works of music and drama, and even *Musikdrama*, the work asserts a foundation and undergirding of the unique power and mission of the German nation.

Anger coins an analogical term, *Gesamtglaswerk*, to describe the significance of a highly particular and consciously representative work, Bruno Taut's Glashaus at the 1914 German Werkbund exhibition in Cologne. She situates the work as a point of reference within widely proliferating arguments from the twentieth century about the relationship between the creative innovations pursued by individual artists committed to visions of modernism, and the repressive, dominating qualities of totalitarian states. She emphasizes that the work's power derives from its ability to create liberating unity, but not repressive totality, out of the specificity of individual experience with the representative modernist artwork: "The way to greater spiritual and intellectual growth—and potential communion with mankind, if not the universe—appears to call for very close looking and experience of something that we cannot see through."

The third essay that focuses on the friction between particularity and totality in the Gesamtkunstwerk is Imhoof's exploration of the dynamics of consumption in German musical film of the mid-twentieth century. Expanding on twentieth-century critiques of mass culture, he asserts that "musical film especially makes clear the iterative and connective function of mass culture." Mass culture brings individuals together, and binds them conceptually, and the three films he explores—*The Blue Angel* (1930), *La Habanera* (1937), and *The White Horse Inn* (1952)—have the capacity, as he argues, to enable "viewers to link their synchronic experience of movie-going with their diachronic consumption of culture." The experience of modern mass culture is thereby itself revealed as a kind of Gesamtkunstwerk, one that renders at least a semblance of social unity out of the consumption of individual products by individual consumers.

Four essays pursue thematically the ways in which performance expresses out of the totality of a work of theatrical or musical art a manifestation of embodied particularity. Joy Calico emphasizes that, contrary to some long-standing readings of Brecht in which opera is given a primarily negative valence, Brecht vigorously and productively pursued operatic works throughout his career, initiating if never completing some two dozen projects that he specifically designated as operas. She makes a compelling case that Brecht's career, pursued analytically to its logical end, demonstrates that "modernist theater, of which epic theater has long been the standard bearer, may be the illegitimate child of opera." It does so firstly by instantiating a new kind of participatory audience contract that links spectatorship into representative and therefore potentially political action, and secondly by theorizing a technique of theatrical representation through gestus that builds from the particularity of the actor's body as received and perceived by the particular spectator a formal structure of sufficient generality to enable political action.

Goodwin and Menninger take on the complex issue of music's memorializing function after World War II. They explore the practice of performers like Yehudi Menuhin and, in particular, Benjamin Britten to analyze how the shared experience of a work of art such as Britten's 1962 *War Requiem* can retrieve something of the lost particularity of the victims of modern mass slaughter. To borrow a figure used by Imhoof, they reveal that music's ability to memorialize emerges through an iterative dynamic that links individual experience and artistic unity: "Memorial music aims to prompt inward transformation on the part of each individual listener, and of the audience as a whole."

Trimingham turns to an institution so clearly politically, aesthetically, and pedagogically committed to the greater unity of the many diverse arts that surface-level analogies to Gesamtkunstwerk seem almost facile: the Bauhaus. With the goal of explaining the complex and contested position of Oskar Schlemmer's theatrical practice within the Bauhaus's shifting institutional and aesthetic parameters, she parallels Vazsonyi in reaching back to Schiller's thought about theater and subjectivity. This analysis makes manifest how, in the world of the Bauhaus, artistic principles without embodied performance became empty concepts, but also how individual embodiments of artistic practice had to be conceived through the strictest ideals of formal order. In Trimingham's trenchant formulation of Schlemmer's goals, "theater was a 'powerful force for order' at the Bauhaus, a 'Schillerian tribunal' decisively countering disembodied approaches to design and idealist notions of form detached from living, arguing always for the body and the human being as central to any humanist quest."

In the fourth and final essay that interrogates Gesamtkunstwerk by focusing on embodied practices of performance, Heisler seeks to retrieve the form so often overlooked in studies of music, opera, and theater, despite its deep links to all of them: dance. In a fascinating parallel with Trimingham's arguments, he chooses the metaphor (derived from Martha Graham's thought) of "reconciliation" to describe how dance emerges into the sphere of Gesamtkunstwerk. He focuses on what he calls "song-ballets": choreographic approaches to song cycles by twentieth-century composers, and in particular on a musical work that incorporates elements in German art from across the nineteenth and twentieth centuries: Richard Strauss's *Four Last Songs*. Heisler sums up how these multilayered song-ballets gather work and performance together through dance's embodiment of formalized movement in a powerful analysis of the work of Maurice Béjart: "Dance brokers reconciliation of distinct ways of being and knowing." As an epistemic process, dance thus unites minds and bodies in a kind of productive Gesamtkunstwerk, much akin to that represented in Calico's analysis of Brecht's complex relationship to opera.

The four remaining essays in the volume explore more conceptually the relationship between totality and particularity in the Gesamtkunstwerk, focusing less on the consequences of embodiment and more on the relationship of the particular work to the space of its possible performances. Pederson hews most closely to a reading of Wagner's own writings to show the tension in his usage of "Gesamtkunstwerk" and "Musikdrama." She builds Udo Bermbach's claims into an argument that emphasizes the dialectics of freedom and unity, and of art and politics, in the Wagnerian ideal: "Because the Volk is a free association of creative people—an 'artistic fellowship of the future' as Wagner put it in *The Artwork of the Future*—only an artwork that is created communally can embody the ideals of a post-revolutionary social order." Still, she demonstrates how the stakes of embodiment remain ever present in Gesamtkunstwerk's shadow, and reveals where Wagner himself went to ground on a perverse rhetoric of embodiment: where he fantasized Jews as the worms consuming the art's decomposing body.

Vazsonyi, building upon his groundbreaking work on the Wagner "brand," provides a fascinating and productive critique of Wagnerian ideology. From his reading of Schiller's ideals of aesthetic education, he derives an approach to Gesamtkunstwerk that emphasizes that work and performance exist only together as concepts: "Any Gesamtkunstwerk that does not involve performance—meaning the *medium* of human, lived, and live experience—is already a departure from and, I submit, a fundamental misunderstanding of the Wagnerian idea." This relationship lies at the core of how Schiller's derivation of the political from the aesthetic becomes transformed into Wagner's totalizing vision and, in concert with the other essays in this volume, how Gesamtkunstwerk retained its political charge through the many manifestations of twentieth-century modernism, and retains it still today.

Rippey's chapter turns to the function of sound—and sound broadly conceived, not just musical sound—as represented in two canonical early German sound films to explore the consequences of spectatorship for political unity. He does this through two films "diametrically opposed" in their political stance, but that parallel each other in representing "the collective experience of sound by formally assembled audiences and amorphous crowds": Slatan Dudov's *Kuhle Wampe* (1932) and Leni Riefenstahl's *Triumph of the Will* (1935). Following Lutz Koepnick and others, he posits a "modernization of listening" through reproductive technologies that, while potentially splitting aurality from visuality and other sensory modes, nonetheless enables sound to be manipulated aesthetically in ways that crowds, both represented and spectatorial, can experience together.

Finally, like Rippey, Wlodarski's contribution also focuses on a film, but one that sought to represent what seemed at the time (and not just to Theodor Adorno) to be something that surpassed in its horror the possibility of all representation: the destruction of human life in the Nazi concentration camps. In her analysis of Alain Resnais's *Night and Fog* (1955), and in particular Hanns Eisler's musical score for the film, she contends that, in overtly deconstructing the Nazi imagery and soundscape analyzed by Rippey in *Triumph of the Will*, Resnais's film and Eisler's score produce a "political retort to totalitarianism that undercuts Riefenstahl's Gesamtkunstwerk and reveals its illusory facades, all the while consciously acknowledging the continued relevance of Wagnerian techniques to twentieth-century modernist film." At a secondary level then, Resnais and Eisler intertextually achieve a kind of performance of political atonement that brings it into contact with works as diverse as *Parsifal* (as analyzed by Steinhoff) and Britten's *War Requiem* (as explored by Goodwin and Menninger).

Leopold Ziegler's dense critique of Wagner in the inaugural 1910 volume of *Logos*, in fact, resonates deeply with the rich reflections, analyses, and critiques in this volume, and highlights further significant aspects of the essays' explorations of the epistemic space enfolding artist, work, performance, and audience. Gesamtkunstwerk, as Ziegler reads it, is necessarily a colossal contradiction, something that demands what it at the same time undercuts: a productive audience. He initiates his argument with a comparison to Mozart's operas, and *The Marriage of Figaro* in particular. Analogously to the achievements of this volume's contributors, he turns the surface-level rhetoric of formal synthesis and unity that adheres to the Gesamtkunstwerk concept upon itself. He argues that *Figaro* takes the most discretely embodied forms of human activity and makes out of them great art, in contrast to Wagner's endless mythologizing and theoretically circumscribed universalizing. "In short," he argues, "le marriage de Figaro unifies essentially everything that seems to sin against the Wagnerian theory of music drama's elemental expression of the purely human."[6] Ziegler then heightens this argument by emphasizing a conflict that even in Wagner's world of mythical universality seems incapable of resolution, or even sublation, and to which Calico, Heisler, and Steinhoff further grant central significance in their analyses: gender polarity. He stages this argument in a directly epistemological fashion as well: "Gender polarity, as the tragic Ur-phenomenon of the world, allows him namely to cognize the impossibility of ever totally resolving the separation of all beings into a multiplicity of individuals."[7] Absolute unity would make form itself unnecessary and thereby evacuate art. A core of multiplicity thus remains always at the heart of the unifying formal artistic impulse, rendering the Gesamtkunstwerk, at its core, a paradox.

In Ziegler's view, Wagner's ultimate failure—and the root cause of the simultaneous fascination and meaninglessness of Gesamtkunstwerk (as Vazsonyi discusses)—is to have only created a new formal hierarchy in the name of totality, one that eats away at the very arts it would deign to heighten, transform, or sublate through unity: "In Wagner's Gesamtkunstwerk, the final verdict is rendered upon singing."[8] Wagner might wish that the meaning of words, as intensified through the operatic voice, resolve into a higher form of mythic signification through the endless melody of his leitmotif technique. However, that wish itself, so Ziegler argues, runs the danger of obviating meaning altogether, rendering the epistemic fantasy of the Gesamtkunstwerk both philosophically and culturally destructive. This is, finally, because it evacuates the process of *productive* listening, the audience's contribution to the artistic process (a point so effectively emphasized by Vazsonyi and Pederson). "In that the poet allows music to become stage drama, he robs it necessarily of its most beautiful effect upon the listener: namely that this listener proves himself through his own form-inventing, productive activity."[9]

Thus we arrive at Gesamtkunstwerk's vanishing point. Can the unifying, even totalizing formal impulse common to so many artistic spheres in the nineteenth and twentieth centuries render out of distracted spectators, listeners, or audiences something more? Does anything remain but broken shards of the Gesamtkunstwerk ideal mapped, analyzed, questioned, and constellated across the spheres of music, opera, film, dance, theater, architecture, philosophy, and history in this volume? Is the necessary failure of any such dream (or fantasy) of totality the boundary condition of all art? Here the words that Walter Benjamin—perhaps the greatest cultural theorist of the discrete, the fragmentary, the detritus of modernity—creates out of a painting by an artist so tantalizingly analyzed by both Trimingham and Anger in this volume, namely Paul Klee's *Angelus Novus*, form a conclusion adequate to the spirit of this project: "This storm drives him irresistibly into the future, upon which he turns his back, while the pile of ruins before him grows toward heaven. That which we call progress is *this* storm."[10]

Notes

1. Website, Deutsche Gesellschaft für Soziologie, accessed 3 March 2015: http://www.soziologie.de/de/die-dgs/geschichte.html#c2857. See also, Robert Proctor, *Value-Free Science? Purity and Power in Modern Knowledge* (Cambridge, MA, 1991).
2. See Herbert Schnädelbach, *Philosophy in Germany, 1831–1933*, trans. Eric Matthews (Cambridge, UK, 1984). Rickert (1863–1936) in particular was centrally concerned with the epistemological stakes of disciplinary knowledge and the utility of concepts in scholarly inquiry. See Heinrich Rickert, *The Limits of Concept Formation in Natural Science*, ed. and trans. Guy Oakes (Cambridge, UK, 1986).
3. Leopold Ziegler, "Wagner. Die Tyrannis des Gesamtkunstwerks," *Logos: Internationale Zeitschrift für Philosophie der Kultur* 1, no. 3 (1910/1911), 371–404. All translations by the author. Despite numerous books and several articles in *Logos* and other prestigious academic journals, Ziegler never achieved *Habilitation* or a professorship. He remained a successful private scholar, however, corresponded widely with literary and philosophical figures including the Jünger brothers, continued to publish widely throughout his life, and closed his career as a winner of the Goethe Prize of the City of Frankfurt (1929) and the West German *Bundesverdienstkreuz* (1956).
4. Significantly for the spirit of this volume, Mann's text was written in December 1949 (and published 6–7 April 1950 in the *Süddeutsche Zeitung*) as a letter to the stage designer and illustrator Emil Preetorius (1883–1973), who had worked and written extensively on Wagner. Thomas Mann, "Wagner und kein Ende. An Emil Preetorius," in *Miszellen* (Frankfurt am Main, 1968), 212–14.
5. "...Bramarbasieren, ewigem Perorieren, Allein-reden-Wollen, über alles Mitreden-Wollen..."; "Ich werde eben wieder jung, wenn es mit Wagner anfängt." Ibid., 213. Translation by the author.
6. "Kurz, le mariage de Figaro vereinigt ziemlich alles, was sich gegen die Wagnerische Theorie eines reinmenschlichen Vorwurfes für das Musikdrama versündigen kann." Leopold Ziegler, "Wagner. Die Tyrannis des Gesamtkunstwerks," 380. The use of French in the original text also serves to refer to the original Beaumarchais play.
7. "Die Geschlechtspolarität als das tragische Urphänomen der Welt gibt ihm nämlich die Unmöglichkeit zu erkennen, die Trennung aller Wesen in eine Vielheit von Individuen jemals gänzlich zu überwinden." Ibid., 386.
8. "In Wagners Gesamtkunstwerk ist dem Gesange das Urteil gesprochen." Ibid., 398.
9. "Indem der Dichter die Musik Bühnendrama werden läßt, beraubt er sie notwendig ihrer schönsten Wirkung auf den Hörer: nämlich daß dieser sich in seiner gestalterfindenden produktiven Tätigkeit erweise." Ibid., 401.
10. Walter Benjamin, "Über den Begriff der Geschichte," in *Illuminationen: Ausgewählte Schriften* 1 (Frankfurt am Main, 1977), 255. Translation by the author; emphasis in

original. "Dieser Sturm treibt ihn unaufhaltsam in die Zukunft, der er den Rücken kehrt, während der Trümmerhaufen vor ihm zum Himmel wächst. Das, was wir Fortschritt nennen, ist *dieser* Sturm."

Kevin S. Amidon is Associate Professor of German Studies at Iowa State University in Ames, and also an affiliate member of the faculty in Women's and Gender Studies. He has published widely on science studies, musical studies, gender studies, literature, and critical theory.

Select Bibliography

Abbate, Carolyn. "The Parisian 'Vénus' and the 'Paris' Tannhäuser." *Journal of the American Musicological Society* 36, no. 1 (1983): 73–123.

———. *Unsung Voices: Opera and Musical Narrative in the Nineteenth Century.* Princeton, NJ: Princeton University Press, 1991.

Abbate, Carolyn, and Roger Parker. *A History of Opera.* New York: W.W. Norton & Company, 2012.

Acocella, Joan. *Mark Morris.* New York: Farrar Straus Giroux, 1993.

Adorno, Theodor. *In Search of Wagner.* Trans. Rodney Livingstone. New edition. New York: Verso, 2005.

———. "Wagner's Relevance for Today." *In Essays on Music,* ed. Richard Leppert and trans. Susan H. Gillespie, 584–602. Berkeley and Los Angeles: University of California Press, 2002.

Adorno, Theodor, and Hanns Eisler. *Composing for the Films.* London: Continuum, 1994.

Ahlstrand, Jan Torsten, ed. *Svenskt avantgarde och Der Sturm i Berlin. Schwedische Avantgarde und Der Sturm in Berlin.* Osnabrück: Felix Nussbaum Haus, 2000.

Albright, Daniel. "Golden Calves: The Role of Dance in Opera." *The Opera Quarterly* 22, no. 1 (2006): 22-37

———. *Untwisting the Serpent: Modernism in Music, Literature, and Other Arts.* Chicago: University of Chicago Press, 2000.

Alter, Nora, and Lutz Koepnick, eds. *Sound Matters: Essays on the Acoustics of Modern German Culture.* New York: Berghahn Books, 2004.

Anger, Jenny. *Paul Klee and the Decorative in Modern Art.* Cambridge: Cambridge University Press, 2004.

Appia, Adolphe. *Staging Wagnerian Drama.* Basel: Birkhäuser, 1982.

Ash, Mitchell. *Gestalt Psychology in German Culture 1890–1967.* Cambridge: Cambridge University Press, 1995.

Bablet, Denis, and Élie Konigson, eds. *L'œuvre d'art totale.* Paris: CNRS Éditions, 1995.

Bach, Steven. *Leni: The Life and Work of Leni Riefenstahl.* New York: Alfred A. Knopf, 2007.

———. *Marlene Dietrich: Life and Legend.* Minneapolis: University of Minnesota Press, 2011.

Balanchine, Georg, and Francis Mason. *Balanchine's Complete Stories of the Great Ballets.* Garden City, NY: Doubleday, 1977.

Barbas, Samantha. *Movie Crazy: Fans, Stars, and the Cult of Celebrity.* New York: Palgrave Macmillan, 2001.

Beasley, Edward. *The Victorian Reinvention of Race: New Racisms and the Problem of Grouping in the Human Sciences.* London: Taylor & Francis, 2010.

Behne, Adolf. *Architekturkritik in der Zeit und über die Zeit hinaus.* Basel: Birkhäuser Verlag, 1994.

Beil, Ralf, and Claudia Dillman, eds. *The Total Artwork of Expressionism: Art, Film, Literature, Theater, Dance and Architecture, 1903–1925.* Darmstadt: Hatje Cantz Verlag, 2011.

Beinssen-Hesse, Silke. "The Ideological Implications of Wagner's Changes to Wolfram's Parzival." *Miscellanea Musicologica* 14 (1985): 131–47.

Bell, Catherine. *Ritual Theory, Ritual Practice.* Oxford: Oxford University Press, 1992.

Benjamin, Walter. "The Work of Art in the Age of Mechanical Reproduction." In *Illuminations*, ed. Hannah Arendt, trans. Harry Zohn, 217–52. New York: Harcourt, Brace & World, 1968.

Benson, Timothy. *Expressionist Utopias: Paradise, Metropolis, Architectural Fantasy.* Los Angeles: Los Angeles County Museum of Art, 1993.

Berman, Russell. "Written Right Across Their Faces: Ernst Jünger's Fascist Modernism." In *Modernity and the Text: Revisions of German Modernism*, ed. Andreas Huyssen and David Bathrick, 60–80. New York: Columbia University Press, 1989.

Bermbach, Udo "Nationalismus in Deutschen Festspielen? Zur Idee und Praxis der Bayreuther Festspiele." In *Poltische Erinnerung. Geschichte und kollektive Identität*, ed. Harald Schmid und Justyna Krzymianowska, 53-66. Würzburg: Königshausen & Neumann, 2007.

———. *Der Wahn des Gesamtkunstwerks Richard Wagners politisch-ästhetische Utopie*, 2nd, revised and expanded edition. Stuttgart: Verlag J. B. Metzler, 2004.

Betz, Albrecht. "Music and Politics: Theme and Variation." In *Hanns Eisler: A Miscellany*, ed. David Blake, 393–405. Luxembourg: Harwood Academic Publishers, 1995.

Bick, Sally. "A Double Life in Hollywood: Hanns Eisler's Score for the Film *Hangmen Also Die* and the Covert Expressions of a Marxist Composer." *Musical Quarterly* 93, no. 1 (2010): 90–143.

Billings, Joshua. "Epic and Tragic Music: The Union of the Arts in the Eighteenth Century." *Journal of the History of Ideas* 72, no. 1 (2011): 99–120.

Bletter, Rosemary Haag. "Expressionist Architecture." In *German Expressionism: Documents from the End of the Wilhelmine Empire to the Rise of National Socialism*, ed. Rose-Carol Washton Long. Berkeley and Los Angeles: University of California Press, 1993.

———. "The Interpretation of the Glass Dream—Expressionist Architecture and the History of the Crystal Metaphor." *Journal of the Society of Architectural Historians* 40, no. 1 (1981): 20–43.

———. "Paul Scheerbart's Architectural Fantasies." *Journal of the Society of Architectural Historians* 34, no. 2 (1975): 83–97.

Borchmeyer, Dieter. "Gesamtkunstwerk." In *Die Musik in Geschichte und Gegenwart* 3, 1282–89. Kassel: Bärenreiter and Metzler, 1994.

———. *Richard Wagner: Theory and Theater*. Oxford: Oxford University Press, 1991.

———. *Das Theater Richard Wagners: Idee—Dichtung—Wirkung*. Stuttgart: Reclam, 1982.

Brecht, Bertolt. *Brecht on Theatre: The Development of an Aesthetic*. Trans. John Willet. New York: Hill and Wang, 1992.

———. "A Short Organum for the Theater." In *Playwrights on Playwriting: The Meaning and Making of Modern Drama from Ibsen to Ionesco*, ed. Toby Cole, 72–105. New York: Hill and Wang, 1960.

Brown, Hilda Meldrum. *Leitmotiv and Drama: Wagner, Brecht, and the Limits of "Epic" Theatre*. Oxford: Oxford University Press, 1991.

Brühl, Georg. *Herwarth Walden und "Der Sturm."* Leipzig: DuMont, 1983.

Brzoska, Matthias. *Die Idee des Gesamtkunstwerks in der Musiknovellistik der Julimonarchie*. Laaber: Laaber-Verlag, 1995.

Bürger, Peter. *Theory of the Avant-Garde*. Minneapolis: University of Minnesota Press, 1999.

Bushart, Magdalena. *Der Geist der Gotik und die expressionistische Kunst: Kunstgeschichte und Kunsttheorie, 1911–1925*. Munich: S. Schreiber, 1990.

Calico, Joy. *Brecht at the Opera*. Berkeley and Los Angeles: University of California Press, 2008.

Carnegy, Patrick. *Wagner and the Art of the Theatre*. New Haven, CT: Yale University Press, 2006.

Carpentier, Nico. *Media and Participation: A Site of Ideological-Democratic Struggle*. Chicago: Intellect, 2011.

Chadwick, Whitney. "Living Simultaneously: Sonia and Robert Delaunay." In *Significant Others: Creativity and Intimate Partnership*, ed. Whitney Chadwick and Isabelle de Courtivron, 30–49. London: Thames and Hudson, 1993.

Chion, Michael. *Film: A Sound Art*. New York: Columbia University Press, 2009.

Chytry, Josef. *The Aesthetic State: A Quest in Modern German Thought*. Berkeley and Los Angeles: University of California Press, 1989.

Cicora, Mary A. *Wagner's* Ring *and German Drama: Comparative Studies in Mythology and History in Drama*. Westport, CT: Praeger 1999.

Clark, Kevin. "Zurück in die Zukunft: Aspekte der Aufführungspraxis des weißen Rössl." In *Im Weißen Rössl: Zwischen Kunst und Kommerz*, ed. Ulrich Tadday, 101–50. Munich: Edition Text & Kritik, 2006.

Cohen-Levinas, Danielle, ed. *Le renouveau de l'art total*. Paris: L'Harmattan, 2004.

Cooke, Mervyn. *A History of Film Music*. Cambridge: Cambridge University Press, 2008.

Corbin, Alain. *Village Bells: Sound and Meaning in the 19th-Century French Countryside*. New York: Columbia University Press, 1998.

Currid, Brian. *A National Acoustics: Music and Mass Publicity in Weimar and Nazi Germany*. Minneapolis: University of Minnesota Press, 2006.

Dahlhaus, Carl. *The Idea of Absolute Music*. Trans. Roger Lustig. Chicago: University of Chicago Press, 1989.

———. "Richard Wagners 'Bühnenfestspiel': Revolutionsfest und Kunstreligion." In *Das Fest*, ed. Walther Haug and Rainer Warning, 592-609. Munich: Fink, 1989.

———. "Wagners Begriff Der 'dichterisch-musikalischen Periode." In *Beiträge zur Geschichte der Musikanschauung im 19. Jahrhundert*, ed. Walter Salmen, 179–94. Regensburg: G. Bosse Verlag, 1965.

———. *Wagners Konzeption des musikalischen Dramas*. Munich: DTV, 1990.

Daub, Adrian. *Tristan's Shadow: Sexuality and the Total Work of Art After Wagner*. Chicago: University of Chicago Press, 2014.

Davidson, David. "From Virgin to Dynamo: The 'Amoral Woman' in European Cinema." *Cinema Journal* 21, no. 1 (1981): 31–49.

Deathridge, John, and Carl Dahlhaus. *The New Grove Wagner*. New York: Norton & Company, 1984.

Del Mar, Norman. *Richard Strauss: A Critical Commentary on His Life and Works*. Ithaca, NY: Cornell University Press, 1986.

Dennis, David B. *Beethoven in German Politics, 1870–1989*. New Haven, CT: Yale University Press, 1996.

———. *Inhumanities: Nazi Interpretations of Western Culture*. Cambridge: Cambridge University Press, 2012.

———. "The Most German of All German Operas': Die Meistersinger through the Lens of the Third Reich." In *Wagner's Meistersinger: Performance, History, Representation*, ed. Nicholas Vazsonyi, 98–119. Rochester, NY: University of Rochester Press, 2003.

Dickerman, Leah. "Bauhaus Fundaments." In *Bauhaus, 1919–1933: Workshops for Modernity*, ed. Barry Bergdoll and Leah Dickerman, 14–39. New York: The Museum of Modern Art, 2009.

Dümling, Albrecht. *Laßt Euch Nicht Verführen: Brecht und die Musik*. Munich: Kindler, 1985.

Eaton, Katherine Bliss. *The Theater of Meyerhold and Brecht*. Westport, CT: Greenwood Press, 1985.

Ersoy, Ufuk. "The Fictive Quality of Glass." *Architectural Research Quarterly* 11, no. 3–4 (2007): 237–43.

Fehrenbach, Heide. *Cinema in Democratizing Germany: Reconstructing National Identity after Hitler*. Chapel Hill: University of North Carolina Press, 1995.

Feiereisen, Florence, and Alexandra Merley Hill, eds. *Germany in the Loud Twentieth Century: An Introduction*. Oxford: Oxford University Press, 2011.

Finger, Anke. *Das Gesamtkunstwerk der Moderne*. Göttingen: Vandenhoeck & Ruprecht, 2006.

Finger, Anke, and Danielle Follett, eds. *The Aesthetics of the Total Artwork: On Borders and Fragments*. Baltimore: John Hopkins University Press, 2011.

Fischer-Lichte, Erika. "Das 'Gesamtkunstwerk.' Ein Konzept für die Kunst der achtziger Jahre?" In *Dialog der Künste: Intermediale Fallstudien zur Literatur des 19. und 20. Jahrhunderts. Festschrift für Erwin Koppen*, ed. Maria Moog-Grünwald and Christoph Rodiek, 61–74. Frankfurt: P. Lang, 1989.

Fornoff, Roger. *Die Sehnsucht nach dem Gesamtkunstwerk: Studien zu einer ästhetischen Konzpetion der Moderne*. Hildesheim: Olms, 2004.

Fox, Jo. *Filming Women in the Third Reich*. Oxford: Berg Publishers, 2000.

Frank, Alan. "Strauss's Last Songs." *Music and Letters* 31 (1950): 305–6.

Fricke, Richard. *Wagner in Rehearsal, 1875–1876: The Diaries of Richard Fricke*, ed. James Deaville with Evan Baker, Franz Liszt Studies 7. Stuyvesant, NY: Pendragon Press, 1998.

Friedländer, Salomo. *Philosophische Abhandlungen und Kritiken 1896–1946*. Herrsching: Waitawhile, 2005.

Frisch, Werner, and K.W. Obermeier. *Brecht in Augsburg: Erinnerungen, Texte, Fotos*. Frankfurt: Suhrkamp Verlag, 1976.

Führer, Karl Christian, and Corey Ross, eds. *Mass Media, Culture and Society in Twentieth-Century Germany*. New York: Palgrave Macmillan, 2007.

Galard, Jean, and Julian Zugazagottia, eds. *L'œuvre d'art totale*. Paris: Gallimard, 2003.

Gay, Peter. *Weimar Culture: The Outsider as Insider*. New York: Harper & Row, 1968.

Gay-White, Pamela. *Béjart and Modernism: Case Studies in the Archetype of Dance*. New Orleans: University Press of the South, 2006.

Giedion, Siegfried. *Space, Time and Architecture: The Growth of a New Tradition*. 5th edn. Cambridge, MA: Harvard University Press, 2008.

Gilliam, Bryan. *The Life of Richard Strauss*. New York: Cambridge University Press, 1999.

Glass, Frank. *The Fertilizing Seed: Wagner's Concept of Poetic Intent*. Ann Arbor, MI: UMI Research Press, 1983.

Goehr, Lydia. "From Opera to Music Drama: Nominal Loss, Titular Gain." In *Wagner and His World*, edited by Thomas Grey, 65–86. Princeton, NJ: Princeton University Press, 2009.

———. *The Imaginary Museum of Musical Works: An Essay in the Philosophy of Music*. Oxford: Oxford University Press, 1992.

———. *The Quest for Voice: On Music, Politics, and the Limits of Philosophy*. Berkeley and Los Angeles: University of California Press, 1998.

Goodwin, Julia Anne. "Breaking Down Barriers: Music and the Culture of Reconciliation in West Berlin, 1961–1989." PhD dissertation, University of Rochester, 2007.

Grey, Thomas. *Wagner's Musical Prose: Texts and Contexts*. Cambridge: Cambridge University Press, 1995.

———. "A Wagnerian Glossary." In *The Wagner Compendium: A Guide to Wagner's Life and Music*, ed. Barry Millington, 230–43. London: Thames & Hudson, 2001.

———, ed. *The Cambridge Companion to Wagner*. Cambridge: Cambridge University Press, 2008.

Gropius, Walter, and Arthur Wensinger, eds. *The Theater of the Bauhaus*. Baltimore: Johns Hopkins University Press [1961] 1996.

Großmann-Vendrey, Susanna. *Bayreuth in der Deutschen Presse*. Vol. 2. Regensburg: Gustav Bosse, 1977.

Groys, Boris. *The Total Art of Stalinism: Avant-Garde, Aesthetic Dictatorship, and Beyond*. Princeton, NJ: Princeton University Press, 1992.

Gutman, Robert W. *Richard Wagner: The Man, His Mind, and His Music*. New York: Harcourt, Brace & World, 1968.

Gutschow, Kai Konstanty. "The Culture of Criticism: Adolf Behne and the Development of Modern Architecture in Germany, 1910–1914." PhD diss., Columbia University, NY, 2006.

———. "From Object to Installation in Bruno Taut's Exhibition Pavilions." *Journal of Architectural Education* 59, no. 4 (2006): 63–70.

Hanslick, Eduard. *Music Criticisms 1846–99*. Trans. Henry Pleasants. Baltimore: Penguin, 1950.

Haus, Andreas, and László Moholy-Nagy. *Moholy-Nagy, Photographs and Photograms*. London: Thames and Hudson, 1980.

Hesse, Hermann. *Musik. Betrachtungen, Gedichte, Rezensionen und Briefe*. Frankfurt: Suhrkamp Verlag, 1986.

Heßelmann, Peter. "Der Ruf nach der 'Policey' im Tempel der Kunst: Das Theaterpublikum des 18. Jahrhunderts zwischen Andacht und Vergnügen." In *Das Theater glich einem Irrenhause*, ed. Hermann Korte and Hans-Joachim Jakob, 77–94. Heidelberg: Universitätsverlag Winter, 2012.

Hinton, Stephen. "The Concept of Epic Opera: Theoretical Anomalies in the Brecht–Weill Partnership." In *Das Musikalische Kunstwerk: Festschrift Carl Dahlhaus*, ed. Stephen Hinton, 285–94. Laaber: Laaber-Verlag, 1988.

Hodonyi, Robert. *Herwarth Waldens "Sturm" und die Architektur. Eine Analyse zur Konvergenz der Künste in der Berliner Moderne*. Bielefeld: Aisthesis, 2010.

Höfig, Willi. *Der Deutsche Heimatfilm, 1947–1960*. Stuttgart: F. Enke, 1973.

Hughes, Gordon. "Envisioning Abstraction: The Simultaneity of Robert Delaunay's First Disk." *Art Bulletin* 89, no. 2 (2007): 306–32.

Hutcheon, Linda, and Micheal Hutcheon. *Opera: Desire, Disease, Death*. Lincoln: University of Nebraska Press, 1996.

Jackson, Timothy L. "Ruhe, Meine Seele! and the Letzte Orchesterlieder." In *Richard Strauss and His World*, ed. Bryan Gilliam, 90–137. Princeton, NJ: Princeton University Press, 1992.

James-Chakraborty, Kathleen, *German Architecture for a Mass Audience*. London and New York: Routledge, 2000.

———, ed. *Bauhaus Culture from Weimar to the Cold War*. Minneapolis: University of Minnesota Press, 2006.

Jameson, Fredric. *Brecht and Method*. London: Verso, 1998.

Jaques-Dalcroze, Émile. *Eurhythmics: Art and Education*. Trans. Frederick Rothwell. London: Arno Press, 1930.

Jefferson, Alan. *The Life of Richard Strauss*. Newton Abbot: David & Charles, 1973.

Johnson, James H. *Listening in Paris: A Cultural History*. Berkeley and Los Angeles: University of California Press, 1995.

Jordan, Stephanie. *Moving Music: Dialogues with Music in Twentieth-Century Ballet*. London: Dance, 2000.

Jost, Christa, and Peter Jost. "'Zukunftsmusik'. Zur Geschichte eines Begriffs." *Musiktheorie* 10 (1995): 119–35.

Kaes, Anton. *Kino-Debatte: Texte zum Verhältnis von Literatur und Film 1909–1929*. Munich: DTV, 1978.

Kalinak, Kathryn Marie. *Film Music: A Very Short Introduction*. Oxford: Oxford University Press, 2010.

Karbaum, Micheal. *Studien zur Geschichte der Bayreuther Festspiele*. Regensburg: G. Bosse, 1976.

Karnes, Kevin. *A Kingdom Not of this World: Wagner, the Arts and Utopian Visions in Fin-de-Siècle Vienna*. Oxford and New York: Oxford University Press, 2013.

Kesting, Marianne. "Wagner/Meyerhold/Brecht oder die Erfindung des 'epischen' Theaters." *Brecht Yearbook/Brecht-Jahrbuch* 7 (1977): 111–30.

Kiesow, Gottfried. *Gesamtkunstwerk—Die Stadt: Zur Geschichte der Stadt vom Mitteralter bis in die Gegenwart*. Bonn: Denkmalschutz Bonn, 1999.

Kinderman, William. "Dramatic Recapitulation in Wagner's 'Götterdämmerung.'" *19th-Century Music* 4, no. 2 (1980): 101–12.

Kirby, E.T., ed. *Total Theatre: A Critical Anthology*. New York: Dutton, 1969.

Kittler, Friedrich. *Grammophon Film Typewriter*. Berlin: Brinkmann U. Bose, 1986.

———. "World-Breath: On Wagner's Media Technology." In David J. Levin, *Opera through Other Eyes*, 215–35. Stanford, CA: Stanford University Press, 1994.

Klee, Paul. *Pedagogical Sketchbook*. Trans. Sibyl Moholy-Nagy. London: Faber and Faber, (1925) 1968.

———. *The Thinking Eye: The Notebooks of Paul Klee*. Trans. Ralph Manheim. London and New York: G. Wittenborn, 1961.

Koch, Hans-Jörg. *Das Wunschkonzert im NS-Rundfunk*. Cologne: Böhlau Verlag, 2003.

Korte, Hermann. "Historische Theaterpublikumsforschung." In *Das Theater glich einem Irrenhause: Das Publikum im Theater des 18. und 19. Jahrhunderts*, ed. Hermann Korte and Hans-Joachim Jakob, 9–54. Heidelberg: Universitätsverlag Winter, 2012.

Koss, Juliet. *Modernism after Wagner*. Minneapolis: University of Minnesota Press, 2010.

Kramer, Lawrence. *Opera and Modern Culture: Wagner and Strauss*. Berkeley and Los Angeles: University of California Press, 2004.

Kropfinger, Klaus. *Wagner and Beethoven: Richard Wagner's Reception of Beethoven*. Cambridge: Cambridge University Press, 1991.

Kuenzli, Katherine. "Intimate Modernism: The Nabis, Symbolist Theatre and the Gesamtkunstwerk." In *Art, History and the Senses*, ed. Patricia Di Bello and Gabriel Koureas, 67–82. Farnham, UK, and Burlington, VT: Ashgate, 2010.

Kühnel, Jürgen. "The Prose Writings." In *Wagner Handbook*, ed. Ulrich Müller and Peter Wapnewski, 565–651. Cambridge, MA: Harvard University Press, 1992.

Lack, Russell. *Twenty-Four Frames Under: A Buried History of Film Music*. London: Quartet Books, 1997.

Large, David Clay, and William Weber, eds. *Wagnerism in European Culture and Politics*. Ithaca, NY: Cornell University Press, 1984.

Lee, David. "A Flash of Enlightenment: A Brechtian Moment in Douglas Sirk's 'La Habanera.'" *Monatshefte* 100, no. 3 (2008): 400–14.

Lehmann-Haupt, Hellmut. *Art Under a Dictatorship*. New York: Oxford University Press, 1973.

Levin, David. *Richard Wagner, Fritz Lang, and the Nibelungen: The Dramaturgy of Disavowal*. Princeton, NJ: Princeton University Press, 1999.

———. *Unsettling Opera: Staging Mozart, Verdi, Wagner, and Zemlinsky*. Chicago: University of Chicago Press, 2007.

———., ed. *Opera through Other Eyes*. Stanford, CA: Stanford University Press, 1993.

Lindsay, Kenneth C., and Peter Vergo, eds. *Kandinsky: Complete Writings in Art*. Cambridge: Da Capo Press, 1994.

Lista, Marcella. *L'Œuvre d'art totale à la naissance des avant-gardes: 1908–1914*. Paris: Comité des travaux historiques et scientifiques, 2006.

Louis, Eleanora, ed. *Oskar Schlemmer Tanz Theater Bühne*. Vienna: Ritter Verlag, 1997.

Lucchesi, Joachim, and Ronald K. Shull. *Musik bei Brecht*. Frankfurt: Suhrkamp, 1988.

Maciuika, John V. *Before the Bauhaus, Architecture Politics and the German State, 1890–1920*. Cambridge: Cambridge University Press, 2005

Maier, Hans. "Political Religion: A Concept and Its Limitations." *Totalitarian Movements and Political Religions* 8, no. 1 (2007): 5–16.

Mann, Thomas. *Pro and Contra Wagner*. Trans. Allan Blunden. Chicago: Faber and Faber, 1985.

Maur, Karin von. *The Sound of Painting: Music in Modern Art*. Munich: Prestel, 1999.

McCormick, Richard. "From 'Caligari' to Dietrich: Sexual, Social, and Cinematic Discourses in Weimar Film." *Signs* 18, no. 3 (1993): 640–68.

McLean, Adrienne L. "'It's Only That I Do What I Love and Love What I Do': 'Film Noir' and the Musical Woman." *Cinema Journal* 33, no. 1 (1993): 3–16.

Melzer, Annabelle. *Latest Rage the Big Drum: Dada and Surrealist Performance*. Ann Arbor: UMI Research, 1980.

Metken, Günter, ed. *Realismus: Zwischen Revolution und Reaktion 1919–1939*. Munich: Prestel Verlag, 1981.

Meyer, Stephen. *Carl Maria Von Weber and the Search for a German Opera*. Bloomington: Indiana University Press, 2003.

Michaud, Éric. *Théâtre au Bauhaus*. Lausanne: Éditions L'Age d'homme-La Cité, 1978.

Millington, Barry. *The Sorcerer of Bayreuth: Richard Wagner, His Work and His World*. Oxford: Thames and Hudson, 2012.

Minor, Ryan. *Choral Fantasies: Music, Festivity and Nationhood in Nineteenth-Century Germany*. Cambridge: Cambridge University Press, 2012.

Moltke, Johannes von. "Evergreens: The Heimat Genre." In *The German Cinema Book*, ed. Erica Carter, Tim Bergfelder, and Deniz Göktürk, 18–28. London: BFI Publishing, 2002.

Morat, Daniel. "Cheers, Songs, and Marching Sounds: Acoustic Mobilization and Collective Affects at the Beginning of World War I." In idem, ed., *Sounds of Modern History: Auditory Cultures in 19th and 20th Century Europe*, 177–200. Oxford: Berghahn Books, 2014.

Morris, Christopher. "'Too Much Music': The Media of Opera." In *The Cambridge Companion to Opera Studies*, ed. Nicholas Till, 95–116. Cambridge: Cambridge University Press, 2012.

Mösch, Stephan. *Weihe Werkstatt Wirklichkeit: Wagners Parsifal in Bayreuth*. Kassel: Bärenreiter, 2009.

Müller, Sven Oliver. "Distinktion, Demonstration und Disziplinierung: Veränderungen im Publikumsverhalten in Londoner und Berliner Opernhäusern im 19. Jahrhundert." *International Review of the Aesthetics and Sociology of Music* 37, no. 2 (2006): 167–87.

———. *Richard Wagner und die Deutschen: Eine Geschichte von Hass und Hingabe*. Munich: Verlag C.H. Beck, 2013.

Münsterer, Hans Otto. *The Young Brecht*. Trans. Tom Kuhn and Karen Leeder. London: Libris, 1992.

Nadar, Thomas R. "The Director and the Diva: The Film Musicals of Detlef Sierck and Zarah Leander: *Zu neuen Ufern* and *La Habanera*." In *Cultural History through a National Socialist Lens: Essays on the Cinema of the Third Reich*, ed. Robert C. Reimer, 65–83. Rochester, NY: Camden House, 2000.

Nattiez, Jean-Jacques. *Wagner Androgyne: A Study in Interpretation*. Trans. Stewart Spencer. Princeton, NJ: Princeton University Press, 1993.

Neumann, Alfred R. "The Earliest Use of the Term 'Gesamtkunstwerk.'" *Philological Quarterly* 35, no. 2 (1956): 191–93.

Neumann, Dietrich. "'The Century's Triumph in Lighting': The Luxfer Prism Companies and Their Contribution to Early Modern Architecture." *Journal of the Society of Architectural Historians* 54, no. 1 (1995): 24–53.

Newcomb, Anthony. "The Birth of Music out of the Spirit of Drama: An Essay in Wagnerian Formal Analysis." *19th-Century Music* 5, no. 1 (1981): 38–66.

———. "Those Images That Yet Fresh Images Beget." *Journal of Musicology* 2, no. 3 (1983): 227–45.

Nieder, Christoph. "Bertolt Brecht und die Oper: Zur Verwandtschaft von epischem Theater und Musiktheater." *Zeitschrift für Deutsche Philologie* 111, no. 3 (1992): 262–83.

Packer, Randall. "The Gesamtkunstwerk and Interactive Media." In *Aesthetics of the Total Artwork: On Borders and Fragments*, ed. Anke Finger and Danielle Follett, 155–67. Baltimore: John Hopkins University Press, 2011.

Pederson, Sanna. "Defining the Term 'Absolute Music' Historically." *Music & Letters* 90, no. 2 (2009): 240–62.

———. "Romantic Music under Siege in 1848." In *Music Theory in the Age of Romanticism*, ed. Ian Bent, 57-74. Cambridge: Cambridge University Press, 1996.

Pehnt, Wolfgang. *Die Architektur des Expressionismus*. Ostfildern: Hatje Cantz Verlag, 1998.

Peucker, Brigitte. "The Fascist Choreography: Riefenstahl's Tableaux." *Modernism/Modernity* 11, no. 2 (2004): 279–97.

Picard, Timothée. *L'art total: Grandeur et misère d'une utopie (autour de Wagner)*. Rennes: Presses Universitaires de Rennes, 2006.

Porges, Heinrich. *Wagner Rehearsing the Ring: An Eye-Witness Account of the Stage Rehearsals of the First Bayreuth Festival*. Trans. Robert L. Jacobs. Cambridge: Cambridge University Press, 1983.

Porter, Cecilia Hopkins. "The New Public and the Reordering of the Musical Establishment: The Lower Rhine Music Festivals, 1818–67." *19th-Century Music* 3, no. 3 (1980): 211–24.

Potter, Pamela. "What Is 'Nazi Music'?" *The Musical Quarterly* 88, no. 3 (2005): 428–55.

Prange, Regine. *Das Kristalline als Kunstsymbol, Bruno Taut und Paul Klee. Zur Reflexion des Abstrakten in Kunst und Kunsttheorie der Moderne*. Hildesheim: G. Olms, 1991.

Puchner, Martin. *Stage Fright: Modernism, Anti-Theatricality, and Drama*. Baltimore: John Hopkins University Press, 2002.

Raskin, Richard. *Nuit et Brouillard: On the Making, Reception, and Functions of a Major Documentary Film*. Aarhus: Aarhus University Press, 1987.

Rausch, Mechthild. *Von Danzig ins Weltall: Paul Scheerbarts Anfangsjahre (1863–1895)*. Munich: Text & Kritik, 1997.

Ravel, Jeffrey S. *The Contested Parterre: Public Theater and French Political Culture*. Ithaca, NY: Cornell University Press, 1999.

Ray, Katerina Rüedi. *Bauhaus Dream-House: Modernity and Globalization*. London: Routledge, 2010.

Reeber, Sharon. "Finding Harmony: What Adolf Hoelzel Learned from European Sacred Art." *Zeitschrift für Kunstgeschichte* 76 (2013): 243–60.

Rehding, Alexander. *Music and Monumentality: Commemoration and Wonderment in Nineteenth-Century Germany*. New York: Oxford University Press, 2009.

Rienäcker, Gerd. *Musik Theater im Experiment, fünfundzwanzig Aufsätze*. Berlin: Lukas Verlag, 2004.

Resnais, Alain. "Für Hanns Eisler." *Sinn und Form*, Sonderheft Hanns Eisler (1964), 371–75.

Richter, Simon. "The Return of the Queen of the Night: Joseph Von Sternberg's *Der Blaue Engel* and *Die Zauberflöte*." *German Life and Letters* 61, no. 1 (2008): 171–85.

Roberts, David. *The Total Work of Art in European Modernism*. Ithaca, NY: Cornell University Press, 2011.

Ross, Corey. *Media and the Making of Modern Germany: Mass Communications, Society and Politics from the Empire to the Third Reich*. Oxford: Oxford University Press, 2008.

———. "Writing the Media into History: Recent Works on the History of Mass Communications in Germany." *German History* 26, no. 2 (2008): 299–313.

Rousseau, Jean-Louis. "From Wagner to Fellini." In *Béjart by Béjart*, ed. Maurice Béjart. New York: St. Martin's Press, 1980.

Rubin, James H., and Olivia Mattis. *Rival Sisters, Art and Music at the Birth of Modernism, 1815–1915*. Farnham, UK: Ashgate, 2014.

Sartwell, Crispin. *Political Aesthetics*. Ithaca, NY: Cornell University Press, 2010.

Savage, Roger. "The Staging of Opera." In *The Oxford Illustrated History of Opera*, ed. Roger Parker, 350–420. New York: Oxford University Press, 1994.

Schafer, R. Murray. *The Soundscape: Our Sonic Environment and the Tuning of the World*. Rochester, VT: Destiny Books, 1994.

Scheerbart, Paul. *Paul Scheerbart: 70 Trillionen Weltgrüsse—Eine Biographie in Briefen 1889–1915*. Berlin: Argon, 1991.

Scheper, Dirk. *Oskar Schlemmer, Das triadische Ballett und die Bauhausbühne*. Berlin: Akademie der Künste, 1988.

Schlemmer, Oskar. *Letters and Diaries of Oskar Schlemmer*. Trans. Krishna Winston. Middleton, CT: Wesleyan University Press, 1972.

Schuetze, Andre. "Der gläserne Raum: Paul Scheerbarts Utopie einer Glasarchitektur." *Seminar: A Journal of Germanic Studies* 48, no. 1 (2012): 31–50.

Schulte-Sasse, Linda. "Leni Riefenstahl's Feature Films and the Question of a Fascist Aesthetic." *Cultural Critique* 18 (1991): 123–48.

Schulze, Holger, ed. *Sound Studies: Traditionen—Methoden—Desiderate: Eine Einführung*. Bielefeld: Auflage, 2008.

Schumacher, Ernst. *Die Dramatischen Versuche Bertolt Brechts, 1918–1933*. Berlin: Rütten und Loening, 1955.

Schuster, Peter-Klaus, ed. *Delaunay und Deutschland*. Cologne: DuMont Buchverlag, 1985.

Seeßlen, Georg. "Blood and Glamour." In *Riefenstahl Screened: An Anthology of New Criticism*, ed. Ingeborg Majer O'Sickey, Neil Christian Pages, and Mary Rhiel, 11–29. New York: Bloomsbury Academic, 2008.

Sharp, Dennis. "Paul Scheerbart's Glass World." In *Glass Architecture by Paul Scheerbart and Alpine Architecture by Bruno Taut*, ed. Dennis Sharp, 7–28. New York: Praeger, 1972.

Shaw-Miller, Simon. *Visible Deeds of Music: Art and Music from Wagner to Cage*. New Haven, CT: Yale University Press, 2002.

Simonson, Mary. "Dancing the Future, Performing the Past: Isadora Duncan and Wagnerism in the American Imagination." *Journal of the American Musicological Society* 65, no. 2 (2012): 511–55.

Smart, Mary Ann. *Mimomania: Music and Gesture in Nineteenth-Century Opera*. Berkeley and Los Angeles: University of California Press, 2004.

Smith, Marian. *Ballet and Opera in the Age of Giselle*. Princeton, NJ: Princeton University Press, 2000.

Smith, Matthew Wilson. *The Total Work of Art: From Bayreuth to Cyberspace*. New York: Routledge, 2007.

Smock, Ann. "Don Giovanni, or the Art of Disappointing One's Admirers." In *Enigmas: Essays on Sarah Kofman*, ed. Penelope Deutscher and Kelly Oliver, 49–66. Ithaca, NY: Cornell University Press, 1999.

Spotts, Frederic. *Bayreuth: The History of the Wagner Festival.* New Haven, CT: Yale University Press, 1994.

———. *Hitler and the Power of Aesthetics.* Woodstock and New York: Overlook Press, 2002.

Stanley, Glenn. "Parsifal: Redemption and Kunstreligion." In *The Cambridge Companion to Wagner*, ed. Thomas S. Grey, 151–75. Cambridge: Cambridge University Press, 2008.

Stegmann, Vera. "Brecht Contra Wagner: The Evolution of the Epic Music Theater." In *A Bertolt Brecht Reference Companion*, ed. Siegfried Mews, 238–60. Westport, CT: Greenwood, 1997.

Stein, Jack. *Richard Wagner and the Synthesis of the Arts.* Detroit: Wayne State University Press, 1960.

Steiner, Gertraud. *Die Heimat-Macher: Kino in Österreich 1946–1966.* Vienna: Verlag für Gesellschaftskritik, 1987.

Steinhoff, Anthony J. "Embracing the Grail: Parsifal, Richard Wagner and the German Nation." *German History* 30 (2012): 372–94.

Stern, Fritz. *The Politics of Cultural Despair: A Study in the Rise of the Germanic Ideology.* 2nd edn. Berkeley and Los Angeles: University of California Press, 1974.

Sternberg, Josef van. *Fun in a Chinese Laundry.* New York: Macmillan, 1965.

Sterne, Jonathan, ed. *The Sound Studies Reader.* London: Routledge, 2012.

Strauß, Dietmar. "Eduard Hanslick und die Diskussion um die Musik der Zukunft." In *Eduard Hanslick. Sämtliche Schriften. Historisch-kritische Ausgabe*, ed. Dietmar Strauß, Band I, 4 Aufsätze und Rezensionen 1857–1858, 407–26. Vienna, Cologne, and Weimar: Böhlau Verlag, 2002.

Sudendorf, Werner. *Marlene Dietrich: Dokumente, Essays, Filme.* Berlin and Vienna: Ullstein, 1980.

Sühnel, Rudolf. *Der Park als Gesamtkunstwerk des englischen Klassizismus am Beispiel von Stourhead.* Heidelberg: Winter, 1977.

Syer, Katherine R. "Parsifal on Stage." In *A Companion to Wagner's Parsifal*, ed. William Kinderman and Katherine R. Syer, 277–338. Rochester, NY: Camden House, 2005.

Szeemann, Harald, ed. *Der Hang zum Gesamtkunstwerk: Europäische Utopien seit 1800.* Aarau: Verlag Sauerländer, 1983.

Taut, Bruno. Frühlicht. *Eine Folge für die Verwirklichung des neuen Baugedankens, 1920–1922.* Berlin: Ullstein, 1963.

———. *Der Weltbaumeister. Architektur-Schauspiel für symphonische Musik*, ed. Manfred Speidel. Berlin: Mann, 1999.

Teck, Katherine, ed. *Making Music for Modern Dance: Collaboration in the Formative Years of a New American Art.* New York: Oxford University Press, 2011.

Thiekötter, Angelika. *Kristallisationen, Splitterungen. Bruno Tauts Glashaus.* Basel: Birkhäuser Basel, 1993.

Thompson, Emily. *The Soundscape of Modernity: Architectural Acoustics and the Culture of Listening in America, 1900–1933.* Cambridge, MA: MIT Press, 2002.

Traubner, Richard. *Operetta: A Theatrical History.* Garden City, NY: Doubleday, 1983.

Treadwell, James. *Interpreting Wagner*. New Haven, CT: Yale University Press, 2003.

Trimingham, Melissa Trimingham. *The Theatre of the Bauhaus: The Modern and Postmodern Stage of Oskar Schlemmer*. London: Routledge, 2011.

Utrecht, Luuk. *Rudi van Dantzig: A Controversial Idealist in Ballet*. Trans. Nicoline Gatehouse. Zutphen: Walberg Pers, 1992.

Vazsonyi, Nicholas. *Richard Wagner: Self-Promotion and the Making of a Brand*. Cambridge: Cambridge University Press, 2010.

Walter, Michael. "Die Musik des Olympiafilms von 1938." *Acta Musicologica* 62, no. 1 (1990): 82–113.

Warrack, John. *German Opera: From the Beginnings to Wagner*. Cambridge: Cambridge University Press, 2001.

———, ed. *Writings on Music*. Cambridge: Cambridge University Press, 1981.

Weber, William. "Did People Listen in the Eighteenth Century?" *Early Music* 25, no. 4 (1997): 678–91.

Weiner, Marc A. *Richard Wagner and the Anti-Semitic Imagination*. Lincoln: University of Nebraska Press, 1995.

Weisstein, Ulrich. "Von reitenden Boten und singenden Holzfällern: Bertolt Brecht und die Oper." In *Brechts Dramen: Neue Interpretationen*, ed. Hinderer Walter, 266–99. Stuttgart: Reclam, 1984.

Westernhagen, Carl von. *Richard Wagners Dresdener Bibliothek 1842–1849. Neue Dokumente zur Geschichte seines Schaffens*. Wiesbaden: Brockhaus, 1966.

White, Iain Boyd. "The Expressionist Utopia." In *Tracing Modernity: Manifestations of the Modern in Architecture and the City*, ed. Mari Hvattum and Christian Hermansen, 256–70. London: Routledge, 2004.

Wilk, Christopher, ed. *Modernism 1914–1939: Designing a New World*. London: V&A Publications, 2006.

Williamson, George. *The Longing for Myth in Germany: Religion and Aesthetic Culture from Romanticism to Nietzsche*. Chicago: University of Chicago Press, 2004.

Wingler, Hans. *The Bauhaus, Weimar, Dessau, Berlin, Chicago*, ed. Joseph Stein and trans. Wolfgang Jabs and Basil Gilbert. Cambridge, MA: MIT Press, 1969.

Zelinsky, Hartmut. "Richard Wagners letzte Karte." In *Parsifal: Texte, Materialen, Kommentare*, ed. Attila Csampi and Dietmar Holland. Reinbek: Rowohlt, 1996.

———. "Der verschwiegende Gehalt des Parsifal." In *Parsifal: Texte, Materialen, Kommentare*, ed. Attila Csampi and Dietmar Holland, 244–56. Reinbek: Rowohlt, 1996.

Žižek, Slavoj, and Mladen Dolar. *Opera's Second Death*. New York: Routledge, 2002.

∾: INDEX :∾

Abbate, Carolyn, 91, 93n12, 149n2, 211
Acocella, Joan, 138
Adorno, Theodor W.: on art and commercialism, 34, 229, 239; and Brecht, 82, 115–16; critique of Wagner, 141, 161, 177n19; on film, 254; on Gesamtkunstwerk and totalitarianism, 8–9, 16n31, 115–16, 117, 121, 128
Adrian-Nilsson, Gösta, 163, 169
Aeschylus, 60
aesthetics: Adorno on, 115, 121; and the Bauhaus, 96, 97, 99, 101, 112n44, 252; and cinema, 11–12, 184, 195; and dance, 135, 137, 140–41, 145, 149; and Eisler, 115, 117, 128; of epic theater, 82, 136; and experience, 4, 105, 119, 184, 189, 197; and Gestalt, 103–4, 106; and memorial music, 207, 208; and modernity, 23, 24–25, 96, 159; and National Socialism, 3, 115, 119, 121, 122, 127, 199, 201, 208; and notions of totality/unity, xii, 2, 58, 60, 82, 100, 162, 183, 221, 234, 254; of performance, 34; and politics, 1, 3, 8, 23, 40, 57, 63, 82, 119, 162, 172, 184, 185, 190, 254; and Riefenstahl, 122–25, 127, 197–99, 201; and Scheerbart, 172; and Schiller, 25–30, 104, 253; and the senses, 186, 188, 190, 200; and society, 24, 100, 118–19, 136, 162; and sound, 184, 254; and Taut, 165; and theater, 62, 64, 104, 201; and totalitarianism, 3, 121, 159; Wagnerian, 2, 21, 25, 31–34, 39, 43–48, 57, 81, 98, 115, 118, 120, 123, 127, 136, 140, 183
agitprop, 193
Albright, Daniel, 89, 134, 153
Allgemeine Zeitung (Munich), 73
Alter, Nora, 230
anti-Semitism (*see also* Jews), 16n31, 49–50, 56, 69, 223, 247
Appia, Adolphe, 73, 77n72, 88, 111n32, 143
Archipenko, Alexander, 165
architecture, 8, 46, 63, 119, 122, 141, 165, 188; and the Bauhaus, 96, 99, 110n6; and glass, 161–62, 171–74; and modernism, 1, 98, 109n4, 110n6, 159; and society, 99–100, 110n15, 112n 38, 112n45; and the theater, 45, 98, 104, 109. See also *Glashaus*; Werkbund, German, 1914 Cologne Exhibition
Aristotle, 40–41
Artaud, Antonin, 143
Ascott, Roy, 22
Ashton, Frederick, 139
audience: and consumption, 12, 87, 229–30, 243; and Einfühlung, 99, 105; experiences of, 84, 105, 208, 210, 217, 251; as expression of community, 71, 83, 98, 185, 189, 196, 213, 254; and film, 11, 195, 229, 236; idealization of, 67, 71, 83, 119, 141, 177n18, 183, 189; *Lehrstück* and, 84, 87; and memorial music, 206, 207, 208, 211, 222–23; and opera, 86; as participants, 34, 45, 73–74, 87, 107, 108, 113n65, 184, 201, 202, 206, 210, 218, 220; performers and, 24, 82, 87, 189; and realization of Gesamtkunstwerk, 5, 6, 7; relation to artworks, xiii, 3, 10, 13, 66, 183, 184, 186, 190, 197, 212, 255; Schiller on, 11; sensory perceptions of 27, 66, 83, 86, 91, 107, 116, 184, 186, 189; as spectators, 85, 90, 121, 201; as symbol of the Volk, 67; and the theater, 67, 97, 187
audience contract, 81, 84, 85, 87, 92, 93n12, 252

auditory field, 192, 194
Auerbach, Lera, *Requiem* (Dresden: Ode to Peace), 221–22
Aufstieg und Fall der Stadt Mahagonny (*Rise and Fall of the City of Mahagonny*), 84, 85, 150. *See also* Brecht, Bertolt; Weill, Kurt
Auschwitz, 124
Austria, 228, 233, 242; dialect of, 236; national songs of, 238, 247n28; people from, 232, 233

Bach, Johann Sebastian, 86, 146, 171
Bach, Steven, 124, 131, 247
Bachakademie Stuttgart, Internationale, 220
ballet, 10, 102, 105–6, 133–34, 136, 137–39, 145–46. *See also* dance; song-ballet
Ballets Russes, 137, 151
Barbas, Samantha, 239
Barenboim, Daniel, 223
Barnes, Clive, 141
Bauhaus, xi–xii, 2, 106–7, 207n8; and architecture, 112n38, 165n22; and dance, 17n36, 102; and Gestalt thinking, 100–104, 106, 109; history, 96–97, 99, 110n6, 111n22, 158; manifesto 97, 99, 100, 111n22, 158; and music, 106; and theater, 9, 95–97, 98, 100–102, 104–5, 108–9, 110n12, 112n45, 253; and the unity of arts, 8–10, 97, 100–102, 111n27; 111n30, 158, 177, 252; and Wagner, 98–100, 105, 109;
Bauhaus Exhibition (1923), 100, 102, 107
Bausch, Pina, 139, 145, 151
Bayreuth circle, xii
Bayreuth Festival, 8, 72, 73, 121, 122, 141; of 1876, 43, 45, 58, 67–68; of 1882, 68, 69, 73; experience of, 33–34, 109, 184, 187, 188, 192, 195; and festivals in ancient Greece, 32, 58, 65; and the German nation, 66, 67, 72, 183; and theatrical production, 67, 68, 89, 185, 187, 189, 197, 201. *See also* Wagner, Richard, musical works: *Parsifal*
Bayreuth Festspielhaus. *See* Festival Theater, Bayreuth, 94, 200
Bayreuther Blätter, 43, 68
Beethoven, Ludwig van, 26, 30, 49, 134, 137, 220, 221
Behne, Adolf, 161, 169, 174, 175, 182n101
Béjart, Maurice, 10, 135–36, 139, 139–49, 152n36, 152n41, 253
Bell, Catherine, 66
Benatzky, Ralph, 233, 238, 240, 242, 244
Benjamin, Walter, 8–9, 16n16, 115, 208, 230, 255
Bergen-Belsen, 206
Berio, Luciano, 220–21
Berlioz, Hector, 50
Berlin, 163, 232, 239, 240; and the Bauhaus, 96, 104, 158; and Britten's *War Requiem*, 212–13, 214–17, and the *Glashaus*, 163; and *Kuhle Wampe*, 190–91, 195. *See also* Gedächtniskirche, Kaiser Wilhelm; Herbstsalon, Erster Deutscher
Berlin Philharmonic Orchestra, 147, 152n36, 206, 214, 217
Berlin Radio Symphony, 148
Berlin Wall, 212–14, 217
Berliner Börsen-Courier, 70
Berliner Sinfonie (East), 214
Berman, Russell, 199, 201
Bermbach, Udo, 2, 36n29, 36n33, 44–45, 63, 66, 69, 253
Betz, Albrecht, 115, 117, 119
Bick, Sally, 116, 129
Bildung, 25, 36–37
biological process, composition as, 48
Bismarck, Otto von, 66
Bizet, Georges, 88, 231, 232, 238
Blake, David, 125, 129, 131
Bletter, Rosemary Haag, 164
Blue Rider group (*Der Blaue Reiter*), 101
Blue Angel, The (*Der blaue Engel*), xii, 228, 230–31, 233–40, 243, 246, 252. *See also* Sternberg, Josef von
Bluemner, Rudolf, 164
Blumenthal, Oskar, 232–33
Borchard, Leo, 206, 207, 223
Borchmeyer, Dieter, 26, 45, 57, 64, 65, 72

Botticelli, Sandro, 47
Boys' Choir of Harlem, 215
brand, idea of artistic, 2, 8, 9, 21, 23, 63, 71, 253
Brandt, Karl, 68, 186
Brecht, Bertolt: 3; and Adorno, 115, 117, 121, 128; and audience contract, xiii, 81, 84–85, 87, 92, 252; and the Bauhaus, 207; and Bach, 86; and consumption, 87; and Eisler, 86, 115, 125–26, 127–28; and epic theater, xi, 8, 81–87, 89, 116–17, 120, 136, 252; and mimesis, 91; and modernism 84, 91; on music and irrationality, 85, 86, 116; and Nietzsche, 83, 89, 91; and opera 8, 81, 83, 84, 86, 87, 252–53; and Riefenstahl, 89; and totalitarianism, 121; and unity, 82; and voice-object, 91–92, 211; and Wagner xii, 8–9, 81–84, 87, 89, 91, 116, 120, 136, 207; and Weill, 84, 235, 238. *See also* audience; estrangement; gestus
Brentano, Franz Clemens, 108
Britten, Benjamin, 139; *War Requiem*, xiii, 12, 206, 207, 208–13, 214–17 passim, 218, 220–22 passim, 223–52, 254. *See also* symbolic casting
Brown, Hilda Meldrum, 82
Brussels, 141, 214
Brzoska, Matthias, 24, 26, 35
Bühnenfestspiel. *See* Bayreuth Festival
Bühnenweihfestspiel. *See* Wagner, Richard, musical works: *Parsifal*

Cage, John, 218
Campendonk, Heinrich, 165
Carmen, 231, 232, 237, 238
Carter, Elliott, 219
Cathedral: and glass architecture, 161, 162, 173, 175, 177n21, 177n25; and memorial music, 224n13; as symbol of total artwork, 11; 97, 99, 103, 111n18, 165
"Cathedral of Socialism," 99, 100, 158, 172, 177n22
Cayrol, Jean, 125
Celan, Paul, 221
Chadwick, Whitney, 168
Chion, Michel, 196
choreography, 135, 136, 137, 141–49 passim, 151n27, 152n36. *See also* ballet; dance
Chytry, Josef, 3–4
cinema, 190, 191, 192, 198, 199, 231, 239, 240, 241; and Adorno, 121; and audiences, 185, 195; and consumer culture, 229, 242; and fascism, 121, 204n42, 238; role of music in 121, 128, 236, 237, 244; and sound, 194, 195, 196, 197, 199, 200, 228, 230, 236; and Wagner, 121, 188, 229, 245n3. *See also* Dudov, Slatan; Riefenstahl, Leni; sound cinema
cinematic experience, 11, 195, 200
cinematographic sound, 12
Cold War, 44, 109
Cologne, 163, 169, 251. See also *Glashaus;* Werkbund, German, 1914 Cologne Exhibition
Cologne cathedral, 157, 160
communication, 26, 139, 187, 195
consumer, 12, 60, 243–44, 252; and (mass) culture, 12, 229, 230, 233–34, 239, 241, 244, 251
consuming films and movie stars, 242
consumption, 6, 11, 251, 252; and audience, 87, 208, 229; and culture, 10, 229, 230, 232, 242; diachronic vs. synchronic, 230, 234, 239, 242, 252; and epic theater, 91; habits of, 12, 229, 230, 239, 241, 243; and ideology, 244; and listening, 229; of records, 230, 238; as unifying force, 229, 230, 234; and Wagner, 229, 239
Cornelius, Hans, 249
Coventry, 209, 210, 211, 213, 216, 221, 223
Coventry Cathedral. *See* Coventry
Croce, Benedetto, 249
crowd, xiii, 185–86, 190; and cinematic sound, 11, 184, 186, 190, 193, 196; and listening, 198
cubism, 165, 166
Currid, Brian, 241, 244
Cuvilier, Marcel, 214

Dada, 101, 113
Dahlhaus, Carl, 27, 44, 53n21

Damrosch, Walter, 137
dance, xi, 6, 234, 253; and the Bauhaus, 97, 102, 104–6, 109n4, 112n37; in the twentieth-century, 10, 101, 135, 136–39, 141, 150n14; and Wagner, 10, 25, 32, 46–48, 51, 78, 83, 133–35, 138, 142, 148–49, 183, 186, 203. *See also* ballet; Béjart, Maurice; Dantzig, Rudi van; Schlemmer, Oskar; song-ballet
Dantzig, Rudi van, 10, 135–36, 139, 145–49, 152–53
Daub, Adrian, 3, 48
Davidsohn, George, 70
Debussy, Claude, 232
Delaunay, Robert, 165–70, 171
Delaunay, Sonia, 165, 166, 168, 171
Delsarte, François, 88, 89
Dennis, David, 120, 131n53
Dessau, 96, 97, 101, 102, 104, 107, 109, 158
Deutsche Gesellschaft für Soziologie (German Sociological Society), 249
Diaghilev, Serge, 137
Diefendorf, Jeffrey M., 213
diegetic and non-diegetic music, 192, 196, 228, 235–39, 244
Diepgen, Eberhard, 216
Dietrich, Marlene, 231, 238–45 passim
Disney, Walt, 129n6
Disneyland, 33
drama: in ancient Greece, 25, 32, 58, 60, 61–62, 133, 183; and dance, 134, 137, 149, 186; and feeling, 105; participation in, 189; and performance, 27, 32; relationship to music, 40, 41, 84, 90, 142, 235, 251, 255; and Schiller, 7, 9, 29–30, 207; social-political role of, 7, 27, 61–62, 68, 72, 207; on stage, 69; and the voice-object, 91. *See also* music drama; theater; Wagner, Richard, prose works: *Opera and Drama*
Draschke, Harry, 221
Dreigroschenoper, Die (*The Three-Penny Opera*), 84, 235, 238. *See also* Brecht, Bertolt; Weill, Kurt
Dresden, 30, 124, 209, 213, 221–22; 1849 Revolution in, 31, 46, 60, 117. *See also* Auerbach, Lera
Driver, Paul, 216
Dudov, Slatan, xii, 12, 184, 190, 254
Duncan, Isadora, 137, 151n17
Dupanloup, Félix, 59
Dutch National Ballet, 145–47

Eichendorff, Joseph von, 135, 144
Eiffel Tower, 167, 168
Einfühling, 99, 105, 108, 112n44
Eisler, Hanns, xii, 10, 86, 90, 115–17, 121–22, 125–27, 127–29, 254
Enlightenment, 23
epic theater, xi, 9, 81–82, 82–92, 116, 117, 120, 136, 252
estrangement (*Verfremdung*), 85, 87, 90, 116, 211
ethics and art, 27–28, 170–72, 217
eurhythmics, 88
expressionism, 96, 101, 102, 109, 165

fascism, 3, 66, 81, 96, 115, 116, 120, 121, 127, 199, 200, 201
Fauser, Annegret, 100
Feininger, Lyonel, 99, 158
Feininger, T. Lux, 103
Feld, Eliot, 139
Ferrier, Kathleen, 209
festival: and ancient Greece 21, 63, 65; at Coventry 209; and French Revolution, 24; in Germany, 24, 35n14, 120; sharpshooting, 236–37 and Wagner, 21, 24, 36n34, 45, 58, 63, 65–66, 108, 109. *See also* Bayreuth Festival
Festival Theater, Bayreuth (Festspielhaus), 11, 33, 66–67, 68–69, 98, 101, 105, 112n45, 141, 184, 186–88, 192, 194, 196, 197, 203n4
Feuerbach, Ludwig, 31, 46, 47, 60, 141
Feuerstein, Marcia, 112n38
film, xii; as total artwork, 8, 28, 123–24, 128, 184, 186, 243; and audience, 190; and the Bauhaus, 104, and music, 90, 116–17, 123, 125, 228–30, 239; and sound, 184, 186–200 passim, 235, 240. *See also* cinema; musical film; *titles of individual films; names of individual directors*

Finger, Anke, 2, 4, 5, 14n5, 22, 23, 60, 99, 130n41, 162, 207
Fischer-Dieskau, Dietrich, 209, 211
Fischer-Lichte, Erika, 22
Florentine Camerata, 40–41
Fluck, Alan, 214
Follett, Danielle, 2, 5, 23, 99, 162, 207
Fornoff, Roger, 22
Forst, Willi, 228, 232–34, 235–37 passim, 242, 243. See also *White Horse Inn*
France, 2, 24, 138
Frauenkirche (Dresden), 209, 221–22
French Revolution, 24, 25, 28–32 passim, 35n14, 98
Freud, Sigmund, 109
Fulbrook, Mary, 213, 225n29
Furtwängler, Wilhelm, 206
futurism, 101

Gächinger Kantorei Stuttgart, 220
Garbo, Greta, 240
Gaskell, Sonia, 145
Gay, Peter, 247
Gay-White, Pamela, 141–42, 143, 144–45
Gedächtniskirche, Kaiser Wilhelm (Berlin), 209, 217
gender, 47–49, 160, 244, 251, 255
Geneva, 59, 223
Germany: Democratic Republic of (DDR), 215; Third Reich (Nazi), 98, 119, 120, 123, 136, 228, 232, 233, 234, 241, 242; Weimar Republic, 96, 98, 212, 231, 238, 243, 247
Gerwitz, Paul, 13
Gesamtglaswerk, 11, 157, 159, 163, 165–67, 168, 170, 171–75, 251
Gestalt thinking, xii, 95, 100, 102, 103–4, 106–8
Gestapo, 116
gestus, 87, 88, 89–91, 252. *See also* Brecht, Bertolt
Giedion, Siegfried, 158
Glashaus, 11, 157–164, 169–75, 176n1, 176n12, 177n15, 177n20, 178n31, 251. *See also* Taut, Bruno
glass, xii, 106, 112n37, 157, 158–59, 163, 164–165, 170, 171–75, 177n15. See also *Gesamtglaswerk*; *Glashaus*; Scheerbart, Paul
Gleichschaltung, 120, 121, 130
Gluck, Christoph Willibald, 41, 151
Gobineau, Arthur de, 56
Goebbels, Joseph, 119–20, 127, 238, 240, 241
Goehr, Lydia, 43, 44, 57
Goethe, Johann Wolfgang von, xi, xii, 9, 30, 31, 103, 108
Göring, Hermann, 127
Gothic architecture, 161, 165, 175, 177, 209
Gottsched, Johann Christoph, 29
Graham, Martha, 10, 135, 145, 152n51, 253
Greece, ancient: 23–25, 28, 30, 32, 58–59, 60, 62; drama of, 32, 40, 41, 58, 60, 133, 183; festivals of, 21, 24, 65–66; ideal of unity in, 2; as inspiration for Wagner, 65, 71; nation and culture in, 62
Grey, Thomas, 33, 34, 44
Gropius, Walter, 95–97, 100, 104, 107, 109n4, 110n6, 111n22, 112n45, 158
Groys, Boris, 159
Guldin, Rainer, 23
Gutman, Robert, 56
Gutschow, Kai Konstanty, 162
Gypsies, 238

Habanera, La, 228, 230, 231–32, 234–35, 237–41 passim, 244, 252. *See also* Sierk, Detlev
Haid, Liane, 232
Hanslick, Eduard, 70, 71
Harbison, John, 220
Harper, Heather, 209
Haydn, Franz Joseph, 238, 247
Heesters, Johannes, 233, 239, 241–43
Hegel, Georg Wilhelm Friedrich, 25, 46, 62
Heibach, Christiane, 27, 105
Heimatfilm, 233, 242
Henry, Pierre, 141
Herbstsalon, Erster Deutscher (First German Autumn Salon), 165, 168, 169
Hesse, Hermann, 135

Hilbersheimer, Ludwig, 159
Hildebrand, Adolf von, 106
Himmler, Heinrich, 127
Hitler Youth (Hitler Jugend), 126
Hitler, Adolf: aesthetic vision of, 119–20, 121; Hanns Eisler on, 127; and *Triumph of the Will*, 122–24, 127–28, 131n62, 198; and Wagner, x, 115–16, 120, 121, 122, 128, 250; and totalitarianism 16n35. *See also* National Socialism
Hochschule für Musik (Berlin), 212
Hoelzel, Adolf, 160, 177n15
Hoffmann, E.T.A., 26, 41, 42
Hölderlin, Friedrich, 25, 35
Holländer, Friedrich, 235, 238, 239, 240
"Horst Wessel Lied," 123, 197
Horton, Lester, 137
Hughes, Gordon, 166–68, 179n50
Humphrey, Doris, 137, 138
Husserl, Edmund, 249
Hutcheon, Linda and Michael, 44
Huyssen, Andreas, 34

idealism: in German thought, 100, 103, 105, 109, 137, 253; revolutionary, 5, and Wagner, 31, 45, 69
identity: collective, 122; national, 30, 32, 124, 215; religious, 222
Isenstadt, Sandy, 180n85
Israel Philharmonic, 220

Jackson, Timothy, 135
James-Chakraborty, Kathleen, 97, 98
Jannings, Emil, 231, 239–40
Janowitz, Gundula, 147, 153n58
Japan: and Britten's *War Requiem*, 213; and Pendercki's *Threnody*, 219
Jaques-Dalcroze, Émile, 88–89
jazz, 107, 235, 238, 239
Jazz Singer, The, 229, 236
Jena, 97, 113
Jenne, Michael, 214–15
Jeunesses Musicales, 214, 216, 225
Jews, 49, 50, 115, 206, 221, 222, 224n3, 253. *See also* anti-Semitism
Joffrey, Robert, 139
Johnson, James H., 187
Jordan, Stephanie, 136
Joseph II (Holy Roman Emperor), 65
Josef, Franz (Emperor of Austria-Hungary), 233
Judge, Mychal, 222

Kabbalah, 222
Kadelburg, Gustav, 232, 233
Kalbeck, Max, 68
kaleidoscope, 160, 162, 164, 177n15
Kandinsky, Wassily, 3, 4, 97, 101–2, 110n12, 164, 165, 179n42
Karajan, Herbert von, 147
Karnes, Kevin C., 2
Kenngott, Louise F., 218
Kesting, Marianne, 82
Keyserling, Hermann Graf, 249
Kinderman, William, 44
Kirchmann, Kay, 101
Kisselgoff, Anna, 141
Kittler, Friedrich, 188, 189, 203n4, 230,
Kitzinger Manifesto, 214
Klee, Paul, 101, 108, 169–71, 180n77, 181n91, 256
Klob, Karl Maria, 72–73
Knef, Hildegard, 242
Koepnick, Lutz, 101, 184–85, 190, 192, 194, 197, 200, 230, 254
Koss, Juliet, 2, 66, 83, 86, 95, 99, 105, 112n44, 113n50, 118, 121, 129, 183, 203n4
Krakow, 220, 223
Kramer, Lawrence, 84
Kuhle Wampe, xii, 11–12, 184, 186, 190–96, 197, 200, 254. *See also* Dudov, Slatan
Kühnel, Jürgen, 43, 64
Kulturnation (cultural nation), 24
Kunstreligion (religion of art), 23, 31

Lamac, Carl, 233
Laparra, Raoul, 232
Leander, Zarah, 228, 232, 234, 237–44 passim
Lee, David, 241
Lehmann-Haupt, Hellmut, 119
Lehrstück, 13, 61, 84–87, 247n49. *See also* Brecht, Bertolt

Leipzig, 203
Leister, Regina, 215
leitmotif, 21, 33, 39, 67, 82, 92, 116, 121, 122, 125, 126, 128, 147, 229, 255
Lessing, Gotthold Ephraim, 29
Levin, David J., 44
Lipps, Theodor, 105–6
Lista, Marcella, 2, 4, 99
listening: as collective practice, 192, 193, 198, 206, 207, 211; modernization of, 184–85, 190, 192, 200, 201, 254; productive, 255; and the theater, 187
Liszt, Franz, 33
Logos: Internationale Zeitschrift für Philosophie der Kultur, 249–50, 254
Ludwig II (King of Bavaria), 64, 65
Luxfer prisms, 160

MacDonald, Brian, 139
Maciuika, John V., 110
MacMillan, Kenneth, 139
Maeterlinck, Maurice, 110
Mahler, Gustav, 111n25, 139, 140
Mallarmé, Stéphane, 111n30, 138
Mallgrave, Harry, 98
Manen, Hans van, 145
Mann, Heinrich, 230, 231, 234, 244; *Professor Unrat*, 230, 231
Mann, Thomas, 16n28, 250
Marc, Franz, 165
Marian, Ferdinand, 232, 247n44
Martell, Karl, 232
mass culture, 4, 12, 121, 153n60, 228, 229, 230, 234, 244, 245, 252
Massine, Lorca, 139
Matz, Johanna, 233, 242
Maur, Karin von, 101
Meinecke, Friedrich, 24
memorial music, 12, 206–8, 209, 212–13, 217–20, 222–23, 252
Mendelssohn, Felix, 206
Menuhin, Yehudi, 206, 207, 223, 252
Messner, Hermann, 70
Meyer, Stephen, 42
Meyerhold, Vsevolod, 88
Meyrowitz, Peter, 191, 194
mickey-mousing, 89
Mimik, 133, 134, 186
mimomania, 89
Minor, Ryan, 35n14
Musikalische Jugend Deutschlands (MJD), 214
modernism, 103, 168, 251, 254; Adorno and, 129; and aesthetics, 159; in architecture, xii, 96, 109, 157, 172, 174, 180n85; and the Bauhaus, 101, 102; and Brecht, 83–84; and dance, 136–37, 151n27; and drama, 121; and Einfühlung, 99; Eisler and, 117; and film, 10, 117, 129, 199, 255; in Germany, 3, 140; and movement, 85, 91; synesthetic, 101, 185, 203n6; and the theater, xii, 9, 82–83, 85, 92, 101, 104, 116, 252; and Wagner, xi, 49, 98, 121, 128, 190, 200
modernity, 2, 31, 34, 95, 141, 184, 185, 195; criticism of, 23, 24–25, 28
Moholy-Nagy, László, 103–4, 108, 111n27, 112n45, 165
Morat, Daniel, 195–96
Morris, Christopher, 40
Morris, Mark, 151, 259
movie. *See* cinema; film
Mozart, Wolfgang Amadeus, 41, 49, 84, 135, 246n26, 254; *Marriage of Figaro*, 254, 255
Mühsam, Erich, 163
Müller, Sven Oliver, 187
Müller, Walter, 233
Mulvey, Laura, 241
Munich, 64, 65
Münster, 213
music drama (*Musikdrama*), and anti-Semitism 16n31; and audience experience, 186, 187, 188, 196; concept of, 21, 40, 41, 46, 48, 50, 51, 58, 92, 255; critique of, 81, 86, 89; and dance, 133, 134, 137, 142, 149; as festival piece, 45, 71; compared with film, 201; as national art, 62, 67; and notions of artistic unity, xi; and opera, 71, 83, 84, 86; relationship to epic theater, 82, 90; and sound, 184, 187, 200; as Wagnerian product, 21, 33, 39, 41, 42, 43, 105, 127. *See also* Wagner, Richard, prose works: *Artwork of the Future*; *Opera and Drama*

musical film, 12, 228–30, 234, 243–44. *See also* film
Musikalisches Wochenblatt (Leipzig), 43
Mutzenbecher, Franz, 160, 177
myth, 57, 62, 67, 75n21, 115, 122, 138, 141, 195, 245n6, 255

national ideal: conceptions of, 24, 60, 124; and German theater, 30, 31, 61, 64, 65; and Wagner, 31–32, 62, 64–65, 66, 251
National Socialism: and film, 228, 238, 247n44; legacy of 3, 121, 208, 212; as political movement, 123, 124, 212, 241; politicized aesthetics of, 119, 121, 122, 125, 127, 208, 254; restrictions under, 206, 222, 241; terrorism of, 117, 124, 128, 254; and Wagner, 9, 44, 116, 121, 122, 127. *See also* Nuremberg Party Rally (1934)
nationalism, 16n31, 27, 69, 124, 195, 218, 238
Netherlands, 146
Neue Evangelische Kirchenzeitung, 70
Neue Sachlichkeit (New Objectivity), 191
Neue Zeitschrift für Musik (Leipzig), 49
Neumann, Alfred, 21
Newcomb, Anthony, 44
Nieder, Christoph, 82
Nietzsche, Friedrich, xi, 8, 43, 81, 83, 89, 90, 106, 136
Night and Fog (*Nuit et Brouillard*): and National Socialism, 10, 124, 254; and *Triumph of the Will*, 90, 117, 125–26, 128, 254; and Wagnerian aesthetics, xiii, 115, 121, 128, 254. *See also* Eisler, Hanns; Resnais, Alain
Nordheim, Arne, 220
Novalis (Georg Philipp Friedrich Freiherr von Hardenberg), 26
Nuremberg, 197
Nuremberg Party Rally (1934), 122, 123, 126, 127

Oehlmann, Werner, 213
opera, 239; Brecht and, 75n19, 81–84, 84–89, 90–92, 252; and dance, 133, 134, 138, 149, 151n27, 253; Eisler on, 116; and France, 100; history of, 40–42, 92n3; as multimedia artwork, 26; under National Socialism, 120, 123; and theater, 8, 25. *See also* music drama; Wagner, Richard
opera house, 186, 187, 188. *See also* Festival Theater, Bayreuth
Oswald, Richard, 232
Owen, Wilfred, 210, 217

Pabst, G.W., 235
Packer, Randall, 22
Panufnik, Roxanna, 223
Paris, 24, 26, 88, 127, 133, 138, 149n2, 153n58, 171, 187
Pears, Peter, 209
Penderecki, Krzysztof, 218–20, 223; *Threnody for the Victims of Hiroshima*, 218–20, 226n51
performance: and Adorno, 121; in ancient Greece, 32, 183, and Bauhaus, 9, 96, 107, 108; and creation of community, 7, 74, 83, 207, 219; as dimension of Gesamtkunstwerk, 7, 8, 27, 33, 63, 185, 221; and noise, 11; practices, 81, 253; and theatrical space, 33, 45, 184; and voice, 147; and voice-object, 91; Wagner and, 27, 32, 33, 64–65, 98, 105, 189, 190. *See also* audience; Brecht, Bertolt; memorial music; reception
Pettitt, Stephen, 215, 217
Peucker, Brigitte, 199, 201
Philharmonie (Berlin), 215, 216, 217
Picard, Timothée, 2, 92n3
Piscator, Erwin, 104
Pius IX (pope), 59
Plomer, William, 211
poetry: in Greek theater, 40; and Kandinsky, 101; as masculine, 47–49; vs. poetics, 26; and romanticism, 26, 105; and Schlemmer, 106; and song 144; and song-ballets, 149; as theater, 143. *See also* Bauhaus; dance; Owen, Wilfred; reconciliation; sister arts; Wagner, Richard, prose works: *Opera and Drama*
politics: Adorno on, 121; and aesthetics, 1, 2, 5, 10, 40, 56, 63, 82, 119, 122, 128, 162, 172, 184, 189, 190; art

and, 10, 119–21, 127, 129, 244, 253; and artistic totality, xii, 1–2, 5, 9–12, 23, 119, 122, 128, 162, 253; and the Bauhaus, 100, 252; Brecht and, 90–91; culture and, 3, 61, 244; in ancient Greece, 59; and cinema (film), 122, 128, 184, 185, 192, 202, 233, 238, 239; and dance, 141–42, 146; and the *Glashaus*, 162; and *Heimatfilm*, 233; in *Kuhle Wampe*, 192–95 passim, 200; mass, 72, 190; and memorial music, 207, 208, 209–13, 214, 215–18, 219, 221, 222, 254; and music, 118; and the nation, 24, 63, 64; and opera, 51, 56; and Riefenstahl, 121–26, 127; and Schiller, 27, 28, 31, 254; and society, 69, 136, 192, 207, 222; and spectatorship, 254; and the theater, 30, 57–58, 72, 98, 252; and utopianism, 27, 51; Wagner and, 7–8, 31–32, 40, 44–46, 50, 56, 61, 63, 69, 183, 254; of Wagner reception, 81, 115–16, 121, 127, 141. *See also* National Socialism; totalitarianism; Volk
Potter, Pamela, 115, 127
Preminger, Otto, 242
Projekt 10, 217. *See also* Berlin Philharmonic Orchestra
Puchner, Martin, 82

Ravel, Maurice, 232
Ray, Katerina Rüedi, 95
reception: of ancient Greece, 24; and audience, 5, 8, 11, 87, 108, 218; of Bèjart, 141; and creation of collectivities, 183; of Robert Delaunay, 169, 171; and experience, 5, 12, 189, 208; and memorial music, 211, 212, 215, 216, 218; of Penderecki, 219, 220; and performance, 12, 81, 207, 208; sensory, 11, 26, 186, 190; and Wagner, 8, 81, 126, 128, 136, 185
reconciliation, xiii, 10, 12, 135, 142, 144, 148, 206–13, 215–23, 236, 253
Rehding, Alexander, 219
Reichskulturkammer (RKK or Reich Chamber of Culture), 119, 120
Reich Labor Service, 198
religion: and memorial music, 210; and relation to theater, 29, 30, 65; and ritual, 66; and Wagner, 31, 45, 61, 69, 98. See also *Kunstreligion*; Wagner, Richard, prose works: "Religion and Art"
Requiem of Conciliation (*Requiem der Versöhnung*), 220. *See also* Bachakademie Stuttgart, Internationale
Resnais, Alain, 10, 117, 124–25, 128, 254. See also *Night and Fog*
Rhine River, 24, 124, 157, 160
Riefenstahl, Leni: aesthetic practices of 11–12, 90, 117, 122–23, 127, 131n52, 184–86, 200–202; and propaganda, 125. See also *Triumph of the Will*
Riegger, Wallingford, 137
Rienäcker, Gerd, 8, 128
Rihm, Wolfgang, 220
Rilling, Helmuth, 220
Roberts, David, 2, 11, 23–27, 31, 61, 65, 97, 98, 99, 122, 124, 208
romanticism: and ballet, 134, 138, 149; and the Bauhaus, 101, 103; in Germany, 2, 29, 137, 140; and notions of artistic unity, 7, 9 12, 21, 23, 25–27, 31, 98, 148, 162; and Strauss, 135, 140, 142; and religion, 23; and theater, 28–29, 207; and Wagner, 10, 26, 44, 105, 133, 201
Ross, Alex, x, 219
Roth, Ernst, 136
Rousseau, Jean-Jacques, 24, 28, 29, 61
Rousseau, Jean-Louis, 142, 143

Said, Edward, 223
Siegel, Marcia, 141
Saint-Saëns, Camille, 232
Sartwell, Crispin, 119, 127, 131n60
Saussure, Ferdinand de, 109
Saxony, 64
Schaefer, Hansjürgen, 214, 215
Schäfer, Alfred, 191
Schauspielhaus (East Berlin), 214–16
Scheerbart, Anna, 173–75
Scheerbart, Paul, 159, 161, 162, 162–64, 169, 171–75
Schefer, Olivier, 128

Schelling, Friedrich Wilhelm Joseph, 25, 35
Schiller, Friedrich: and aesthetics, xiii, 9, 25, 27, 104, 222, 253; and artistic unity, 9, 33, 113n47, 243–44; and audiences, 11; and theater xi, 7, 9, 25, 28–30, 32, 34, 37n42, 104–5, 207, 252–53; and Wagner, xii, 7, 21, 28, 30–33, 36n33, 130n27, 254; works: "Ode to Joy," 221; *On Naïve and Sentimental Poesy* (*Über naïve und sentimentalische Dichtung*), 28, 31; *On the Aesthetic Education of Man* (*Äesthetische Erziehung des Menschen*), 25, 29–30, 104, 113n47, 130n27, 253; "The Theatrical Stage Contemplated as a Moral Institution," 29
Schinkel, Karl Friedrich, 23, 98
Schlegel, Friedrich, 25–26
Schlemmer, Oskar: aesthetic ideals, xii, 100, 101, 104–6, 252; and the Bauhaus, 96–97, 100, 106–7, 112n38, 252; and dance, 104, 109n4; and Gestalt thinking, 102–4, 106; and music, 106–7; and the theater, 9, 95–96, 102, 108–9, 112n45, 113n57, 113n65, 253
Schmidt, Andreas, 215
Schober, Thomas, 101
Schoenberg, Arnold, 3
School of Fine Art (Weimar), 97
Schopenhauer, Arthur, 31, 44, 46, 57, 134, 146
Schreyer, Lothar, 96
Schuetze, Andre, 158, 159
Schumacher, Ernst, 82
Schumann, Robert, 139, 140
Schützenfest. *See* festival, sharpshooting
Schwarzkopf, Elisabeth, 147
Schwinger, Wolfram, 219
Seeßlen, Georg, 199, 200
Semper, Gottfried, 98
sensory experience, 26, 161, 184, 185, 200. *See also* reception
sensory field, 188, 192
sensory hegemony, 195
Serait-ce la mort?, 135, 139, 142–48. *See also* Béjart, Maurice
Shakespeare, William, 71, 82
Shaw, George Bernard, 89
Shaw-Miller, Simon, 23, 35
Sierk, Detlev (Douglas Sirk), 228, 231–32, 234–35, 237, 240, 247. See also *Habenera, La*
Simmel, Georg, 249
sister arts (poetry, music, dance): as metaphor for artistic unity, 7–8, 25, 32, 46–48 passim, 51, 83, 133–40 passim, 142, 144, 149, 183, 201
Smart, Mary Ann, 88–91 passim
Smith, Matthew Wilson, 4, 61, 66, 72, 73, 82, 86, 112n45, 113n47, 116, 119, 122, 123, 130n27, 131n52, 134, 153n60, 186, 187, 189, 201, 203n4, 207, 245
Solti, Georg, 223
song-ballet, 133, 135–36, 139–40, 143, 146, 149, 253. *See also* Béjart, Maurice; Dantzig, Rudi van
Sophocles, 60, 82
sound: acousmatic, 197; amplified, 188; and the body, 88, 91, 92, 143; diegetic, 192; edited, 191, 193, 194, 254; experience of, 101, 184, 185, 190, 201, 254; and film, 12, 123, 196, 197, 230, 234–40 passim, 254; as noise, 11, 184, 185; non-verbal vocal, 185, 193; qualities of, 196, 199; recorded, 195, 197, 230, 245; and singing, 41; symbolic, 216; and the theater, 101, 106, 188; Trahndorff and, 133, 186
sound cinema (sound film), 184, 228, 229, 230, 239, 240, 254
sound field, 192, 194, 195
sound–image relationship, 90, 126, 127, 128, 129, 196
soundscape, 11, 184, 185, 191–98 passim, 200–201, 245, 254
soundstream, 185, 188, 197, 200
sound studies, 184, 203n3, 230
soundtrack, 12, 117, 123, 193, 228, 229, 230, 234, 236–39, 244
Soviet Union, 209, 210, 212, 215
spectator: Adorno on, 121; as audience, 45, 83, 98, 122, 186–88, 255; and participation, 45, 109, 130, 208, 251; relationship to the creative process, v, xiii, 86, 89, 109, 114n66; and

spectatorship, 83, 95, 198, 200, 252, 254
Spotts, Frederic, 119, 208
Staatskapelle (Dresden), 221
Stabreim, 39
Stern, Fritz, 69
Sternberg, Josef von, 228, 230, 231, 235–37, 240. See also *The Blue Angel*
Stewart, Potter, 13, 150
Stockholm, 234
Strauss, Richard, 136, 139, 140, 150n14; *Tod und Verklärung (Death and Transfiguration)*, 144, 145; *Vier letzte Lieder (Four Last Songs)*, 10, 133, 135–47 passim, 149, 253
Strauß, Dietmar, 50
Sturm, Der (Berlin), 161, 163, 165, 166, 169, 170, 171, 173
Stuttgart, 106, 177n15, 220
Suppé, Franz von, 238
surrealism, 101
Sweden, 232, 234, 237, 240
Switzerland, 66
Syllabus errorum, 59
symbolic casting, 12, 131, 207, 209, 210, 212, 220
symbolism, 110, 138, 142, 144
synchresis, 196–97

Tagesspiegel, Der (Berlin), 213
Tate, Jeffrey, 215
Taut, Bruno, xii, 11, 157–65, 169–74, 251. See also *Glashaus*
Tchaikovsky, Piotyr Illyich, 67
Tear, Robert, 215
theater: in antiquity, 24, 25, 28, 65, 71; and architecture, 98; as artistic space, 28, 33, 63, 67–69, 82; and audience 11, 84, 85, 87; and the Bauhaus, 9, 95, 97; Brecht and, 82; experience of, 82, 98; and the festival idea, 24, 45, 58, 65–66; and Germany, 31, 32, 57, 60, 66, 71, 72; opera and, 8, 82–83, 91; performance of, 64, 82; and politics, 57; reform, 64–64, 67; relationship to dance, xi; relationship to music, xi, 86; and Schelling, 25, and Schiller, xi, 25, 28–32; as social–moral institution, 28, 29, 58, 61, 82; as transformative experience, xi, 98; and Wagner, 31, 32. *See also* drama; epic theater; Festival Theater, Bayreuth
Thiekötter, Angelika, 162
Thompson, Emily, 184
Times, The (London), 215, 217
Tokyo, 213
Tönnies, Ferdinand, 249
totalitarianism, 3, 10, 15n18, 16n35, 72, 117, 121, 124, 127, 254
Trahndorff, Karl Friedrich Eusebius, 133, 186, 201–2
Treadwell, James, 44
Triadic Ballet. *See* Schlemmer, Oskar
Tristan chord, 22, 126
Triumph of the Will (Triumph des Willens), 3, 11, 12, 90, 117, 122–23, 125–26, 131n60, 183, 184, 186, 196–200, 201, 254. *See also* Riefenstahl, Leni
Troeltsch, Ernst, 249
Tudor, Antony, 139
Tynam, Kenneth, 240

Universal Film AG (Ufa), 238, 240

Vaness, Carol, 215
Velde, Henry van de, 97, 110, 111
Vergangenheitsbewältigung, 217
Versöhnungsmusik (music of reconciliation), 213
Vienna, 2, 111n25, 240, 242; opera houses in, 64, 65, 73
Vienna Youth Choir, 215
Vischer, Robert, 105
Vishnevskaya, Galina, 209, 210
visual field, 192, 197
voice: and choreography, 147, 148; and consumer culture, 234, 239, 241, 242; as embodied, 143, 148, 149, 211; in film, 228, 231, 239, 240, 244; non-verbal, 185, 193, 194; as sound, 185, 188, 194, 199
voice-object, 91–92, 211
Volk: as artistic community, 118–19, 141, 189, 253; as audience, 189, 194, 196; in film, 123–24, 200; German notion of, 32, 67, 71; as myth, 200; and

National Socialism, 119–20, 124; as political community, 32, 62, 183, 196; the theater and, 61, 71; Wagner on, 44, 60–61, 66, 69, 127, 183–84, 189–90, 201. *See also* audience; music drama; reception; theater; totalitarianism
völkisch, 67, 124
Völkischer Beobachter (Munich), 120
Volkstrauertag (Memorial Day), 212

Wagner, Cosima, 30, 56, 66, 89, 251
Wagner, Richard: Adorno on, 82; and ancient Greece, 23–24, 28, 58, 59–60, 62, 71; and anti-Semitism, 16n31, 49, 56–57, 253; and audiences, 11, 87, 105, 108–9, 177n19, 186, 187, 189, 196, 201, 218, 229, 242, 255; and Bayreuth, 34, 65–67, 67–71, 72, 141, 183–85, 189, 195, 197, 203n4; Béjart and, 140–44; Brecht and, 81, 83–84, 86, 87; and dance, 10, 47, 133–34, 137–38, 148–49; Eisler and, 115–16, 117, 125–26, 128; and the feminine, 47–49; festival idea of, 21, 24, 32, 36n34, 45, 58, 63, 65–66, 189; and German nationalism, 61–62, 66, 67, 71, 120, 183, 251; and gesture, 88, 89, 90, 91, 133–34; and labels for his oeuvre, 21–23, 33, 39–40, 42–43, 57, 71, 253; and the market, 34; and modernism, 1–2, 23, 121, 189–90, 200, 251; and myth, 57, 62 (*see also* Wagner, Richard, prose works: *Opera and Drama*); and National Socialism, 3, 105, 119, 121, 122, 127; Nietzsche and, 83, 89, 90, 136 (*see also* Nietzsche, Friedrich); and notions of artistic unity, x–xii, 5–8, 42, 47, 48, 58, 60–61, 70, 98, 103, 183, 202, 244; on opera, 40–42, 51, 61, 118, 142; and performance, 27, 33, 252, 253–54; and politics, 44–46, 56, 69, 98, 117–18, 183, 184, 189, 253; reception of, xii, 8–9, 81, 82, 84, 98, 100, 101, 116, 121, 122, 128, 136, 249; and religion, 31, 52n11, 61, 69, 98, 113n65; and romanticism, 23, 26–27, 100; and Schiller, 21, 25, 27–29, 30–32, 75n19, 130n27; and Schopenhauer, 44, 46, 57; and social community, 107, 118–19, 184, 251; and sound, 184–88, 191, 195, 197; and staging, 111n32; and the theater xiii, 6, 28, 58, 60, 62, 64–65, 82, 97, 103–5, 186; utopianism of, 2, 11, 13, 27–29, 31, 51, 57, 60, 98, 107, 118–19, 157, 183, 206; and *Zukunftsmusik*, 50, 59. *See also* Adorno, Theodor F.; Bayreuth Festival; leitmotif; song-ballet
Wagner, Richard, musical works: *Götterdämmerung*, 66, 67, 68; *Lohengrin*, 4, 12; *Meistersinger von Nürnberg, Die*, 57, 67, 120, 123, 127, 131n53, 133; *Parsifal*, xii, 7, 8, 23, 56–58, 66–71, 72, 73, 133, 185, 251, 254; *Rheingold, Das*, 57, 60, 66, 67, 92; *Ring des Nibelungen, Der*, 23, 43, 58; *Siegfried*, 67, 68, 137; *Tannhäuser*, 116, 123, 133, 138, 149; *Tristan und Isolde*, 22, 23, 123, 125–26, 127, 140, 188; *Walküre, Die*, 57, 60, 66, 67, 90
Wagner, Richard, prose works: *Art and Revolution* (*Die Kunst und die Revolution*), 31–32, 57, 61–62; *Artwork of the Future, The* (*Das Kunstwerk der Zukunft*), 32, 39–44, 46–47, 50–51, 57, 60, 62, 69, 83, 133–34, 149; "Eine Mitteilung an meine Freunde" (A Communication to my Friends), 49, 58, 63, 134; "Das Judenthum in der Musik," 49; *Opera and Drama* (*Oper und Drama*), 39–43, 47–51, 57–58, 60–62, 64, 69, 134; "Religion and Art" (Religion und Kunst), 31, 45, 69; "Über die Bestimmung der Oper," 31; "Was ist Deutsch," 72; Zurich writings (see *Art and Revolution, Artwork of the Future, Opera and Drama*)
Wagner, Wieland, 143
Wagnerism, 2, 84, 100, 111n25, 127, 249
Walden, Herwarth, 163–65, 168–70, 172–73
Warrack, John, 42
Watkins, Glenn, 220
Weber, Carl Maria von, 42
Weber, Max, 249
Webern, Anton, 139, 140

Wedekind, Frank, 231
Weill, Kurt, 81, 85, 235, 238
Weimar: and the Bauhaus, 96, 102, 107, 112n38, 158; School of Fine Art, 97, 111n22
Weimar culture, 239, 240, 243
Weiner, Marc, 44, 56
Wensinger, Arthur, 103, 107
Werkbund, German, 157; 1914 Cologne Exhibition; 110n6, 157, 159–61, 162, 169, 174, 251
Westernhagen, Curt von, 37
White Horse Inn (Im weißen Rössl), 228, 230, 232–39 passim, 241–43, 252. *See also* Forst, Willi
Whitton, Kenneth S., 211
Wilkening, Martin, 215
Willcocks, David, 213
Williams, Simon, 188, 201
Williamson, George, 245
Windelband, Wilhelm, 249
Wischmann, Marianne, 236
Wöfflin, Heinrich, 105
Wortklang (word–sound), 133, 186

Zelinsky, Hartmut, 56
Ziegler, Leopold, 249, 254–56
Zukunftsmusik (music of the future), 50, 59. *See also* Wagner, Richard
Zurich, 31, 42, 46, 64, 73, 183
Zurich writings. *See under* Wagner, Richard, prose works